BEETHOVEN

AMS PRESS

NEW YORK

PORTRAIT OF BEETHOVEN AT THE AGE OF
TWENTY-ONE

(*From a miniature in the possession of Sir George Henschel*)

BEETHOVEN

BY

PAUL BEKKER

Translated and Adapted
from the German by
M. M. BOZMAN

MCMXXV
LONDON & TORONTO
J. M. DENT & SONS LTD.
NEW YORK: E. P. DUTTON & CO.

ML
410
.34
B323
1971

Reprinted from the edition of 1925, London and New York
First AMS EDITION published 1971
Manufactured in the United States of America

International Standard Book Number: 0-404-00728-7

Library of Congress Catalog Number: 75-175938

AMS PRESS INC.
NEW YORK, N.Y. 10003

PREFACE

THIS book is of especial interest to English readers at the present time, when public appreciation of Beethoven's genius, after a curious partial eclipse, shows unmistakable signs of reviving. And for a presentation of the modern estimate of Beethoven and his work, no one could be better fitted than Mr. Paul Bekker, the well-known Berlin musical critic. For nearly a score of years he has exercised a great influence over the German musical public by his writings. So far, none of his books have appeared in English, and it is particularly fortunate that the first to do so should be this fine study of Beethoven, which has won universal praise and popularity, running speedily through numerous German editions.

There are certain artists whose genius and humanity can be reflected and presented to the world, once for all, in a single exhaustive biography. Mozart's genius was of this simpler type; Otto Jahn has presented us with all that is necessary for the understanding of the Salzburg genius. But such a biography has not been, and can never be, written of Beethoven. His genius is so many-sided, yet so subtle and intricate, that it is bound to make a new appeal and arouse a fresh response in each new generation. Mr. Thayer's biography, as Mr. Bekker admits, shows a wide appreciation of the nature of the subject, so long as it is confined to the unadorned historical narrative of Beethoven's life and leaves æsthetic criticism alone. Nottebohm similarly provides us with a useful account of the facts relating to the works. These books are of permanent value as a store-house of facts, from which the students of various generations may draw, when seeking to form an æsthetic judgment of Beethoven. It is therefore in no spirit of disparagement of these works that the paramount importance of such æsthetic judgment is emphasised. Any estimate of such a genius as Beethoven's must of necessity be transitory and subjective; it

can lay no claim to universality; but its existence is justified, its aim achieved, if it assists clear thinking in the age for which it is written. It is from this view-point that Bekker approaches his subject. His work is an attempt to present Beethoven as he strikes the modern mind, and it is intended in this way to supplement earlier criticisms. Furthermore, Bekker's estimate is that of a practising musician; he claims to interpret Beethoven's works in the light of personal experience, not indeed through the proper medium of the orchestra or the pianoforte, but through the written word.

As regards historical facts the author has been content to rely on traditional sources. A comparatively short space is devoted to the "Life." Bekker does not believe that Beethoven the "man" and the "musician" are of equal importance to posterity. They are, of course, two complementary, and in many respects strikingly contradictory, aspects of a single personality; the "musician" supplies many shortcomings in the character of the man, and Bekker has made no attempt either to smooth out the contradictions or to present a pleasing portrait of his subject according to conventional or sentimental standards. Beethoven the "man," moving in the actual world, was in many respects different from Beethoven the "musician," moving in an ideal world of his own creation, and any attempt to reconstruct a picture of the "man" from the works is foredoomed to failure. Bekker accordingly presents the two aspects separately, without attempting a complete synthesis. The "Life" is, however, transitory; its interest for us to-day is secondary. The works are immortal and contain all that was best and greatest in the man, and it is to the works that Bekker devotes his book.

In particular, it seems to me that Mr. Bekker rightly emphasises many points never sufficiently marked before; Beethoven's attitude towards key-colour, for instance. Throughout his discussion of the works, the author lays considerable stress on Beethoven's choice of keys, a matter in which he certainly followed a very definite procedure. This is fully proven by the evidence of the works themselves.

As for Beethoven's outlook on opera, Bekker disperses the legend that Beethoven was frightened away from operatic composition by the poor success of *Fidelio*. The composer was certainly not of the fibre which was discouraged by failure to obtain a public success. The Petition to the Opera Board of the Court Theatre in 1806 is one of the most remarkable documents in musical history. In it Beethoven pledges himself " to compose annually at least one big opera and also to deliver each year a small operetta, divertissement, choral or orchestral work in addition." This does not bespeak a man disheartened by the ill success of *Fidelio*. Not even the rejection of his petition drove him away from his operatic plans. He continued his discussions with poets—Grillparzer, Varnhagen, Körner, Collin, Treitschke and others. Even a prize for a suitable libretto, apparently for Beethoven, was offered in the spring of 1812. Beethoven attempted without success to get an opera commissioned for Berlin, through the singer Milder-Hauptmann, who had sung *Fidelio* there with unexpected success. He held decided views on the value of magic and the supernatural on the stage, which were in his opinion subsidiary to human interest. In one of his letters he says that he much preferred a great historical subject, especially from the Dark Ages, like *Attila*. *Alfred the Great* was considered; even the subject of Macbeth was contemplated. In returning Collin's second libretto on a fairy subject, *Bradamante*, Beethoven wrote: " Now as to the question of magic, I cannot deny that I am prejudiced against that kind of thing, because it so often demands that both emotion and intellect shall be put to sleep." This dislike of magic caused him to reject two Indian plays offered him by the famous Orientalist, Hammer-Purgstall. It is not without interest that we find that the Schikaneder who offered Beethoven an honorarium and free lodging in the Theater an der Wien, and gave Beethoven his first opera-commission, was the same man who had struck a bargain with Mozart and launched his *Magic Flute*.

The fact of the matter was that Beethoven always carried too many big works in his mind at the same time. Though he never wrote any opera after *Fidelio*, his dramatic studies were all-important to his music, since through them he found his way, as Mr. Bekker puts it, " *through* the drama, and *beyond* the drama, to heights whence he could view the real essence of things, where the material fell away and his discerning spirit could find the underlying and informative idea." Mr. Bekker's exposition of the evolution of the "poetic idea" in Beethoven's music, particularly in the symphonies, is very finely set forth; and he seems to me to have given us more of the true essence of Beethoven's music than any other writer has done.

A. EAGLEFIELD-HULL.

CONTENTS

PART I

BEETHOVEN THE MAN

CHAP.   PAGE

I.   Biographical 3

II.   Beethoven's Personality 38

PART II

BEETHOVEN THE MUSICIAN

III.   The Poetic Idea 61

IV.   Pianoforte Works and Concertos . . . 80

V.   The Symphonies 146

VI.   Dramatic Works and Overtures . . . 200

VII.   Vocal Works 251

VIII.   Chamber Music 277

APPENDIX I

Summary of Events of Beethoven's Life in Tabular Form   343

APPENDIX II

Tabular Summary of Beethoven's Works . . . 360

Index of Names 381

Index of Works 386

PART I
BEETHOVEN THE MAN

CHAPTER I

EARLY authentic information as to Beethoven's life is remarkably scarce. His contemporaries were preoccupied with the world-shaking political and social events of their day to the exclusion of the " historic sense," and no amount of painstaking research has since been able to recover the material which they failed to conserve. Many details of Beethoven's life-history consequently remain obscure, and even the day of his birth is unknown ; it may have been the 15th or 16th of December 1770, for on the 17th of that month he was baptised in the church of St. Remigius at Bonn.

His youthful circumstances resembled those of Mozart in a way that invites comparison. Both composers were the sons of musicians in the employ of princes of the Church, and, from the earliest appearance of talent, each was educated for his father's profession and was destined for the service of his father's patron. For both boys, their home was also their place of artistic training and testing, the natural fulcrum of their earliest public ventures. Artistic stimulus was richer and more varied in the vigorous capital city of Bonn than in the smaller court of Salzburg, but against this advantage to Beethoven must be offset the sordid domestic troubles which weighed upon his youth and deprived him of the one thing which fully indemnified Mozart for all else—the self-sacrificing care and insight of a father who possessed sufficient discernment to recognise and advance his son's exceptional gifts as a musician, without neglecting his general education and breeding. Beethoven possessed no such counsellor and friend to guide his first steps either in life or in art. Although he had teachers to instruct him in the various branches of music and later on won friends, in whom he aroused the warmest personal interest and with whom he enjoyed spiritual intimacy, the lack of a good father—teacher and friend

3

in one—to care for his youthful normal development handicapped his later life.   From the dawn of consciousness he was strange to the social aspects of life, a lonely nature thrown back upon himself.   Those who were nearest him in blood were furthest from him in spirit, and there can be no doubt that the hardships of his youth nurtured the seeds of the eccentricity and moodiness which marked him later on and estranged many of his friends.

Among Beethoven's relatives there was one to whom all the rest looked up with pride and reverence—his grandfather, Louis van Beethoven, who had come as a young singer from Holland to Bonn and had risen by degrees to the position of *Kapellmeister* to the Elector.   Serious minded and vigorous, he united in himself the characteristic virtues of the family, and the happiest memories of Beethoven's childhood were centred in his honourable and patriarchal figure.   When in riper years he settled in Vienna, he had the old man's portrait sent to him from Bonn and preserved it to the end of his life.   Louis' son, Johann, inherited few of his father's gifts, but was a true son of his mother, whose drunkenness in later life obliged her husband to confine her in a convent ; a vintner's business carried on by Kapellmeister Beethoven to supplement his professional income was probably a source of temptation to his wife and son.   When in 1767 Johann married Maria Magdalena, daughter of the Elector's personal cook and widow of one Laym, a valet of Ehrenbreitstein, Louis opposed the match, but later there appears to have been a reconciliation and the old man was godfather to Johann's two elder sons.   His pleasure in his grandchildren was, however, not of long duration, for in 1773 he died, and with him the good star of the house set.

Johann van Beethoven's tall and imposing presence accorded ill with a conceited and shiftless personality.   He owed his position as tenor in the royal choir entirely to his father's influence, for he was as lacking in artistic talent as in strength of character. He had no sense of responsibility for his children's education and welfare, and encouraged and exploited the talents of his eldest son merely to satisfy his own vanity and greed.   In later years he went to pieces, and but for Ludwig's vigorous interposition would have ended his days in the gutter.

At the beginning of her married life, Beethoven's mother may have exercised a soothing and restraining influence over her husband, but later she had much to endure from him and suffered terribly in enduring. Maria Magdalena van Beethoven was one of those gentle women who suffer, silent and unresisting, till they sink into the grave. " What is marriage," said she to a young friend, " at first a little joy, then a chain of sorrows." She had to endure not only spiritual trouble but actual want, for her husband's income was small and their family regularly increased. Ludwig Maria, born in 1769, died in infancy and was followed in December 1770 by Ludwig, the second son ; between that date and 1786 five more children were born, of whom two only, Kaspar Anton Karl and Nikolaus Johann, survived.

Throughout his life Beethoven held his mother in hallowed memory and spoke of her always with the tenderest reverence, with a painfully acute sense, perhaps, of her unenviable life with his brutal father. She remained for him the chief of the very few happy associations of his childhood's home. " Each year the feast of St. Mary Magdalene (her birthday and name-day) was kept with due solemnity. The music-stands were brought from the *Tucksaal* and placed in the two sitting rooms overlooking the street, and a canopy, embellished with flowers, leaves and laurel, was put up in the room containing Grandfather Louis' portrait. On the eve of the day, Madame van Beethoven was induced to retire betimes. By ten o'clock all was in readiness ; the silence was broken by the tuning-up of instruments, Madame van Beethoven was awakened, requested to dress, and was then led to a beautifully draped chair beneath the canopy. An outburst of music roused the neighbours, the most drowsy soon catching the infection of gaiety. When the music was over the table was spread and, after food and drink, the merry company fell to dancing (but in stockinged feet to mitigate the noise) and so the festivities came to an end." We have this pretty birthday idyll from a young inmate of the house occupied by the Beethovens ; it gives us a glimpse of the family life in which these merry-makings alternated with certain ugly scenes, but where normal and peaceful domesticity was unknown. Madame van Beethoven's soothing and gentle personality could not in the long run counteract the disastrous effect upon the family life of her husband's unstable temperament. The cares of the household and of her many children hindered her from close intimacy with any one of them, and we have no evidence of that deep understanding between Magdalena van Beethoven and her eldest boy which is often found between the mothers of great men and their sons. Ludwig's affections clung the more to his gentle mother as he saw her the victim of his father's selfish tyranny; it was a childish love born of intense pity, but no more. He was emotionally as shy and reserved with his mother as with others, and she was apparently like others, incapable of penetrating his reserve or winning his confidence.

Beethoven thus grew up amidst sordid cares and emotional storms, his few moments of happiness growing fewer as his father's increasing drunkenness cast an ever-deepening shadow over the family. Even the boy's developing talent brought no pure, unselfish joy to his nearest relatives, but only the hope of turning them to some kind of material profit.

We do not know when the first stirrings of Beethoven's genius became apparent, but in his high-flown, ceremonial dedication of three pianoforte sonatas to the Elector (published in Speyer in 1783 when he was thirteen) he writes: " Since my fourth year, music has occupied the first place among my youthful studies." As his father, however, understated his age by two years to provoke wonder at this youthful prodigy, it would not be safe to draw from this dedication any definite conclusion as to the beginning of his studies. Undoubtedly he was forced to apply himself to music at a very tender age, and his father's heartless speculations on possible fame and gain spoilt, to a great extent, the child's joy in his gift; many a time he was driven sobbing to his instrument. Johann van Beethoven schemed to extract immediate profit from his son's genius. His profession had brought him into touch with cultured people and made him well aware of the advantage of a good general education; yet, although he might have procured such advantages for his son without difficulty, he made no attempt to do this. It is true that for a short time—till about his eleventh year —Ludwig probably went to the *Tirocinium*, which was a kind of preparatory school for the gymnasium, and there received scanty instruction in the rudiments, but we have not reliable information as to his schooling nor even as to his early musical attainments. A concert notice has been preserved according to which little Ludwig, with an older girl, one of his father's pupils, appeared in public at Cologne on March 26th, 1778. This was his first public venture, but we know nothing of the programme, nor of the success of the evening, nor of the boy's subsequent activities. Although he showed unmistakable signs of great gifts, he had not Mozart's marvellous precocity. His father was incapable of understanding the boy's real nature and talents, but he kept him hard at work at clavier and violin alternately until he realised that he had nothing further to teach his son. There followed a rapid succession of teachers, a yet more complete condemnation, if that were possible, of the father's confused and ill-judged educational system than the harshness which he used when himself instructing his young son. An old organist and contemporary of Kapellmeister Beethoven, Van der Eeden, was induced, probably for friendly reasons, to undertake the further teaching of little Ludwig, but there is no indication that he was able to do much for his gifted scholar. He was succeeded by Tobias Friedrich Pfeiffer, a young waster and jack-of-all-trades with some ability as a singer, actor and instrumentalist. His disorderly behaviour had obliged him to leave city after city, and Bonn was to prove no exception. His licentiousness qualified him as boon-companion to Johann van Beethoven; he lodged in his house, drank with him and instructed his son. His methods as teacher were far from gentle. When the two men returned at midnight from rioting in the grog-shops of the town they would wake their pupil, drag him weeping from his bed and begin a lesson which often lasted till morning. In this way Ludwig's art was made a misery to him under the very eyes of his father. Under other conditions, Pfeiffer, with his wide experience and considerable gifts, might have been no bad teacher, but as things were the results can hardly have been salutary. Pfeiffer's reign lasted about a year, at the end of which time Bonn became too hot to hold him. Another inmate of the house, Francis George Rovantini, a young and talented fiddler, took his place till his death at the age of twenty-four in the autumn of 1781. It is said that Beethoven next received organ tuition from Brother Willibald Koch, a Franciscan of considerable musical fame, and that he became friendly with several other organists and received advice and encouragement from them. The boy must gradually have realised that his education had been hitherto superficial and his sense of its inadequacy must have increased as his genius ripened. Choice of a profession he had none; he was unschooled, except in music; and a musician he must become, whether he wished it or not, since every other way was barred to him. His voice was probably not strikingly good, for if it had been his father would in all likelihood have forced him to enter the choir; and of the various instruments which he had studied, the organ seemed to afford him the best chance of early independence. Johann van Beethoven must have been alive to this aspect of the case, for his money troubles had increased with his family, and he counted on assistance from his eldest son at the earliest possible moment.

About this time Ludwig, after a long series of more or less insignificant teachers, was fortunate in securing one who was a teacher indeed, Christian Gottlob Neefe, a man who exercised a real influence over him and fully recognised his great gifts. The coming of Neefe into his life marks the end of Beethoven's troubled childhood, and at the age of eleven he began to feel his way in a world beyond the narrow family circle. His outlook broadened, the spirit of independence in him—partly innate, but undoubtedly increased by bitter early experience—grew stronger with a growing hope of freedom.

The incidents of Beethoven's life at this period, including the origin and duration of the Neefe connection, are obscure. Neefe was in Bonn from October 1779 as musical director to the Grossmann Theatrical Company which had been invited thither by the Elector, Max Friedrich, under promise of his patronage. Attempts to form a German national theatre were at that time in the air, and the Elector of Cologne was following the fashion set by Vienna and Mannheim.

It was then usual for actors to undertake light opera and musical comedy as well as spoken parts. In the Grossmann Company were several renowned artistes; Grossmann and Opitz were considered fine actors, while among the women was the youthful Friederike Flittner (later Unzelmann), an actress of outstanding talent. The young conductor arrived at Bonn with a reputation already won. He was the son of a tailor and had risen by his own efforts from very poor circumstances, becoming first a law student and afterwards a pupil of Johann Adam Hiller, the musical comedy composer, at Leipzig. His own success as a composer was considerable, and the most renowned theatrical managers of the day were soon competing for his services. When he accepted the invitation to Bonn he probably cherished the hope of an additional and lucrative post in the Elector's service, a hope soon fulfilled, for in February 1781—despite the fact that he was a Calvinist—he received a written promise of the place of court organist at the next vacancy, and about a year later, upon the death of Van der Eeden, he got the appointment. Our first really reliable information as to Beethoven's lessons dates from this time. Neefe tells us that the boy, Beethoven, deputised for him at the organ during a journey of the theatrical company to Münster, where the Elector was staying, and paid for his lessons by helping his teacher in this way. In a contribution to *Cramer's Magazine*, March 2nd, 1783, upon the state of music in Bonn, Neefe writes : " Louis van Beethoven, son of the aforementioned tenor, is an eleven-year-old boy of great promise. He plays the clavier with facility and power, reads well at sight, and, in short, plays for the most part Sebastian Bach's *Well-tempered Clavier*, to the study of which he was introduced by Herr Neefe. Those who are thoroughly conversant with this collection of forty-eight Preludes and Fugues (which may almost be considered the *ne plus ultra* of music) will realise the significance of this. As far as his other duties have allowed, Herr Neefe has also instructed him in thoroughbass and has now set him to the study of composition. For his encouragement he has allowed him to publish in Mannheim nine variations upon a march for the clavier. This young genius deserves support and should go far ; if he progresses as he has begun he will become another Wolfgang Amadeus Mozart."

Before Thayer's tireless research work threw light upon the dark and contradictory accounts of Beethoven's youth at Bonn, Neefe's share in his education was undervalued. In the light of what we now know, Neefe's influence upon his pupil's career can hardly be overestimated. His learning was neither very profound nor comprehensive, but he was eminently practical.

The relationship between teacher and pupil is not difficult to understand—common sympathies and common interests drew them together.   Neefe, then in his thirtieth year, was versatile and clever, with the culture of his day at his fingers' ends, and took an interest in the talented but unfortunate boy-musician, finding time in his busy life to give his kindly feelings practical effect by teaching him and making him his deputy.   Beethoven for his part found Neefe no mere pedantic instructor, but an inspiring companion who opened his eyes to the oneness of life and art.   Neefe was a severe critic of Beethoven's early attempts at composition, but he was never a capricious tyrant, and his strictness was due solely to his high artistic standard; its effect upon a boy used hitherto merely to ignorant adulation must have been altogether wholesome.

The unhappiness of Beethoven's family life had made him shy and reserved, but about this time other good influences joined with Neefe's tuition to work a change in his life.   In 1782 he made the acquaintance of a young medical student, Franz Gerhard Wegeler, who, though he did not care for music, conceived a warm liking for the young musician five years his junior and introduced him to the von Breuning family, where he first found the happy domestic atmosphere that was so lacking in his own home.   With these people he was soon at ease, and the liking was mutual.   Frau von Breuning was a widow, twenty-eight years of age, the mother of four children, Christopher, Eleonore, Stephan and Lenz.   Her husband, Herr Hofrat Emanuel von Breuning, had died in 1777 in an attempt at saving life from a castle on fire.   The eldest boy, Christopher, was one year, and the youngest, Lenz, seven years, younger than Beethoven, but despite differences in age a warm friendship grew up between him and the little von Breunings; he was a constant guest in the family and became one of its free yet orderly circle.   Frau von Breuning exercised a strong influence on the character of the growing boy, who felt only too acutely the imperfections of his upbringing.   In her house he found opportunities of making up some of the gaps in his schooling, while in the gentlest way she corrected his defects, taught him to control his unusually headstrong temper and to acquire the manners of polite society.   Until his mother's death his intercourse with the von Breunings was not quite so free as it became later, but at this time the foundations of his lifelong friendship with them were laid and his first serious artistic studies began.

His life was now more eventful, and several of his compositions, notably three pianoforte sonatas dedicated to the Elector, appeared in print. Neefe's own activities expanded; in April 1783 he was asked to deputise during leave of absence for Kapellmeister Luchesi, and he left his young assistant to fill his place in Bonn both at the organ and at pianoforte rehearsals in the theatre. In the meantime Max Freidrich, delighted with the performance of the players, had taken the whole company, now under the management of Frau Grossmann, into his service. Beethoven accordingly was now serving the Elector in the double capacity of deputy-organist and cembalist in the theatre. In February 1784 he plucked up courage and presented a petition, warmly supported by the lord high chamberlain, for appointment as assistant court-organist. Documentary evidence leaves the result of this petition unclear. It seems that a mere entry on the official list of court musicians was promised to Beethoven, when the death of Max Friedrich in April 1784 brought about a complete change of circumstances. The players were discharged, Luchesi returned from leave, and Neefe resumed his place at the organ, while his assistant, recently so much in demand, seemed suddenly to have become superfluous.

The new Elector, Maximilian Franz, youngest son of the Empress Maria Theresa and brother of the reigning Emperor Joseph II, was determined to economise. High salaries were somewhat reduced, Luchesi resigned forthwith, and Neefe would have done the same, but Max Franz, realising his worth, retained him at the old rate of pay. Beethoven, too, stayed on. The pay-lists of the time give us the exact constitution of the Electoral choir. It consisted of thirty-five persons, the Kapellmeister, two organists (Neefe and Beethoven), ten vocalists, eight violins, two violas, one 'cello, two double-basses, one flute, two clarinets, two horns, three bassoons and an organ-blower. The omission of oboes is curious; these were added in January 1785. Beethoven's salary is noted as 150 *gulden*, showing that his appointment had been concluded and that he now had a settled income, small indeed, but nearly sufficient for his needs.

Max Franz's accession had been awaited with anxiety, but it soon became plain that the new ruler of the Cologne Electorate would prove a benefactor to his subjects. He was an enlightened prince, kindly and tolerant towards men of all faiths despite his high spiritual office, and he was eager to make his capital city a centre of intellectual activity and sound learning. By an imperial decree the High School of Bonn already possessed the status of a university; Max Franz instituted thorough reforms in school and law courts, and lost no opportunity of promoting their welfare. He had grown up at the Viennese court, where the arts, especially music, were enthusiastically cultivated, was himself a capable player of the viola, and in his new dignity became a generous patron of the arts. The mistakes of his predecessor forced him to retrench in the early days of his reign, and Max Friedrich's theatrical undertakings were provisionally abandoned, though with reluctance. Instrumental music was, however, his chief interest; it flourished amazingly under his encouragement, for the private residents of Bonn soon followed the lead of the court. Life in the capital under its amiable young ruler must have been an animated and gay affair. The sense that church government prevailed ceased to occupy the foremost place in the minds of its inhabitants and intellectual interests became the fashion, exercising a refining social influence. We have no exact account of Beethoven's doings at this time, but he must have shared in the social prosperity of his town. He probably continued to receive lessons from Neefe, while he added to his salary by taking pupils himself. But his chief interest, apart from his duties as an organist, must have been original composition. Many anecdotes are told of his life at this period, of which only one is credibly vouched for; it relates how he made a wager with Heller, the singer, to " put him out " in his singing of the Lamentations on Good Friday by audacious modulations on the accompanying organ. Beethoven won his bet and was let off lightly with a " gracious reprimand " when the affair was explained to the Elector.

Apart from this incident there is no indication, however, that Max Franz took any special interest in Beethoven. Shortly afterwards an important event occurred in Beethoven's life— his journey to Vienna in the spring of 1787. It was not, apparently, suggested by the Elector, nor did he offer financial assistance, but the origin of the visit and all questions connected with it remain obscure despite much patient research. We do not know how Beethoven got the money for the journey—he may have been able to save up for it himself. The dates of his departure from Bonn, of his arrival in Vienna and his business in that city are also unknown. A wealth of anecdote has grown up round the incident, making it doubly necessary to remember that established facts are few. Beethoven undoubtedly met Mozart, though there are several divergent accounts of the meeting, and when later Ries questioned him about it, Beethoven himself had no very clear account to give. Beethoven improvised before Mozart, but the latter imagined that he was listening to a carefully prepared performance and contented himself with a few cold and formal words of praise. This annoyed Beethoven and put him upon his mettle. He asked Mozart to give him a theme and forthwith developed and embellished it with such astounding originality that Mozart cried to the friends assembled in the next room : " Keep an eye on this man—the world will hear of him some day ! "

If Mozart had come to know Beethoven more thoroughly, the acquaintance might well have ripened into friendship ; but fate separated them. Urgent letters from his father recalled Beethoven to Bonn, where his mother, who had long suffered from lung trouble, lay at the point of death. He left Vienna early in June, borrowed money in Augsburg to complete his journey, and arrived in Bonn ill and depressed. His mother was still living, but her days were numbered and she died on July 17th, 1787. The family fortunes were at a very low ebb. Two sons, aged eleven and thirteen years, were still dependent on their shiftless father. Most of the parents' few possessions had found their way to the pawnbrokers or second-hand dealers, and the eldest son's income was far too small to supply even bare necessities. At this crisis a family friend, Franz Ries the violinist, came to Beethoven's aid, and thanks to his support the most pressing expenses were met. Karl, the elder of the two boys, was destined for the musical profession, while the younger, Johann, was apprenticed to the court apothecary. For a time father and sons lived together with a housekeeper, and Johann and

Ludwig shared expenses. Johann van Beethoven's vice increased upon him, however, and Ludwig was obliged to proceed against his father in the interests of his two young brothers. The answer to Beethoven's petition to the Elector is still in existence. It orders that Johann van Beethoven be suspended from the electoral service, and that for the future only the half of his salary be paid to him; the other half, together with certain accessory payments, to be paid to Ludwig in trust for his brothers' education. It was also decreed that Johann should leave Bonn, but at his own request he was allowed to remain in his son's house, where he lived on under tutelage, a shiftless waster without, apparently, a single redeeming virtue.

Although Beethoven did not formally and openly take charge of the family affairs till November 1789—that is to say two years after his mother's death—there is no doubt that there was a series of domestic crises in the interval and that the official disciplinary measures which he was at last forced to set in motion were only the climax of the quarrel which finally destroyed all sympathy between father and sons. To his family cares Beethoven added a gnawing sense of disappointment with his own achievements. He had sacrificed much to his expedition to Vienna and felt that he had obtained no corresponding results. His health was poor —he was still a growing lad—and he began to imagine that he had inherited lung trouble from his mother. He ceased to find satisfaction in his work in Bonn, realising that it asked of him far less than his capacity warranted, and the tormenting sense that he could find no room to develop nourished a disposition to melancholy —not uncommon in men of genius during adolescence—of which he begins to complain in his letters, from about his seventeenth year. He longed more than ever for friends and for work which would stimulate him and give him self-confidence. Both wishes were fulfilled sooner than he could have hoped, the gloom of his home-coming from Vienna gave place to a brighter mood, and so beneficial was the effect upon him of more congenial society and more fruitful occupation that, despite his unhappy family circumstances, he came to look back upon the years spent at Bonn between his first and second journeys to Vienna as the happiest of his life.

His friendship with the von Breunings and with Wegeler was

once more taken up and increased. Formerly his mother and his mother's troubles had kept him at home to some extent, but he now entered into his friends' family life without reserve. He spent whole days with them, explored with them the beautiful surroundings of Bonn and visited their friends and relatives. Their sympathy, their understanding, their cheerful friendliness and care never failed, and under their influence his melancholy soon gave way to the natural high spirits of youth, only damped from time to time by the thought of the music-lessons which he had to give in various aristocratic families and which he heartily detested. When he was seized by what Frau von Breuning expressively called his " raptus," he avoided the friendly house in the market-place and gave his ill-humour the rein ; but her motherly kindness never failed to overcome his obstinate and passionate humours. She exercised a quieting charm over him and, although he was perverse and refractory with others, he submitted to her, the more willingly that he was not by any means blind to his own failings and lack of self-mastery.

Through the von Breunings he made other acquaintances both morally and practically useful to him, his friendship with Count Ferdinand Ernst Gabriel Waldstein, a young man eight years his senior, being of lifelong importance. Count Waldstein came to Bonn in 1784, probably as a friend of the Elector, with the intention of joining the Teutonic Order of which Max Franz was Grand Master. He served his year of novitiate and was solemnly invested in June 1788. From this time onwards his active participation in Beethoven's affairs is unquestioned, but there is little doubt that the two men became acquainted much earlier, through the von Breunings, and that Waldstein had already given the young artist proof of his generous sentiments towards him. He honoured and encouraged with his friendship one who, in a social sense, was far beneath him. He gave him a grand piano ; and many presents of money, formerly supposed to have come from the Elector, are now known to have been made by Waldstein in Max Franz's name, out of a delicate regard for Beethoven's feelings. Waldstein was the first and probably the most disinterested of Beethoven's many aristocratic patrons. There is a note of fatherly advice in his intercourse with Beethoven—the Count was older and had the advantage in education and experience—yet their whole relationship makes it perfectly clear that he was fully conscious of the infinitesimal value of such things as birth and knowledge of the world in the face of genius.

Social intercourse of this kind improved Beethoven's standing and gradually brought him notice. At the same time his professional opportunities increased. In 1788 Max Franz found himself in a position to revive his predecessor's theatrical plans. The artistes whom he summoned to Bonn—unlike Max Friedrich's troupe—were chosen rather for operatic than dramatic ability, and the orchestra had to be adapted to meet the greater demands upon it. The *konzertmeister* (leading violin), Joseph Reicha, a gifted and keen musician, became director, and under his intensive training the Bonn orchestra soon attained a high level of artistic efficiency. The Elector " discovered " in Münster two cousins named Romberg and attached them to his own choir; and young Anton Reicha, a nephew of the director, was invited to Bonn and created a stir among music-lovers in the capital by his great musical and intellectual gifts. In this way a nucleus of promising and talented musicians was formed in Bonn. Beethoven's place amongst them was not prominent; he was considered but one among many; yet the stimulus of such a circle was extremely good for his developing genius. He composed several works, later published in Vienna (among them, in 1791, a setting for a romantic ballet of Waldstein's), but his name did not appear at the performance of the work, and it seems likely that his compositions were not taken so seriously as those of some of his fellow-musicians and that he was valued chiefly as a pianist. He played the viola in the theatre orchestra; and, although this gave him no chance of personal distinction, it did give him the opportunity of hearing and studying closely all the important operas, lyrical dramas and melodramas of his time. More significant still for his future, he gained a practical knowledge of the elements of orchestral technique. He could have had no sounder training; no lessons or theoretical studies could have supplied its place; and from four years of it Beethoven obtained enough suggestive ideas and practical experience to last him a lifetime.

It was a time of great happiness in many ways. Harmless flirtations, friendships with his colleagues, work in the church and theatre provided plentiful and varied interests. Many famous foreign artistes travelled through Bonn and gave performances there, and in this way Beethoven got to know several of the most renowned prima donnas of the day. In December 1790 he saw Joseph Haydn, who was fêted in Bonn, as he passed through on his way to London. In the autumn of the following year the Elector and his court, accompanied by members of the royal choir and orchestra (Beethoven among them), took ship up the Rhine and Main to Mergentheim, where Max Franz stayed about a month to hold a Chapter of the Teutonic Order. For Beethoven the memory of the expedition was invested with all the charm of romantic youth. While on this journey he met at Aschaffenberg the Abbé Sterkel, the most noted pianist of the day; and his own talent first found recognition beyond the borders of his native city. Upon his return he took up his old life again for a short time, but a change was at hand. In July 1792 Haydn passed through Bonn once more, on his return journey from London; his attention was drawn to a cantata of Beethoven and his interest was caught by the great promise it displayed. It is not known if any practical agreement was then concluded between them, but Beethoven undoubtedly felt that he could remain in Bonn no longer. He had, at any rate, learnt what Bonn had to teach him and had enjoyed the last of his boyish years there. He was now sure of his own talent and felt the need of a wider scope, harder tests and a loftier goal than Bonn could afford him. In November 1792 he set out for Vienna with indefinite leave of absence for purposes of study and with assurance of monetary support. Sudden political changes may account for the readiness with which this leave of absence was granted. At this time the French army of occupation had reached the bank of the Upper Rhine and was drawing very near to Bonn, forcing the Elector to leave his residence. Early in 1793 Max Franz returned amidst the jubilations of his people; but in the autumn of 1794 he was obliged to flee for the second time. He never saw his lands again and died in exile at Hetzendorf near Vienna on July 26th, 1801.

Beethoven arrived in Vienna on November 10th, 1792, after an adventurous journey. Political events had favoured his departure from Bonn, but were by no means propitious to his

c

finances. The promised stipend of one hundred ducats dwindled to one quarter of that amount. In his altered circumstances the Elector could do no more than promise his continued support provisionally. Beethoven's difficulties were further increased by the death of his father a few weeks after his departure. Beethoven's petition that the payment of half Johann's salary might be continued for the support of his two younger sons was granted, but in the first quarter of 1794 these payments also ceased. Maximilian saw that the Electorate was lost, but hoped still to retain the bishopric of Münster. His retinue was greatly diminished, and Beethoven, though not dismissed, was retained on the rolls "without salary." Thus he found himself, after a short residence in the capital of the Holy Roman Empire and German nation, deprived of all financial support and thrown entirely upon his own resources. This alone was sufficiently depressing, but further troubles awaited him. He had come to Vienna with great expectations, honourably greedy for knowledge and hoping at last to be able to complete his musical equipment, but he was bitterly disillusioned. Haydn's lessons fell far short of his hopes. The famous man failed altogether to understand his scholar's personality, nor did he teach the theory of music with the accuracy which Beethoven desired. He concealed his disappointment from Haydn as well as he could, but as soon as he realised that mistakes were being passed over in his work he began to look for other teachers. At first he went secretly to Johann Schenk, composer of *The Village Barber*; but when Haydn's second journey to England left him free, he placed himself under Johann Georg Albrechtsberger, *Kapellmeister* of St. Stephen's Cathedral, one of the most learned and thorough musical theorists in Vienna at that day. At the same time he took lessons from Salieri, an ingenious Italian operatic composer, whose instructions, confined to song composition, involved no strenuous work, and served chiefly as a relief from the hard study demanded by Albrechtsberger. We have fairly exact information as to Beethoven's studies at this period; Nottebohm has brought them together and discussed them critically. These studies were carried on till about April 1795 and comprise various branches of counterpoint, canon and fugue in no very regular order. Neither teacher nor pupil appears to have taken much interest in the lessons, which were apparently plodded through from a sense of duty on both sides. Albrechtsberger's subsequent remarks about Beethoven are not very cordial, and Beethoven's feeling for his teacher never exceeded a certain politely cold admiration.

While he performed dull exercises under this master with assiduity, though without enthusiasm, the musical life of Vienna, on the other hand, influenced him strongly. At first he was strange to the people and customs of the town, but the fact that he took lessons from a dancing-master, as well as from the severe Albrechtsberger, proves that he had social ambitions. In those days, indeed, the houses of the nobility were the only places where a practising musician could find scope for his gifts, since a " public " in the modern sense there was none. Music was cultivated almost exclusively by a rich aristocracy, and particularly in Vienna these people did much to raise the artistic standard. Noble families supported private choirs and orchestras of all descriptions from the most numerous and complicated to string quartets or wind-bands. According to rank and riches, each possessed a *Hauskapelle*, which helped to pass time agreeably in summer, when they withdrew to their castles and estates, and in winter, when they resided in Vienna, contributed to the social prestige of the family. In a land thus soaked in musical culture, a pianist of Beethoven's powers could not long pass unnoticed. We do not know whether Waldstein's recommendation first gave him the entrée to the palace of some great nobleman ; but he was no sooner received than his worth was recognised and his reputation grew with amazing rapidity. A year after his arrival, his position as the first pianist of Vienna was almost unchallenged. The competition of Gelinek, an able performer nicknamed the " variation-smith," of Wölffl, a pupil and imitator of Mozart, and of Steibelt, a specialist in tremolo, only served to enhance his fame. This man and that approached, or even surpassed, him in details of technique, but in imaginative interpretation Beethoven left them all far behind and displayed the compelling greatness of true creative genius. He was hailed on all hands as an enthralling improviser and a brilliant sight-reader. He won as much admiration in the academic soirées of van Swieten, a lover of Bach and Handel, as in the "modern" concerts of Lichnowsky, Liechtenstein, Browne and Schwarzenberg. His services were also in request for the very few public concerts (some four in the year) arranged in the interests of charities. A journey in the summer of 1796 made him known in Prague and Berlin; whether he ever played in public in Leipzig or Dresden is doubtful. He had pupils among the foremost aristocratic families of Austria.

The best proof of Beethoven's self-confidence and trust in his own future at this period is the fact that in 1795 he made a proposal of marriage to a former colleague at Bonn, Magdalena Willmann, now famous in Vienna as a singer. Her refusal— ostensibly because she considered him "too ugly"—does not appear to have caused him any great grief. He continued to take part in the social round, and his letters of the time are almost arrogant in their consciousness of power. He felt that his star was in the ascendant and that nothing could bar his triumphal way. For the time being he was free of practical worries. He lived with Prince Lichnowsky, who gave him a salary of six hundred *gulden*, treated him like a son of the house, and tolerated his attacks of "raptus." In lordly mood he set up a horse and then forgot its very existence till the groom surprised him with a huge bill for fodder; in short, he lived royally and care-free from day to day. He soon made a circle of like-minded friends, music-loving amateurs and young musicians including Zmeskall von Domanowecz, Court Secretary and an able 'cellist; Krumpholz the fiddler; Häring; Eppinger; Kiesewetter, singer and writer; Mozart's pupil, Hummel; and Schuppanzigh, leader of Lichnowsky's private quartet. Beethoven was hearty and jovial with them all, yet there is a faint note of conscious superiority in his most friendly utterances. He dominated them even in his most expansive moments and, with the possible exception of a young musician and theologian, Karl Amenda, he made no such close friends as he had made in Bonn. Wegeler had for some time been settled in Vienna; later on Reicha, and Stephan and Lenz von Breuning came to the capital. These were followed by Beethoven's two brothers, he having undertaken to find them employment. Among the Viennese nobility, Prince Lichnowsky's brother, the artistic Count Moritz Lichnowsky, and the jolly Baron Ignaz von Gleichenstein were

Beethoven's very good friends and patrons. The days passed pleasantly and harmoniously in Vienna, his one trouble being the extreme difficulty of obtaining recognition as a composer.

Vienna was then the music market of the world, and it was by no means easy for new compositions to attract notice or win favour.   Interest in Mozart's rich legacy was still fresh ; Haydn's activity was undiminished, while Salieri, Gyrowetz, Weigl and Eybler were composers of some ability.   They were not all natives of Vienna, but long residence had given them a footing not possessed by the newcomer, Beethoven.   Moreover they conformed easily to the taste of the period after the pattern of Mozart and Haydn, while Beethoven's work was full of what were then considered novelties and audacities which stretched traditional conventions to their limit.   The Viennese saw no need for such strongly individual innovations in composition.   They were willing to forgive them in a virtuoso, but they were too well content as yet with the superfluity of productive (if not creative) talent of the older school to trouble themselves about a young composer's eccentricities.   It took a long time to overcome this attitude, and it was probably rather from policy than from modesty that Beethoven held back the publication of his works. He printed a set of pianoforte variations, but he saw to it that his more important works were first performed several times in the houses of various noblemen, so that their hearers became accustomed to them and the list of subscribers grew, before attempting publication.   Thus his official Opus I, three trios dedicated to Prince Lichnowsky, did not appear till 1795, and it was quickly followed by further works which had for some time been kept back—the first pianoforte sonatas, compositions for various combinations of instruments (among them the septet which so much amazed his contemporaries), the first quartet and the first symphony.

Beethoven was gradually forced to recognise that he could not, as composer, hope for the instant and general recognition which had greeted him as pianist.   As the inward convictions, upon which his work was based, became more secure, he felt that the highest tribunal before which it could be judged lay within himself, and he came to regard the condemnations of conventional criticism with indifference.   On the other hand, he was not deaf to the well-meant advice of his near friends. He had opportunities in plenty of putting his work to practical tests and he made the most of them. On Fridays the Schuppanzigh Quartet met at Prince Lichnowsky's. It consisted of four young musicians all under twenty years of age; Ignaz Schuppanzigh, the leader, was born in 1776, and Nicolas Kraft, the first violin, in 1778. His place was frequently taken by his father, Anton Kraft, while Prince Lichnowsky himself replaced Sina, the second fiddle. Franz Weiss, born in 1788, was the youngest, and later became the most renowned viola player in Vienna.

These musicians were always at Beethoven's command, and he was able to test and experiment with his work to his heart's content. A little later, Prince Lobkowitz, a young spendthrift who ran through his whole fortune in twenty years, took over this quartet party as the nucleus of an orchestra which he placed at Beethoven's disposal for purposes of rehearsal. He was able to bring his pianoforte compositions to the test of his own expert powers as a pianist; the pains which Prince Lichnowsky took to practise Beethoven's pieces in order to refute the allegation that they were "unplayable" were not really necessary. There was keen competition for the copyright of Beethoven's works, first among Viennese publishers and later among foreign publishers; and this made a very favourable impression upon the public. The "professionals" still shook their heads, partly from jealousy and partly from stupidity; but the signs of the times were against them. A genius of the most absolute originality was amongst them; everyone who got to know the new works felt their amazing charm, and the very puzzles and difficulties which they presented were an incentive to closer study.

Beethoven began to extend his activities beyond the borders of purely instrumental work to opera. In 1800 he received a commission to compose ballet music for Vigano's ballet, *The Men of Prometheus*. It was his first important connection with the stage. At the same time he wrote some great vocal music. *Adelaide*, composed in 1796, was followed about 1800 by the oratorio, *The Mount of Olives*. He was engaged also upon the second symphony, and an opera, in collaboration with Emanuel Schikaneder, was projected. Beethoven's star brightened in the heavens, the conquering might of his art was irresistible. In his thirtieth year he had won a position seldom attained by others in old age. There seemed nothing between him and the very highest honours.

At this moment the tide of his fortunes turned. It was as though the gods were jealous and, since the artist was unassailable, struck at the man. In the Heiligenstadt Will, Beethoven has left us a most heartrending picture of his inner life at this time. It is dated October 6th, 1802, and was made under pressure of a constantly increasing fear—the fear of deafness. The first symptoms of ear trouble appeared sometime in the latter part of the 1790's. He began to suffer from more or less severe attacks of partial deafness, the cause and significance of which were not understood by the physicians. Early in the nineteenth century the symptoms increased in gravity and Beethoven was forced to face the fact that total deafness was slowly but surely approaching. He strove against the disease with all his might, sought the advice of physicians, tried the calming effects of country holidays and resorted to strong mineral baths. It was all in vain. He was the helpless victim of an incredibly malign fate. A mood of absolute despair seized him ; not even his pride could support him, and for a time he collapsed utterly. The crisis came at a time of intense creative activity, and nothing but belief in his high destiny and the immortal worth of his work kept him from suicide.

His fate was terrible indeed, but the mood of despair did not last long. He had a strong and vital will, and he knew that, whatever earthly joys might be denied him, the joy of creation was his for life. With this thought to support him he determined to master his fate. He now became more creatively prolific than before deafness overtook him ; various types of pianoforte and chamber-music works followed hard upon each other ; the *Eroica* was projected, and in 1803 he took rooms in the theatre *An der Wien* in order to write an opera for Schikaneder. At first his activities as a performer went on almost as before. With the violinist, Bridgetower, he played the A major sonata—then but just completed—which he dedicated later to Rudolph Kreutzer. He entered into a contest with Abt Vogler, which gave the Viennese the entertainment of comparing and contrasting the two great masters of the keyboard. Schikaneder commissioned both to write opera, but the agreement was made void by a change of management. Baron Braun, however, Schikaneder's successor, renewed the contract with Beethoven, whose imagination was fired by the libretto of *Leonora*. The completed work gave him endless trouble from its first, and only, three performances on November 20th, 21st and 22nd, 1805. It was poorly staged and insufficiently rehearsed, and these faults, together with many weaknesses of text, produced a very bad impression. The hopes attached to it were disappointed, and even when it was produced again on March 29th, 1806, after thorough revision, it was scarcely more successful. In this form it was repeated but once, on April 10th, 1806, after which Beethoven quarrelled with Baron Braun, demanded the return of the score, and severed his connection with the theatre.

Forced as he was by a whole series of unfortunate circumstances to abandon operatic composition, Beethoven turned with keener ambition to instrumental music, in which he was acknowledged master and had no need of compromise and caution. He had reached the maturity of his creative powers, and the next few years gave to the world the 4th, 5th and 6th symphonies; the overture to *Coriolanus*; pianoforte sonatas, Op. 53, 54 and 57; the trios, Op. 70; the *Mass in C major*, commissioned by Prince Esterhazy (first performed in Eisenstadt on September 13th, 1807); the triple concerto, Op. 56; the G major pianoforte concerto, Op. 58; the violin concerto, Op. 61; the choral fantasia, Op. 80, and the Rasumowsky quartets, Op. 59. The dates of composition can, of course, only be given approximately, for many, such as the C minor symphony, were projected and sketched out years before their completion.

Many lesser compositions, such as songs, arrangements of old music, made for sheer love of the work, and settings of Irish, Welsh and Scottish melodies, commissioned by the Edinburgh publisher, Thomson, were produced during the same period. At a concert held on December 22nd, 1808, an imposing array of Beethoven's works was performed for the first time, among them the fifth and sixth symphonies, the *Choral Fantasia*, the G major piano concerto and the *Gloria* and *Sanctus* from the *Mass in C.* It was an occasion of public homage to Beethoven's genius.

During this period many changes occurred in the circle of his personal friends and patrons. He broke off relations with Lichnowsky, when in the autumn of 1806 the Prince required him to play to French officers at his estate near Troppau in Schleswig. On the other hand, he had become more intimate with the wealthy Count Rasumowsky, Russian ambassador and art patron. Count Rasumowsky now engaged the former Lichnowsky Quartet for life. Beethoven controlled. it to a great extent and wrote Op. 69 for it. Other friendships ripened and other new friends were made, among them the sympathetic Hungarian, Countess Erdödy, and Baroness Ertmann, long considered the ablest amateur woman pianist in Vienna, who interpreted his work with deep understanding of its spiritual implications. He was unboundedly grateful to her and called her his " Dorothea Cecilia." Through his friendship with Nanette Stein, now settled in Vienna and married to Andreas Streicher—a boyhood's friend of Schiller—he became very intimate with the best pianoforte-maker of the day. He was welcome both as man and musician in the families of two doctors, Malfatti and Bertolini, while among members of his own profession, Marie Bigot the pianist, Röckel the tenor and Kapellmeister Seyfried were his closest friends.

Beethoven prospered socially and financially, yet he increasingly felt the need of a secure income which would give him freedom for creative work independent of audiences or pupils. In the spring of 1807 a committee of great nobles took over the management of the Court Theatre, and Beethoven asked for the post of composer to the theatre with a fixed yearly salary. No answer was made him and Beethoven's wish seemed unlikely to be fulfilled, when in the autumn of 1808 King Jerome of Westphalia invited him to become Kapellmeister at his Court in Cassel. Many considerations influenced him to reject this offer, among them his increasing deafness, his inherent dislike of the dissolute tone of Jerome's gay court and the uncertain political situation ; but he was undoubtedly attracted by the high salary suggested. He was apparently on the point of accepting, when the Viennese aristocracy awoke to what was happening.

They knew that they possessed a treasure in Beethoven and were determined that he should not be allowed to depart without a struggle. Three of them came together and offered him a secure pension, payable till he should receive an appointment, but " if such appointment should not take place, or if Herr Ludwig van Beethoven should be prevented through accident or old age from practising his art, the said gentlemen guarantee him this pension till his life's end." The compact was concluded on February 26th, 1809. In return for the sum of four thousand *gulden* payable yearly, Beethoven undertook to make Vienna, or some other Austrian city, his permanent place of residence and not to leave the country without his patrons' consent.

Of his three patrons, Prince Kinsky, Prince Lobkowitz and the Archduke Rudolph, Beethoven had most in common with the Archduke, who had been his pupil on the pianoforte and in composition for some years. Rudolph appreciated his teacher's greatness of soul to the full and proved a sincere and disinterested friend. He was the only one of Beethoven's acquaintances whose enthusiastic devotion sometimes bordered on flattery. The hearty and unrestrained intercourse between the two men made Beethoven's subordinate position easier to bear; he expressed his sense of gratitude and dependence at times in striking fashion, knowing that the Archduke was incapable of misunderstanding him or of hurting his proper pride. It was probably the Archduke's idea to keep Beethoven in Vienna by the grant of a pension, and he was certainly the only one of the three patrons who continued to pay the full sum guaranteed till Beethoven's death. Beethoven was constantly in difficulties with his other two patrons. In September 1811 Prince Lobkowitz's affairs were put into the charge of guardians and payments from him ceased for several years. Scarcely a year later, Prince Ferdinand Kinsky died from a fall from his horse, and Beethoven had to resort to a tiresome law process to get the sums due to him paid. When in 1815 he was once more in full receipt of his income, it consisted of 3,400 *gulden* in notes, amounting to 1,360 silver *gulden*, having shrunk to less than half its original value following upon the finance patent introduced in 1811. If, however, he had accepted the offer from Cassell, the depreciation would have left him even worse off.

These perpetual money troubles left Beethoven very much as he had been before the grant of the pension, and forced him once more to do business with publishers. A time of artistic unfruitfulness was the result. His inspiration had already been diminished by the troublous times in 1809, when Vienna was besieged and Haydn died. Gradually, however, his spirits began to revive, and when Bettina von Arnim arrived in Vienna in May 1810 he was full of plans for the future. She was a woman of extraordinary intuition, knew the artist soul through and through, and possessed more of Beethoven's confidence than any other friend throughout his life. Even if the form in which Bettina has given us Beethoven's comments on life and art is fabricated, or at any rate subsequently touched up—even if the originals of two out of her three Beethoven letters, which are doubtfully authentic, never existed—it would still be impossible to doubt that Beethoven's spirit speaks in Bettina's words. No contemporary probed the mystic sources of his genius so deeply as this strange woman, the mystifying prophetess of the German Romantic movement.

Either through Bettina's instigation, or following some impulse of his own, Beethoven began to take an increased interest in contemporary literature and consequently in song composition. He saw much of the Brentanos at this time, and during 1811 and 1812 he became more intimate with a little group of poets at Teplitz, including Tiedge, Varnhagen, Rahel, Elise von der Recke and the somewhat hysterical Amalie Sebald. About the same time he met Goethe, whom he had long honoured from afar. The work of composition once more progressed steadily. Certain occasional works to which he had been commissioned, such as the music for Kotzebue's festival play *The Ruins of Athens* and *King Stephen*, made but slight demands on his time, while some great instrumental works, the B flat major trio, Op. 97, the violin sonata, Op. 96, dedicated to Rode the violinist and the Archduke Rudolph, and two of his last three symphonies were nearing completion. Enough new work was ready to justify another concert such as that held in 1808, but attempts made, early in 1813 to secure a hall suitable for the purpose were unsuccessful, and Beethoven, depressed by attendant worries and still more by disputes with the trustees of his two princely

patrons, was strongly inclined to visit England. Mälzel, a
clever mechanic and astute business man, the inventor of the
metronome and other excellent musical appliances, hoped to
travel with him, realising that Beethoven's fame would help to
draw public attention to himself and his inventions. The plan
seemed a promising one, and although the journey had to be
delayed on account of Karl Beethoven's serious illness, both
Beethoven and Mälzel clung to the idea. The main difficulty
was to raise money for necessary expenses, and money neither of
the prospective travellers possessed. Mälzel, however, was a
man of resource and suggested that they should turn the general
enthusiasm over Wellington's victory at Vittoria to account.
Beethoven was to compose a great battle-piece for Mälzel's
panharmonicon (orchestrion) ; it was to be performed in Vienna
with all possible *éclat*, and means for the journey would be theirs.
Beethoven saw the lucrative possibilities of this suggestion and
set himself to compose battle music for Mälzel's *panharmonicon*.
He was so pleased with the result that he instrumented it for the
orchestra and decided to have it performed with the A major
symphony. The concert took place on December 8th, 1813.
All the most renowned musicians in Vienna took part, including
Sphor, Schuppanzigh, Romberg, Mayseder and the noted
double-bass player, Dragonetti. Salieri conducted from behind
the scenes, Hummel and Meyerbeer played the kettledrums,
Moscheles the cymbals and Beethoven directed the whole. The
care bestowed on the enterprise was amply rewarded and
Beethoven suddenly found himself the hero of the hour ; the
battle music created a greater sensation than all seven symphonies
put together. The results exceeded all Beethoven's expectations ; the concert was repeated three times, each time with
greater success, and Beethoven abandoned his project of visiting
England. Mälzel, with whom the whole idea had originated,
felt himself robbed of the fruit of his labours and secretly set
about collecting the score, part by part, so that he could, if he
wished, perform it independently. Beethoven discovered this
and protested, accusing Mälzel of purloining the score. Mälzel
retorted by claiming the battle music for his orchestrion, and the
case dragged on till 1817, when a friendly settlement was reached.
    Beethoven's popularity was now unassailable. For once in

his life he had been businesslike and speedily reaped his reward. The public could not have enough of him, and the authorities at the Court Theatre suddenly remembered *Leonore*. Once more it was remodelled, the text was revised by Treitschke, and the opera produced on May 23rd, 1814. It was received with enthusiasm, the performance was several times repeated, and it was chosen as the opening piece for the following winter season. The Congress of Vienna was imminent and the city was full of visitors. One of them, a certain Dr. Aloys Weissenbach, laid before Beethoven a poem of welcome to the royal guests. He composed for it with great rapidity, and on November 29th *Der glorreiche Augenblick* (The Glorious Moment) was performed with *Wellington's Victory* and the A major symphony; the concert was twice repeated. About the same time, Beethoven wrote the music for a display at the Königliche und Kaiserliche Riding School and various other small pieces. He returned once again to serious work in the E minor sonata, Op. 90. Beethoven was "lionised" in the *salons*, and the Russian Empress, for whom he improvised a *Polonaise*, granted him an audience. At the castle he accompanied *Adelaide* and the canon from *Fidelio* before the assembled princes and was loaded with presents. He received further offers of business connections with England through two enthusiastic English admirers, Sir George Smart the conductor, and Neate the pianist. Early in 1815, to his great relief, the disputes with Prince Lobkowitz and with Kinsky's heirs were finally settled. A society calling itself "The Friends of Music" commissioned him to write an oratorio and paid him a substantial sum in advance, which he did not take up, however, as the work was never carried out. The Viennese authorities gave him the freedom of the city, with relief from all taxation, and he received a series of honours and recognitions to the detriment, apparently, of his creative work. A setting for Goethe's *Meeresstille und glückliche Fahrt* (Calm Sea and Prosperous Voyage), a few songs and canons, and the 'cello sonata, Op. 102, were all that 1815 produced. Nevertheless Beethoven's courage and artistic consciousness were undoubtedly strengthened and deepened during this period.

On November 15th, 1815, his brother Karl died, leaving him the guardianship of his young son, and on the following January

19th Beethoven pledged himself solemnly to undertake all the duties of a father towards the boy. He little guessed what influence this promise was to have upon the future course of his life.

Most of Beethoven's biographers have been unsparing critics of his two brothers. The single exception is Thayer, whose discovery of certain facts led him to attempt to make their conduct towards their famous brother appear less detestable, or at any rate humanly understandable. In the effort to be fair and to clear away the prejudices of several generations, he draws them in rather too favourable a light. The old estimate may have wronged them in detail, but it is impossible to blink the main fact that neither Karl nor Johann had a trace of spiritual kinship with the genius whose name they shared. The apothecary and the cashier were too clearly their father's sons, as poorly endowed intellectually, less brutal indeed, but with a compensating meanness and paltriness of outlook which made them at times utterly contemptible. Even if we allow that Beethoven may sometimes have misjudged them, and that his relations with them were occasionally exacerbated by his own unreasonable transitions from absolute confidence to offence and suspicion, yet the general impression of their greed and selfishness remains. Beethoven had no real illusions about them and was seized from time to time with disgust at the unequal relationship, but he felt the blood tie strongly. He helped them in sheer goodness of heart and shut his eyes, as far as he might, to their failings, till some rude shock made their true character painfully clear. Karl and Johann were not to blame for having no share of their brother's genius, and their failure to appreciate it or to foster it with brotherly kindness may be pardonable, but their absolute thanklessness for all the advantages which they drew from it, their deliberate exploitation of Beethoven's affection, which they repaid with petty spite, is a thing for which they stand condemned before the tribunal of history.

The younger brother, Johann the apothecary, was the worse of the two, possibly simply because he attained independence earlier and consequently did not need to conceal his true character, possibly, too, because he was the less able. In later years when he acquired property at Gneixendorf he sent Ludwig a card on which was written "Johann van Beethoven, Landowner," and Ludwig replied," Ludwig van Beethoven, Brainowner "; it was a neat piece of self-portraiture on the part of both brothers. Karl's connection with Ludwig was more intimate and personal than Johann's. He occasionally did business of various kinds for his brother and had wit enough to recognise Ludwig's love for him, little as he returned it. It was his trust in this love which made him appoint Beethoven to the guardianship of his son when he came to die. Beethoven took the trust very seriously and modified his manner of life in order to fulfil it. The boy's upbringing gave him a new object in life and he made artistic as well as personal sacrifices for his sake. His care for Karl proved a perpetual drain on his resources, and his intense interest in his nephew's fate undermined his health and weakened his creative powers. He had household worries, lawsuits and domestic intrigues to contend with. When these difficulties were overcome at the cost of tremendous nervous expenditure, it began to be clear that his hopes were to be disappointed and that the boy for whom he had suffered and given so much was unworthy of his pains.

When Beethoven first took charge of his nephew, the child was nine years old, good-natured and talented (though probably less talented than Beethoven in his blind affection supposed), but he had had little chance of developing well in his disorderly and quarrelsome family. His mother was a frivolous and deceitful woman, and Beethoven soon recognised that she had a bad influence on the boy. His plan of education was directed to eliminating this influence so far as possible, and the more the " queen of the night," as he called her, tried, by all kinds of subterfuges, to cross his plans, the more passionate, ruthless and determined Beethoven became in attempting to separate mother and son. These disputes naturally reacted unfavourably on little Karl. Wherever Beethoven placed him, whether he put him to school or took him into his own household, the mother spun her subtle webs and succeeded from time to time in getting hold of the child. For a moment it seemed that the law would take her part against Beethoven. His appeal to statute law was dismissed on the ground that Beethoven, not being of the nobility, was subject to the jurisdiction of the municipal council. Deeply aggrieved at being relegated thus to a forum of burgesses, and knowing that the council took the mother's part, Beethoven felt that Karl was as good as lost to him, when he at length received a favourable judgment from the court of appeal. His guardianship of the child was ratified and the mother was debarred from access to him. Karl was now his own, and, in his exceeding joy at this fact, Beethoven forgot his former troubles and anxieties. The proceedings had dragged on till April 1820, and from the artistic point of view the victory was dearly bought. The year 1817 was almost entirely barren of composition, domestic problems having been too acute; but there was subsequently a gradual revival of artistic interest. Beethoven sketched out the plans of certain great sonatas and symphonies, and in the summer of 1818 he traced the main outlines of a *Mass*, intended to celebrate the expected enthronement in 1820 of Archduke Rudolph as Archbishop of Olmütz. The work, however, took four years to complete, and the finished score was at last presented to Beethoven's distinguished pupil on March 19th, 1823.

During the last few years of creative activity, his most important works were the ninth symphony (completed in 1824); three string quartets (in E flat major, A minor and B flat major), commissioned by and dedicated to Prince Galitzin of Russia, and the string quartets in C sharp minor and F major. Besides these he composed a number of occasional works, including the overture and closing chorus of the *Weihe des Hauses* (Blessing of the House), written for the opening of the Josephstädter Theatre); variations upon certain waltzes of the publisher Diabelli, composed at his request; trio variations upon the theme of *Ich bin der Schneider Kakadu* by Müller, a humorous composer, and several small pieces such as the *Gratulations Menuett*. Other works were projected, but did not get beyond the first rough sketches; some not so far. Among these were a Bach overture, a tenth symphony, a *Mass* in C sharp minor, a series of oratorios, *Sieg des Kreuzes, Die Elemente, Judith, Saul*, an opera, *Melusine* (upon Grillparzer's text), a requiem and a sonata for piano duet.

We know something of these plans from the " conversation books " kept by Beethoven during his later years, little octavo notebooks in which visitors scribbled their remarks. He resorted to this method of conversation in 1819, when his hearing became so bad that the spoken word reached him no more. Those notebooks, which have been preserved, provide a picture of the kind of conversation which he held during the last eight years of his life, only the visitors' remarks, of course, being recorded. His social intercourse was far from restricted. He had become in course of time one of the " sights " of Vienna, and every visitor to the city with any interest in art eagerly sought an introduction. Travelling musicians thronged to see him, bringing scores to put before him, eager to discuss musical news and events, so that, deaf as he was, Beethoven was kept well in touch with the world of art. Marschner came ; the enthusiastic Rellstab ; Weber, whom Beethoven received with affectionate respect; Liszt, then a twelve-year old boy, whose reception was not particularly favourable ; Rossini, the idol of the time ; Ferdinand Hiller ; Franz Lachner ; the two Zelters ; and that keen observer, Rochlitz. They came to pay homage to genius ; Beethoven allowed them to entertain him with great good humour, but in intercourse with near friends and colleagues he seemed often to revert to the high-spirited unceremonious tone, the jovial manner, of his youth. Schubert's friend, Anselm Hüttenbrenner, visited him, but we do not know whether Schubert himself did so. It is certain that there was no close intercourse between the two composers, and it was not till Beethoven lay on his deathbed that he realised that the " divine spark " burned in this man, who had lived near him so long unnoticed, and who eighteen months later was to follow him to the grave.

Hüttenbrenner came from Graz as an emissary from Frau Marie Pachler-Koschak, one of several ladies artistically and personally near to Beethoven, though with none did he overstep the bounds of sympathetic friendship. Time had wrought many changes in Beethoven's circle, some of his old friends having died, while Zmeskall was confined to his room by sickness and Schuppanzigh had for several years been settled in Russia. A new generation had grown up, but of the friends of his youth, Stephan von Breuning remained, and chance brought them more closely together during the last year and a half of Beethoven's life.

In October 1825, Beethoven took apartments in the so-called *Schwarzspanierhaus*, in the neighbourhood of which the von

D

Breunings were settled, and the two households held constant intercourse. Stephan von Breuning's twelve-year-old son Gerhard (whom Beethoven nicknamed " Ariel " and " Hosen-knopf ") later set down his recollections of those days in a book, *Aus dem Schwarzspanierhaus*, which has a great air of proba-bility. About this time a number of younger men, who had grown up under the spell of Beethoven's music, began to form a circle about him. Among these, he was particularly intimate with Anton Schindler and Karl Holz, who were only too glad to be of use to him as some return for what they felt to be the honour of his friendship and confidence. Hitherto he had relied alternately upon his brother Karl and upon a young accountant, Franz Oliva (to whom he dedicated pianoforte variations, Op. 76), for secretarial help and business advice. In 1820, Oliva left Vienna. His personal relations with Beethoven are somewhat obscure, but it appears that for some time before Oliva's depar-ture their former close friendship had been upon the wane. However that may be, his place was taken in 1819 by Anton Schindler, a sound, average man and musician, honestly devoted to Beethoven, but too limited to be capable of anything like friendship on equal terms with the Master he honoured. We owe the preservation of much valuable verbal and written infor-mation about Beethoven to him, although he was not the man to obtain deep insight into his mind and character. The material which he collected so zealously is not on that account to be despised. Despite his somewhat jealous affection, his place in Beethoven's personal regard was gradually taken by a younger acquaintance, Karl Holz, who, gifted and clever, though given to wild fancies, was more able than the precise Schindler to understand Beethoven's peculiarities and to stimulate and amuse him. We know too little of Holz's character to form a judgment, but it is clear that personal bitterness has led Schindler to over-colour his picture of the riotous living to which, according to him, Beethoven, in his need of distraction, was led by the dashing Holz.

Beethoven had now lost touch almost completely with the Viennese public. His increasing deafness made public per-formance impracticable for him, and he could appear on the platform only as composer. When it was proposed that the ninth symphony and a new *Mass* should be given for the first time in Berlin, a large number of Viennese music-lovers presented an address to Beethoven asking him to organise a concert, so that Vienna, his second home, might not lose the honour of the first performance of these works. He was very much touched by the form of the address and consented. The ninth symphony and parts of the *Mass* formed the principal items on the programme; but the concert, which took place on May 7th, 1824, proved a bitter disappointment to the ageing composer. He had much trouble in finding a suitable concert-hall and orchestra, the business negotiations encroached very much on his time, and the monetary result was unexpectedly small. Payment of expenses left a net profit of only 420 *gulden*, and a repetition of the concert proved yet more disappointing; Beethoven was only saved from actual loss by a guarantee of 500 *gulden*.

The artistic results were more encouraging, although Beethoven was unable to enjoy them to the full, for he could hear nothing and a woman singer had to turn him towards the audience so that he might at least *see* their applause. By November 1822 he was completely deaf, and at a rehearsal of *Fidelio* he was asked to lay down the conductor's baton to prevent confusion. This affliction was hard for him to bear, but, unfortunately, it was not his only physical ailment. Almost every year his health suffered some fresh assault; he was attacked in turn by jaundice, rheumatism, an obstinate eye trouble, and peritonitis. He did not know, however, that most of these illnesses were but symptoms of a slow but deadly disease, cirrhosis of the liver.

Constant interruptions to his productive work naturally affected his financial position adversely. Ten subscribers contributed 50 ducats each for the *Mass*, and the publisher's fees for the new work were high for those days; but even so his income barely sufficed for his daily wants. During the Congress, Beethoven had saved up money which he had invested in eight bank-stocks of 1,000 *gulden* each, and which he intended to leave to his nephew. Early in 1823, pressed by extreme necessity, he at last decided to sell one bank-stock; but nothing could persuade him to reduce his intended legacy further. When during his last lingering illness he was in actual want of food, he applied for help to the London Philharmonic Society rather than touch the capital which he regarded as Karl's property. His intense love for his nephew survived the strain which was put upon it by the young man's behaviour during his uncle's last years. Karl undoubtedly inherited his mother's frivolity and lack of moral responsibility. After short and desultory study at the University he left it for the Polytechnic; but he failed to apply himself to work there till he was faced in the autumn of 1826 with the prospect of an examination for which he was totally unprepared. Fear of the discovery of certain hidden debts and of his uncle's perpetual admonishments and reproaches drove him to despair and he decided to take his own life. His attempt failed, and after a short illness he was able to follow his new wish for a military career; but the affair was a shattering blow to Beethoven. Outwardly he bore up under his troubles, and late in the autumn went for a holiday with his convalescent nephew to Gneixendorf, near Krems, his brother Johann's little estate. The seeds of mortal disease were in him, however, and early in December he returned, gravely ill, to Vienna. Symptoms of dropsy appeared, the disease advanced very rapidly, and, although he did not receive the best medical attention, there is little doubt that he was beyond the help even of the best. A little before the end he was cheered by a gift of £100 from the London Philharmonic Society; it was one of several kindnesses which he received from England—others being the present of a Broadwood grand from Thomas Broadwood, a partner of the firm, and an *édition de luxe* of Handel's works from Stumpff, a harp-maker of London—and his feelings for that country had long been very warm.

In the spring of 1827 his health grew rapidly worse. He underwent four operations, after which the doctors declared that they could do no more for him. Beethoven knew that death approached and faced it in the spirit of his own words, written in 1802—" Come when thou wilt, I will meet thee with courage." He concluded his worldly affairs. Helped by his nearest friends, yet with the greatest difficulty, he made a short will on March 23rd. The next day he signed a contract with Schott for the C sharp minor string quartet and received the last sacrament with trustful resignation and devotion. He had a hard conflict before him; his strong body did not easily submit to the forces of dissolution. By the evening of March 24th he lay unconscious, breathing with difficulty—a harrowing spectacle to the few friends who took turns to watch by his bedside. His nephew was not among them, but remained with his regiment at Iglau. The death agony was prolonged over two days. A little after noon on March 26th, Schlindler and Breuning, worn out with grief and watching, went out for a little to choose a burial place. Anselm Hüttenbrenner stood alone by the deathbed, while a violent storm of thunder and lightning raged overhead. The dying man suddenly raised himself, clenched his fist threateningly, and sinking back breathed his last.

Ludwig van Beethoven's earthly course was finished. Like the great prophet of the Old Testament, he ascended to heaven in a chariot of fire.

CHAPTER II

BEETHOVEN'S PERSONALITY

THE general tendency to idealise the figure of a great man has resulted in the creation of a portrait of Beethoven which bears little resemblance to reality. He is depicted as making his difficult way through life, an unpractical and eccentric dreamer— a picture easily constructed with the help of a few anecdotes and allusions to his deafness. How, indeed, could such a man, lost in a world of his own imagining, have any conception of human nature, of the every-day business of life? Rather would he withdraw yet further within himself at the first rude touch of reality!

The results of historical investigations, however, build up a very different image. Many interesting particulars of Beethoven's life are now established, free from fictitious embellishments. In view of these facts it is clear that he has hitherto been presented to us in a falsely romantic light, and the need to dispel this is obvious. Few musicians, indeed, have shown such a grasp of objective reality. Beethoven was inclined to severity rather than indulgence in his estimate of his fellow-men (hardly the characteristic of an idealistic dreamer!) and his conduct, though it may seem strange at times, reveals throughout a strong sense of purpose and a fundamentally discerning and dispassionate spirit.

Certainly Beethoven was not the man to become immersed in every-day affairs. His art stood for him above mundane matters, and it might well happen that in the ecstasy of creation he was sometimes lost to all around; that at such times he was oblivious of his friends, and, indeed, during the composition of the *Mass*, so neglectful of his appearance that he was arrested and put in custody as a vagabond, bears witness to the overwhelming power of his inspiration, but not at all to its unhinging quality. Such events, moreover, are exceptional; they afford no basis for general conclusions.

Special care for his appearance was certainly never one of Beethoven's characteristics. When scolded as a child for his disordered and soiled garments, "What does it matter?" he answered; "when I am a man I shall not bother about such things." Intercourse with the von Breunings and their circle may have had a good influence upon him, and during his first stay in Vienna he seems to have made an effort to comply with the usages of society. In his records of that time there are many notes of expenditure on a fashionable wardrobe. Lessons from a dancing-master, too, show that even Beethoven once paid homage to the Graces. They can hardly be said to have smiled on him. All his efforts after refinement were doomed to failure by his uncouth nature and excitable, impetuous temperament. All his life long, fragile ornaments were unsafe in his vicinity. His very efforts after elegance were not so much a natural impulse as a concession made to the cultured, in order to gain admission to their salons. Once his object was achieved, he reverted to his unceremonious self, indifferent to the sit of his wig, or to the fact that his behaviour outraged the laws of etiquette. He lived with Prince Lichnowsky and enjoyed all the benefits of an intimate hospitality; yet he hated the restrictions of the communal board. "I have to be at home regularly by half-past four to change my attire, shave myself and so forth—I cannot endure it," he complains to Wegeler. He would rather live after his own fashion and dine at an inn; constraint of any kind is hateful to him; attentions disgust him, and extreme politeness he finds almost as offensive as arrogance. He left Baron Pronay's villa at Hetzendorf, where he was staying during the summer of 1823, after a short stay, in order to escape the owner's manifestations of respectful devotion. He scorned social conventions; his artist's pride raised him above them. In 1804 he was invited to meet Prince Louis Ferdinand of Prussia, then staying in Vienna, but when he found that his place was not at the Prince's table, he started up brusquely and left the house. Shortly afterwards he enjoyed the satisfaction of an invitation from the Prince, who selected for himself a place between Beethoven and the hostess of the former evening.

Inevitably this overweening self-assurance grew with his

growing conviction of his own artistic merits. His neglect of externals, however, was subject to phases. After a period of complete disregard of appearances, Beethoven would be suddenly seized again by a desire to play the polished gentleman. These changes may generally be explained by his creative mood. When he was enthralled by a great work, it possessed him to complete forgetfulness of the outside world and its claims ; but the composition once completed he gradually returned to the normal, became alive to his surroundings, and cheerfully resumed social intercourse.

Beethoven certainly must have presented an odd ·picture when dressed in the height of fashion. When he had a companion, his extravagant gestures and rough loud voice arrested the attention of passers-by. When he strode alone on his usual daily walk through the streets of Vienna, his appearance was strikingly grotesque. Lyser has given us a description of Beethoven on his rambles, founded on Gerhard von Breuning's very trustworthy account of the musician's last years. We see him as he hastens through the streets, his short sturdy figure clad in fashionable white stockings and light pantaloons, a vest of the same colour, a white neckcloth artistically arranged round a wide stand-up collar, a big, curly-brimmed hat and a flowing blue frock-coat with brass buttons. The pockets of this same coat are heavily laden, causing it to flap open and show the lining as he walks. They contain a bulky sketch-book in quarto, an octavo " conversation " note-book, a thick carpenter's pencil, an ear-trumpet and other necessities. He passes on, his hands folded behind him, the upper part of his body bent forward, his head tilted up. Suddenly he stops in his walk, draws one of the books from his pocket, and begins to hum to himself, now softly, now loudly, gesticulating as he makes his notes. The walk is then resumed ; and if Beethoven is no longer gazing into the sky, but has his glance turned earthwards, he twists his face into a smirk of admiration at the sight of a pretty girl.

That Beethoven was no Adonis is vouched for, not only by his contemporaries but by such portraits of him as we possess. A considerable number are extant, particularly of the composer in later years when his increased reputation afforded a motive for more frequently portraying him. Unfortunately none of these portraits can be taken as reliable expositions of Beethoven's personality. The art of portrait-painting was at that time but little developed in Vienna, and, moreover, Beethoven was far too impatient a model to give a painter opportunity of making a really penetrating study. As a revelation of his essential nature the majority of the not inconsiderable number of Beethoven's portraits are practically valueless to-day. Neither Stieler's idealised, sentimentally melancholy picture of the composer with his *Mass*, not Dietrich's stiff conventional drawing and bust, nor even Mähler's well-meaning but amateurish performance can be regarded as true to life. It is uncertain whether the reputed silhouette of Beethoven at sixteen years of age, made at Bonn, is actually of him or of one of his brothers. The death-mask is worthless, for Dannhauser was not able to take it till after the temples had been sawn out and the features and skull distorted. There remain Schimon's oil-painting, Kloeber's lithograph, Höfel's copper-plate engraving after Letronne's drawing, and the bust modelled by Klein for *Streicher's Magazine* from the mask taken for that purpose in 1812. This last gives the most faithful picture of Beethoven's head with its conch-shaped chin, deformed on the left side by pock marks, prominent cheek-bones, wide, thick-lipped mouth, short thick nose, and proudly arched forehead. The regal brow was, indeed, the only external feature which could arouse admiration. " What a beautiful brow he has !" a lady exclaimed once to the assembled company. " Well then—salute it ! " answered the master, bending towards her. Many years after his death the thickness of the outer walls of Beethoven's skull aroused comment. A reconstruction, however, was found, on the exhumation of 1863, to be impossible. Those bones which had been sawn through for the purpose of a scientific examination of the brain were completely distorted by the dampness of the grave.

The mask preserves the general contour of the face accurately enough, but the best is irretrievably lost—the arresting gaze of the fiery and most expressive eyes. A wonderful and noble power beamed from their luminous depths ; above all when, as Rochlitz pictures him in creative mood, he seemed, with head thrown back and uplifted gaze, to seek in infinity expression for the fancies thronging him. No artist has succeeded in showing us what these eyes with their immense range of expression were really like. Letronne has doubtless best caught the penetrating gaze with which Beethoven would sometimes probe a visitor, whilst Kloeber and Schimon sought rather to represent the visionary. Both, too, show the same thick, wavy, unkempt hair. But of the light that once dwelt beneath those brows, the Jove-like ray which once shone there, we can only catch a faintly reflected glory in the memoirs of contemporaries.

Imagination must come to our aid to give us, with the help of a few isolated indications, a vivid idea of Beethoven's appearance. The sturdy thick-set frame and brown vivacious face were a picture of native forcefulness, before illness and mental struggles engraved them with the marks of incurable disease. Beethoven's career proclaims an essentially sound and robust nature. There are no outward indications of a sensitive temperament, no trace of fastidiousness—he would spit out of the window or by an oversight into a mirror!—and, indeed, his personal habits were often so careless that Stephan von Breuning's wife had a rooted aversion to accepting an invitation to lunch in his rooms. Lack of cleanliness in such matters did not worry him, but every morning he washed from head to foot, humming, singing or bellowing, as he composed the while. He then sat down to his desk, or as an alternative, whatever the weather, went for a long country walk, which, when the creative spirit was strong upon him, was often prolonged till nightfall. In summer when he was in the country, he would lie in a shady spot gazing into the heavens or would run across the fields, declaiming and beating time—as once at Gneixendorf, where a span of oxen fled terrified from the uncanny spectacle to the amazement of the honest peasant who led them. At table he was frugal and no epicure. "Why so many dishes?" he asked Stumpff. "Man is little better than any other animal if his chief pleasures are confined to those of the table." He thought fish a great delicacy and often presented his friends with what he himself valued so highly. He liked good wine and sacrificed to Bacchus at times without becoming his slave.

Beethoven indulged a taste for luxury chiefly in the choice of rooms. He attached, indeed, no importance to interior appointments, demanding neither elegance nor great comfort, only plenty of space to move in, but the situation of the room was a matter of the greatest moment to him. He insisted on an open and pleasant outlook, with windows not overlooked, at a short distance from the country. These requirements were not easily satisfied, and thus Beethoven frequently changed his lodgings, sometimes without due notice. As he usually migrated during the summer to some pleasant spot in the neighbourhood of Vienna, Heiligenstadt, Hetzendorf, Mödling, Döbling or Baden, he was often tenant of three separate dwellings—a quite considerable establishment for a man of his means.

These summer migrations are hardly to be explained as periods of physical recuperation, for Beethoven worked even harder in summer than in winter, when he had many distractions and could, for the most part, only elaborate ideas shaped in the summer. Beethoven's passion for the country sprang from a deep-rooted craving for recollectedness, for communion with the world of unspoilt nature. His works show many signs of his love of nature, its strongest, most masterly expression being the *Pastoral* symphony. When, later in this book, we come to consider this work we shall find opportunity to touch on the very special relationship in which Beethoven stood to external nature. There is much oral and written testimony that to him, brought up as he was in a most beautiful countryside, communion with nature was a vital need. At the same time it is clear that Beethoven sought nature in the first place as the antithesis of the restraints of town, and not for beauties of landscape. The essential charm of country life lay for him in its utter freedom from social considerations, its unhampered impulses, its peace. He felt but little need for change, and was only occasionally induced, on medical advice, to leave the immediate neighbourhood of Vienna for Teplitz, Karlsbad or Franzensbad.

Beethoven travelled but little. Except for a trip to Holland made during childhood with his mother, the journey to Prague and Berlin towards the end of his nineteenth year was his only considerable expedition. There was no lack of schemes. Not only was a visit to England, with its bright monetary prospects, frequently deliberated in his later years, but he had an inclination to visit Italy and Sicily and often dreamed of an adventurous and triumphant tour. All such plans were shattered, not only by Beethoven's own irresolution, but by the many practical difficulties. The profits from any such undertaking were doubtful; Beethoven's increasing deafness would have made a travelling companion indispensable, with a consequent increase in expenses. Moreover, Beethoven himself, his brother Carl, or his nephew was usually taken ill at the very moment decided upon, so that, in his later years, but for his summer holiday, Beethoven did not leave Vienna.

He thus remained throughout his life confined to one narrow sphere of personal activity. This state of affairs could not be anything but favourable to his finances. As a matter of fact, once Beethoven had obtained a footing in Vienna, he was safe from actual want. He could dictate his own terms to his publishers, and the capital of 8,000 *gulden*, saved from the time of the Congress, formed a reserve fund when receipts dwindled through a period of illness or lessened productiveness. He complained, indeed, frequently of his straitened circumstances, and he has been taken at his word to a degree unjustified by facts. Truth to tell, Beethoven's conduct in money matters was one of the weak spots in his character, and cannot be presented in a favourable light. Like many another man of genius whose predominating interest lies in the realm of ideas, he overestimated the value of money. He would never prostitute his art to pecuniary needs, but he was often unscrupulous to a degree which cannot be explained away. He was, of course, absolutely within his rights in making the best bargain he could for his own works. Correspondence relating thereto reveals him as a practical business man, extraordinarily good at accounts and competent at arranging favourable terms. Indeed, it is manifestly absurd to represent him as inexperienced in affairs and imposed upon on every side. On the contrary, he was one of the first musicians to stand up to his publishers and to reap the highest possible reward of his labours. But he was not always satisfied with what he could justly claim.

He not infrequently broke his word, struck a bargain and then withdrew on receiving other offers; he took payment in advance for work which he did not carry out, and for his own purposes roused expectations which he knew could not be fulfilled. There are few more regrettable episodes than that of the publishers' rivalry for the great *Mass*, which Beethoven promised, almost simultaneously, to six firms, only to hand it over to a seventh in the end. The request for monetary support, couched in the most moving terms and sent to London from his death-bed, is a conscious misrepresentation of the state of affairs; even the fact that it was prompted by love of his nephew cannot excuse it.

Signs of a fine magnanimity are not lacking, however, as some mitigation of this darker side of Beethoven's character. A proof of his inherent generosity is found in his support of Carl's mother when she fell on evil days, despite all the wrongs she had done him and the quite righteous detestation he felt for her. The fact that he unselfishly lent certain of his works to the Ursulines at Graz to be performed for the benefit of their charities shows that he could be full of zeal in a good cause, and his correspondence with Councillor Varena concerning this affair is one of the finest memorials we have of Beethoven the man. He was always ready to give, even if equally ready to take—a trait often either completely ignored or passed over in silence. This had a disturbing effect on personal relationships. In money-matters he often shows himself in a most unfavourable light both to his brothers and to his nearest friends. One of the most disagreeable scenes in his life is that in which, disappointed by the small takings of the concert of May 7th, 1824, at a dinner given shortly after to his intimate friends, he reviled them with such wounding expressions of distrust that they, who had rallied faithfully round him in all his difficulties, got up silently, leaving him alone with his nephew. Beethoven's increasing deafness may have strengthened his suspicious habit of mind, but it was an innate defect of his character and constantly led him to impute blame to others for untoward happenings. Just as he could not rejoice in solitude, so, too, he always needed someone on whom to vent his vexation. Whoever came across his path at such times paid for it; no rule of politeness, no sensitiveness of feeling, constrained Beethoven to an exercise of self-control.

It was no light task to be Beethoven's friend. Only the consciousness of serving a great and essentially noble artist could compensate his intimates for the many unwarrantable injuries they received from him. Such servitude was an essential condition of inclusion in his circle; he needed friends to distract, amuse and support him in the daily round. " I must have some confidant, or life is a burden to me," he writes to Brunswick. A sure instinct always led him to choose congenial spirits. He judged them aright and estimated them at their true value. Even so, he sometimes came to grief in his treatment of them, through a too boorish display of his own superiority. He would perversely wound the little weaknesses which he perceived in them and thus estranged many who would willingly have remained his friends.

Friends, in the full sense of the word, intellectually his equals, truly appreciative of his art, Beethoven never possessed. He could never form such a bond as that which existed between Goethe and Schiller. Enthroned in lonely majesty, whom could he have found who would dare to reach out a hand to him? And had it been otherwise, had he discovered in the youthful and apparently undistinguished Franz Schubert a branch of the same great stock of master-artists from which he himself had sprung, would they not both have lacked speech, the great medium for the exchange of thought? Beethoven had but slight command of language. His comments on his art, culled from letters and diaries, deeply thoughtful though they are, and surprisingly illuminative, are as it were " impressionist " and wrung out with difficulty. The clear-sighted power of an affectionate nature like Bettina's might, indeed, illumine the depths of Beethoven's emotions and thoughts with some strange flash of insight, and interpret through her own personality what she saw in him, but Beethoven was not made for the stimulating intimacies of a heart-to-heart friendship. He drew his inspiration from the depths of his own personality and was far too impetuous and headstrong to submit to any external influence. A dominant nature, born to despotism, he could brook no other tyrant nigh him.

Inevitably his capacity for human friendship was limited. The tale of those with whom he was unreservedly intimate is but small, and confined to the friends of his youth. The Breunings and Wegeler, his Rhineland friends, were those for whom he always entertained the liveliest affection. To them, in the first years of the life in Vienna, was added the young theologian Amenda. However long intercourse with these few might be broken, and even though occasional differences threatened to loosen or even break the tie, harmony was always re-established, and Beethoven, on the heels of a breach for which he was often to blame, would display his most attractive qualities. He would then find words of a most touching tenderness and give the noblest expression to a friendship founded on perfect sympathy.

Widely separated from these cherished companions of his youth were his Viennese friends. For the former he felt unreserved affection; he condescended to the latter—and made use of them. He was at pains to overlook their failings. " Never show to men the contempt they deserve; one never knows to what use one may want to put them," he reflects to himself in the 1814 diary. He did not, however, always live up to these calmly diplomatic principles! In time, firm ties were formed in Vienna also. Gradually Gleichenstein, Brunswick and Zmeskall became something more to him than " instruments on which to play as it pleased him "—as he once wrote arrogantly to Amenda. They were witnesses of the storms he lived through, the griefs which rent him. They befriended him generously; custom and a life in common bound them to him and bridged many disparities between them. But they never attained the perfect intimacy of the earlier friendships, which continued throughout his life and preserved the glamour of those bygone happier times upon which the master, in his days of lonely exaltation, loved to dwell in retrospect. An exile, called forth to the conquest of the world, he saw in these friends the fatherland he was never to revisit. The men whom later he learnt to know and value may have been no less estimable than his companions at Bonn, but they could never be to him what these had been; they could only occupy a part of his existence, they could take no root in his heart.

He had lost for ever the ready and joyous susceptibility of youth.

There were, too, only a few in his circle of Viennese acquaintances whose friendship deepened with time. People like Schindler or Holz counted for nothing with him. They were born "hangers-on" and their reward lay in mere association with the Master. Beethoven treated them peremptorily—masterful, irritable, inconsiderate according to his mood. He rightly felt them beneath his confidence and affection. He played with them as the lion with the mouse, and it was almost ludicrous when that honest subaltern, Schindler, preened himself complacently upon being one of Beethoven's intimate circle. He was no more than his master's lackey—but certainly he was a very faithful and honourable one, treasuring and preserving every crumb that fell from his table. Beethoven's pupil, Ferdinand Ries, prided himself, too, on the master's favour. But he was as little able as Anton Schindler to bridge the gulf that separated their personalities. The son of a former fellow-student at Bonn, he had been taken up and taught by Beethoven out of gratitude for a favour once conferred by his father. What is more, Beethoven was irate when he found that Ries was in want and had suppressed the fact. "Why do you hide your poverty from me? None of my friends shall starve while I have anything." Ries repaid him with a blind devotion. Later on, he made influential friends for Beethoven in England, and, as a musician, worked for the recognition of his master's works, thereby securing to himself Beethoven's undying goodwill. The latter had a disposition far too humane ever to forget those whose services he had accepted. Schindler, like Ries, received frequent proofs of his affectionate solicitude. Beethoven was no ingrate and his inferiors never seemed to him unworthy of remembrance. Even from his death-bed he proffered help to Schindler, then in needy circumstances: "At least take food from me—it is given with all my heart."

Thus his spirit of wide humanity was reflected in his treatment of those who had but slight claim on him. His heart was big enough to welcome and entertain all with whom he came in contact. To the beloved comrades of the Bonn days alone was he united in bonds of closest friendship, for with them alone he felt as a man among men, and voluntarily relinquished all the privileges of genius.

Beethoven's relations with women arose naturally from his friendly impulses. He regarded Eleonore von Breuning, daughter of his motherly friend, Helene von Breuning of Bonn, and, later, Wegeler's wife, with a brotherly affection. His trusted counsellor in all matters of his wardrobe or his household was practical, shrewd Nanette Stein, wife of the ingenious pianoforte-manufacturer, Andreas Streicher. Intellectual interests formed his chief link with the ladies of the Brentano family circle, and especially with Bettina von Arnim; and such was the case with the clever and sensitive Amalie Sebald of Berlin, whom he met at Teplitz in 1811–12. His acquaintance with Dorothea von Ertmann, a most sympathetic interpreter of his pianoforte works, had an important influence on his art. Marie Bigot and Marie Pachler-Koschak were also exponents of his work whom he valued highly, while the Countesses Erdödy and Therese Brunswick, in the rôle of aristocratic patronesses, were among his most intimate friends.

There is proof enough, however, that Beethoven's feelings for women often overstepped the bounds of friendship. " Beethoven was never without a love-affair, and with him love was usually a passion," Wegeler affirms. But we cannot discover where he found a favourable hearing. A single document found among his effects after his death gives evidence of a deep-rooted and apparently reciprocated passion, but impenetrable darkness broods over the affair. The letter to the " Immortal Beloved," as he styles her, is vaguely dated, bears neither place nor year, and leaves room for boundless conjectures as to her identity. Diligent efforts have been made to discover which of the ladies of Beethoven's circle could have thus enslaved him. First in chronological order comes Magdalene Willmann, the singer, whom he knew in Bonn, and to whom tradition has it he made an offer of marriage in 1795. The next to be considered is the young Countess Guilietta Guicciardi, who was Beethoven's pianoforte pupil at the beginning of the new century, and was rather his friend than his " flame." That there was a love-affair between Beethoven and Guilietta cannot be doubted on the evidence of Beethoven's own words on the subject to

E

Schindler. "J'etais bien aimé d'elle, et plus que jamais son époux." Still it is doubtful if Guilietta Guicciardi can be identified with the "Immortal Beloved." Other clues seem to indicate the Countess Therese Brunswick. But, whoever the recipient of the mysterious letter may have been, it would be an extravagance to assign to this love-affair the nature of a tragedy. It can only be regarded as an episode in Beethoven's history.

He made matrimonial plans in plenty without suffering from any very lasting emotions. After being rejected by Magdalene Willmann, and, apparently, in the spring of 1810 by Therese Malfatti, the daughter of his friend the doctor, he occasionally expresses a longing for peaceful married happiness. " Only grant me love, that gift which alone brings joy to life ! O God, let me but find her who shall strengthen me in all virtue, who is destined to be mine ! "—so runs an entry in the Baden diary—" when M. drove past me, and methought she threw me a glance." So he blazes up suddenly, as suddenly to forget the incident. He writes to Ries : " All blessings on your wife ; alas, that I have none ! There is but one woman for me, and her I shall probably never possess ; yet I am no woman-hater." There is no deeper pang in this than a somewhat complacent note of resignation. Beethoven was not the man to wreck his life for a woman. Love was never the driving force in his purposes.

His art shows no indication of erotic tendencies. His music is outside the realm of sexual impulses. Even in the opera *Fidelio* it is the theme of loyalty rather than of love that sounds throughout. We know, on his own showing, that it would have been impossible for him to use such subjects as *Figaro* or *Don Juan*. There must have been some deep-rooted instinct which constrained him to hold his art thus aloof. For him only the hero existed and he ignored the hero's liege-lady. How can one explain such an extraordinary characteristic—one doubly surprising in a man of Beethoven's powerful and voluptuously-gifted nature ?

That his morals were not of " the strictest, most bourgeois rigidity," as Wagner asserts, Beethoven's own words testify. " Sensual enjoyment, without spiritual affinity is and remains bestial : one is left thereafter with no trace of noble emotion but rather with remorse." The words indicate that Beethoven himself did not pass through life in the character of " *der reine Tor* " (the pure fool—the " innocent "). His moral code recognised no restraint imposed from without. If it led him in later years to control those impulses recognised as belonging to the lower nature, it was but in response to the fundamental instincts of his being, which pressed for a concentration of every available faculty on creative work. The rejection of certain of life's common pleasures in which he had once shared was decreed for him by his recognition of his mission as an artist, which not only compensated him for the forfeiture of earthly love, but taught him in time to see this forfeiture as necessary. In the course of a conversation about Guilietta Guicciardi he says to Schindler in 1823 : " Had I been willing to surrender thus my vital power and my life, what would have been left of the best and noblest in me ? "

Herein lies the answer to all questions relating to the part played by love in Beethoven's life. The erotic instinct in him, sublimated, soars to the heights, expands to infinity ; the common mating impulses are transformed into a desire for the love of all mankind, leaving no room for other interests ; he scorns alike frivolity and a narrow morality. They seem to him alike too petty to be fused or resolved in music. The sense of self is exchanged for a sense of cosmic being ; the desire of man for woman which Beethoven found too paltry, not too immoral, for his genius is transfigured into a spiritual embracing of the whole world. " *Seid umschlungen Millionen.*"

Dithyrambic joy, ecstatic rapture, is the essence of Beethoven's genius. He ranges through the whole gamut of passion. He sinks to bottomless pits of despair, he soars in unfettered bacchanalian joy. Periods of inconsolable dejection follow hours of extravagant delight. This swift change of mood is typical of the artist, as of mankind. His temperament imposed upon him a wide range of emotions. His deeply sensitive nature made him respond restlessly to every passing mood. Nevertheless it would be a foolish and one-sided estimate of Beethoven which would class him as a melancholic. The dull apathy and weakness which give birth to melancholia were foreign to his nature. After surmounting the catastrophe of 1802 he felt himself master of his fate. His immense vitality overcame all obstacles, and though later years brought him every kind of trouble, he never again sounded the funereal note of the Will. Did the demons " with straight and with crumpled horns " grant him but a little respite, straightway his natural good-humour and sturdy courage were reasserted.

Beethoven's coarse-grained humour was displayed not only in conversations with his contemporaries, but in his letters, in which many examples of it are to be found. In fact, Beethoven only occasionally succeeded in being " intellectual." He loved to laugh long and loud in his own uncouth style, so that Spohr, who was sensitive, disliked being in ladies' society with him. Beethoven himself was well aware of this peculiarity but made not the slightest effort to overcome it. On the contrary, he enjoyed reducing some exquisite carpet-knight to a state of nervous embarrassment with his clumsy ways and free-and-easy manners. " Our age needs mightier spirits to scourge these mean-spirited weaklings—much as it goes against the grain with me to offend a single soul," he writes to his nephew, when the appearance of a satire on the publisher Tobias Haslinger drew much odium upon him. Savagely as he dealt with this pitiable " Jew of the musical world " in a sudden spasm of rage, it was not his usual style. He delighted in puns ; some indeed he could never resist. A play upon " Noten " (needs) and " Nöten " (notes) he would not forgo for anything. In this he shows a happy childish *naïveté*, a capacity for whole-hearted delight in trifles. The rustic strain in his nature is displayed in his vulgarly humorous remarks about his intimates. Too often unrestrained coarseness must have taken the place of wit. Zmeskall, in particular, of whom he was " quite devil-ishly fond," and who used to mend his pens for him, had occasionally to endure a flood of quite exceptionally offensive comments as a mark of special affection. But when Beethoven was really angry, his fury knew no bounds. No term was too downright to express his rage. The classical example of this in a letter is his answer to a copyist who had been guilty of some insolent comments on the musician. The culprit is deluged with the most abusive epithets, and his impertinence is summarily characterised: " It is as if a swine should try to instruct Minerva ! "

Beethoven had no respect for high or low. He arraigned Church and State, the political party in office and the ruling powers at Court, just as loudly and indifferently at the inn table as he railed at the manager in the theatre or his servants at home. Sheer rage was to him an absolutely necessary means of relieving his feelings. The gift of moderation was denied him by his upbringing, but when he lost his temper, his most common fault, he was eager to effect a reconciliation and hastened to make amends. Usually he rushed to as great extremes as in his anger ; his submission was absolute, his self-reproach disproportionate, and he could not rest till he had won full pardon.

The deficiencies of his upbringing are apparent in many ways. In childhood he had been imperfectly educated and later efforts to supply the omissions were only partially successful. His letters show that he had a poor command of language and could never spell correctly. Clumsy expressions, arbitrary and haphazard punctuation, disregard of orthographical laws, and extremely illegible handwriting in his letters often defy all the efforts of the decipherer. Especially in later years, Beethoven's quill set down such extravagant hieroglyphics as baffle the most expert examination. These fantastic lines and curves, these grotesque characters, sometimes almost on top of each other, sometimes separated in the most ludicrous manner, are in fact the expression of an energetic but undisciplined brain, whose words conceal more than they reveal.

With a few exceptions, Beethoven's letters bear the character of " improvisations." The art of letter-writing, as a branch of literature, as it was so frequently exercised at that time, was unknown to him. His correspondence is mainly concerned with news, occasionally interspersed with general reflections, prompted by the matter in hand. Such sentences occur without any preamble amongst dry business-like memoranda or observations on current gossip. Rarely indeed does Beethoven indulge in deliberate philosophical reflections upon his relations with the world, his religious convictions, or his attitude to his fellow-men. For such purposes he prefers his diaries to letters,

confiding his thoughts to the former, often in the form of pithy
aphorisms.   The existence of these diaries shows clearly how
greatly he lacked friends in Vienna in whom he could unreservedly confide and from whose conversation he could expect
solace.   Instead, in moments of affliction, when even his art
could give him no consolation, he sought to master his feelings
by setting them down on paper.   Now and then his reading
stimulated him to make notes.   These are largely mere quotations from works in his own library.   Beethoven was an ardent
book-lover, not because he wanted superficial entertainment,
but because he had a keen desire for education.   When he was
offered Scott's novels as a diversion during illness, he rejected
them contemptuously " because the fellow only wrote for
money."   He was specially fond of the classical historians.
Plutarch and Xenophon always inspired and delighted him
afresh ; Ovid, Horace, Homer, Plato and Aristotle were always
to his hand.   He read them of course in translation, for he
knew so little of the humanities that he had to have even the
Mass rendered into German for his composition.

His interests, however, were not confined to the ancients.
He wanted to keep in touch with his own age.   Goethe and
Schiller, as well as Klopstock, Seume, Tiedge and Matthisson
were his constant companions.   He asked Breitkopf and Härtel
to forward their newest publications.   " So far none of the
treatises have been beyond me.   Without making the least claim
to scholarship, I have endeavoured since childhood to steep myself
in the spirit of the best and wisest of every age.   Shame to the
artist who does not consider it his duty to achieve at least so
much."

He preferred works of natural philosophy and repeatedly
studied Sturm's *Betrachtungen der Werke Gottes*, and Kant's
Naturgeschichte und Theorie des gestirnten Himmels.   Probably
it was this work which first interested him in Kant.   Wegeler
had often vainly entreated him to attend the lectures on Kant's
philosophy in 1796.   The more Beethoven in later years withdrew from the world, the more he found in Nature alone the
peace denied him elsewhere, and speculative works aroused his
keenest interest when they related to visible natural phenomena.   He was deeply interested, too, in the Oriental studies

of the famous translator, Hammer-Purgstall, and the numerous researches into Oriental religions and culture of distinguished contemporaries. His writing-table was adorned with short extracts from Schiller's *Sendung Moses*, and quotations as to the existence of God, written out in his own hand and neatly framed.

Beethoven rarely makes allusion to his own attitude to religion. He disliked discussing this theme with others. " Religion and thorough-bass are both things that settle themselves—there is no need to discuss them further," thus he rebuffs Schindler's forwardness. Occasionally we find in the diaries some statements about God, but they are more mystifying than illuminative. He has made full avowal of his faith, not in words but in the music of his great *Mass*; we must seek there if we wish to comprehend Beethoven's relations with his God, and we shall find that Haydn erred when he called Beethoven an atheist. Certainly Beethoven's ideas on God and religion were far removed from Haydn's happy piety. Beethoven's faith was the result of a lifelong battle against doubt and temptations of every kind; it was a conviction of a higher and divine power won only after a bitter struggle. His religious beliefs, firmly grounded as they were on the root principles of Christian faith, were yet free of dogma, the fruit of independent, critical and inquiring thought.

Beethoven thus had many intellectual interests. He sought in every realm of knowledge that which is worth the knowing, delving in the rich treasures of the ancients, devoting himself to the consideration of religious problems, taking a genuine interest in good, new work in order to overcome as far as possible the faults of his upbringing. But this picture alters when we turn to the records of the Conversation-Books, when we see him no longer alone but with his friends and associates. These records have value for the inquirer, for they serve to confirm and elucidate certain events in Beethoven's career. Despite their disconnectedness and Beethoven's inadequacy in words, they remain as the most faithful reflection we possess of his way of life. They show that in general his life was one of dull mediocrity, seldom offering anything better than the common daily round, aimless conversations and dry business questions and interviews. His intellectual environment was shockingly inferior, the sphere in which he lived afforded little artistic stimulus. Acquaintances come from other towns to pay their respects to the Master or to arrange for performances of his work in their native places. They tell him how famous he is, he receives them with gracious condescension. In spirit he withdraws from them, and the incense duly offered by some paltry traveller is received as his due by the lonely man rather than by the great artist.

In his later years, Beethoven was not free from vanity. He was disappointed when the Prussian King merely sent him a ring on the dedication of the ninth symphony instead of bestowing the hoped-for Order. When the Swedish Academy conferred on him honorary membership, he himself requested the editor of several papers to announce the dignity. But he did not think only of his own advantage—" as far as practical affairs are concerned, one must work and live that others may reap the benefit." In all his thoughts and resolves, Beethoven's nephew was always in his mind. The youth occupied an important place in the conversation notebooks. In these we find town gossip discussed, family matters talked over, publishers' business debated: a serious note is seldom sounded. With Grillparzer, too, the conversations usually turned on the commonplace, though there are some valuable comments on the relation between text and music in opera, arising from the contemplated *Melusine*. The poet Kuffner apparently had a brilliant idea for an oratorio, entered into zealously by Beethoven, who always welcomed suggestions of this kind from others, and an absorbing conversation followed. Then in the midst of such a talk, " Frau Schnaps," the old housekeeper, would poke her head round the door and demand her weekly wages because it was Saturday. Or else, perhaps, that idle gossip, Schindler, would arrive, and the atmosphere, erstwhile so clear, would grow clouded: the light would die from Beethoven's eyes, his gaze would range no further than the limits of the narrow street. " At those very moments of highest inspiration, when I am most conscious of rejoicing in my own world of art, these earthly natures drag me down again. I am overwhelmed by the petty details of daily life."

Amidst these daily trivialities, Beethoven lived surrounded by " infernal powers " which compelled him " to turn earthwards the gaze he fain would direct heavenwards "; but he found his happiness in an inward visionary world, and the older he grew the more he dwelt therein.   Externals, the banalities of his surroundings almost ceased to impinge on his consciousness. Even his most intimate friends could only touch his exterior personality ; his genius stood aloof from them.   Women once played a part in his life, but it was now over.   His eye was still held by their beauty and charm, but they could no longer touch his soul.   The world could but furnish him with the necessaries of life, the means to satisfy his very unpretentious claims.   Of this he himself made sure.   The older he grew the more Beethoven showed signs of a deliberate, calculating and cold egoism.   Nevertheless the harder and more inflexible he seemed, the stronger did the burning tide of creative power surge within him.   The more insignificant his surroundings, the more powerfully did he rise above them.   His air of indifference and impassivity was but a cloak for the wealth and tenderness of his inward life.   There was tragedy for him, however, in the fact that he could not successfully maintain this division of material and spiritual interests.   For the sake of the nephew whom he loved, he was obliged once more to submit to the forces of life over which he had triumphed.   This devotion was the single human weakness which clung to him ; unlike all other emotions, he could not master it and withdraw within the temple of his art.

Beethoven had some insight as an educationist.   His letters to the authorities of the schools to which he sent his nephew Karl reveal more judgment and more thought on educational matters than is generally attributed to him.   What he lacked was the strength of mind to carry out his own theories.   All his resolution was shattered by a coaxing word from Karl, a tearful or sulky expression.   The most foolish and indulgent mother could not have been more lenient to Karl than this severe and passionate man ; and with all youth's determination to have its own way, the nephew fostered his uncle's weakness.   When flattery and cajolery proved fruitless, threats and defiance were brought to bear.

Beethoven was well aware of his own weakness and endeavoured to retrieve his lost authority with entreaties and reproaches, for which he would immediately afterwards apologise. He longed for his nephew's confidence and society, he " would not like to feel that he had expended so much to give the world a merely commonplace man." But Karl was not born for intimacy with a genius. He found his uncle's complaints wearisome; Beethoven's anguished cry, " Do but come—that my heart may cease to bleed for you," struck him only as the fretful outburst of a troublesome old fool. He made no effort to hide his feelings from his uncle. Beethoven received unequivocal proofs of his nephew's indifference, and yet he could not give him up. Love compelled him to endure to the end and, with heroic self-control, to repeat the unending struggle.

Thus Beethoven, who had already solved the riddle of the sphinx, became at the end the sport of fate. He knew that he had done his duty as a man and as an artist; but he was overcome by a bitter sense of the uselessness of all effort. He recognised the eternal mutability of things, and, worn-out, he murmured on his death-bed: " *Plaudite amici—comœdia finita est.*"

Only the earthly comedy was over, with all its confusions and contradictions, mistakes and petty cares. Only the mortal frame sank into the grave, whence soared the liberated spirit, proclaiming in his works the message of eternal freedom and joy.

PART II
BEETHOVEN THE MUSICIAN

CHAPTER III

BEETHOVEN was not a revolutionary musician. He was born in the " *Sturm und Drang* " period, but he was not of it. He felt indeed no need for rebellion; the work of his predecessors did not restrict him, it saved him from wasting time and energy on experiment. Haydn was more daring in this respect, he was more inclined to novelty for its own sake than Beethoven, and liked constant variety of form. He liked also to surprise and amuse his hearers and had an eye to change in the manner of presentation. Beethoven was naturally more conservative and avoided anything speculative wherever possible. When he varied from tradition he did so in no spirit of wilfulness, but in obedience to the demands of the poetic idea which inspired him and upon which his whole work was based. Music was to him an exquisitely and delicately adapted vehicle for the expression of a spiritual and intellectual creed, a faithful mirror of his inner life and experience. Words and their attendant images, the limitations inseparable from exact definition, are not evaded but are spiritualised and transcended and expressed upon a higher plane of abstraction through the power of music. Instrumental tone is used to reflect and interpret the occurrences of a world far removed from actuality, a world, however, which is an abstract representation of an actual region of the intellectual and emotional life, and is consequently subject to the motions and laws of its prototype. It should be possible, therefore, to understand some, at least, of the secret springs of music by translating them into terms of their analogies in human consciousness. A piece of music develops in a certain way in strict accordance with a corresponding sequence of thought, and this sequence of thought, when closely considered, is found in its turn to correspond with the creative artistic process. This process begins with a definite spiritual impulse which gradually takes shape in suitable artistic form. The intelligent observer, who is not content with mere sensuous enjoyment of the finished work, will attempt to reason from the form before him back to the initial impulse which gave it being. In this way he may grasp the origin, course and goal of the artist's thought.

Is it, however, possible in practice to work back to the original impulse in this way? May not the artist himself have covered up his own traces, hidden or falsified them? We are not, of course, considering the chance *incident* which gives rise to a work; this usually has no more than anecdotal interest, though occasionally it throws a side-light upon the subject. Interest of a deeper kind attaches to the character of the spiritual forces which give meaning and direction to a composition. The composer may destroy corporeal evidence bearing on his work, notes, sketches or letters, but he cannot disguise its spiritual origins, for the content of a composition is necessarily laid bare through the emotional witness of the music itself. Careful study of the music inevitably gives insight into the mind of the composer. Whether the artist himself has followed his own processes consciously or otherwise is of secondary importance. The reflection of his own mind is there, must be there, if his work is to reach the minds of his hearers. The more perfectly it incorporates the originality of the artist, the more clearly is his image perceptible to us and the more earnestly we gaze upon and consciously assimilate that reflection, the deeper will be our knowledge of the composer's mind.

Beethoven entertained no doubts as to the psychological bases of his art. As Neefe's pupil he had early received and accepted the doctrine of a necessary correspondence between things musical and things spiritual in the mind of the musician. This was a point of view to which he clung throughout his life. Neefe was both by nature and by training a musician of the type which is distinguished rather for philosophic and æsthetic interest in the art of music than for exact knowledge of musical science. There is no doubt that Beethoven was strongly influenced by Neefe's teaching, for in later years his interest developed and expanded upon the lines suggested by Neefe; he studied æsthetics, was ready to argue upon the subject and to defend certain clear convictions. There is a widespread but erroneous idea that Beethoven approached his art only from the practical side, that he set aside or even despised theoretical discussions as to essence and content. On the contrary, he constantly sought an æsthetic basis for artistic expression. He endeavoured to think clearly, to get at the meaning of things, to develop the artistic instinct on logical and regular lines. His work is sprinkled with question marks; letters, diaries and conversation testify alike to his keen critical intellect and grasp of æsthetics. Unfortunately the majority of Beethoven's associates were intellectually insignificant, so that the recorded results of his thinking have come down to us for the most part only in some comment preserved by chance, some brilliantly illuminating remark, but when he came in contact with more independent and stimulating minds, he quickly took fire and became more communicative. With the poet, Hofrat Kuffner, he discussed oratorio, with Grillparzer opera, and those parts of the note-books which touch on these conversations show that Beethoven's mental activity was keen and his judgment acute upon various æsthetic problems.

Schindler records at length the substance of certain conversations with the poet-composer, August Kanne, one of those half-geniuses whose many gifts prove their ruin. Beethoven argued with Kanne about the key, Kanne denying, Beethoven affirming, its definite inner significance. He defended his position on logical grounds, claiming that each key is associated with certain moods, and that no piece of music should be transposed. So far he agreed with Schubart's theory of æsthetics, although he differed in certain details as to the character of the major keys. Such subjects are occasionally touched upon in his letters. He associates the greatness of Klopstock, for instance, with the solemn D flat major key. He chose the keys for his works with the greatest care. He did nothing, indeed, at haphazard; everywhere one notes his strong " will to definition," his considered design, even in detail.

It did not occur to him to regard his work as " absolute " music, in the false sense of that term, meaning music for its own sake, devoid of content. In later years he complained to

Schindler that the times were imaginatively bankrupt. " When I wrote my sonatas," he said, " people were more poetic and such indications (of the music's meaning) were superfluous. At that time everyone recognised that the *largo* of the third sonata in D (Op. 10. iii) expressed a melancholic state of mind, that it portrayed every subtle shade, every phase of melancholy, without the need of a title to give a clue to the meaning, and, similarly, everyone saw that the two sonatas, Op. 14, represented a struggle between two opposing principles, an argument between two persons; its interpretation is as obvious as that of the other work." About the same date, Beethoven, presumably in connection with his complaint about the decay of imagination in music-lovers, declared his intention of giving poetic titles to his earlier works. One can scarcely regret that he did not carry out his plan. Such titles would have helped intelligent listeners very little, while the addition of a written " programme " would not make up for lack of imagination in the unintelligent. For a proper understanding of Beethoven's work prolonged and sympathetic experience and intense mental application are essential; hints in the form of a programme and tags of verse will carry no one very far.

A short-sighted view of æsthetics has wrongly deduced that definite content in music is unnecessary and that a clear intellectual grasp of pure musical creations is impossible. Feeble and unclear thinking of this kind was entirely foreign to Beethoven. He demanded intellectual co-operation. He regarded listening to music as a living experience, and with him the terms " to compose " and " to write poetry " were interchangeable. " Read Shakespeare's *Tempest*," he replied, when questioned as to the meaning of the D minor sonata, Op. 31. ii, and the F minor sonata, Op. 57. When composing he kept a definite mental image before him and worked to it. His works were " inspired by moods which the poet translates into words and I into music; they rage and storm in my soul till they stand before me in the form of notes of music." On the title-page of his *Name-day Overture* he writes with naïve self-confidence not " composed " but " made into poetry by Ludwig van Beethoven."

It is but a short step from such a view-point to " programme-music." Beethoven is, indeed, more of a programme-music writer than is generally supposed. The gap which exists to-day between " programme " and other music was unknown to him. He knew and valued the possibilities of a programme and accepted it as a part of his musical heritage. Where it suited his purpose he used it ; where it did not, he dispensed with it. He brought free artistic judgment to bear on each problem of musical expression as it arose. There is a strong naturalistic tendency in his work which strikes the modern listener, particularly in the grotesque *Battle* symphony. The piece is inferior, is scarcely worthy indeed of a place in Beethoven's work ; yet it contributes to an understanding of the composer's æsthetic position. Many of his contemporaries accepted it in good earnest, while Beethoven himself had apparently no mean opinion of its merits. He was ready enough to condemn his own work when it seemed worthless to him, yet he undoubtedly took unusual pains to advertise " Wellington's Victory " and to get it favourable recognition. He embarked on a wearisome law case to secure his copyright, dedicated the composition to the Prince of Wales, and was highly offended at receiving no thanks from that quarter. Business interests may have had something to do with his action, yet there is no doubt that he gave the piece a far higher place than modern judgment would allow. It is a copy-book example of a primitive form of programme-music, such as is to be found frequently enough in the work of Kuhnau and of composers from Bach to Leopold Mozart, Krebs, Dittersdorf and Vogler. Essentially this implied a realistic representation of outward events such as a Bible story, a sleigh run, one of Ovid's Metamorphoses, a thunderstorm, or a battle. That Beethoven should have followed such models as late as his forty-third year, goes to prove that he could not compose quickly, he needed time and deliberation to produce great work. He had no time to think over the " Battle of Vittoria," no time to sort and arrange his material. If circumstances had not thus forced him to compose hurriedly the *Battle* symphony might have been a most interesting contrast to the *Pastoral* symphony. Even as it is the score is instructive. It proves that Beethoven worked from the representation of realistic impressions which he gradually purged of their crudity

F

as he laboured upon his subject. The *Battle* symphony is an example of his work in its crude state.

The heights which he could attain in programme-music, when he spent time and effort upon it, are revealed in the *Pastoral* symphony. Here we have a conventional programme, not differing in form from the work of former generations. Scenes of country life which afford opportunity for tone-painting are strung loosely together without any particular grace of thought, and, from the poetic point of view, it has little more value than the *Battle* symphony, but here Beethoven has had time to assimilate and work upon his material, to subject it to the refining and formative power of his genius. Furthermore the subject delighted him, reminding him of his own experiences of the secret charms of nature, which he savoured with the sentiment proper to a true disciple of Rousseau. His " programme " was a foundation upon which his own imagination could build, the tangible course of an intangible train of imaginative thought. This programme within a programme is designated by Beethoven as " an expression of feeling." He tells us expressly that " Anyone who has the least understanding of the countryside will know at once what the author wishes to express." Emphasis upon the author's " wish to express " and upon the necessity of responsive thought in the hearer proves that the composer's poetic intention oversteps the limits of a conventional title. Beethoven is silent about his programme, not because he has none, but because he takes it for granted that his hearer will understand his meaning and that descriptive words are superfluous.

There is, nevertheless, something æsthetically hybrid about the *Pastoral* symphony. The composer's imagination was hampered and limited to some extent by the necessity of suiting his emotional expression to the different sections which he had previously marked out. He realised this difficulty himself and as a rule subsequently avoided a programme divided into scenes or sections. He substituted short characteristic titles, sufficient to give his fancy an objective without confining it strictly to a certain course with fixed halting places. *Napoleon, Egmont, Coriolanus, Leonora* thus provided themes upon which Beethoven's mighty imagination could exercise its full powers untrammelled.

A spark was sufficient to kindle his poetic fire. The impression is none the less vivid because he painted with a bold sweep of the brush and did not tie himself to detail. He had transcended words and no longer needed their support. Why should he seek to fold the full-blown rose in the bud once more ? He had substituted bold emotional painting for the detailed picture series of the older programme-music, and the superiority of his method was self-evident. Beethoven discovered a new æsthetic basis for programme-music which in his hands became emotional revelation instead of superficial description.

He produced a considerable number of works of this type. Each enshrines a particular poetic conception and each bears witness to Beethoven's view of a particular problem. They form a connecting link between the lower type of programme-music, from which they differ by their greater imaginative freedom, and the music without a programme, the meaning of which they help to make clear. They mirror certain ideas, certain habits of thought which provide a clue to Beethoven's inner life.

The world revealed to us is one of tremendous events and visions. It is manifested in many forms, but a single principle vitalises the whole. This principle is the heroic struggle for absolute freedom of personality, and it persists throughout Beethoven's programme-music, diversely clothed by the imagination, like manifold variations upon a single *leitmotiv*. Handel had worked before him upon not dissimilar lines. His personality also was strong, straightforward, sympathetic, capable of appreciating greatness, and on this account he had Beethoven's wholehearted admiration. Handel took his material, without exception, from the remote past. Heroes of the Old Testament or of classical antiquity fired his imagination. His ideal man was a powerful spectacular figure, imposing his will upon the world of lesser men surrounding him, and he represented such heroes with sculpturesque effect. Beethoven's idea of a hero was essentially different. Handel's conception found in him an echo, but Beethoven's own message was less massive and gigantic. He was more interested in the inward workings of the hero's soul than in his startling effect upon his fellows. He sought special characteristics, probed into motives, compared and assimilated them to his own thoughts and opinions, so that his portrait became a critical study. He took account of his hero's circumstances and surroundings and attempted to reconstruct mentally the world in which he had lived and worked. Living as he did in a time of upheaval and revolution, political events held first place in his interest.

Beethoven is frequently described as a republican, without reference to the fact that he was by nature uncompromisingly, almost arrogantly, aristocratic. He was, indeed, a curious mixture of the aristocrat and the democrat. Like every true artist, conscious of his high calling, he believed in the principle of authority. He went as a freedom-loving Rhinelander to Vienna and there saw the full disadvantages of the old, aristocratic, political order. While there he heard news of an oppressed people's violent bid for freedom, of their abolition of abuses such as were perpetrated daily before his eyes. He heard of the rapid progress of liberated France and saw that a Republic, such as had long been considered an impracticable Utopia, was possible for a modern state. Looking back he compared it to Greece at the height of her glory—to the artist's golden age of human culture. He thus became a theoretical republican, partly from hatred of the abuses of the monarchical system, partly from sympathetic enthusiasm for a political ideal of the future, but his democratic opinions could hardly have stood the practical test. His pride as an artist knew no compromise, and he would have set his face like flint against any notions of equality or fraternity which would allow others to approach his throne without due respect. He was, moreover, creatively inspired, not by the movement of an entire people towards freedom, but by the nobility of certain outstanding leaders. In his works he celebrates the political hero who leads his people through battle to freedom and happiness. At that time Beethoven believed in the coming of such a hero. He believed, too, that freedom thus achieved was the end to which human development tended, and that the deeds of the expected leader would represent the most exalted plane of practical human endeavour.

Beethoven turned his gaze from the affairs of nations and peoples to the affairs of the sexes and of the family. Here

again, even in the tenderest idyll, he dealt with human idiosyn-
crasies upon the heroic plane. He was interested in love as a
plighting of eternal troth between a man and a woman, as a
self-sacrificing devotion able to withstand the hardest test.
Unselfish love between husband and wife, as distinct from mere
sensuous attraction or desire for possession, was his theme and
gave him a fresh source of spiritual inspiration. The idea
behind the *Leonora Overture* is that of freedom of the individual
achieved through loving sacrifice; it is the " heroic theme "
once more in a new form, in relation to the lives of two people
instead of to the common weal. Glorification of personal freedom follows glorification of political freedom; the *Leonora
Overture* follows the *Eroica*. The next development was a
philosophical contemplation of the self. Victory is no longer
won by a hero as representative and saviour of his fellows, as
in the *Eroica*, nor by the love between a man and woman, as
in *Leonora* and *Fidelio*, but by a hero who stands alone in a
hostile world. *Egmont* and *Coriolanus* are Beethoven's great
tragic creations. They stand not for outward freedom but for
freedom of will, and, though victorious, their victory proves
their ruin. They indicate a period of transition in Beethoven's
inner life, a period when he believed deliberately chosen annihilation of self to be the desirable consummation of effort.
Yet he drew fresh power from the depths of a pessimism which
threatened to overwhelm him. He gained a new assurance
and proceeded to greater heights than had hitherto been within
his reach.

Despair over the world's travail and over his own fate now
lay behind him; he had pierced the veil of life and had looked
fearless upon the naked truths of existence. It did not break
him; he did not become either a perpetual penitent or a
prophet of the transitoriness and nothingness of earthly things.
He had done with life's hard problems and he lifted his eyes
to free and sunny heights. He still loved this present life
for the very struggles and sorrows which it brings, for through
pain he had found joy. A new heroic ideal began to dawn
in him. He seems to have felt himself lifted above earth's
confusion, to have received a promise and foretaste of eternal
bliss. In his own person he became an incarnation of his

own ripened conception of the heroic character, raised above
the many griefs and scanty joys of this troublous life, yet not
out of love with it.   The love of life, which no sorrow could
stifle, rings through his last works, bringing, to those who are
able to hear, news of the salvation and joy which he had found,
whose praises he sounds in a pæan of ecstasy.

Beethoven's programme-music affords a comprehensive view
of his work as a whole, but it is not the only window to the
world of his thought.   His operas and songs are a valuable
supplement to his instrumental programme-music.   They are
not numerous, but they are grandly conceived and are artistically very perfect.   His dramatic works are so closely associated
with his programme-music as to be critically barely distinguishable.   The overtures of *Egmont* and *Leonora* give the essentials
of the work to follow in concentrated form.

His greatest lyrical vocal work, on the contrary, the famous
Mass in D, far surpasses his instrumental programme-music
with its inherent limitations.   In intention it is the most powerful and ambitious of his works.   It is based on a formula
originally intended to be the confession of faith of an ideal,
universal human society, but he makes it the perfect expression
of one man's faith—his own.

Beethoven's relations with the organised religion of his day
were always cool.   Neither as man nor as artist could he blindly
accept dogmas as true and indefeasible.   He was brought up
in a formalised Catholic doctrine whose narrowness left him
coldly indifferent.   Protestantism was too prosaic to appeal to
his hot artist's imagination.   As a result he kept aloof from
church matters and he satisfied his religious needs in con-
templating Nature, which revealed to him more than the words
of any priest had been able to do.   The more he penetrated
the metaphysical sources of life the deeper became his philosophic understanding of the relationship of the individual to
the universe ; the higher his spirit climbed to transcendental
regions, where he discovered that the true Godhead dwelt
within man, the more he longed to express his new vision of
things in terms of the old creed of Christendom.   He found
that what was narrow and limited in the Christian doctrine
was not of its essence, but had been artificially grafted upon it

by shortsighted and illiberal interpreters. As a free-thinking artist who had thrown off petty superstition he now attempted to give artistic expression to his own religious perceptions through the forms of the Mass. Freed from the limitations of creed, he dared to make use of the lofty words which had served for centuries as the symbol of faith in God. Nature was Beethoven's divinity; from her he had learned to accept all phenomena as reflections of the Godhead. He felt himself to be a chosen vessel of supernatural revelation, a hero, a saviour, who had suffered, and rising, had felt the divine life within him. In Beethoven's faith, in his sense of the god in man, was something more than the pantheism of Spinoza and Goethe. It was closely bound up with the idea of personality. To the doctrine of Nature in God and God in Nature, of God immanent in the universe, he added a mystical apprehension of God as dwelling in one single artistically creative individual.

The sum of his message was freedom, artistic freedom, political freedom, personal freedom of will, of art, of faith, freedom of the individual in all the aspects of life, and he gives it symbolic expression through the heroic idea in drama and in poetry. It is the link which connects the apparently lonely musician with his great contemporaries and companions-in-arms, Kant, Fichte, Humboldt, Stein, Schiller and Goethe. It is the same note which sounded to battle in the War of Liberation and which twenty years earlier had rung clear through the tumult of the French Revolution. We find it again in Beethoven's private life and character. He had nothing of Haydn's submissiveness, nothing of Mozart's contented, child-like dependence, nothing even of Bach's attitude of blunt, honest professionalism. He preserved a jealous, personal independence, taking what the world offered as due tribute and giving what he had to give as an act of grace. He was more obstinate and autocratic than any previous musician, with the possible exception of Handel, who somewhat resembled him in this respect; and he proclaimed the individual's unalienable right to act freely within the body politic. He strove for an ideal of conscious freedom in faith and knowledge, echoing the battle-cries of his epoch, " the Rights of Man " and " all men are born free and equal." Freedom, as he understood it, however, did not mean libertinism and caprice. A lively sense of responsibility should co-exist with the right of self-determination, and the individual may not consider that the world was made for his sole pleasure. The man who over-steps the bounds of his natural powers finds his own nemesis. Thus *Coriolanus* perishes through inordinate pride of power, and Napoleon's name is erased from the score of the *Eroica* because he made himself a tyrant. Beethoven's idea of freedom rests upon a firm ethical basis. It is a happiness to be achieved only through a stern conflict with fate, the very opposite of effeminate self-indulgence; for only by self-discipline and steady devotion to duty can the depths of the true self be revealed and qualities be developed which make hard-won freedom worth having. The sense of responsibility rests upon the consciousness of duty to oneself and others, upon Kant's " cate-gorical imperative." Active fulfilment of duty causes an exalted serenity which brings the best qualities of the self to perfection, despite all the storms of life. It is a buoyant, idealistic creed, suggesting faith and hope in things beyond our understanding, reaching out to the mysterious Power, in which love and majesty are one. It sets a goal and promises a reward, but it leaves to each man the finding of a rule of conduct, based on his own will to freedom, his own will to duty. It may be summed up in the words of Kant, " The moral law within us, the star-strewn heavens above us."

Thus Beethoven developed the poetic idea and expressed it in his programme-music and songs in a manner comprehensible to the senses, but he was not confined to music of this type. His characteristic handling of material made a further develop-ment in the direction of abstraction logically inevitable. The whole body of his thought could not be contained in the pro-gramme themes which chance suggested and which he used so frugally, nor in his vocal music. Many of his spiritual experiences, expressed in music, were inexpressible in words. For these it was useless to seek suitable texts or titles. They are, nevertheless, conveyed immediately to the mind through the ear. Objectivity, hard and fast intellectual concepts, every-thing material is set aside. Beethoven no longer speaks in parables, but proclaims the faith attained through parables.

He has found the realities behind appearances and now reveals them, stripped of material disguises, through the musician's world of sound. Only one sensible symbol remains—the form of the tone-phenomena, form not in its narrow, pedagogic, but in its widest sense as a deliberate, artistic organisation of all the elements available to music at that time, melody, rhythm, harmony, tone-colour, dynamic, phrasing. Analysis of the forms thus constructed and a close study of their inherent emotional and spiritual effects will bring æsthetic understanding of this last section of Beethoven's creative work. In his non-programmatic instrumental music, which forms the greater part of his work, Beethoven uses the most mysterious and yet the most direct of all means of human communication. He has himself provided a few signposts such as " *Marcia funebre sulla morte d'un eroe*," " *La malinconia*," " *Das Lebewohl*," which are very nearly " programmes." Comments such as " *ermattet klagend* " (lamentation sinking to exhaustion), " *nach und nach wieder auflebend* " (reviving little by little) in the last A flat major sonata, " *Heilige Dankgesang eines Genesenen an die Gottheit* " (devout thanksgiving to God on recovery from sickness) in the A minor quartet, " *beklemmt* " (" straightened," in the biblical sense), in the cavatina of the B flat major quartet, and " *schwergefasster Entschluss* " (resolution in face of difficulty) in Op. 135, exceed the limits of the customary musical directions. How revealing are the remarks inserted in the great A flat major sonata—" *Etwas lebhaft und mit der innigsten Empfindung* " (rather lively and with the most intense feeling), " *lebhaft, marschmässig* " (lively, with a marching swing), " *langsam und sehnsuchtsvoll* " (slowly and with yearning), " *geschwind, doch nicht zu sehr und mit Entschlossenheit* " (quickly, but not too quickly and with decision)! They are a strange development from the generalised *tempo* suggestions of tradition. They are almost programmatic in their clearness and definition, and form a kind of summary of the contents of a poem which is sketched out only on broad emotional lines.

Beethoven's use of the stereotyped Italian terms is also significant. He uses *molto legato*, *espressivo marcato*, *ritardando*, *a tempo*, *dolce* and *cantabile* with the utmost prodigality, using them to express his poet's meaning rather than as mechanical indications to the performer. Calculated "effects" are indeed steadily rejected, and in the last pianoforte concerto the one opportunity for virtuosity which he had hitherto preserved— the cadenza—is omitted. The work is a delicately and intricately conceived organism in which the personality of the exponent finds no opportunity to spread itself. Hitherto the composer's directions had been used and regarded as hints from which the performer could proceed to his own individual interpretation; they now become ineluctable commands. They have ceased to serve as the scaffolding of a programme, but they give the emotional meaning of the composition in crystallised form. They may be compared to the projecting towers and spires of a submerged city, rising above the surface of the waters and inciting imagination to seek for its hidden glories through depths of ocean. Beethoven soon found the traditional Italian terms inadequate. He sometimes strung them together into whole sentences, dealing with the intricate score, part by part. He indicated the rhythm of groups of bars, and for a time expected miracles from the use of the metronome. He hunted out complicated Italian phrases and, where these were insufficient, he employed German comments. In the end, he came to use all these methods simultaneously, the metronome, Italian and German marks of expression.

This careful attention to detail implies more than the fear that his work might be misinterpreted or inexactly rendered. He believed indications of *tempo* and style of performance to be just as much an organic part of his work, an expression of his poetic meaning, as signs of pitch and phrasing. The complete artist, he took nothing for granted; he would allow no vagueness, knowing exactly what he wished to express and how to make every detail contribute to his meaning.

Just as Beethoven made poetry out of the old mechanical "marks," so he increased the expressiveness of musical dynamics. Dynamic as a means of suggesting emotional grades was, of course, known to former generations of musicians. The earliest instrumental music borrowed the method of contrasting tones of various strengths from choral music, as Gabrielli's sonata, *Pian e forte*, shows. Echo effects, moreover, were very popular, and a similar principle lies behind the contrast of *solo* and *tutti* in the old form of concerto. Nevertheless, light and shade were usually only crudely and broadly differentiated. As the emotional range of instrumental art increased, there arose a demand for some means of expressing the variations, the rise and fall of emotional tension. The symphonic composers of Mannheim were certainly not the original discoverers of *crescendo* and *diminuendo*, yet they were the first to make a science of musical *nuances*, of the free play of light and shade in sound. Their intellectual range was not great, with the result that they exploited swelling and diminishing tonal effects, the inversion of marks, till the art of light and shade became mere virtuosity; they made, in short, an end of what should have been merely a means. Gluck, Mozart and Haydn used the new-won facility with real significance. Haydn's use of dynamics, his enchanting *sforzati*, his two crescendo points, the rapid alternations of loud and soft, are the chief determinants of his emotional effects. Even Haydn's inspired handling, however, pales before the intensity with which Beethoven makes dynamic expression serve his meaning. Shades of emotion too delicate to find expression in terms of melody, rhythm or harmony are perfectly mirrored in Beethoven's dynamics. Abrupt transitions of mood, which one would believe it impossible to link up, are made convincing by dynamic changes; for example, in the third and fourth movements of the C minor symphony and in the last movement of the *Egmont* overture. His dynamic methods are as serviceable and delightful for the expression of lesser, more delicate, emotional impulses— for the sudden turning of a rising tone-mass, for the stifled pangs of restrained passion, the unexpected damping and extinction of hot emotion, alternations of vacillation and decision —as for bolder contrasts. He estimates the value of these things with absolute exactitude and presses them into the service of his central idea, the poetic idea, which gives unheard-of persuasiveness to the language of dynamics and musical marks of expression. Through these means, it also controls form in the narrower sense of the word, careful juxtaposition and sequence of rhythm, melody, harmony and colouring. Here, again, Beethoven built upon the work of his predecessors, transfiguring it in the light of creative genius. In his hands these media attained fresh significance; one feels, indeed, that their origin, construction and *raison d'être* are revealed for the first time. Beethoven's characteristic forms owe their originality not so much to their outward scheme of construction as to the superiority with which they adapt themselves to, and reflect, ideas which they were built to enshrine.

Thought associations and emotional associations alternate in Beethoven's work. They even cross, unite, separate, contrast with each other and supplement each other; but they remain essentially and recognisably distinct. On the one hand is pure lyricism, confined to the exposition of purely emotional impulses; on the other, a more explicit, more descriptive, more argumentative side of musical art. The latter arises in intermingled trains of thought, the former is direct and simple in origin; the former makes for breadth, the latter for the heights and depths. They find expression respectively in Beethoven's two most important musical forms, *sonata* and *variations*.

The sonata form represents " drama " in instrumental music. Its construction is determined by a multiplicity of intellectual activities, by spiritual conflicts, by spiritual events, peaceful or tragic. It arises in the interaction of contradictions, in the energy of conflicting claims and assertions. Within the framework of the sonata, an organically developed action, a logical sequence of scenes, an exact exposition of character, takes place. It is unnecessary to conceive this dramatic action in absolutely material terms, yet its existence as the constructive principle of the sonata cannot be disregarded without misrepresentation of its æsthetic character.

Variation is the sonata's artistic antithesis. It does not bring a number of melodic entities into relation, but takes a single melody and analyses it. It grows, not by addition of matter from without, but by inward subdivision; its changes all spring from the same root. The essential quality of a single underlying concept is displayed in a series of metamorphoses. It consists, not in the mingling of many elements, as in the sonata, but in the analysis of a single element. It thus exploits one selected mood to the limits of thought, but it lacks the fructifying effect of contradiction. The æsthetic character of the variation is passive, that of the sonata active; but the former, perfected by Beethoven and blended with fugal elements of pure emotional expansiveness, is the highest form of lyrical music. It springs from the original lyrical form, the song; and may be resolved into its elements, mood-atoms, which revolve for a time about a centre, like planets round the sun, to be presently re-absorbed into the mass from which they were detached. Sometimes this activity presents the vitality, richness and variety of phenomena of a great planetary universe; at other times it appears the product of a whim, a merely superficial, kaleidoscopic play. The latter is the variation form more frequently to be met, but Beethoven contributed to deepen it, to free it from mere virtuosity, to make it a great medium of emotional expression. He bent the thought-architecture of the sonata to his will and ennobled the emotional range of the variation, thereby giving eternal value to the two greatest musical forms, other than programme-music.

The active and comprehensive tendencies of the sonata determine the relationship of its several parts. It remains for the musician's skill to construct a higher synthesis out of the contradictions of these parts, and the sharper the contrasts offered, the more strikingly will the idea of the whole be reflected from the several angles. The consequent need of change in the form of the movements explains why Beethoven gradually made the variation (as the greatest possible contrast to the sonata phase) the most important member, after the leading development movement, of the cyclic sonata form.

Between these two extremes stands, as a connecting link, the *rondo*, a hybrid of variation and sonata. It differs from the variation form in being based on not one but several concepts; yet it strings them together but loosely, avoiding the strict logic of the sonata. The *rondo* consists in an almost rhapsodical multiplicity of moods; it may occasionally be used to express spiritual depths, but is usually confined to a stimulating play of pleasant, trifling thoughts or feelings. It had a long history behind it when Beethoven took it over, probed, as usual, to the root of its value and achieved wonders with it. His creative capacities were various and inexhaustible. He was not always upon the heights or in the depths, but knew and prized the norm of life and thought. He found the *rondo* useful, for not every thought can support the merciless logic of the sonata-form proper, nor every emotion endure the keen analysis of the variation form.

Beethoven's genius rescued him from the degrading power of the commonplace in everyday life, even when it pressed upon him most heavily. It is customary to overlook this aspect of his life; yet the picture of Beethoven, as man and musician, is incomplete without it. Reaction from the high tragedy of his dreams, from high intellectual tension, from ecstatic visions, took the form, not of pleasant, ordinary light-heartedness, but of resounding, almost hysterical outbursts of laughter; moods of super-sensitiveness gave place suddenly to explosive, demoniac humours. As a pianist, Beethoven had a knack of breaking in upon the hush which followed his imaginative interpretations with peals of harsh laughter, bringing his hearers back from supernal regions to earth with brutal suddenness, and he did the same thing as a composer. He abolished the quiet elegance, the cheerfulness and grace of the old minuet, substituting terrific natural force, freed from narrow rhythmic conventions, restless, sometimes darkly passionate, sometimes full of wild joy, sometimes showing the reverse side of things with quiet humour, sometimes resolving deep pathos in lightly swinging dance-rhythms. It ceases to be a dance of polite society, formal and conventional, and becomes a dance of elemental spirits. From the old minuet, with its drawing-room associations, is derived the humorous musical poem—the characteristic *scherzo* of Beethoven.

We have now touched on all the principal forms used by Beethoven. They were based on the nature of things; they were no mere devices, but characteristic embodiments of certain poetic ideas through the symbols of music. They provided the æsthetic foundations of a highly abstract art. In Beethoven a composer arose who completely understood the possibilities of that art and ruled its forms with the absolute confidence of an infallible despot. He knew the secret forces of his spiritual kingdom. He worked with unremitting critical consideration, tireless experiment, a constantly increasing consciousness of his own enormous power. He was artist enough to enforce his will without breaking with tradition, and was able to improve upon forms which came down to him in an apparently complete and unadaptable state. He breathed his own spirit into them, till it filled them almost to bursting point. The might of his inspiration made light of the rules of etiquette. The last secrets of a soul, of an elemental stormy personality, are revealed without reserve. The impulse to self-revelation came from within, not from without. He made himself the subject of artistic exposition, choosing as his medium an art magically expressive of all thoughts and feelings of mankind—wordless, instrumental music.

CHAPTER IV

PIANOFORTE WORKS AND CONCERTOS

BEETHOVEN's work is based on the pianoforte : therein lie its roots and there it first bore perfect fruit. Nevertheless he abandoned this sphere of activity before any other, and the majority of his pianoforte works were produced before he was forty. Till then, each year saw the appearance of a number of compositions for the pianoforte, but an interval of almost five years separates *Das Lebewohl* (Farewell) sonata from the E minor sonata, Op. 90. After this, production was very slow till it quickened a little in the eighteen-twenties. These years gave us the last great works from the E major sonata to the *Diabelli* variations, each a supreme effort to force the instrument, with all its deficiencies, to express the ageing composer's meaning. It had once been his most trusted friend, but it was unable to satisfy the increasing demands made upon it. Beethoven's intellect outgrew the expressive capacity of the pianoforte. The strings jangled and broke— one almost expected to see the whole instrument fall to pieces under the hands of the demon pianist—and it could respond but faintly to the demands made upon it by his creative will. He closed the pianoforte sadly. " It is and always will be a disappointing instrument," he said.

Beethoven's interest in the pianoforte declined in proportion to his growing demand for richness and plasticity in sound-material. Force of outward circumstances also contributed to the estrangement. His activities as a performer were restricted by his on-coming deafness. After his fortieth year or there-abouts, he ceased to perform in public ; and even in private he was less and less often to be heard. The pianoforte, having thus lost its value for him as a direct means of com-munication, forfeited its position as favourite, and became simply one instrument among many, and in certain essentials definitely inferior to others, for Beethoven's purposes. At the same time an enforced separation of the creative from the interpretative artist began in Beethoven; to this he submitted unwillingly enough, but it proved to have important consequences for the future of music. Hitherto it had been taken for granted that composer and virtuoso should be one; evil chance now provided an example to the contrary, and proved the historic origin of the present-day distinction between productive and reproductive musical activity.

The change thus initiated, represented not only an artistic but a social resolution. Pianoforte music was established on a new and better basis. It ceased to be merely a medium for display of the composer's facility; his personal virtuosity sank into the background and he lost the temptation to advertise his own particular " points." Much " occasional " work had been done in the past, the virtuoso desiring to shine before academic authority, fellow-students and friends, or select social circles. Solo instrumental works composed upon a purely artistic impulse were unknown, and even work on a greater scale was almost always done " to order." Bach's creative activities were bound up with the office he held for the time being and changed with changes of office. Haydn's symphonies and quartets were composed as duties, and the custom of " ordering " an opera persisted in a few instances right into the nineteenth century. This state of things, however, gradually changed; the composer's independence increased with a new, free relationship between artist and public and with the opportunities afforded by an extended music-market. Mozart was among the first to write symphonies at his own pleasure, and the greater part of Beethoven's orchestral work sprang entirely from personal initiative. Poetic imagination could no longer be " commandeered," and in later years Beethoven fulfilled orders for work on a big scale only when they jumped with his own wishes. His instinct was wholly for self-determination and against compulsion.

He was the first to compose for solo instruments without a practical personal end in view, and solely because an instrument interested him as a means of communicating his inspirations. He put forth work on its own merits, without reference to any particular performance or to the personality of any particular interpreter. Social changes made this procedure possible, and

G

his deafness hastened the process; but Beethoven's own outlook and character were the principal forces by which he established for all time the distinction between serious composition and the music of mere virtuosity.

Like all the changes for which Beethoven was responsible, this originated not from preconceived design but from gradually dawning inward conviction. Though he lived to become indifferent to the interests of the virtuoso, as a young man he had a strong inclination to the study of pure technique, a joyous pride in mastering the mechanism of his art and in overcoming self-imposed difficulties. The change in his attitude was due partly to the fact that he had exhausted the possibilities in virtuosity, that the instrument had no more problems to offer him. It did not come about suddenly; not for many years did the technician and pianist in Beethoven give place entirely to the speculative composer. The later works show an increasing, conscious subordination of the personality of the performer to that of the composer; yet the majority of the pianoforte works are clearly designed with an eye to the exigencies of his own performance, poetic in inspiration indeed, but full of a lively interest in technical problems, of joy in sheer tone-material. These works lift a corner of the veil which time has dropped, and give us a glimpse of Beethoven the virtuoso, with his personal merits and peculiarities, his preferences and weaknesses. He wrote them with an eye to the display of his own powers as a pianist, a fact which must always be taken into consideration in the study of his pianoforte music. It affords a side-light upon his personality, not obtainable from the orchestral works, which sprang from a purely artistic impulse to communicate his thoughts. The connection between Beethoven the pianoforte composer and Beethoven the virtuoso was very intimate. His playing bore the same sort of relation to his composition as does the glance of the eyes, the tone of the voice to a man's personality.

What are we to think of him as a pianist? Was his great reputation due to the glamour of his personality alone, or did he really introduce something new in technique and expression? Did he initiate a new epoch in pianoforte playing?

Beethoven's fame as a pianist dates from his second period of residence in Vienna. We have little information as to the impression produced by earlier performances; and such as we have, though complimentary, is not enthusiastic. When he played in public as an eight-year-old child he made no striking impression ; he was recognised as gifted, but was certainly not regarded as a phenomenon like Mozart. Public opinion at the time does not appear to have taken into account the difference between Beethoven's careless upbringing and Mozart's carefully considered and brilliantly successful training to a particular end, although these facts had an important bearing on the subsequent development of the two composers.

Beethoven grew up in a narrow circle, his vision circumscribed, without the opportunity of hearing famous models. His capacity was acknowledged and encouraged and Count Waldstein gave him a grand piano, but he remained at best a merely local celebrity in Bonn, to which his activities were confined till his twenty-first year, when he is said to have made a concert-tour with his mother in Holland (in the winter 1781–1782) of which we know practically nothing. The journey of the court of Bonn to Mergentheim was in all probability his first opportunity of performing before a new audience. Hitherto he had lacked the stimulus, so important to a virtuoso, of intercourse with men of talent. His public, too, had not been an experienced or exacting one ; he was the sole musical celebrity in his small circle. He must have had a genius for self-education as well as special gifts as a pianist. This alone could account for the enthusiastic praises of Chaplain Junker in Mergentheim in 1791. He speaks of the " pleasant fellow, of sensitive temperament, who would certainly become a great virtuoso because of the inexhaustible wealth of his ideas, the absolutely original quality of the expression in his playing and his amazing facility. His playing is so utterly different from the usual methods of the pianist, that he seems to be striking out an entirely new way of his own."

A way of his own ! These words, uttered by a plain man scarcely conscious of their deep significance, express the essence of Beethoven's virtuosity. As a pianist he achieved a " way of his own " not in spite of, but because of, his isolation. A lesser man would have remained stationary for want of encouragement, or would have been spoiled by the uncritical praise of friends. Beethoven, on the contrary, found himself, and evolved an absolutely personal style. Important cultural influences, when they came his way, assisted but did not deflect his natural development, and when he was suddenly transplanted from the comparative obscurity of Bonn to the brilliance of Viennese musical circles, he took the lead almost at once and won an unassailable position above all rivalry.

The Vienna of Beethoven's youth was a city of elegant and highly developed musical culture. The Mozart tradition was very much alive, and new pianists were judged by the standard of his tuneful, sensitive and nobly graceful manner. Distinguished technicians such as Clementi, Wölffl, Lipavski and Gelinek raised the level of technical facility without superseding for an instant the interpretative standards set by the great Salzburg master. Beethoven possessed little in common with Mozart's style, which had some eighty years of tradition, bound up with the delicately constructed Viennese type of instrument, behind it. Neefe's instructions were probably based on the method of Philip Emanuel Bach, which, in contrast to the soft and pleasing Viennese style, was strong, expressive, colourful in touch and energetic in attack. Beethoven's connection with the organ may have strengthened his fingers and sharpened his appreciations of the beauty of the singing touch. His hand, thickset, sinewy, scarcely capable of stretching a tenth, with short fingers flattened in front, was not naturally adapted for the grace of the "gallant" school with its tender *cantabile* execution and light and limited dynamic. His technique demanded from the outset a more ringing resonance; abounding, effervescing energy rather than pleasant dalliance and coquettish *bravura*; it does not sway and glide; it stamps and rolls. At the same time it is bold and rich in new combinations, based not upon flattery of the instrument with an eye to superficial effect but frequently wrung from the instrument as it were thanklessly and in despite. His tone was free from the rapidly cloying sweetness, the flattering grace of the accomplished Viennese virtuoso. His *cantilena* was stirring, full-toned and sustained like organ notes; the tones ran together in long unbroken melodic lines "like the drawing of a violin bow." His touch was very delicate and suggestive, and his sense of tone bordered on the orchestral. He extended the range, not only of forms, but also of pure tone clang, and introduced finer shades. The great breadth of his ideas demanded a transformation of the tone-values of the keyboard, for his standpoint was widely different from that of the older schools.

To give adequate expression to his imaginative originality, Beethoven needed a specially responsive instrument, and he rejected one after another as unsatisfactory for his purpose. The claviers used by him in Bonn were probably designed according to the prevailing taste and therefore ill-adapted to his need. The " grand " given by Count Waldstein was probably the work of Stein of Augsburg (at that time attracting attention as a rival of the Viennese makers), who was endeavouring to give greater fullness and intensity of tone to his instruments. Beethoven was greatly interested in Stein's grand, and visited him at Augsburg on his first journey to Vienna. Stein's daughter Nanette, who was skilled in her father's craft, settled later in Vienna with her husband, Andreas Streicher, a friend of Schiller's, and Beethoven became intimate with this family. To satisfy his demands, Streicher embarked on a series of experiments, and the result proved that Beethoven had been on the right track. Reichardt tells us that in 1809, Streicher " abandoned the soft and too easily yielding touch of other Viennese instruments, and at Beethoven's advice and request produced a touch of greater resistance and more elasticity, so that a good performer had increased control over the sustenance and joining of the tones, and could obtain more delicate touch and repetition. He put a better and more complicated instrument into the hands of the virtuoso who aimed at something beyond mere light brilliance of style."

There was a great difference between the services of Beethoven and those of Bach to the science of instrumental construction. The latter understood the business from the practical and technical side as well as any instrument-maker, while his far-seeing artist's eye and acute, speculative, somewhat over-subtle intellect gave him an advantage over the mere mechanic in discovering possibilities of improvement. Beethoven, on the contrary, did not trouble about the details of construction. He pointed out to the mechanic some end which he thought desirable and left him to find the way to achieve it. He was never wholly satisfied with results, for the more the industry accomplished the more he expected of it, and the mechanism always lagged behind his desires. He was best pleased by the massively constructed English " grand " which he saw in Berlin in 1796, but it was long before his desire to possess one was fulfilled. There are three historic " grands " known to have belonged to Beethoven, the first of which came from Erard's Parisian factory. It may have been given him in 1803 by Prince Lichnowsky, who bought a similar instrument for himself at that date. It is a feebly constructed instrument, and it is unlikely that Beethoven prized it very highly. In the early 'twenties he gave it to his brother Johann, having in 1818 received a " grand " from the London manufacturer, Thomas Broadwood. It was a trichord instrument, astonishingly strongly built for those days, and Beethoven was enthusiastic over its low notes. His delight in this instrument may have fanned his dying affection for the piano to flame once more, and in this way have given rise to the great B flat major sonata begun about that time.

The Broadwood remained his favourite even when it was almost worn out and the Viennese maker, Graf, built him a new four-strung instrument fitted with a special resonator. The two pianos stood " belly to belly " in the " Schwarzspanierhaus," mute witnesses of his last days of life and inspiration.

Beethoven's connection with piano-building shows clearly enough the line which his ideas of reform took. They were all in the direction of increase of resonance, augmentation of tone-capacity, and richness of tone clang. He desired a more expressive, intellectual and colouristic instrument. We are not surprised that the tendency was not immediately understood and that his audience seized upon certain eccentricities in his playing and criticised them adversely. Beethoven's style must have appeared very extravagant and *baroque* to musicians reared in the tradition of eighteenth-century taste, whereas it was in reality under the compulsion of his tremendous creative ideas. As is often the case, the ordinary public, less loaded with technical knowledge and prejudices than the musical profession, was the first to recognise a new phenomenon. Beethoven experienced this recognition both as composer and virtuoso. While his works were being played with enthusiasm by the Viennese nobility, and his fame was spreading among amateurs all over Germany and England, they were pedantically condemned in the *Allgemeine Musikalische Zeitung.* The narrower type of professional continued these strictures, even when his reputation as a pianist was firmly established. At the beginning of the nineteenth-century, Romberg denounced his rough, harsh style of playing, and Cherubini supported this unfavourable opinion in 1805. Compared with Wölffl's coolness and smoothness, Beethoven's technique was " less delicate, bordering at times on vagueness "; but the contrast with the most famous pianist of the old type, Hummel, was yet more violent. Beethoven's freer use of the pedal displeased those who could not understand the need of new blends of colour. His technical audacities were less disconcerting in his later years, when they lost some of their absolute certainty. Pleyel found the *mot juste* when in 1805 he said, " *Il n'a pas d'école, il ne faut pas le regarder comme un pianiste.*" Yet that able critic, Tomaczek, called him " the king of piano-playing." Both were right, for Beethoven was not a pianist in the then accepted sense. He lacked traditional method, and no teacher was ever able to impose it upon him. He gradually evolved a method of his own, which, when found, proved superior to all others. It was not a subordination or adaptation of the performer's personality to the requirements of the instrument; the performer mastered the instrument, forcing the mechanism to respond to his demands upon it. These demands steadily increased, poetic intuition forcing a way through the most obstinate technical difficulties. The poetic sense was the life of Beethoven's performance as of his composition; and it appeared most vital when expression was freest. All witnesses, indeed, are agreed that Beethoven's improvisations were absolutely unique. Even Mozart's most fanatic admirers allow him a place near their idol in this sphere. It is from this standpoint that any estimate of Beethoven as a performer should begin. Our interest centres less in his achievements as a pianist than in the overpowering impression he created when giving free vent to his imagination in improvisation.

Since Beethoven's day, improvisation as a part of the pianist's activity has been almost forgotten; as an independent branch of the art it has been entirely suppressed. In the early days of music it was not so, and free improvisation was sedulously cultivated as part of the musician's equipment. It was, indeed, the original form of virtuosity, when player and composer were one, and music owed much of its attraction to that fact. The wells of imagination bubbled up in the presence of the listener, so that immediate participation in the mysteries of the creative act, together with delight in superficial dexterity, were, for the public, the chief attractions in the musician's performance. The later custom of writing down the score, as a slight indication of the original idea, was designed chiefly for the benefit of less gifted and imaginative instrumentalists. Improvisation was still held to be the severest test of a great musician's genius. A less-gifted musician covered his lack of originality by designating the score as a mere " sketch," which he filled out to his mind. Most of the older scores are, indeed, mere indications, showing that supplementary work on the performer's part was taken for granted, and the *cadenzas* of instrumental concertos are surviving relics of the age of improvisation.

This now lost art was Beethoven's proper domain. His mastery therein was undisputed, and even the malcontents, who would not allow that he was, in the strict sense, a pianist, admitted the power of his improvisations. During his first visit to Vienna, Mozart, who received a set piece somewhat coolly, was moved to prophecy when he heard the free flow of Beethoven's imagination. He needed no specially inspiring theme. Almost any theme served for him as a key to the realm of imagination. It is recorded that on the occasion of a contest with Steibelt, an arrogant trick-pianist, Beethoven strode to the instrument, took the 'cello part of the quintet just played by Steibelt from the music-stand, hammered out a theme from a few insignificant notes, and broke into such a tremendous imaginative improvisation that Steibelt, annihilated, slunk from the room and took care to avoid contact with Beethoven for the future.

A number of well-attested anecdotes tell of Beethoven's almost incredible skill in improvisation, of its unfailing effectiveness in widely varying circumstances. He had no doubts of his own power to create an impression. When a concert tour was planned out he would undertake conducting and improvisation only, leaving " clavier-playing " to his pupil Ries. His interest in the performance of already scored pieces was slight, and he knew that he could safely leave it in the hands of zealous disciples who made an exact study of it and performed it better, perhaps, than himself. In all his public concerts, with the exception of a few " composition evenings " during his last years, improvisation was the chief item on the programme. He would break thereinto when he was in the mood, whether or not it formed part of the pre-concerted plan, and at a performance of the quintet for pianoforte and wind-instruments, Op. 16, at a pause in the music, he suddenly began a bold improvisation, to the embarrassment of the other artistes, who anxiously awaited their entrances— but to the delight of the audience, who entered into the spirit of the somewhat high-handed jest.

The rush of Beethoven's ideas at a given moment and their apparently inexhaustible capacity for metamorphosis are alike amazing. Inspiration, once kindled, seemed unquenchable. Image succeeds image, the spirit ascends in ever-widening circles, forsaking actuality, climbing towards eternity, like an eagle soaring into the sun. Beethoven forgot concert-room and audience, the world of time and space fell away. At times he would touch the keyboard in passing, and, his imagination suddenly taking fire, he would remain beside the piano entranced, without change of his awkward position, playing, playing cease-lessly at the spirit's imperative behest. Thus he first played the *Eroica* variations ; thus for a few friends he improvised, not in the concise form in which they are now scored, and for two hours more he maintained the same theme. Ries tells a similar story about the origin of the last movement of the F minor sonata, Op. 57. The two men had taken a long walk, during which " Beet-hoven hummed to himself, at times roared to himself, high and low without actually singing a note, the whole way. When I asked him what he had in mind he said, ' I have just thought of a theme for the last *allegro* of my sonata.' The moment we entered his room, he rushed to the clavier without so much as removing his hat. I sat down in a corner and he forget me immediately. For an hour or more, he raged through the glorious new finale. When at last he rose, he was amazed to see me there, and said, ' I can give you no lesson to-day ; I must go on with this.' "

The fertility of Beethoven's imagination suggests the conjecture that many valuable ideas were lost, vanishing from the moment of their birth. One of his friends expressed some such thought at the close of an improvisation, but he laughed in a superior way and immediately, to the hearer's amazement, repeated his performance. This remarkable incident, more difficult to understand perhaps than the gift of improvisation itself, proves the absolute consciousness with which Beethoven's mind worked, even in what appears to us as the twilight of creation. It is therefore probably true to suppose that Beethoven's apparently instantaneous improvisations were the result of a previous correlation of the apparently new ideas. He was ever too economical an artist to allow a treasure, once won, to run to waste. Whatever material he thought worth preservation, he put by for future greater uses, so that far less was lost than superficial consideration might lead one to suppose.

Beethoven's wonderful plastic genius is shown as much by the forms in which he clothed his improvisations as in the inventiveness with which he marshalled his ideas. Less talented musicians, forced to improvise by the fashion of the day, often took refuge in a stereotyped form of variation. Beethoven used a new form almost every time. Czerny has indicated several of the most striking types of his improvisations. The Op. 77 fantasia in G minor is one of many examples of his method of stringing thoughts together, as the whim took him, of following the caprices of a changing mood, yet rounding the work to a whole. He seems, as usual, to turn half unwillingly to the keyboard. He begins without smooth harmonies or pleasing anticipatory passages. The fingers break at once into rapid descending *allegro* runs, as if to brush away morose thoughts and banish them with imperious gestures. The excited introduction is interspersed with expectant pauses—no one knew so well as Beethoven the expressive force of the pause with its uncanny power of creating tension. A plaintive melody begins with yearning sevenths and ninths, and finds a close in a delicately fading cadenza. The rolling scales, the sorrowful singing come again in a lower key—the melancholy mood deepens. A solemn D flat major *largo* is heard, broad basses, deeply mystical, a close-knit restful middle part, a reverent, hesitant melody, a questioning half-close. Has the soul found its balance and its rest ? The answer is an emphatic No. More violently than before, the scale descends into the depths. The *largo* melody reappears with a hint of consolation, clothed in etherial colours of flutes and clarionets. An evasive close interrupts the consoling train of thought. The dark shadows of the opening gather, but their power is broken. Now they lead on to a vigorous upward movement of the spirit, and thereupon carry over to a reflective song-like theme. The player's joy in tone awakes. He avoids the usual periodic close, and the full sounding E flat major chord charms him into repeating it uninterruptedly for four bars, ever more tenderly, till it appears to die away in dreamy, almost recitative-like phrases. There follows a decisive awakening. Lively runs appear ; the fires of virtuosity are fanned. After a short hesitation follow introductory chords, simple ascending triad themes characteristic of Beethoven, first in D minor, then in F major, written for both hands with determined *bravura*. Even here the poet finds no lasting content. Again he breaks off suddenly, and as suddenly returns to his indecisive brooding. He takes his fill of one single tone, but half timorously attempted harmonies lead to no new ideas. The opening scale is repeated in a ghostly whisper. The dreamy play with one slow trembling tone is reasserted, and it seems as though the musician were on the track of some enfranchising thought that continually eludes him. Fantastic tone-pictures occur in restless wavering sounds, through which a questioning melody rises momentarily to sink back in dreamy meditation. It does not, however, end now in an indecisive repetition of sound. The spell has been broken, but the melodic line raises itself from bar to bar. One more thoughtful pause precedes an enchanting B flat major melody which detaches itself from the pensive one-tone motive. This is the variation theme. The composer has now found what he sought, and the full joy of creation reawakes. The melody, repeated, is displayed in new ways, clothed in sweet tone arabesques, and shared in grotesque guise by the bass, always preserving its joyous song-like character. The rolling opening scales appear once more, purged of their depressing effect. Free from dissonance, they accord with the key and lead through delicately humorous deviations to an inventive intonation of the song in C major, and thus, transposed into the reconciling B flat major, they bring to a close the half triumphant, half elegiac *coda*.

Czerny, who considers this poetic work (now almost forgotten) as typical of Beethoven's method of improvisations, does it an injustice in describing it as a potpourri, or loose train of ideas. The way that the B flat major melody, the kernel of the whole, is developed organically from the apparently insignificant one-tone motive, the way that the characteristic opening scale frequently reappears in fresh guise, framing the whole from first to last and adapted to each change of mood, makes it absurd to speak of the work as a haphazard, luxuriant mozaic of ideas. Despite its multiplicity of theme-materials the Fantasia possesses an inner unity and displays a readily recognisable and highly poetic sequence of thought throughout.

This particular form gave wide play to the imagination; yet Beethoven did not regard it in any way as a model for subsequent work. Czerny quotes, as another example of Beethoven's improvisation, the free variation-form " such as that of the *Choral* fantasia or the choral finale of the ninth symphony, both of which give a true picture of his method of improvisation." He adds a third and a fourth example of the *genre*.

" There was the form of the first movement or the final *rondo* of a sonata, in which he closed the first part in a regular manner and constructed a middle episode, etc., in the same or an allied key, but in the second part left himself quite free, and yet made the very most of the inspirational motive. In the *allegro tempo* the whole was entwined with *bravura* passages, for the most part even more difficult than those to be found in his works."

His most important improvisational forms were all comprised in the types which Czerny classified as " sonata-movement," " variation " and " rondo." Beethoven was able to improvise in forms for which long and strenuous thought was usually indispensable. This observation leads to the *a posteriori* conclusion that improvisation must have greatly influenced his pianoforte compositions in the narrower sense, or rather, that improvisation and composition are blended in the pianoforte works. His playing was a creation for, and in the presence of, an audience, a free activity which reacted in its turn on composition. The high-water mark of the old type of virtuosity was reached, but at the same time its doom was pronounced. We can understand why Beethoven cared little for the public performance of his own work, why he preferred to leave it to others and to confine himself to free improvisation. He transformed free improvisation by giving it an artistic law, and at the same time, by his scores, provided a multiplicity of exercises and problems for a reproductive and interpretative development of an art foreign to him, unknown, indeed, in his day and which was to take its origin from his creations. He perfected and destroyed the art of improvisation. He was the last virtuoso of the old style and the founder of the new.

Improvisation, controlled and ennobled through the organising power of form—form, winged by the exhilaration of improvisation—these were the basic elements of Beethoven's pianoforte music, the two poles of its being. Improvisation is the stronger of these powers, but this does not mean that Beethoven, a most careful and reflective worker, dashed off his pianoforte compositions in a few hours at the keyboard and then wrote them down. Ries' story of the finale of Op. 57 shows that something of this sort occurred very occasionally; yet even in this particular case only a close comparison between the improvisation heard by Ries and the finished score could show how far strict self-criticism modified the first imaginative impulse. It is, however, important to recognise that these works were based on the concept of ideal improvisation and that they owe their characteristic blend of natural, instantaneous emotion and artistic, carefully thought-out construction, to their double source.

Improvisation demands unconditional surrender to the mood, the whim, the accidental impression, of the moment; whereas the most perfect form of instrumental music, the sonata, requires a firm basis of intellectual data and a strictly logical development of the chosen train of thought. It is organic and well-knit, whereas improvisation tends to be disconnected. The latter represents intuition; the former, purpose and logic. In Beethoven's pianoforte music the two contrive to co-exist. From the union of fantasia and sonata springs his most original creation, the fantasia-sonata.

It was neither wilfulness nor desire of originality for its own sake which led him to this exquisite poetic form. Just as he

hated violent and enforced novelty, just as he was content to wear
the perruque and bag fashionable in his youth, so he respected
the artistic fashions of his time. He conquered established
forms, mastering every detail of their construction, before he
attempted imaginative reconstructions of his own. As an artist
he was never hasty or unbridled, and he thought long before
replacing the old by the new. He never departed from tradition
without urgent necessity ; he left the beaten track reluctantly ;
but when he did, he pursued his own course boldly.

We will now consider the early group of pianoforte compositions ending with Op. 22, the " little " B flat major sonata.
These works extend over a period dating from Beethoven's
childish beginnings in Bonn to his first grand concert in Vienna
in 1800. The group comprises thirteen variations ; four pianoforte concertos (of which two are preserved only in a garbled
form); sixteen solo and one four-handed sonatas ; besides a
number of lesser pianoforte compositions. Most of the chamber-
music composed during this period, e.g. the Bonn pianoforte
quartet, the trios, Op. 1 and 11, the violoncello sonatas, Op. 5, and
the violin sonatas, Op. 12, are designed for the co-operation of the
pianoforte. Beethoven's own instrument is herein dominant,
and his interest in other branches of music is comparatively
slight. Only one symphony, chamber-music works for wind
instruments, string trios, the quartets, Op. 18, and a few choral
works appear beside the pianoforte music. Here is practical
proof that Beethoven was preoccupied with the clavier ; it was
the centre of his thought and composition, and his own playing
was the basis of both his industry and art.

Beethoven's first work was in the form of variations : " Nine
variations upon a March by Dressler," as he called the first
modest attempt which Neefe had printed in Mannheim " to
encourage " the eleven-year-old composer. The work is nothing
more than a series of quite ordinary play-figures, but it shows
notable facility in the handling of a rhythmically and harmonically
uninspiring theme. The sonatas, dedicated to the Elector Max
Friedrich, are a great advance, not only in technical daring and
delicacy of phrasing in the figures, but in a surprising variety
of motives, all demanding expansion. The most remarkable of
these sonatas is that in F minor, a first sketch for the *Pathétique*.

The *larghetto maestoso* of the introduction recurs in the *allegro*; and the *allegro* theme, ascending vigorously from the second bar onwards, has a dull, hammering bass accompaniment. The mournful F minor key had already cast its spell over Beethoven's imagination. A knowledge of suffering, appalling in a twelve-year-old boy, trembles through the quiet *andánte*, and rages through the excited, urgent, *unisono* passages of the *presto*. This minor *presto* with its preordained *appassionata* close is as different as possible from the traditional jollity of the finale. It carries out the basic mood of the first movement in a more fantastic manner. It makes a poem of the whole little work to which, despite a certain precocious *naïveté* and clumsiness, it is impossible to deny greatness of conception and earnestness of feeling.

Other very early pianoforte compositions, an unfinished C major sonata and two " slight " two-movement pieces, all dedicated to Eleanore von Breuning, are less important than the F minor sonata. Certain other trifles, published years later, as Op. 33, have little intrinsic value. It is, indeed, doubtful whether the date " 1782 " on the original manuscript is authentic. It is almost impossible to believe that a twelve-year-old boy could have been responsible for such miniatures as the C major *scherzo*, with surging bass-harmonies in the minor, or the tender A major *andante*, with mystic bass melody in A minor, or the rhythmical *piquant* piece in D flat major. The assured skill of the pianoforte piece alone points to a later date of composition. Nottebohm places the D major *allegretto*, " *con una certa espressione parlante*," in 1802.

Apart from a pretty but not specially interesting A major *rondo*, two dry preludes published as Op. 39, and a few inconsiderable variations in the taste of the period, no great solo piece for the pianoforte appeared till the Op. 2 sonatas of 1796. They may have been composed earlier, for they bear undoubted resemblances of thought to other works of the Bonn period, though Beethoven took the *adagio* of his F minor sonata and a few themes in the C major direct from pianoforte quartets composed in 1785. There are several opinions as to the order in time of these sonatas, but all are agreed that they are the first of Beethoven's solo compositions which have intrinsic value. Earlier work is of interest in displaying his course of development, but these show some-

thing of his essence.   Immaturity is past, and the whole force
of his personality is now at work.   The artist is now in command
of his own tremendous flow of ideas and is able to give them sure
form and shape.   The three differ absolutely from one another
(though bracketed together as one *opus*, Op. 2, according to
prevailing custom), each having a character, a force, a plan and
an object of its own.

The four-movement scheme, *allegro*, *adagio* (or *largo*), *scherzo*
(entitled *minuetto* in the first) and *rondo*, is common to all, though
filled each time with a different content by the composer.   Colour
and physiognomy are indicated by key ;   mournful passion in the
F minor, sunny gaiety in the A major, and joyful brilliance in
the C major sonata.   In the first the *allegro* is composed of two
themes only, of which the composer makes the most.   With the
main theme, ascending in short, energetic crotchet rhythm, now
urgent, now lost in gloomy reverie, he contrasts a plaintive song-
melody in which the dissonant minor ninth is prominent.   A
rhythmical and emotional background is supplied by lightly
vibrating basses—which in the first theme was given by
firmly struck chords.   There is little digression of any sort,
the two contrasting themes dominating the movement till its
mournfully resolute close.

The *allegri* of the A major and C major sonatas are very
different, being full of lively delight in technique.   Both display
an abundance of motives, which in the C major sonata are of an
openly sensational character.   In intoxicating runs, effective
bravu a tests, insignificant openings leading to brilliant octave
passages, striking discords and high-spirited trills, Beethoven
exhausts the resources of his virtuosity.   The languid song-
theme taken from the third pianoforte-quartet produces little
impression.   An improvisation in the form of a *cadenza*, extended
to a *coda*, closes the movement.   The opening movement of the
A major sonata, which begins with a series of even, prelude-like,
lightly scurrying octaves, is a more distinguished work.

The *scherzi* are not as good as the preceding movements.
The roguishly graceful A major *allegretto*, with a melancholy
minor melody in the trio, and the humorously imitative C major
scherzo are inferior to many of the *Bagatelles* in Op. 33.   The
F minor minuet, with its syncopated bass, its sharp, abruptly

changing accentuation and twilight tone-colour, has more individuality.

The closing movements are more significant than the *intermezzi*, each being a characteristic fulfilment of the opening *allegro*. The rondo of the C major sonata is full of the joy of life. It possesses a spiritual, singing melody, designed to contrast with the virtuosity of the main theme, and closes with a witty coda. Exceedingly graceful, despite its impetuously rhythmical middle part, the A major rondo is a masterly combination of poetic charm and architectonic sense. Both the C major and A major final movements are, however, only mere after-pieces; but the F minor *prestissimo* has higher value. It is a free continuation of the opening movement, not of its thematic content, but of its mood. The energy which was carefully restrained and held in reserve in the first movement is here released in surging passion. The performer cannot do justice to the frequently underestimated first part without bearing the finale in mind. The work is a display of temperament, of so explosive a kind that it sets the soul in an uproar. It marks the point where improvisation—submission to the mood of the moment—and hard thinking can be made to unite. A little more and they must separate, but here they weigh evenly in Beethoven's work.

The slow movements display the widest outlook. The two *adagios* and the *largo* are marked by an almost religious solemnity. The old-fashioned *andante* was inadequate for Beethoven's exalted pathos; it needed a broad stream of song, the long, slow breaths of the *adagio* and *largo* to express it. The slow movements of the F minor and A major sonatas are full of a deep longing for peace, but the *adagio* of the third sonata is yet more significant and is undoubtedly the most valuable piece of work, after the F minor *prestissimo*, in the whole of Op. 2. A theme announced, as it were falteringly, with questioning dominant closes at the end of each phrase, a dreamy dialogue between bass and treble, yearning suspensions and dissonances in a melody spasmodically indicated, a bracing of the self to greater activity and a sinking back into ethereal dreams at the close, provide a succession of highly poetic moments. The variety of moods within a single movement, the sensuous charm of the clavier tone at its best, had a magical

H

effect upon Beethoven's contemporaries, particularly upon the youth of the day.

The threefold Op. 2, however, was but the first step in Beethoven's steady progress towards a sonata-form of monumental greatness. There was much that was new in Op. 2, yet the following E flat major sonata, op. 7, marks a distinct advance; only the final movement, a graceful counterpart of the A major rondo, remarkable for a startling change to B major at the beginning of the *coda*, has any suggestion of the earlier works. The third movement, neutral, though described as *allegro*, is, on the contrary, absolutely new. The principal part is more intricate than the earlier *scherzi*; the motives are worked out with delicate art and quiet humour. The shadowy, secret and harmonious *Minore* is one of the earliest examples of Beethoven's love of rhythmic tone. It is possible that this part was not originally designed for the sonata but was meant to stand alone as a musical trifle.

The first *allegro* is an early example of Beethoven's typical, long-drawn-out, thoughtful sonata-movement, emphasising sharply the dramatic character of the sonata-form. There is still a superfluity of ideas. The heroic opening motive resolves itself into a rising and falling line of quavers, is scattered and its inherent strength left undeveloped till the "exposition" and *coda*. The *coda* is the most important part of the movement. In this work Beethoven's tendency to prolong the struggle of opposites right into the *coda* and give this its most decided expression there, becomes for the first time apparent. In his day this sonata was called the "enamoured one," a somewhat unsatisfactory designation. The contrast between the manly, challenging beginning and the gentle, pleading song-melody gives the work an unmistakably heroic and elegiac character which is, indeed, openly declared at the close.

Once more the *adagio*, "*largo con gran espressione*," crowns the whole. It achieves emotional heights, new even to Beethoven, and orchestration would best bring out its manifold dynamic gradations, which are scarcely expressible through the medium of the piano. The work is a poem of loneliness.

Beethoven wrote only three solo pianoforte pieces in *largo* form, these being the D major movement, Op. 2. ii, the C major *largo*, Op. 7, and the D minor, Op. 10. iii, the theme of which, centreing in the keynote of D, was explained to Schindler in after years by Beethoven as the portrait of a melancholic; it makes a poignantly great picture. As he grew to maturity, he used the *largo* less and less frequently. It appears in chamber-music up to the D major trio, Op. 70, but in work for the pianoforte alone it is employed only very occasionally in the form of a prelude, as in the opening of the D minor sonata, Op. 31. ii, and the intro-duction to the fugue of the great B flat major sonata; as an independent movement, it was discarded in solo sonatas after Op. 10. Did Beethoven come to regard the tremendous pathos of the *largo* as a piece of youthful rhetoric? Did he find its emotionalism and solemn earnestness overstrained? It is certain that the *largo* movements of the earlier works had no direct successors; they were the first of a series of forms discarded by Beethoven after he had extracted the utmost from them.

In Beethoven's next period there are notable evidences of unrest. Hitherto he had clung to the four-movement scheme, taking it for granted as a working basis; but he seems at this time to have felt it burdensome, and to have sought a simpler form, not by way of return to the old three-movement form of *allegro*, *andante* and final rondo, but by a thorough remodelling of the form of each movement. The minuet is wanting in two C minor sonatas, Op. 10. i and Op. 13; in the F major sonata, Op. 10. ii, and the E major sonata, Op. 14. i, the long movement is replaced by an *allegretto*; in the G major sonata, Op. 14. ii, the finale is omitted, and the work ends with a *scherzo* in the form of a rondo. Of the seven works Op. 10 to 22, only the D major sonata, Op. 10. ii, and the B flat sonata, Op. 22, retain the four-movement form, and even in these adherence to tradition is but superficial. In the three sonatas of Op. 10, Beethoven attempts a decisive change of the principal movement, constructing the " exposition " upon an entirely new theme. This development had been hinted in Op. 7. The old type of sonata built on a dual theme begins gradually to give place to a new form, not yet exactly defined, but transcending the twofold theme and com-prehending an indefinite number of imaginative ideas and thought associations. So much inventiveness subjected the form to strain. By adding a third or fourth to the traditional pair of equally important themes, he diminished the possibility of exhausting the thought content of the main theme. This result of the innovation is apparent in the C minor and F major sonatas, Op. 10. In both works the opening movement is sketchy. Valuable material (a vigorously dramatic main idea in the C minor sonata and two idyllic song themes in the F major) is more or less wasted. The movements are not thoroughly worked out, questions are raised and dropped, the disadvantages of improvisation are made only too plain, and both works, despite the greatness of their ideas, must be set down as second-rate. Beethoven meets with better success in the first movement of the third sonata, Op. 10, the D major, with its fiery opening theme. The energetic "exposition" theme is at least rhythmically related to the main thought. The first motive so completely dominates the work that the new "exposition" theme comes as a welcome intensification. The movement has a splendid unity and "swing." The somewhat conventional secondary theme is practically negligible and the mysterious closing motive throws up the brilliant colouring of the whole by skilful shading.

We have already discussed one of the two slow movements of the Op. 10 group—the D minor *largo*; and the beautifully euphonious A flat major *adagio* of the C minor sonata is worthy to stand beside it. In the E major *adagio*, Op. 2. iii, questioning and answering motives run parallel and intermingled as in a dialogue; here they succeed each other in order. The resulting contrasts are not highly dramatic, but the simple *adagio* song of earlier times is rendered more lyrical, more poetic.

Instead of a slow movement, the second sonata of this group has an F minor *allegretto*, with a D flat major trio inserted; ostensibly composed in 1798, there is much in it which points to a later date of composition. It inevitably reminds the hearer of the C minor symphony, and it was certainly in advance of Beethoven's imaginative range at that time. The companion sonata in D major (Op. 10. iii) possesses a graceful, trifling minuet and a very effective trio in which the left hand encircles the right, which sustains the harmony, with bold, broken chords.

The rondos in Op. 10 are also remarkable. The jolly *presto* of the F major sonata with its high-spirited, capricious, pulsating rhythm is a foretaste of the " *Wut über den verlorenen Groschen* "

(A fuss about a lost penny). The *prestissimo* of the C minor sonata is richer in content. It is a puzzling, gloomy piece, hiding far more than it reveals, and it leaves an uneasy impression with the hearer despite the reconciling major close.

The D major rondo is similar in construction, though very different in character. As in the C minor piece it grows out of an urgent, aphoristic motive. The cheerful secondary themes appear rather too light by contrast with the pensive main theme which, in a mysterious, syncopated episode in the *coda*, finally resolves itself into mystical rocking sequences of harmony, until the final bars lead the work back with energetic *bravura* to the sunny gaiety of D major.

When these works were appearing, Dionys Weber, a strict professor of music, lived and taught in Prague. Among his scholars was young Ignatius Moscheles, who had been brought up to think Mozart, Clementi and Bach (Philip Emanuel, of course) alone worth study. "About this time," Moscheles tells us in his reminiscences, "I heard from some fellow-students that there was a composer recently come to the fore in Vienna who wrote the most curious stuff in the world—a *baroque* type of music, contrary to all rules, which no one could play and no one could understand; the composer's name was Beethoven. To satisfy my curiosity as to this eccentric genius, I betook myself to the lending library and procured a copy of Beethoven's *Sonata Pathétique*. I had not enough money to buy the work, but I secretly copied it out. I found the novel style so attractive, and my admiration was so enthusiastic, that I so far forgot myself as to mention my new discovery to my teacher. He thereupon reminded me of his precepts, and warned me not to play or study eccentric productions until my style was formed on more reliable examples. I disregarded this advice and acquired Beethoven's works one by one as they appeared, finding in them such consolation and delight as no other composer was able to give me."

There is a delicious *naïveté* about this narrative; the same thing must have been occurring on all hands—the rigid, mistrustful teacher, the pupil with his enthusiasm for novelty, and Beethoven's work as the forbidden fruit between them. The *Pathétique* and the *Lebewohl* are the only two sonatas to which Beethoven himself gave titles. *Pathétique* is not a programme, but a characterisation of style which might be applied to other works composed before Op. 13. The C minor sonata, Op. 10, the *allegro* of the F major sonata, the finale of the F minor sonata, Op. 2, and the *largi* of Op. 2, Op, 7, Op. 10. iii are all "*pathétique*." In Op. 13, Beethoven expressed the essential contents of all these works in a single poem. The stormy pathos of Beethoven's youth, which he gives us here, is quite unlike the pathos of his maturity. It was not born of suffering, of renunciation or of any great spiritual crisis. It springs from boyish pessimism and *Weltschmerz*, from the restlessness of youth, seeking it knows not what. Its key-note is not bitter experience, but bitter desire for experience. Feigned tragedy formed the style of Beethoven's earlier works, and the further he emerged from the world of foreboding dreams, the more real tragedy entered his experience, the less "pathetic-ally" was it expressed. His presentation of tragedy increased in grandeur and lost nothing in emotional impressiveness as he expressed it in a natural idiom, without the aid of "pathos." In the early work, however, he made artistic and conscious use of pathos to produce a certain effect and accordingly himself entitled his sonata *Pathétique*.

It is significant that this particular piece should have made so deep an impression on Beethoven's contemporaries, while to-day it is regarded as the anti-type of all Beethoven's later work. He certainly made the listener's part an easy one when he composed this sonata ; it is a bold fresco, so powerfully expressive that the dullest hearer is compelled to understand it. It is not a tragedy, but the prelude to a tragedy. Just before the final catastrophe it breaks off, Beethoven taking up the tale years later in his last sonata, the C minor of Op. 10, the far-distant goal to which the *Pathétique* pointed. This latter beats upon the doors of true tragedy but cannot enter in ; nevertheless it is a true poem. The composer deliberately works up his own emotion, but it is genuine emotion. He calls it pathos, acknowledging its deliberate effort after effect, but at least it was no borrowed effect. The noble melody of the *adagio* (a kind of pendant on a bigger scale to the middle movement of the C minor sonata, Op. 10) leads on to a more cheerful and hopeful mood, while the final rondo, its motive allied to the secondary theme of the first movement, once more gives prominence to the restless yearning

of the principal movement, displaying it broadly in changing
light and shade but affording no solution. The *Pathétique*, like
the closely allied C minor sonata, is inconclusive; it is full of
unsolved problems and undecided conflicts. Beethoven advances
a little way into the realms which his genius has discovered, but
he is not yet complete master there. That way, however, was
to lead him to his greatest artistic triumphs, and the value and
interest of these early tragic works lie in the glimpse they afford
of the glories to come.

Beethoven's " pathetic " period in pianoforte music closed with
Op. 13. He turned for a time to definitely cheerful subjects, and
the two Op. 14 sonatas and that in B flat major in Op. 22 prove
his power to express gaiety. He is often mistakenly regarded as
a purely tragic figure, whose works are all self-revelatory in the
extreme; but this is a one-sided estimate which does less than
justice to the great composer's delight in life and the joys thereof.
His grasp of tragedy would be less powerful had he not known
the joys of the world and the senses. Traces of that divine gaiety
which in later life carried Beethoven through all troubles and
solved tragic problems are to be found in his earlier work, though
in a less exalted state, and must be taken into account as genuine
attributes of the man. This branch of Beethoven's work was
more in line than the rest with the taste of his day, but it is none
the less true Beethoven.

The E major sonata, Op. 14. i, opens with a pleasant, sentimental
theme, unfolding itself in quiet fourths. The movement comes
to an end without evincing any striking contrasts of content.
The themes enhance and supplement one another, but the mood
is fully stated in the first theme and thereafter merely para-
phrased. The middle movement consists of an E minor *allegro*,
gently touched with melancholy, the softly swaying motion of
which points to the coming E minor sonata, Op. 90. The dancing
rondo which closes the piece is a return to liveliness—though not
immediately—and has an apparently unassuming epilogue worked
out with exquisite delicacy.

The G major sonata begins with a livelier motive. Here
again the opening mood is preserved throughout the movement,
but the theme is more flexible than that of the E major sonata,
particularly in the " exposition," where it appears in many guises,

sometimes as the lightest whisper, sometimes roisteringly jolly. There is no *adagio*; an *andante*, the first example of the variation introduced into Beethoven's pianoforte music, appears in its place. Its form is very simple, consisting of a march theme, very tuneful in the middle phrases. It is sometimes draped decoratively, sometimes broken by syncopation, sometimes broken up into syncopated harmonies. A similar type of variation, though on a bigger scale, appeared later in the F minor sonata, Op. 57. A piquant, highly rhythmical *scherzo*, in rondo form, effective to perform and charming to hear, with an amusing bass solo thrown across, closes the work. The features of the third and fourth movements being blended, a special finale is unnecessary; the dancing merriment of the *scherzo-rondo* says the last word and rounds off the whole.

The B flat major sonata, Op. 22, is a sudden return to the four-movement form. Beethoven was thoroughly pleased with it and dedicated it, full of fatherly pride, to " my most dear and honoured brother," the publisher, Hofmeister. There must be some special interest in a work which the composer of the *Pathétique* regarded thus. The two works have very little in common. The first movement, however, is quite unlike the *allegri* of the two Op. 14 sonatas. After two false starts, a series of ascending chords announce a swinging theme, a jubiliant motive in Beethoven's most characteristic style. The whole work pulsates with energy and conscious power, disregarding troublesome doubts. Even the suggestion of mystery at the close of the " exposition " is merely an artistic device to enhance the brilliance of the recapitulation. Few of Beethoven's works display such confident, conscious joy in existence. The movement is clearly written for the pianist and is full of musical vitality. So, indeed, is the whole work. The marvellously spiritual and tuneful E flat major *adagio*, a foretaste of the *nocturne* of the romantic period, the minuet in the style of the *ancien régime* and the capricious trio, are none the less enchanting that they show the poet-composer in non-controversial mood. The final movement is one of a series of rondos, beginning with that of Op. 2 in A major and including the last movement of the E flat major sonata, Op. 7, that of Op. 22, and that of Op. 90 in E major, all of which are flexible, decorative, based on simple harmonies, graceful without being superficial, although deeper stirrings are repressed to allow a peaceful, joyful mood to bear sway. The rondo of Op. 22 is the last and most exquisite expression of a period of intensely conscious happiness. It followed upon the vague restlessness of the " pathetic " period, when the artist had once more found himself and was producing works which showed his contentment with things as they were.

Beethoven's first group of pianoforte works thus ends on a peaceful and harmonious note. Two sonatinas published as Op. 49 (of which the first anticipates the septet minuet), two rondos, Op. 51, and a two-movement sonata for four hands, Op. 6, have not yet been mentioned. All the important works of this period are in sonata-form, a fact which distinguishes them from the succeeding group. When Beethoven departs from the four-movement scheme, omitting *scherzo*, *adagio* or finale, he does so in accordance with the character and needs of a particular work ; he makes no display of originality, leaves out a single movement only when it is genuinely superfluous, and returns to the four-movement construction when the content of the work allows it. Whatever liberty he took in the arrangement of the parts, he retained the first movement as the principal and characteristic movement of the whole sonata. Even in this matter he allowed himself freedom in detail. Ideas formerly expressed at length are now compressed in the form of brief motives, the key relationship between main and secondary themes is from time to time altered to suit the composer's purposes, while the " exposition " and *coda* occasionally appear in quite a new guise. The very richness and variety of thought sometimes strains the form to the utmost, without actually breaking it or rendering it unrecognisable. The first movement remains the foundation and starting-point of the whole work.

After Op. 22 Beethoven suddenly abandoned this principle. He composed a group of sonatas which can scarcely be called sonatas, as they do not begin with a sonata-movement. He beheaded the sonata-form and supplied a beginning of his own. The old construction had been weakened somewhat by his treatment of the final movement, but this violent attack upon its most essential part disorganised it entirely. Like all Beethoven's apparent innovations, he based it upon old example, in this case Mozart's. What was it in this model which interested and attracted Beethoven?

As Beethoven found it and improved upon it, the sonata-movement was the most highly developed musical form. The pianoforte works which we have discussed show what he achieved in that form and how deeply he could identify himself with it. The fact that he discarded it shows that he must in some way have found it a hindrance. He wanted a free way for his ideas, and came to despise signposts; he wanted, in fact, to escape the bonds of a logical scheme, to give free rein to his fancy, to improvise, not only in a single movement, but with absolute freedom throughout a multiple form. The sonata-movement, as he had used it hitherto, made this impossible, because it gave the work a definite character from the beginning, a character which succeeding movements could supplement but not change. Beethoven rebelled against this determinative quality in the first movement. He wanted a prelude, an intro-duction, not a proposition. He did not wish to commit him-self in the first movement to a certain sequence of thought. Improvisation, as he now began to see it, might gradually assemble the scattered thoughts, gradually work up a mood, till clear and definite concepts appeared.

He did not, however, at once find this type of improvisation which begins tentatively and gradually establishes its own clear goal. It was not till the second and third work of the new group, the two Op. 27 sonatas, that he gave plastic expression to the artistic conception of a gradual sunrise through the mists of mood. The preceding work, the A flat major sonata, Op. 26, merely suggests it as a future possibility. It is a curious kaleido-scopic piece of work without any well-defined centre. Like the Mozartian model from which it was taken, it begins with a variation, followed by a *scherzo*, a funeral march and a closing rondo. The parts are not at all closely interwoven. According to tradition, the *Marcia sulla morte d'un eroe* was inspired by the funeral march in a very popular opera by Paër; and the rondo which follows it so oddly, by the brilliant virtuosity of Cramer, at that time staying in Vienna. There may be a grain of truth in these tales, for Beethoven lived very much in the world and may well have been influenced by topical events, a new pianoforte technique, or another's composition. Be this as it may, the funeral march in this work was very definitely "composed"—it was not a poem in the sense of the great march in the subsequent *Eroica*. The older piece is not on this account, however, to be despised. Its burdened rhythm, the solemnly pacing melody of the middle part, the powerful, lifting bass, the suggestion of drums and trumpets in the *trio* make it a great piece of work. It is music, first and foremost, and objective musical values give it its special charm and popularity. It is not a piece of self-revelation.

The opening variations are based on a confident, upward striving, peaceful and exalted theme, passionless in character till the anticipatory 'cello phrase of its second part introduces a note of yearning. Its charm depends on sensuous effects, beauty of melody and delicate gradations of dynamic. Some themes hint at mystery and their charm consists rather in what they leave unsaid than in what they express; Beethoven's melody is particularly rich in suggestions of this kind, but other themes are welcome for their clear beauty with no touch of the enigmatical, and the theme of these variations belongs to this class. It must have been a difficult task to evolve fresh images from the narrow range of mood possible to this theme, but Beethoven's constructive fancy was equal to it and produced a series of charming dream pictures. The *scherzo*, with the mysterious harmonies of its *trio*, belongs to the same dream world. The rondo is the most difficult part of the work to understand. Some whim of improvisation may have led the composer to tack it on to the funeral march; its fairy-like tenderness, only occasionally marked by stronger accentuation, its quiet humour, its dependence for effect on skilful performance make it the counterpart of the closing movement of the F major sonata, Op. 54, and its capricious delicacy is often similarly misunderstood.

The tendency to dreamy improvisation is yet more striking in the succeeding work, the E flat major sonata, Op. 27. i. The composer seems to begin with no fixed purpose. The right hand sustains a simple, unassuming melody, the left supplying lightly indicated accompaniment. The whole becomes a song and is repeated. The artist's imagination now seems to take

fire and, preserving the opening rhythm, gives richness of tone
and colour to the folk-tune-like melody. And so for a brief
period only. The first mood soon reasserts itself, expressed
more decoratively. Suddenly, however, the *improvisatore* pulls
himself together ; through his prelude rushes a storm of chords.
This energy breaks into runs working up to a questioning
seventh, which in vain attempts to disperse the dream rapture ;
the shadowy figures reappear and dreaminess again prevails.
The performer's hands appear to grope for unrelated chords
heard from the distance. Faintly, in E flat major, with actuality
left aside, the realm of fantasy is entered. Weird forms remind
one of the mood of the *scherzo* of the C minor symphony and
of the F minor *allegretto*, Op. 10. ii. In the middle movement,
lively dance-rhythms are heard, and again the ghostly triad
motive of the *allegro* follows, syncopated and almost unrecognisable. In a *fortissimo* passage these elements are momentarily
blended, only to be quenched in sudden darkness, out of which
emerges a yearning melody, a poignant prayer. A development indicates that dreams have been resolved into conscious
realities. A swinging, jubilant passage culminates in a sustained
trill, and here begins the main movement. As in so many
other closing movements, the form is the rondo. But there is
an amazing disparity between this and former compositions.
The former were simple epilogues ; but here the decisive
meaning of the whole work is given out with sane humour.
Never before did he pour such a prodigality of ideas into the
rondo form or let humour loose therein. A rhythmic security
dominates the whole piece, notably in the *sforzati*, and characteristically in staccato bass octaves. With delicacy and
originality, a re-statement of the principal theme is introduced
by bold modulations in dropping thirds. When humour is
at its height the prayer melody reappears, now in E flat major,
his heroic key, like a happy memory of benefits received. There
is a resounding closing *presto*, giving a foretaste of the fugue
theme in the A flat major sonata, Op. 110. The first movement of sonata Op. 7 was the earliest expression of the powerful
energy which he developed in E flat key. There it dealt with
dramatic emotion ; here it deals with heroic and sane humour.
The close association between this sonata and the companion

work in C sharp minor (they appeared almost simultaneously) should in itself have been sufficient to discredit certain foolish legends which have gathered about the latter and which attribute to it definite autobiographical significance. It is true that Beethoven's work regarded broadly is autobiographical, bearing witness to thoughts and feelings which occupied him at different periods of his life, but to attach anecdotes to individual works—as, for instance, that the C sharp minor sonata tells of a love affair—is manifestly absurd. If the C sharp minor sonata grew out of a tragedy of the heart, how is the E flat major sonata, which was composed during the same period, to be explained? For a long time the latter work was misunderstood and undervalued by comparison with the C sharp minor fantasy, whose popularity probably accounts for the growth of the legends attached to it. The two compositions are a typical example of Beethoven's capacity for producing pairs of works, alike in form but quite unlike in content. Other such pairs are the F minor and A major sonatas of Op. 2 ; the C minor and F major sonatas, Op. 10 ; the G major and D minor sonatas, Op. 31; the C major sonata, Op. 53, and F minor sonata, Op. 57 ; and, yet more markedly, symphonies 3 and 4, 5 and 6, 7 and 8. A purely artistic impulse of reaction from the preceding work is sufficient, without romantic fiction, to account satisfactorily for the birth of the C sharp minor sonata. Organic correspondences are self-evident. Both works possess a slow introduction, both have an *intermezzo* in *scherzo* form, which appears to side-track the opening mood, and in both a tremendous finale, comprising the pent-up forces of the whole, comes to full expression, the only difference being that the E flat major finale is introduced by an *adagio*.

In content, the two works are supplementary, like Michelangelo's *Giorno* and *Notte*. The greater popularity of the C sharp minor fantasia-sonata, with its gravely harmonised *adagio*, its mournful, despairing melody, its pathetic attempt at gaiety in the *allegretto*, its heady, feverishly excited *presto*, is easily understood, passion being easier to grasp and superficially more effective in art than humorous insight.

In the closing movement of the C sharp minor sonata, Beethoven returned to the stricter sonata form. He had completed his experimental circle; beginning with the classic sonata, he concentrated on the first movement; his interest next centred in the following movements, and the first movement finally disappeared from his field of vision. As soon, however, as he had made the finale the principal movement, he returned to the sonata by way of the rondo and grappled once more with the problem of the first movement, bringing to the task much fresh experience derived from the fantasia-sonata, which was his creation. The introduction of the main theme in the manner of improvisation in the C sharp minor finale was destined to have an important influence upon future sonata construction. The theme is not, as formerly, "given out" complete from the outset; it develops as the work proceeds. The apparently introductory opening of the C sharp minor finale gradually forms itself into a theme through a series of periodic repetitions. We hear it coming into being, as in the D minor sonata, Op. 31. ii, where a seeming inadvertent chord is worked into the pivot of the whole.

The apparent simplicity which allows us thus to assist at the birth of a work is in reality an intense refinement of art. Beethoven, of course, had thought out the theme and the whole work to the last detail before sitting down to the piano; what appears as improvisation to us is an amazingly delicate and skilful artistic illusion. The composer sees the end from the beginning and is absolute ruler of the figures which seem to arise by chance.

Beethoven perceived that the one way to a further development of pianoforte composition lay through this seeming return to primitive improvisation; it was also the only method by which the technical capacities of the pianoforte could be used to the full without violence to the essential character of the instrument. In the year in which the Op. 31 sonatas were composed, the second symphony was completed; the *Eroica* was contemporaneous with sonatas Op. 53, 54 and 57. Beethoven saw two possible courses before him. His symphonic ideas could no longer find adequate expression on the pianoforte, and of the fifteen great sonatas still to come only three (the D major sonata, Op. 28, the E flat major sonata, Op. 31. iii, and the famous B flat major sonata, Op. 106) are in four movements ; but for imaginative work in the form of fantasies, the pianoforte was better adapted than any other instrument. He had mastered the problems of improvisation in his fantasia-sonatas and he no longer needed the explanatory *quasi una fantasia ;* he was able to use the strict sonata form in improvisation. He pressed this art to its limits and then abandoned the pianoforte.

The apparently improvised introduction, leading up by degrees to a statement of the main idea of the work, demanded considerable structural modifications in the form. Themes thus gradually emerging needed the whole of the first part to establish their musical entity. An increasing wealth of secondary motives also demanded room for expansion. The result was that the " exposition " increased in length and there was a tendency to postpone the dramatic climax of the work till the very end of the movement. A first " exposition " was no longer sufficient to bring out the contrasts fully, and a second " exposition " came into being, while the coda-epilogue became by degrees the climax of development. As early as in the E flat major sonata, Op. 7, the action culminates in the coda. In the C sharp minor fantasia, freely imaginative *cadenzas* give further amazing brilliance and power to the coda. The composer's skill here is beyond praise ; he displays his powers to the full at the very moment when it would seem they might be entirely exhausted.

Beethoven's originality both as composer and virtuoso was now fully developed. Despite increasing deafness his powers were at their height. Contests and wagers with Wölffl and Vogler, the reappearance of Hummel, his intercourse with Clementi and Cramer had all proved stimulating. His technique increased in breadth and audacity. Figurative passage technique began to give place to an expressionist technique hitherto unknown. Mere ornament disappeared, but gradations of tone increased in subtlety. Doubled hammer displacement (*due* and *una corde*) played an important part in Beethoven's pianoforte colourism, the pedal enhancing the carrying power of the tone. The style remains, on the whole, homophonous ; but a richer and more colourful harmony points, among other symptoms, to an increasing tendency towards the polyphony of the last period.   Beethoven's execution also shows a change, strict adherence to time giving place to a freer use of *rubato*. He was approaching the zenith of his artistic brilliance.   He was yet of and for this world.   Hermit-like moods were but transitory, and he was still ambitious for fame and public recognition ; his hopes were set upon the present rather than upon the future.

The next group of sonatas show his frame of mind.   They are great works and show Beethoven, self-confident, happy in his work as man and artist, his life unclouded save by merely passing shadows.   The group begins with the fantasia-sonatas and ends with the Op. 90 sonata.   In the interval were produced the works of his prime of manhood, the fulfilment of all earlier experiments and exercises.

The first sonata of the group, Op. 28 in D major, followed hard upon the fantasia-sonatas.   It has been called the " Pastoral " sonata, a name which neither belies, nor yet fully expresses, its content.   It would be hard to find any short title to fit this dreamy, reflective, meditative work.   In the first movement the thoughts flow almost imperceptibly into one another ; even the " exposition " shows but a slight increase in vividness and definition.   A mood of restful content pervades the movement.   It appears to be based on a single broad theme which proceeds in circular motion and ends at the point where it began.   An *andante*, suggesting resignation, in a minor key follows.   A graceful, rhythmical major *intermezzo*, introducing a more cheerful mood, appears near the close, only to be overcome by the minor mood once more, and the movement ends in gentle melancholy.   The contrast enhances the gay opening of the *scherzo*, which is set to a mood of high-spirited jest and contains a *trio*, in the folk-song manner, which is one of the most delightful examples of the type.   Even Beethoven must have found it difficult to add a significant finale to a work whose range of mood seemed so satisfactorily worked out in the first three movements.   As a matter of fact, the final rondo is by no means one of his happiest efforts, despite certain beauties of diction.   The pastoral bass rising above a pedal note, with the descending melody (like that of the main theme), the later inversion of this bass as a top part and the mysterious opening of the coda, all show the master's hand. The underlying thought, however, fails to add anything fresh to the preceding movements and it ends as a mere display of virtuosity. Was the four-part design of the work a mistake ? The *scherzo* as it stands would not have provided a suitable close, and Beethoven apparently attempted a new kind of imaginative rondo. He did not aim at a rondo which should contain the climax of the piece, as in Op. 27, but at one which should serve as a counterbalancing factor of equal value with the principal movement. A rondo of such a kind was hinted in the first D major sonata, Op. 10. iii. Beethoven more nearly embodies his idea in Op. 28, but even here he does not quite succeed.

His next work, the G major sonata, Op. 31. i, is far removed from sonatas Op. 26 and onwards, in quality of emotion. It was originally designed as a string-quartet and is spiritually akin to the two sonatas of Op. 14 in the same key. The work is conceived in a jovial vein. Thematic syncopation, disconnected rhythms, the bold emergence of the main theme, the easy tripping secondary theme with its parodistic interchange of major and minor, the humorously blustering " exposition " and terse coda combine to produce an atmosphere of gay surprise rather than of deep sensibility. Here, as elsewhere, the hearer, for his own pleasure, must not demand something which the composer does not intend to offer.

The second movement is an *adagio grazioso* (a somewhat paradoxical title for Beethoven) which is strongly reminiscent of Haydn's *Uriel* aria from the *Creation*, at first with what Nottebohm calls a " guitar-like " accompaniment, and later on decorated with elaborate *coloraturas*. We get nothing characteristic of Beethoven before the melancholy pathos of the episode in C minor. If the work were not that of a pianoforte virtuoso one would be inclined to question the use of its voluminous modulations and dissonant transitions. A pleasant, playful rondo follows as a close. Just before the end it suddenly becomes interesting, breaks off in the midst of a phrase, dissolves into reverie, reacts into life, and once more dies away in dreams. The imaginative metamorphoses to which this harmless theme is subjected are astonishing, until one realises that the pathos is merely a pose, a sly jest on the composer's part.

I

The next sonata, that in D minor, Op. 31. ii, forms a strange contrast. It is a dark and terrible piece of work. Mystical conflicts are foreshadowed in various forms. The first phrase ends with a sane *adagio* bar, followed by a return to mysticism, and then by a change of the first theme into C major. The strife breaks out afresh; the climax is reached, and a *largo* theme of tremendous expressiveness emerges which, in its turn, is aggressively challenged by an apparently new motive. Gradually the excitement dies down, and the mournful repose of the opening reasserts itself in association with the *largo* movement. The gruesomeness of the atmosphere is enhanced by the *arpeggio* passages. The recapitulation introduces the main theme by way of recitative. A series of chord passages suggesting suppressed excitement leads on to a grand yet simple close.

The poetic mood of this great work is sustained in the other movements. As in the first movement, a solemn *adagio* is introduced by a preluding chord. Soaring harmonies are resolved into a peaceful song in F major. Here the tone-colours are enchanting. The last movement is specially characteristic of Beethoven. Formally, it corresponds to the sonata scheme, but its content is a fugitive motive in semiquavers. The second theme is similar—a fantastic night-piece shot with light and shade.

Beethoven used the key of D minor in his pianoforte sonatas only four times : in the *Largo*, Op. 10. iii, in the *Andante*, Op. 28, and in the first and last movements of Op. 31. ii. Against these four D minor movements must be set six F minor and seven C minor movements, all of a profoundly passionate character; those in F minor are mournful, wild and temperamental, while those in C minor are intensely dramatic. The D minor movements, on the other hand, are suggestively tragic, implying implacable fate, accepted with melancholy in the *largo*, with gentle resignation in the *andante*, and with fury in the two movements of Op. 31. ii. Beethoven had now said all he had to say in the D minor key through the pianoforte ; but it was to be the key of the glorious D minor fantasia—the first movement of the ninth symphony.

Apart from the fatalistic, tragic element, there were many

other moods for which he could still employ the pianoforte. He turned once more to cheerful thoughts and to the E flat major key in which he loved to express them It is notable that this work, Op. 31. iii, in four movements, has no slow movement. The *allegro, scherzo, minuet,* and *presto* abound in freshness. The *scherzo-rondo* begins on a lively march with a characteristic emphasis on the last quaver of each bar. The bass recalls the *largo* of Op. 7 and the *andante* of Op. 28. Whether self-evolved or borrowed, certain *staccato* effects are common in his later work, notably in the A flat major *scherzo,* Op. 31. iii. The whole movement is a strikingly original exhibition of humorous fantasy illustrated by a master of virtuosity.

The minuet—*moderato e grazioso*—is a tender song-melody; yet surprises arise in the *trio.* Striking contrasts of register are developed with a return to the tender simplicity of the minuet. In the finale free rein is given to the mood of happiness. It is a kind of German tarantella. The introductory subject is given out in one-bar phrases, while the main theme, a simple hunting-song, hurries along in irrepressible joy. A short coda, with typical pauses, formally rounds off the piece. This, however, is not a true close; just as with the D minor finale, things are left in the air. Each of these works represents culminations of excitement, reaching out to the infinite, sadly and joyously.

"I am by no means satisfied with my works hitherto, and I intend to make a fresh start from to-day," said Beethoven, according to Carl Czerny's account, to his friend Wenzel Krumpholz, the violin-teacher. Czerny believes that the remark was made shortly before the appearance of Op. 31, "in which," he says, "one can trace the partial fulfilment of his new resolution."

If Czerny dates Beethoven's work aright, and these sonatas did actually appear shortly after this announcement, the first two at least must have been already completed and were probably rather the cause than the result of his effort to find a way more satisfactory to himself. Internal evidence supports this conclusion, for the G major sonata is on the whole less significant than some earlier works, and the D minor sonata, though perhaps the climax of the "fantasia-sonata" group, is not "new" in any sense in which Beethoven could have used the word. That Beethoven was actually seeking a new way at the time, is proved by a letter to Breitkopf and Härtel, October 1802, in which he writes, "I have composed two variation works. . . . Both are handled in an entirely new manner and each differs in this respect from the other. . . . Let me not recommend them to you in vain, for I assure you that you will not regret it if you accept them. Each theme therein is treated in a different way from the others. Usually I scarcely realise when my own ideas are new, and hear of it first from others; but in this instance I can myself assure you that I have done nothing in the same manner before. . . . I make this proposal to you because I know that your firm deals especially in works of distinction." When sending the work he asked that it should be published with a preface. He wished that "it should be made clear to the uninformed that these variations are very different from others"; and on this account he would not provide them with a number but would place them among his "greater works"—"the more so that the themes also are my own."

This reiterated insistence, unusual with Beethoven, upon the novelty of his work, fits in well with Czerny's story. What, however, was the exact meaning of Beethoven's words? Why was he dissatisfied, what "new way" did he propose to find, and in what was the new manner to consist?

He himself provides a clue to the answer. Upon a preliminary sketch for the theme of Op. 34 he makes the following note. "Each variation in different time—or passages executed by the left hand and then similar, or different, passages in the right, and vice versa." The clue lies in the word "passages." They had almost entirely vanished from Beethoven's pianoforte music; the poet relegated them to the background; the virtuoso now once more brings them to the fore. It was indeed the virtuoso in Beethoven who sought a new manner and dictated the style of the forthcoming period. The difficult problem of giving technically brilliant (in the performer's sense) expression to the style which he had evolved from improvisation had charm for him. Since the fantasia-sonatas, his facility as a pianist had been the absolute slave of the poetic idea; it now attained independence as a constructive element once more. The *scherzo-rondo* and finale of the E flat major sonata mark the beginnings of the new phase. This work really belongs, indeed, to the new group; it was not originally intended to be included in the same *opus* as the G major and D minor sonatas, and was not so numbered until two years after its publication. It should be classed with the two famous cycles of variations.

This new development is psychologically easy to understand. From the moment that Beethoven consciously set the poetic idea in the foreground, he had come to regard virtuosity (except in the case of the less important G major sonata, Op. 31) merely as the necessary medium of a new type of musical expression. As he attained absolute freedom in this expression the desire naturally arose to enhance it by technical perfections, to set off its beauties with greater effect and brilliance. He never wrote for merely superficial effect, but neither had he an ascetic scorn for arresting devices. He had the greatest respect for virtuosity as a means to an end, and his pianist's imagination helped him as composer to discover a new variation technique. Thus originated Op. 34 and 35, the *scherzo-rondo* and finale of the sonata in E flat major; and, as the crowning triumph of the "virtuoso period," the magnificent pair of concert-sonatas, Op. 53 and 57. Both before and after these compositions Beethoven was responsible for many distinguished tone-effects upon the pianoforte (quite apart from the wide range of his thought), yet never again did he achieve such entire congruity of poetic and instrumental expression. He made perfect use of the pianoforte as an instrument; thought and sound coincided absolutely.

The variations Op. 34 and 35 show more virtuosity, a more free and luxuriant treatment of the theme, a bolder architectural style than their predecessors, although certain earlier works, such as the *Waldmädchen* variations, those upon Grétry's *Fièvre brûlante*, upon themes from Süssmayr, Weigl, Righini and, notably, Salieri's *Stessa stessissima*, far surpass the usual type of variation in general construction and sensitive interpretation of the theme, while many details point to the style of the later period. It is very natural that Beethoven's reviving interest in virtuosity (a virtuosity never detached from poetic intention) should have found first expression in the variation-form, before more complicated forms could be tackled. He worked upon the plan of " every variation in a new key " although he did not always carry it through to the letter. He kept to the scheme in Op. 34, where he passes from F major through a series of alternating minor and major thirds through D, B flat, G and E flat major and C minor before returning to the key of the theme. It provides the student of Beethoven's handling of the scale with an interesting example of his method of fitting every variation with a new key, and at the same time developing the variation idea as a whole from differences between the keys. Op. 34 expresses in miniature Beethoven's æsthetic theory of the key; and it may, indeed, have been designed to that end.

The E flat major variations upon the *Prometheus* theme, later used in the *Eroica*, are nearer to improvisation. The bass part of the theme is heard first, second, third and fourth parts being then added to it; the introduction, indeed, is a little cycle of variations in itself. A well-marked melody next appears, interpreted and enhanced by every device of virtuosity, and rising, after a grandly conceived fugue, to a solemn and splendid climax. The poetic idea underlying this work finds supreme expression in the finale of the *Eroica*, but in itself it is a fine example of the monumental and stately character of Beethoven's virtuosity, of his tendency to bold, fresco effects. His self-revelation in the succeeding sonatas was yet more powerful. Great and imposing effects are aimed at to the exclusion of any more intimate appeal, and broad lines alone are used with strict economy. Only a master could have found such a middle way between the symphonic and the " improvised " sonata; imagination had completely mastered the old form and had thus successfully achieved the new.

In the C major sonata, Op. 53, dedicated to Beethoven's old friend and patron Count Waldstein, a hitherto unknown world of sound was revealed. The first movement does not attempt to deal with any very deep or serious issues; a lively, energetic and active mood is presented, though with a certain reserve. The content of the following movements is conditioned by the first; it consists, as is to be expected, in joyful certainty of victory. Beethoven originally intended the piece in F major, now known as the *Andante favori*, for the slow movement of this work; its peaceful and happy character, as well as its great demands upon the technique of the performer, well qualify it for the purpose; although it is perhaps inferior to the corner-movements in intensity of expression. The *andante* was, however, rejected on account of its unusual length, and an *adagio molto* introduces the closing movement. The *adagio* begins in a pensive, dreamy vein, suggestive of hidden grief. A 'cello *cantilena*, gently interrupted by wood-wind, is heard once and no more. Compelling, wide, ascending intervals emerge from the opening obscurity, mounting upwards till the first tone of the rondo is heard, when earnest tension dissolves in gaiety and grace. A simple song-theme (some investigators think it a Rhenish folk-song), a purely delightful melody repeated without a definite close in a joyous trill, is wreathed in sweet, harmonious ara-besques. This melody is, however, too delicate to bear any heavy harmonic accompaniment. It gradually loses its light colour-ing; two passionate secondary themes appear, the first in A and the second in C minor. The power of the first song grows by opposition. It rises to a hymn of immeasurable joy (C major is Beethoven's joyous and triumphant key), and ends as a pæon of immortal exultation.

As in Op. 27 the C sharp minor sonata follows E flat major, and in Op. 31 the D minor follows the G major sonata, so here a mournful piece, the F minor sonata, Op. 57, is bracketed with one that is joyous. The F minor was not completed till 1806—two years after the *Waldstein*—yet sketches for the two works show that it was projected almost immediately after the latter. It is another proof of the fact that the creative spirit in Beethoven always had these two aspects, these two languages. In the F minor, as in the C major sonata, the first notes reveal to us the artist's mind; the inspiration was too powerful, too insistent to be hidden for a moment by any preliminaries. The elemental quality of the first movement is due to a great extent to its power-fully persuasive emotional rhythm. Dynamic has a more important place here than in any previous work. Not only does Beethoven use the language of the *sforzati*, of broadly extended transition shadings, to the utmost; but he creates a monumental impression by wide expanses of colour, by ground-tones laid on with a broad sweep of the brush. The twelve opening bars, veiled in *pianissimo*, the sixteen-bar *fortissimo cadenza* before the coda, together with such colouristic inspirations as the two closing bars with the flickering thirds A flat to C, in the descant, and the deep, restful *contra* F beneath it, are triumphs which fully explain why Beethoven waited nearly twenty years before again composing in F minor for the piano ; even then he wrote not a sonata-movement but only a *scherzo*.

As in Op. 53, the two last movements in this work are organically united, though the *andante con moto* does not thereby lose its independent value. It is one of the most enthralling works ever composed by Beethoven. It is constructed upon the principles of the variation. The theme is developed by ascension to higher octaves and points to the *arietta* in Op. 111. We have called Op. 34 a miniature picture of Beethoven's æsthetic philosophy of the key ; the Op. 57 variations express the æsthetics of the various D flat major registers. In no previous work did Beethoven use mixed chromatic colours so freely. It was also the last time that he expressed the full passion of his genius in a pianoforte work. It reminds one of the second of the sonatas dedicated to the Elector—of the first work of the Op. 2 group ; for it fulfils the youthful promise there displayed. It is Beethoven's last will and testament in the key of F minor.

Another branch of Beethoven's art, the pianoforte concerto, came to perfection during the great " virtuoso " period. He composed seven works in this *genre*, of which the two earliest have come down to us in an incomplete form. The E flat major concerto, probably composed in Bonn, possesses the piano part only, while that in D major, dating from about 1790, consists only of a first movement. It is unlikely that any of Beethoven's best work is thereby lost. The two earliest of these works, the B flat major concerto, Op. 19, and the somewhat later C major concerto, Op. 15, conventional in subject and insignificant in technique according to modern standards, are merely interesting as indicating the course of Beethoven's development. Even the triple-concerto in C major for piano, violin and violoncello with orchestra, composed in 1805 (the period which produced *Fidelio* and the great concert sonatas), belongs to the same out-of-date group. It was probably an occasional work written for Beethoven's new pupil, the Archduke Rudolph, and was intended to be a renovation of the *concerto grosso* style ; but, despite some interesting points of detail, it lacks both the forceful statement of theme and the close-knit development of thought which one expects to find in his work. The C minor concerto dating from 1800 has points of interest, the arrangement of keys being particularly noteworthy. The composer must have had some very special intention in following a C minor *allegro* with an E major *largo* and a C minor rondo. Beethoven frequently set C major and E major side by side—in the first and second movements of the C major sonata, Op. 2, and within the first movement of the Waldstein sonata, for instance—but an E major piece between two C minor movements is quite extraordinary. The dictatorial, almost threatening opening with its reverberating fourths gives the clue to Beethoven's intention. The fact that the concerto-form represents a dialogue is clearly emphasised. The orchestra does not merely accompany ; it argues with, supports, or contradicts the soloist. The passage-work develops from natural forceful restatements, while the vanity of the virtuoso is subordinated to the work as a whole. A somewhat sentimental *largo*, the theme of which is decorated with luxuriant *coloratura*, is contrasted with the austere and energetic *allegro*. This in its turn, with its dying E major close, forms a striking contrast with the wilfully defiant rondo, which opens with a solo passage for the piano. In later compositions, Beethoven's transitions were more delicate, yet this work was far above the level of the contemporary solo-concerto, in which, since the death of Mozart, the soloist had been the dominating factor, the orchestra providing an entirely subordinate accompaniment.

The C minor concerto is a type of the traditional solo-concerto ennobled by depth of thought, but Beethoven's three last concertos, the two pianoforte concertos in G major and E flat major and the violin concerto in D major, border upon the " symphonic concerto " for orchestra and solo instrument. The intrusion of the mannerisms of improvisation is striking in all these works, particularly in the G major concerto, with its mournful E minor *andante*, in which effective emotional contrasts are obtained by a dialogue between the ruthless, continuous *unisono* of the strings and the tuneful complaining of the pianoforte, martial *tutti* rhythms gradually make themselves heard while the soloist still prolongs his dreamy, elegiac tones. It was probably the most poetic concerto at that time in existence and is said to have been inspired by the idea of Orpheus supplicating the powers of the underworld. Both the opening *allegro* and the march-like rondo give a personal note to the opposition between orchestra and solo instrument and show a method of interwoven motives as unusual in the solo-concerto of that period as were emotional depths. The whole work is characterised by quiet, reflective gravity, by a latent energy, capable from time to time of expressing intense vitality, but usually preserving the mood of tranquillity.

Beethoven's only violin-concerto forms a connecting link between the G major concerto and its poetic complement, the powerful E flat major concerto, Op. 73, composed three years later. Shortly after its completion, probably in accordance with the suggestion of his publishers, he arranged the violin-concerto in D major for the piano, but it formed no valuable addition to his pianoforte work. In the first place the solo-violin part is transcribed almost note for note for the pianoforte, thereby naturally losing much of its effectiveness ; but even if Beethoven had adapted and modified the work the arrangement could hardly have been successful, for the character of the violin and its relationship to the orchestra demand from the first a treatment entirely different from that employed by Beethoven for his pianoforte concertos. The very different tone values of the pianoforte mark it off from the outset from the orchestra, but the violin lacks this basic independence. It is an organic member of the orchestra, needing its support ; and may be effective as leader, but hardly as opponent of the orchestra. On this account the relationship between *tutti* and solo passages must be differently constituted in violin and pianoforte concertos, and it is not possible to translate the one into terms of the other.

From the very first the violin concerto shows a difference in plan from the two last pianoforte concertos. In these latter, Beethoven places pianoforte and orchestra from the beginning as combatants facing each other in the lists ; but the violin concerto opens with a broadly designed orchestral prelude from which the solo-part is later gradually differentiated. Before this occurs, the rich thought material underlying the work is displayed and its course indicated. Beethoven must have written the work lovingly and in moments of very happy inspiration. The *allegro* begins with a nobly pathetic march, a tense knocking motive for the kettledrum, continued through the whole movement, now energetic and menacing, now tender and persuasive. The themes are absolutely suited to the character of the violin as Beethoven understood it; the tuneful, lyrical quality is emphasised, virtuosity suppressed. Some years earlier, in two violin romances with orchestra, in G major, Op. 40, and in E major, Op. 50, he had used that instrument's capacity for *cantabile* with great effect. In the concerto, with ends in view higher than in these two isolated *adagios*, he gives the violin its full value as queen of the orchestra in worth and in grace. The main theme is sometimes dreamy, sometimes majestic and brilliant, rising at the close to the perfection of melody. As in the G major pianoforte concerto, Beethoven makes the slow movement of his violin-concerto a kind of imaginative dialogue in the manner of improvisation. In this instance, however, the solo instrument and orchestra do not in any sense contradict each other but alternately corroborate each other. The climax is reached in a violin melody of enchanting beauty and spirituality, whence the orchestra suddenly brings us back to earth and to the cheerful, somewhat lengthy, but forceful closing rondo.

The interest of the pianoforte arrangement of this unsurpassed violin concerto lies chiefly in the *cadenzas* therein introduced in which Beethoven repeats several times the characteristic introductory knocking motive for the kettledrums. He composed *cadenzas* also for Mozart's D minor concerto and for his own pianoforte concertos with the exception of the E flat major concerto in which the *cadenza*—the opportunity for free improvisation on the part of the performer—is necessarily excluded by the structure of the work. It would perhaps be truer to say that the piece already possesses *cadenzas*.

The E flat major concerto begins with improvisation, with rippling passages between broad orchestral harmonies, before the powerful *tutti* prelude is heard. The form of this concerto is sometimes said to have been inspired by the " military concerto " so common at that period, and undoubtedly the heroic character of the themes, the dominance of warlike rhythms and the secondary place allotted to lyrical episodes (in contrast to the G major concerto, in which the lyrical mood predominates) lend colour to the idea. A joyful atmosphere prevails throughout the work and the secondary theme is not, as elsewhere, a contrast to the main theme, but a more tuneful expression of the same subject. Beethoven has expended special love and care upon this secondary theme. We get many variants of it in the course of the work. It is interpreted first with a suggestion of hushed mystery in E flat minor, is repeated in soft chords upon the horns, a terse bass being sustained by the kettledrums, is remoulded in the dreamy C flat major episode for the solo part with harp-like, sweeping notes, and at length rings out from the full orchestra in powerful, marching rhythm. It is a remarkable use of the variation style within the framework of a concerto movement.

The B major *adagio* forms a true contrast to the *allegro*. The *adagio* is most delicately coloured throughout; strong contrasts are avoided even more than in the previous movement; the theme is deeply experienced and but indicated with imaginative reserve. Here again the pianoforte part begins with improvisation, and later takes over the noble and vital melody from the preluding orchestra. As the closing notes die softly away a bold harmonic change leads with no apparent interruption to a joyous rondo, the theme of which is announced first dreamily, hesitatingly, by the solo instrument, afterwards in a full torrent of gaiety.

The surprisingly numerous improvisation passages in these last three great concertos, the G major, D major and E flat major, prove that Beethoven, however closely he adhered to the concerto of the old school, had certain innovations in mind. With this end in view he pursued the same course as he had done with the sonata—he explored the old form to the uttermost before attempting to recreate it. He brought all his imaginative powers to the task.

The fantasia, Op. 80, for pianoforte, orchestra and choir is in the form of free variation, beginning with a reminiscent prelude upon the pianoforte with which the orchestral instruments are gradually associated in softly approaching marching rhythms.

A simple song-melody is heard (Beethoven took it from a setting for G. A. Bürger's " *Gegenliebe*," composed about 1796); the pianoforte announces the theme and the orchestra develops it with variations to an imposing *tutti* in which the solo instrument at length joins. The variations are worked out in an unusually broad and complex form. The most striking features are a passionate minor movement, a sustained *adagio* and a lively march; there is a further prelude, after which the choir enters with " *Schmeichelnd hold und lieblich klingen unseres Lebens Harmonien.*"

Beethoven projected this curious work as early as 1800. It was played for the first time upon the historic night in 1808 of the first performance of the fifth and sixth symphonies. Does it mark a transition to some new form of concerto sought by him? It is impossible to say, for this work was the first and last of its line. Beethoven returned with the E flat major concerto to the beaten track once more. A sketch for a D major concerto, dated 1815, was never completed. He may have lacked the impulse supplied by active performance, for although the evening of the Academy concert in 1808 was not actually his last appearance upon the concert-platform, it marked the official close of his career as a virtuoso. After that date he was occasionally to be heard before small audiences at performances of chamber music or as accompanist, but he never again performed his E flat major concerto in public. On February 12th, 1812, Carl Czerny played it for the first time in Vienna, and Theodore Körner writes that " A new pianoforte concerto by Beethoven was not successful." We learn, however, that in Leipzig, where it was performed in December 1810, probably for the first time, " it inspired a very numerous audience with such enthusiasm that they could scarcely content themselves with the usual expressions of recognition and appreciation."

Beethoven's virtuoso period thus closes on these two notes of enthusiasm in one place and rejection in another. His choral fantasia, Op. 80, stands like a mark of interrogation before these two opposing judgments. He had brought virtuosity—as he from his tremendous vantage point understood it—to the greatest perfection of which it was capable. After this his interest in the concert-platform declined. He still liked to improvise, but loss of hearing circumscribed all such activities. Upon this phase of Beethoven's life the curtain falls.

Beethoven had done with the piano as a concert-instrument. He no longer attempted to put it to great uses, but, though he found the tone of the clavier too thin and flat to clothe his monumental imagination, he still recognised its intimate, expressive charm.   It was more suited to a small circle of friends in a drawing-room than to a large audience in a concert-hall.   Once more it became the most personal of instruments for chamber-music, perfect in miniature and *genre* pieces, for the expression of sentiment and humour.   This conception resulted in a group of sonatas of a two-movement type, hitherto employed only in sonatinas. Such are Op. 54, Op. 78 and Op. 90. In the only three-movement sonata of this period, Op. 81, the second and third movements are run together as in Op. 57.

The sonata, Op. 54, shows the most marked kinship in form with earlier work and may be regarded as transition work.   Both date of composition and difficult technique link it with the " virtuoso period," while form, expression and content indicate the approaching change.   Standing as it does between those two tremendous works, Op. 53 and 57, and separated from them numerically only by the triple-concerto and the *Eroica*, it has the aspect of a neglected step-child of Beethoven's muse.   Regarded apart from this connection, it is seen to be one of his most exquisite and characteristic works—one of those compositions whose beauties do not emerge without close study but which then take a tremendous hold upon the student.

It consists of no more than a minuet and a rondo, but what a minuet and what a rondo !   Both movements are in F major— not the contemplative F major of the *Pastoral* symphony, but the sunny, gay F major of the eighth symphony.   The delicately humorous first movement is followed and completed by a very lively *allegretto-finale*.   It forms a pendant to the A flat major rondo, Op. 26, and, like it, is a piece of highly intellectual playfulness ; it is, however, more original, more forceful and more sarcastic than the earlier work.

In the F major sonata, Beethoven's concern with technical problems is clearly shown in the *staccato* octaves, in the delicate ornamentation of the first movement, in the chromatic chord breakings and speeding-up devices of the finale; but in the following work, the F sharp major sonata, Op. 78, he makes far less claim upon the acrobatic capacities of the performer. For a time he discards tone-combinations suggestive of the orchestra, and the pianoforte-tone acquires more independence. There is a striking increase in delicacy of touch. The tender contrasts of the subsequent works demand an almost hypercritical weighing, not only of degrees of strength, but also of tone-characters. Widely discursive runs, full-handed harmonies and powerful chord-passages give place to a decorative filigree technique. Themes and figurations appear to be reversed. Miniature work of extreme precision replaces the broad fresco technique. An amazingly exquisite sensibility succeeds the great emotional storms, and the whole breathes the spirit of an earlier time when the clavier was still the instrument of a quiet exchange of thought between soul and soul.

This atmosphere predominates from the first in Op. 78. Beethoven returns to the slow introduction which he had long disused. A decorative and fanciful F sharp major melody prepares us for what is to come. It is a prelude pure and simple, and does not reappear; but it indicates the mood of the subsequent *allegro*, a mood of intensely felt, yet still and unrebellious, emotion. Major themes rise and fall in graceful, wavelike lines. Not till the beginning of the short development section do we get certain swiftly passing clouds in the minor key. After this the exposition is repeated and flows on peacefully and steadily to the short, fanciful and idealistic epilogue which closes the movement. As in Op. 54, the peaceful and cheerful first movement finds its contrast in a somewhat stormy closing movement. It is one of several examples of a combination of rondo and *scherzo* in two-four time, created by Beethoven at the height of his powers. This most interesting hybrid form appears for the first time in the G major sonata, Op. 14. It appears again in Op. 31. iii, in the present instance, and as late as Op. 110. Beethoven lends the rondo the tripping rhythmic character of the *scherzo*, makes it more pointed and epigrammatic, and presents a more rapidly changing series of images. The *scherzo*, on the other hand, through the admixture of the rondo, becomes capable of more luxuriant expansion, of a more many-sided exposition of the subject, than had been possible in the narrow minuet pattern from which it had been developed. The movement is but frugally provided with themes.

Closely allied to this work in content, though composed five years later, is the E minor sonata, Op. 90. Beethoven's notes upon the movements were in German, not in Italian. " With liveliness, with much feeling and expression," he wrote above the first movement, which is in three-four time, and over the rondo, " not too fast and very tunefully." It may have been chance which led him to begin the use of German, instead of foreign marks of expression, with this work; but it may have been something in the work itself which made him feel that the stereotyped Italian *formulæ* were insufficient. The almost superabundant polyphony of this movement forms an exquisitely designed contrast with the following rondo in E major. Outwardly this movement corresponds in build with the older dance rondos of which the last example is to be found in Op. 31 ; but here a new and more noble significance is conferred upon the old form by melodic expression, and it becomes the medium of a pure lyricism far surpassing the mere entertainment associated with the older rondos. The whole is based upon a straightforward, deeply spiritual song-melody, repeated again and again like a strophe, thrown into high relief by curious episodes and contrasted effects, till it completes a circle and returns to the beginning once more. It is one of the most artistically perfect simple movements which Beethoven ever wrote. Certain passages, such as the pensive imitatory episode before the final appearance of the chief theme, transitions based on bold enharmonic, and other episodical work, point to the last quartets.

The sonata in E flat major, Op. 81, the last but one of this group, exhibits an equal intellectually brilliant technique in miniature. It is the only programmatic pianoforte work of Beethoven and its " programme " is as unoriginal as its execution is significant. In accordance with the spirit of the times he had to pay a musical tribute to the Archduke Rudolph, " *hochver-ehrten* " (highly honoured), partly from genuine personal sympathy, partly from political necessity, upon the occasions of his departure, exile and return ; and he could do so in this particular form without the shameful concessions to which the *Battle* symphony later forced him. As in the F sharp major sonata he begins with an *adagio*, which in this case has a close connection as regards motive with the following *allegro*. It begins at once with the musical motto of the work—the descending series of notes—G—F—E flat—with the text inscribed " *Lebewohl.*" A single theme appears in various guises, sometimes in inversion, sorrowfully distorted by the lowering of the third, sometimes in reassuring major notes, like a consoling exhortation. A short epilogue forms the close. The parting has taken place, but the voices of the parted friends still linger, the harmonies cross each other. This passage, frequently attacked on account of its confusion of tonic and dominant chords, is nevertheless one of the most ingenious pieces of tone-painting in all the literature of music, and is for the performer in reality merely a problem of touch. Sensitive hands are absolutely necessary for all the work of this period ; the chords should melt into each other, like the last words of farewell dying away in the distance.

In the *andante*, even more than in the first movement, Beethoven gives prominence to chromatic progressions, dissonance-making appoggiaturas and harmonies. The *andante* opens with a plaintive melody, reminiscent of the opening *adagio*, answered by a consolatory motive in G major. These alternate till the sorrowful voice wavers, rises expectantly and breaks off short, to give place to rapidly ascending runs, accompanied by beckoning rhythms which announce the return of the exile. A tenderly joyful melody rises to open jubilation and a strong series of chords proclaims his approach. Once more the sorrowful, dissonant appoggiaturas are heard, but they are now carried by joyfully excited figures. The secondary theme imitates the rocking movement of the main subject, which rises at the close of the movement to intense significance.

Works of the latest group clearly show Beethoven's increasing tendency to the strictly logical development of one single idea throughout, his pointed treatment of the motive down to the least detail. Op. 54, yet more Op. 78 and 81, and even the enchanting sonatina, Op. 79, with its country-dance-like *allegro*, melancholy *barcarole* in G minor and ornamental *vivace* (which reappears in Op. 109), are all clearly conceived after the pattern

K

of logically coherent, yet free and profuse, speech. This
peculiarity is most striking in Op. 90. The themes are ethe-
realised into small thought-particles which do not attain architectonic forms by means of graduated structure, but are spun
out to endless lengths and thus present an unbroken flow of
development built up of the smallest parts. Motival spinning
is, indeed, no new thing in Beethoven's work; he learnt it from
Haydn and employed it from his earliest days, but this motival
working, which consists in the artistic and well-thought-out
dissection and reconstruction of the theme, is essentially different
from the new type of psychological motive development, which
represents a continuous and progressive process of musical
thought. This penetration of the emotional content of an
entire work by strict thought-processes, this elucidation of
emotional values, not by means of varying temperamental
ebullitions, but by an intensely keen logical analysis, is the
æsthetic principle underlying the following works. It explains
both the slow ripening of the compositions and the ever-increasing prominence of the polyphonic style during the period to
come. Beethoven received the stimulus to this species of formation from the symphony and the string-quartet. At this time
he had already completed eight symphonies, the Rasumowsky
quartet, Op. 59, and quartets Op. 74 and 95. Beethoven applied
the experience gained in this work to the pianoforte, seeking to
blend it with the methods of expression which he had already
learned to apply to that instrument. Up to Op. 90 he employed
the new manner, as it were experimentally, within the narrow
limits of the *genre* piece, but thereafter he felt the need of the
greater forms to express his ideas through a greater volume of
sound. He accordingly returned once more to the old forms, and
the fantasia-sonata, the grand concert-sonata reappeared in his
work, further enhanced by the power of the new motive development. Thus Beethoven brought the fruits of his experience in
orchestral and chamber-music to bear upon the pianoforte, the
last sonata-poems for the solo instrument resulting therefrom.

The series opens with the fantasia-sonata in A major, Op. 101,
which is, as regards the principles upon which it is constructed,
a faithful replica of the E flat major sonata, Op. 27. Here again

are three introductory movements, the *allegretto ma non troppo* of the new work answering to the *andante* of its predecessor ; the *vivace alla marcia* to the *allegro molto vivace*. Both *adagios* are introductions to the closing movements, which in both works are the goals to which the previous developments have been leading. Beethoven no longer uses the phrase " *quasi una fantasia* "—he has long taken the form for granted—but instead he supplies a number of marks of expression in German which render any further attempt at elucidating the work superfluous. From the *innigen Empfindung* (with deeply felt emotion) of the opening, to the *lebhaft marschmässige* (like a lively march) of the *vivace*, the *sehnsuchtsvolle* (yearning) of the *adagio* and the *Entschlossenheit* (with determination, *or* resolution) of the rondo, the programme of the fantasia is completely expressed, and completely expressive of Beethoven. The prototype, Op. 27, shows similar ascending gradation of content ; but in the later work the development of the motive in each individual movement is incomparably more forceful. The tender, gliding, quartet-like conduct of the parts, the free yet never restless harmonic flow, the prominence of light, sweet colours, the absence of any marked dynamic contrasts, lend a dreamy atmosphere to the whole. Consciousness of cold reality is stilled —in the hush delicate and remote vibrations become perceptible to the senses.

The *vivace*, too, belongs to the realm of fantasy. It opens with a lively, quick melody—a rhythmic indication of a march. Fleeting, vanishing visions arise, which attain firm outline for a moment at the close. The *trio* melody breaks off incomplete. A digression, in form of a canon, closes on a questioning note, and the stirring march part is resumed. It is followed by a short, *adagio-intermezzo* (like that in Op. 53), continued in a yearning, mysteriously coloured motive. Reminiscences of the gentle theme of the prelude are introduced, but, at the closing phrase, the composer attains new power. The effort to fight a way through dreams and fancies, spiritual, gay and sentimental by turns, to fully conscious creative activity—this forms the poetic " argument " of the work. The theme of the closing movement shows rather courageous than joyful determination. The peaceful gaiety of the composer is first expressed in the work. A tender line of melody is maintained, and soon the energetic main subject becomes little more than a trifling pleasant subsidiary theme. The protasis expresses liveliness and joy, when suddenly the opening motive destroys the gay mood. A brooding minor *fugato* begins in the bass and, mounting, weaves a shadowy dance about a single idea, which suddenly, with a gesture of elemental force, resumes its former aspect and leads to a jubilant close.

In order to present with exactitude the course of development, either in this or the preceding movements, it would be necessary to analyse the work bar by bar, to trace the changing aspect of the motive in every detail of an entrancing technique. Here we can do no more than point to the fact that Beethoven developed a whole sonata-movement of mighty dimensions from the prolongation of a single theme and that the whole highly intellectualised process was nevertheless permeated from first to last with imaginative meaning. The argument flows on without a trace of rhetoric, without appeal to sentiment, yet tremendously impressive. Beethoven's pathos in his later years rises above all superficial " effectiveness "; it was a pathos latent in the thought behind the work, a world of exalted emotion in which any touch of exaggeration is nevertheless avoided.

Working as he was in this self-created world of music, some memory came to the composer of the great concert-sonatas of his earlier days, of himself seated at the pianoforte, each note obedient to the will of the great virtuoso despot. Once more he felt the passion for monumental construction, which had produced Op. 53 and 57; but he could feel it only through the power of imagination, for, isolated by deafness, he was the great virtuoso no longer; nor did he stand, as formerly, in any close relationship to the outer world and its happenings. The passion now aroused in him was the passion of artistic imagination, not of sensation and temperament. In this world of imagination he conceived of an instrument bearing some superficial likeness to the pianoforte of his memory, but far surpassing anything that mere mechanism could produce. The Broadwood " grand " which Beethoven possessed at this period may have spurred him on to these audacious conceptions, but, be that as it may, he wrote one more concert-sonata which, as it was the child of pure imagination and was heard by its composer only thus, can never be fully grasped and enjoyed, save through the imagination. This work shows Beethoven's conception of the ideal pianoforte, and shows, moreover, that he could set problems only partly soluble by an advance in technique. There was never a more powerful musical expression of the strife between mind and matter. The composer, standing above the world of actuality, wrestles with the deficiencies and limitations of the mechanism of the pianoforte which would drag him down and imprison his fancy. Both composer and instrument have their victories; both have their defeats. The composer conquers as to the idea, for he writes to the idea alone; but at the moment when the idea should be perfectly realised he has to acknowledge defeat.

Thus arose the B flat major sonata, Op. 106. The work is a battle song, combining the joyous energy of Op. 53 with the demonic passion of Op. 57. An heroic *allegro* is succeeded by a fantastic *scherzo-intermezzo*, an *adagio* sounding the very depths of lamentation and a triumph song of the unconquerable will, such as none but Beethoven has attempted to sing either before or since. It begins in an atmosphere of titanic conflict, the powerfully rhythmic principal subject being announced in tremendous ascending chords. A pleading answer is heard, becoming more urgent from bar to bar. The first mood, however, reasserts itself; a new and strongly defined subject appears, its stamping rhythms overcoming every opposition. They die away in soaring octaves, from which the main subject arises once more, softened by modulation, in D major. Ascending harmonies attach themselves to the D major change and gliding melodious quaver passages have a pacifying effect, and find expression in a peacefully flowing G major *cantilena*. This mood appears to triumph in a festal close, when, at a sudden change to B flat major, the weighty rhythms of the opening reassert themselves once more. They suppress the motive of the close which is heard ever more faintly. A combative *fugato* rises up to a series of wild outcries. A second subsidiary theme, stated softly in B major, is unable to establish itself. Once more the forces of conflict occupy the stage till the main theme is again reached, and dominates all else. "Power is the moral law of man's being," runs a passage in a letter to Zmeskall, and the phrase might stand as a text for the first movement of Op. 106.

The *scherzo*, with its abrupt, restless, hurrying rhythms, its mysterious swaying harmonies, its seven-bar periods, the fantastic *presto* between *trio* and *scherzo* repeats, the tremolo which shakes itself, as it were, before the return of the principal subject, the *presto-coda* with its bold chromatic shifting from B to B flat, the ghostly close—it is all these points which make this work the summit of Beethoven's pianoforte *scherzi*. From Op. 28 onwards he had avoided the pure *scherzo* and used it only in combination with the rondo. Here he turns to the almost-forgotten form once again, a form which he had only got to know thoroughly through orchestral and chamber-music. This *scherzo* takes him back to it. The *scherzo* is to be found in its perfection in the second movement of the ninth symphony, where it expresses elements of rhythm and colour which can but be indicated upon the pianoforte.

The first movement pays homage to the spirit of combative strength; the *adagio* is the apotheosis of pain, of that deep sorrow for which there is no remedy, and which finds expression not in passionate outpourings, but in the immeasurable stillness of utter woe. A solemn introduction of a bar (subsequently added by Beethoven) forms a kind of up-beat to a long-drawn-out F sharp minor melody; rising in yearning, sinking in resignation, it attains no definite close. We feel the religious atmosphere of the second *Mass* about us; the mood of consolation, of reliance in supernatural promises, as it exists in the *Benedictus*, finds expression not merely in the character, but in the very key and melodic trend of the answering theme. More agitated rhythms take up the dignified plaint in a new F sharp minor melody, instinct with pain. Consolation is expressed in the bass and repeated in the higher parts in D major. The cry of sorrow grows more urgent, the song rises more longingly, more hopefully, till it once more sinks to the depths in chords of the diminished seventh. The first melody reappears in the major, but brings with it no peace. Restless modulations lead back to the opening theme, whose steady solemnity is now animated by highly expressive supplicating demi-semi-quavers. Even at the change to F sharp major, the consoling voices cannot hold the lead. Ever and again the cry of sorrow rings out, more piercing, more urgent for the useless attempts to allay it. No comfort is vouchsafed, save that which is self-won in the mystical illumination of the F sharp major harmonies.

Beethoven frequently uses his slower movements to express sorrow, but he never closes upon that mood. He always fights his way through to an active emotion, whether it be dark passion, joyous transfiguration or strong resolve. The so-doing represents for him freedom from the too heavy burden of passive emotion, a means of salvation in the midst of catastrophe. How can he find this liberating musical act after the experiences of the F sharp minor *adagio* ? What form could here be sufficient ? What subject could claim and hold the attention ? As later, in the ninth symphony, he here sets the *scherzo* before the *adagio*, lest it should be entirely overshadowed by it. There remain the rondo and the variation, of which the last, as a purely lyrical form, is out of the question after the *adagio*, while the rondo is excluded as too slight. Only some particularly powerful and decisive intellectual effort could find a way back to life from the bottomless emotional depths of the *adagio*. A form was needed capable of expressing unshakable will to creative existence, earnestness, strenuous activity without a hint of frivolity. Beethoven found what he needed in the *Fugue*.

" There is no art in making a fugue," he declared upon one occasion to Holz ; " I made them by the dozen in my student-days. But imagination asserts its rights, and nowadays a new and truly poetic element finds a place in the traditional form." It was this poetic element which Beethoven found, when he had to express a " yea-saying " to life with sufficient force to answer to the tremendous song of sorrow which he had just completed. A similar development is to be found later in the B flat major string quartet, Op. 130. There, following the advice of friends, Beethoven subsequently omitted the closing fugue and substituted a rondo. In the sonata, however, the fugue remains ; and although this movement presents the most difficult problems in performance, its retention gives a noble unity to the work which would have been otherwise lost.

The opening *largo* leads on with free improvisation and gradually increasing liveliness to the *allegro risoluto*, in which an ascending trill prepares for the fugue theme. Beginning with vigorous defiance, this leads through abruptly broken descending runs to a restless, rebellious figure which continues till the entry of the answer. A counter-subject, ascending with vigorous octave leaps, joins the answer and is built in, stone by stone, with the cyclic structure of the fugue, which represents the triumph of creative will over all the powers of emotion. Isolated lyrical episodes interrupt the restless activity of the main subject, and so does a tender restraining G flat major phrase, which prepares the way for the theme which now begins again with redoubled might. Further on, it culminates in what Bülow calls the "melancholy B minor episode" and "triumphing D major entrance" of the theme. After a stormy passage, leading to A major, comes a mystic, "pensive," thinly-written *intermezzo*. Highly complicated thematic intricacies, inversion and contrary movement combined, carry on to the *stretto* with its thundering, jubilant trills in the bass, which, after a short *poco-adagio* meditation, rise victoriously to the heights and close the work on a note of unexampled strength.

All his life Beethoven experienced the obstructiveness of material things most bitterly when dealing with the pianoforte. No other branch of his work shows such a restlessness of research and experiment as the pianoforte sonatas. Beginning with the symphonic sonata, he proceeds by way of the improvisation, the concerto, and the chamber-music sonata to a blend of the symphonic and concerto styles. Just at this point, however, when gathering up the heights and depths, the strength and tenderness within him into a single mighty confession of faith, he was fated to feel the deficiencies of the pianoforte as a means of expression most bitterly. Even his growing conviction that his work was fitted for the future rather than for his contemporaries could not blind him to the fact that the colossal Op. 106 represented the furthest attainable summit of pianoforte expression, though not perhaps of pianoforte technique.

Beethoven had thus achieved a goal; to him no further advance was conceivable. But he had by no means exhausted the possibilities of the most problematic, yet most stimulating, of instruments. He had written his last symphonic concert-sonata, but there remained the fantasia and the chamber-music sonatas. He turned his attention again to these two types, the three-movement and the two-movement forms, and here we have his last will and testament as a pianoforte composer, a document which marks not only an end, like Op. 106, but which is significant for the future. Beethoven destroyed the symphonic multiplicity of the pianoforte sonata once for all; he carried it back to enlargement upon a single poetic subject (corresponding to improvisation), which he now unfolded with all the force of a sure expression-technique of motive, in a blend of the styles of chamber-music and improvisation. We have the results in three last sonatas, Op. 109, 110 and 111.

Schindler tells us that Beethoven, "in the late autumn of 1820, returned from a summer holiday at Mödling, where, according to custom, he had industriously collected his ideas, sat down at his desk and wrote the three sonatas, Op. 109, 110 and 111, 'at a sitting,' as Beethoven expressed it in a letter to Count Brunswick, reassuring his friend as to his mental welfare." Schindler, indeed, doubts that "at a sitting," and the sketches and conversation note-books prove that Beethoven's remark is to be taken *cum grano salis*. The sonatas appeared during the course of a year, the first in 1820, the last in the winter of 1821–22. Apart from the overture, Op. 124, they were the sole work of that period which is able to rank in importance with the *Mass in D* and the ninth symphony (to which they bear an inner resemblance) and may well have appeared to Beethoven as spiritually very closely connected.

In the E major sonata, Op. 109, we once more encounter the fantasia-sonata, of which it is an even more striking example than Op. 101. The prelude begins with wave-like figures (the *vivace* theme of Op. 79 reappears here) and is twice interrupted by a short emotional *adagio* passage. The lively movement has no definite close, but dies away in hovering harmonies. A passionate *prestissimo* follows with stamping basses and an excited ascending theme. Yearning motives are interpolated, and not till just before the repeat of the main subject does a pacifying episode, taken from the bass motive, make its appearance. This, however, merely prepares the way for a passionate restatement of the opening subject and the piece closes in wild, onward-pressing chords.

This restless introductory movement is followed by an *andante*, conceived as a variation-theme, " singing, with intense emotion," expressive of absolute happiness and peace, passionless desire, which finds its fulfilment, not in conflict with hostile powers, but in the activities of the creative imagination. Imagination vitalises the theme and conjures up a series of bright and varied images. In the closing variation, the theme becomes exquisitely tender in tone, reassumes its original form, and the imagery of dreams gives place to utter peace.

This work, which is exclusively lyrical, contrasts vividly with the A flat major sonata, Op. 110, a composition much varied in content. The first movement, *moderato cantabile, molto espressivo* (it is always *espressivo* in Beethoven's later period), points more strikingly to the past than any other movement composed at that time. There is no motival development of the subject. Grace and sensibility dominate the movement; there is very little dark shading. It resembles the dawn of a brilliant day, the course of which is still unknown. The *allegro molto* which follows is more forcefully accentuated, but the mood is still undeclared. Neither the beautiful and melodious first movement in A flat major, nor the spirited F minor *scherzo* provide any clue to future developments or ultimate goal. The veil is lifted, however, with the opening of the solemn and mournful *adagio* in B flat minor. The instrument begins to speak as it spoke in the D minor sonata. A deeply sorrowful recitative is heard, followed by another, expressing consolation. It has a questioning close, as though seeking to probe the cause of sorrow. Now begins a " song of sorrow " in A flat minor, with dull palpitating harmonies; a lift towards C flat major brings momentary peace, but it sinks once more to the depths of grief which gave it birth.

The composer pursues a course similar to that which he marked out in the bridge-passage from the *adagio* to the finale in Op. 106. As age approaches he wrestles with sorrow in the might of free creative thought. In Op. 106 both grief and consolation were of supernatural magnitude; here the scale of things is less tremendous, the sorrow is the sorrow of a man, not of a super-human being, and the consolation has not the soaring sublimity of Op. 106, where titanic emotions oppose each other. The theme begins with quietly confident ascending fourths, culminating in an assured expression of conscious power. The evil spell is, however, not yet broken. An abysmal fall follows and the sorrow song is heard once more, " weary, lamenting," in muffled G minor harmonies, the melody even more intense and urgent than before, the echoing chords yet more eerie in effect. At length the dark minor key is resolved into the more encouraging major. " Gradually reviving," the theme first establishes itself in the inversion, until, with increasing assurance, it assumes its earlier form and climbs to the heights as a hymn of triumph and thanksgiving.

" My dear boy, the startling effects, which many ascribe solely to the natural genius of the composer, are quite frequently easily achieved by the right use and resolution of the chord of the ' diminished seventh,' " Beethoven is reported to have said to Carl Hirsch, a grandson of Albrechtsberger, to whom he taught harmony for a short period, in grateful remembrance of his one-time master. The speech is probably authentic, for it answers exactly to Beethoven's own practice. Chords and intervals of the " diminished seventh " were for him, as for his contemporaries, the most powerful means of expressing pain and sorrow. He closed the introduction of his earlier sonata in C minor, the *Pathétique*, Op. 13, with a chord of the " diminished seventh."

In Op. 111 Beethoven stands from the outset upon heights to which the earlier work pointed. He wastes little time over preliminary phrases, but launches at once into his subject. The opening chord is the most agonised dissonance in Beethoven's musical vocabulary. Cleft rhythms follow; wide, darkly majestic, " diminished sevenths " are clamped together. A phrase rings out like a groan above the palpitating sforzati bass. Through the mysterious brooding dusk comes a faint sound as of distant thunder; suddenly the powerful chief theme breaks forth, boldly modelled and uncannily arresting; it calls up a picture of a bull charging with lowered horns. There is a short, threatening pause—and the battle begins. There are wild, ascending unison passages, unprecedented in Beethoven's work since Op. 57. The " diminished seventh " dominates the exposition. With a tremendous leap the combat appears to have reached its climax and a lighter A flat major subject appears ; but the storm breaks out afresh. A second entry of the motive of promise and hope in the light-coloured C major key brings no alleviation. The basses drag the subject down to the darkest depths of the minor, while the first theme continues on its triumphant way until its force is spent and it dies away in sheer exhaustion. Its own uncontrolled fury has annihilated it. A short C major epilogue sings the death-song of a fighter who is a victim to his own inordinate lust of combat.

A remote similarity exists between this and another work by Beethoven in C minor, the overture to *Coriolanus*. Both portray head-strong energy ; both are dramatic monologues. Such contrasts as are introduced are all of a mollifying description ; the main subject alone holds, and is held, by tragedy. In *Coriolanus*, the salvation and transfiguration of a will whose own greatness has been its destruction are not shown, being outside the purview of the composer, but in the sonata they are suggested by the C major close. The will, worn by earthly conflict, is translated to realms of light, its strength purified and transfigured. Lenz expresses the antithesis as " Defiance and submission," while Bülow carries the thought even further, describing the contrast as " Sansara—Nirvana." Neither seems to have quite hit the mark ; for in the second part of the sonata is neither the passivity of " submission," nor the " Nirvana " negation of desire. Rather, the same force is active in both movements, working in darkness in the *allegro*, but enlightened in the *adagio*, where there is no self-forgetting surrender of the *ego*, but a continuous active striving as of a truly personal energy, cleansed from earth's stains. The " Nirvana " mood was foreign to Beethoven ; the force of personality always triumphs in his work. It does not find expression necessarily, or solely, in violent activity ; at times, as in the Op. 111 variations, it is represented by a continuous striving to the heights ; but this striving has all the character-istics, the wishes and hopes of an indestructible personality ; and it is clear that the two movements were not planned philo-sophically, but upon a purely artistic impulse. There is the same underlying conception of action and re-action, which in earlier years produced mutually complimentary " pairs " of works from Beethoven's hand; though here the two aspects are blended in one to produce a single grand and lofty work.

The essentially active character of the second movement—far removed from anything resembling passivity—is, with its strong upward-striving trend, so marked in the theme that the whole direction and plan of the variations is at once revealed. As in the former, so in the latter movement, the melodic line rising from C to G indicates the course of development of the whole. The song is heard, increasingly spiritualised, dematerialised. High notes call up a vision of ideal unapproachable heights, the accompanying rhythms flow along, sweeping, harplike; high above all, a trill suggests the glitter of stars, while among them all runs the melody like a silver thread—the thread woven between earth and heaven by the aspiration of a great soul.

Op. 111 is Beethoven's farewell pianoforte sonata. It is hard to estimate the possibility of his return to the pianoforte after the completion of the great string quartets and the projected tenth symphony, even if longer life had been granted him. In spite of certain expressions of distaste, his interest in the instrument was certainly not entirely quenched. After Op. 111 he composed two collections of *Bagatelles* for the pianoforte, Op. 119 and 126. They were produced at various dates; some of them bear the impress of his preoccupation with the string quartets very markedly, and although they are unequal they exemplify, almost without exception, the delicate miniature technique of Beethoven's later period. Other works which appeared between the sonatas, such as the C minor variations (1806), the *Polonaise*, Op. 89 (written for the Empress of Russia in 1814), the D major variations, Op. 76 (the theme of which reappears as the *Turkish March* in the *Ruins of Athens*), besides a number of little pianoforte waltzes, minuets and contra-dances, are genuine products of the genius of Beethoven, which is reflected unmistakably even in the smallest mirrors. Beethoven has, indeed, composed very little " weak " work. His powerful critical faculty allowed few inferior conceptions to pass muster, and the triple-concerto, Op. 56, is one of very few examples in which it is clear that technical effort actually outweighs inspiration. Much more frequently the fault lies with the critic who fails to grasp the mood of the work, the purpose of the composer.

Beethoven's last pianoforte works have suffered much from such lack of sympathetic insight on the part of players and audiences, and here again it is significant that the tragic pieces have been understood more readily than the humorous. Hans von Bülow did the great service of bringing to light certain works, particularly those in the style of the last period, which had been almost entirely forgotten, and of restoring them to their due place of honour.

Two last humorous pieces are notable; one, the G major rondo entitled "*A fuss over a lost penny—a wild caprice*," is instinct with rough humour; the other, the *Diabelli Variations*, with humour of a lofty and reflective type. Robert Schumann discovered the rondo. It was found among Beethoven's literary remains and issued as Op. 129. It is a clever combination of variation and rondo, in which his inventiveness and inexhaustible flow of paradoxical ideas issue in unabashed high spirits.

The thirty-three variations on a waltz by Diabelli are a marvellous picture of the high spirits of a great mind. Bülow writes of them enthusiastically as " a perfect microcosm of Beethoven's genius, an image indeed, an abstract and epitome of the whole world of music. All the results of the long evolution of musical thought and imagination, from the most exalted reverie to the most saucy humour, are to be found in all their incomparable richness and variety in this eloquent work. It is a subject for endless study; its contents provide the necessary pabulum for generations of musicians. No author in the world has left so shining a witness, not merely of undeclining, but of actually increasing creative power upon the threshold of old age." Bülow has indicated each magnificently conceived part of this mighty structure, and a study of his analysis, which is made with a fine and loving insight, is absolutely necessary for those who wish to enter the thought-world underlying this tremendous work.

In the enthusiasm of the discoverer and propagandist, however, Bülow has overlooked one fact, and that is that the piece ought not to be played. In this respect, it is the counterpart of the B flat major sonata, Op. 106. There the clash between creative will and tone-material occurred over a tragic subject; here it is the quintessence of humour which laughingly disregards the insufficiencies of imperfect mechanism and soars on the wings of imagination high above the world of actuality. Both the B flat major sonata and the *Diabelli Variations* are written for an instrument which never existed and never will exist. In these works Beethoven moves in an abstract world of music ; he plays not with sounds but with conceptions of sounds, using the language of the pianoforte symbolically. Actual physical tone is but a coarse materialisation of the artistic idea, given here to the mind's ear alone. These two works are the most immaterial creations of human art hitherto. We see instrumental music carried to the point of actual perfection, and carried beyond it by the urge to the immaterial ; physical sound is rejected and an experiment is made with tone-abstractions which can only be grasped intellectually. In the B flat major sonata, Beethoven passes through a tremendous outburst of sorrow and violence to the pure, cool heights of incorporeal tone. In the *Variations* he sets out from a jolly, common-place waltz, the work of the worthy composer and publisher, Diabelli, who had given it out to fifty well-known musicians of his time as a theme for variations. Some very good work was achieved by several composers of repute, Franz Liszt among them ; but a collection of these variations only serves to emphasise the gulf which separates the best of them from the work of that solitary genius who, setting out from this good homely piece, finds his way beyond the bourne of time into the ocean of eternity.

While doing justice to the speculative originality of Beethoven's music, more especially in this particular composition, we must at the same time allow the justice of the pianist's complaints as to the disturbing peculiarities of his work when taken phrase by phrase. It is perfectly true that, with increasing age, Beethoven " instrumentated " worse and worse, both for the orchestra and for the pianoforte, and that, as Reinecke has remarked, he often piled high and low registers upon each other without the connecting middles necessary on acoustic grounds. This is partly to be accounted for by his deafness, his loss of practical control through the ear ; but it had also a deeper cause —the transcendentalism of his imagination increasing as his affliction isolated him. The sensuous aspect of sound became for him a secondary matter ; he felt in abstractions alone.

Thence arose the asceticism of his pianoforte writing and the " acoustic abominations " which Bülow attempts to argue away. The same condition of mind is observable in the harmony, melody and rhythm of his later period. He is haunted by the ghosts of tone, which stimulate him to the most exquisitely delicate cerebral perceptions. Both in form and content his music becomes purely metaphysical, piercing to the greatest depths which the imagination of the composer could perceive or reveal.

Beethoven began with a strong sense of the actual and practical ; he ended in complete withdrawal from the world. His pianoforte compositions arose originally out of the requirements of an active performer—at the last he wrote work not technically, but musically, unplayable. He grafted the improvisation upon the strict form as a liberating and fructifying element ; but in thus marrying it with form he destroyed improvisation as a separate entity. He transfigured free improvisation, but robbed it of all its value by consciously using it to produce an artistic illusion. A broad historical survey discloses two divergent paths of development, both taking their departure from Beethoven's pianoforte music. One leads to the modern virtuosity of faithful reproduction, the player giving himself up to the service of another personality, adopting that person's ideas and blending them with his own. By this method the player speaks as through a mask, and his performance becomes " transmission " in the best sense of the word. The leading representative of this type of virtuosity, since the days of Beethoven, was Franz Liszt, an artist whose most significant work was thus reproductive. The other path leads to the musician who is solely a composer, and whose sense of kinship with the performer grows ever less. The line of Schumann and Brahms is representative here. Between the two groups stand such musicians as Chopin, Mendelssohn and Weber, three virtuoso-composers who further developed, and exhausted, Beethoven's ideas on improvisation, though in a comparatively narrow and specialised manner. They have no successors and they appear in the history of musical development as mere appendages of the towering greatness of Beethoven.

He, indeed, united all these aspects of music in himself.

He was the last great virtuoso of the old school, and his works were the greatest produced in an epoch when the creative and interpretative artist were commonly one. As far as we know, Beethoven never, except in his earliest days, played the compositions of another, and he never wrote a work for the pianoforte of which he did not conceive himself to be the best possible interpreter. It makes no real difference to us whether Beethoven did or did not, as a performer, answer to his own ideal; or whether, in later years, his performance deteriorated on account of his deafness, or his neglect of the technical side of his art. What matters is the certainty that in the pianoforte works we possess an absolutely subjective confession of faith from a practising artist. They give us a glimpse into his workshop. Through them we get authentic tidings of his wishes and purposes; they form a diary of the deepest, most individual and intimate description. The sonatas are in the nature of a soliloquy; what he there revolved alone he gave to all the world in fuller perfection, through a richer means of expression than the pianoforte could offer, in his orchestral and chamber-music.

L

CHAPTER V

THE Symphonies rise like a great nine-pointed peak from the mountain range of Beethoven's works; they do not perhaps pierce the clouds at the altitude of some of his other works, but they are visible from the greatest distances. The first Beethoven symphony was first performed on April 2nd, 1800, the last, the ninth symphony, on May 7th, 1824, so that about a quarter of a century, from his thirtieth to his five-and-fiftieth year, comprises his whole symphonic work. In his youth and in his last years he produced nothing in this branch of music. The complete story of his development as a composer cannot, therefore, be read in the symphonies, but they form a comprehensive cycle of his work during his prime, when he surveyed the world about him most keenly and rendered an account of what he saw through his art. No other work of his has so many, and such vital, points of contact with the wide range of human culture, or has made so deep an impression upon the artistic consciousness of the masses. The symphonies are the most popular of Beethoven's works, indeed they are the most popular of all serious instrumental music.

Their success was due, in the first place, to the concentration of creative power which they represented and which, by contrast with earlier work, seemed stupendous. Beethoven's symphonies were few in number as compared with Haydn's hundred and more, or with the short-lived Mozart's forty, not to speak of the still greater numbers totalled by some of their contemporaries. Beethoven worked far more slowly upon his symphonies than did these composers. Mozart wrote his three last and best symphonies within three months, and Haydn at nearly sixty years of age composed his twelve famous London symphonies within a few years. Such swiftness of conception and execution was impossible to Beethoven. The eighth symphony occupied about five months, but the others took far longer, and the ninth symphony, from its first conception to its completion, covers more than ten years. Beethoven's desire to concentrate, select and pack his material into the shortest possible formula, which made his task such a severe one, arose from his new conception of the basis of symphonic work.

Mozart and Haydn wrote for musical amateurs, for a particular caste of critical patrons of art. Their compositions graced the social gatherings of a privileged class, sometimes in the form of serious symphonies, sometimes as light entertaining *Cassations*, *Divertimenti* and *Serenades*. Not till later years did Haydn begin to recognise a wider public. Beethoven, however, set out with this conception. His ideas were too big for the narrow bounds of the music *salons* of the nobility, and he did away with the intimate and chamber-music character which had hitherto clung to the symphony. He calculated on a far wider sphere of influence, and exchanged the range of thought and feeling of a particular class for the whole range of human interest of his period. That period, with its high cultural ideas, its worship of human freedom, moral and intellectual, is the source whence Beethoven drew his symphonies. He conceived them in a spirit of conscious intellectual community and sympathy with the life and progressive forces of his time. They are a confession of his outlook upon common human problems, not, like the sonatas, a subjective revelation of his own particular nature. He strips away everything personal and seeks the eternal and typical in the problems before him. He recognises this common element underlying all the individual dissensions as to spiritual ideals among the men of his time, and reflects it as in a mirror, in the great symphonic form. The symphonies might well be described as speeches to the nation, to humanity. Because the sense of human solidarity then existed as a strong and unbroken force, it inspired the greatest composer of the time to write symphonies which, in the width of their appeal, far surpassed any previous work of the kind. Because Beethoven absorbed and turned to good use the *stimuli* he thus received from without, he succeeded in making the instrumental symphony, hitherto addressed to small and select circles of amateurs, the art-form of democracy. Herein lies the significance of the symphonies in the history of human culture. The Beethoven symphony is an Atlas, which carries upon its shoulders the whole public musical life of the nineteenth century. General public interest, hitherto confined in sacred music to the *Mass*, the cantata and the singing of the Passion, and in secular music to opera and oratorio (apart from suites of folk tunes, serenades and church organ music, vocal music predominating), was now won for symphonic instrumental music. Generations of musicians had popularised other forms, but to Beethoven alone belongs the honour of completing the work which Haydn began and carrying the symphony to the summit of its greatness. In doing this he created a new musical public. The wide appeal of Beethoven's symphonic music reaches its climax in the choral finale of the ninth symphony, which, ideally, demands that the audience should join in the singing, as in the chorales of Bach's cantatas and Passion music.

As with the sonatas, so too with the symphonies, it was the inner promptings of his soul that taught Beethoven to understand and to master the problems before him. The sonatas were primarily problems of form, and were meant to give varied expression to every least motion of the composer's most intimate heart of hearts. The symphonies are primarily problems of matter, and they mirror the diversity and extent of the outward vision just as the sonatas reflect each change in the inward. In the sonatas, Beethoven reasons with himself; in the symphonies, with the world, and this world is, at first, that of Haydn and Mozart, though seen through Beethoven's eyes. As with the sonatas, he had first to assimilate the form in order to resolve it later on into its elements and construct it anew. He followed the steps of his predecessors before striking out a path for himself. He began, therefore, with an " amateur's " symphony of the accustomed type; yet he worked neither as an imitator, nor as a student performing an exercise. He followed the path marked out; yet he did so with the self-assurance of a ripe and independent personality.

At the very beginning of the first symphony he avoids the conventional form of opening chord. Beethoven scorns to enter by the well-worn portal of the tonic. His C major symphony opens with a chord of the dominant seventh of F major, a harmonic audacity which struck strangely upon the ears of contemporaries, although it had already been used by Bach. This rousing opening is followed by a peaceful passage, which stamps the following *allegro* with a basic mood of grave recollectedness. The exposition is very promising, and the main subject, firm, vigorous and progressive, triumphantly overcomes the opposition of the sustained chords of the wood wind. Themes of a like structure are to be found (not infrequently) in contemporary music, but the interruption by pensive " wind " chords is peculiar to Beethoven and highly characteristic. The thought is forceful, pithy and developed with originality, but it lacks opposition through which it might come to greatness. A graceful, trifling second subject, weaving itself about the groups of instruments like an arabesque, has a somewhat distracting effect, but the gloomy, melancholy aspect which the gay motive takes on in the basses suggests graver conflicts to come. The first subject asserts itself energetically, however, and the shadows vanish till the sunny images are clouded once more in the " working out " section. The main subject, robbed of its forceful harmonic background, struggles with a contrasted, wavering, syncopated motive, but at length, as though impatient of further hesitation and uncertainty, breaks through with decision and asserts itself successfully up to the short and cheerful coda. The music bears unmistakably the stamp of Beethoven, but has not the tremendous power of his later work. It is, however, greatly in advance of contemporary productions, and its grave yet cheerful manliness must prevent us from calling it a " youthful work " in any derogatory sense.

The *andante*, which now follows, deepens the impression of earnest activity, conveyed in the first movement, to pensive contemplation. A simple lyrical theme is heard, touched with the spirit of resignation. The second violins enter softly and the gradual addition of the various parts reminds one of the similar opening of the *andante* of Mozart's G minor symphony. In Beethoven's *andante* the parts are introduced in a kind of *fugato* and are further developed in alternating moods of gravity and pathos. The range of emotion is not very great, but it is very thoroughly explored, and rises at the surprising change to D flat major to a solemn climax which is not far short of great.

In form, the *andante* resembles the symphonies of the eighteenth century; but the third movement breaks new ground in symphonic music. The theme (probably derived from a collection of German tunes) rises light as a feather, the capricious dynamic plays with all kinds of paradoxical ideas, and the swaying rhythmic life of the whole gives the lie to the old-fashioned designation of *Menuetto*. A new spirit possesses the work, stripping the old minuet of its conventional restraint and making it a free dance-form. Not the outward gestures of the dance, but the very pulse-beat of the dancer is rendered. Emotions change with overwhelming suddenness; concentrated vitality is expressed in every beat, and no such detailed and reasoned development is necessary as in the case of a less close-packed sequence of ideas. The principal movement and the trio are opposites, in the true Beethoven manner, the one stormy and rapid, the other swaying, with arresting grace, upon soft, long-drawn-out chords for the wind. The thrill of the main movement is softly echoed in mischievous fugitive figures for the violins. Without breaking in upon the idyll, they form a lively addition to the gradually swelling chorus of harmony and prepare for the return of the first section.

The predominance given to this movement within the symphony, by its originality of form and of treatment of the subject, is the more striking, in that the finale is notably inferior, not only to the third, but also to the first two movements. It has, however, a few traits characteristic of Beethoven, the most remarkable of which is the caustic wit of the introduction. The first violins ascend the scale, parodying the pathos of the *adagio*, and then, upon a sudden whim, break into the *allegro*. This introduction seemed so audacious to a contemporary conductor that he omitted it from his performance of the symphony. The bridge passage to the coda through a sharp incisive *fortissimo* pause on the diminished seventh deserves attention. Apart from these details, the finale is scarcely distinguishable from the better sort of contemporary symphony. It is apparently the earliest part of the work. Studies dating from 1794 and 1795 were originally intended for an opening movement, but were used for this finale.

The immediate and widespread success of the C major

symphony goes to show that Beethoven's contemporaries over-looked the germs of promise for the future in the work and were principally concerned with those features which accorded with the taste of the period. It was first performed in Vienna on April 2nd, 1800, and shortly afterwards spread its composer's name throughout Germany. In January 1802 it was praised in the *Leipzige Allgemeine Musikalische Zeitung* as " intellectual, powerful, original and difficult, but here and there somewhat over-rich in detail." In 1805, in the same newspaper, it was held up, by contrast with the much-criticised *Eroica*, as a " noble work of art. All the instruments are splendidly used, an unusual wealth of ideas is magnificently and gracefully dis-played and yet consistency, order and light reign throughout." Many other critics of the time made Beethoven's first symphony the measure of the value of those which followed, and always upon the ground of its conservative elements. Even the second symphony suffered by the comparison. It was felt that the first symphony " has more value than the second because it is carried through with unforced ease ; whereas in the second, the effort after the new and striking is far more obvious. It must, however, be understood that neither work is wanting in striking and brilliant beauties."

The markedly cool reception of the second symphony had some justification according to the existing standard of taste. The means of expression which Beethoven employed were distinctly " futuristic " for those days ; the character and content of the work, on the contrary, were confined, for the most part, within the limits hitherto observed. It was one of those rare cases in which Beethoven's development as a technical musician outran his development as an imaginative composer. The " effort after the new and striking," upon which the contemporary critic commented so derogatorily, is indeed perceptible, but the clearly conceived goal which could justify these efforts is lacking. Beethoven does not here steer his ship into uncharted seas, seeking undiscovered lands, but cruises about erratically in well-known waters. It is not surprising that, with his musical genius, he has been able to improve upon his first symphony in freedom of treatment of the symphonic form and of the means of expres-sion which it offers ; but the fact that he merely experiments with these means, and does not employ them to any very exalted end, gives the D major symphony a curious and uneasy position between past and future, and makes it, perhaps, inferior to the first as a symphonic entity.

The work opens with a full orchestral unison, and its exceptionally broadly-designed introduction contains a multi-coloured succession of subjects, some peaceful and joyous, some rough and vigorous, such as, for instance, the " sheet lightning " theme which returns in the *allegro* and points to the majestic and mournful D minor theme of the ninth symphony. The thoughts of the composer seem to well up from the depths of some powerful emotion not clearly comprehended by himself. He is possessed by that mood between dreaming and waking, which is the mood of improvisation, and, indeed, this introduction is an improvisation for the orchestra, a free imaginative fantasia, woven for the most part of joyous colours, and only here and there darkened by the shadow of a graver mood. The same desultory play of contrasts also dominates the *allegro*. The underlying ideas are more original than those of the C major symphony. The orchestration, in particular, is the work of a master of orchestral characterisation. The ideas are perfectly suited to the instruments. As in the first movement of the C major symphony, the main subject is developed by means of contrasts. There is no lack of interesting imaginative details and surprises, to some of which contemporary critics took exception.

The following movements contain similar moments of inspiration. The harmonic mobility, the free play of tone, the brilliant instrumental effects of the *scherzo*, the amazing F sharp episode in the middle part of the *trio*, the mysterious F sharp change in the coda of the finale—all these are characteristic inspirations of Beethoven's genius. The subject of the last movement, with its sharp contrast of brusque energy and careless gaiety, also bears the impress of his personality. The luxuriant, almost over-sweet *adagio*, with its alternations of gentle melancholy and childlike playfulness, is the crown of the whole work, and shows Beethoven's genius working upon levels whereto only the very greatest attain. In this symphony, with its wealth and power of emotion, its dazzling beauties of instrumental tone, combined with the free treatment of a form, bent and distended by the burden of ideas, the Viennese type of symphony comes to ripe perfection, perhaps even to over-ripeness. It contains the germ of all the symphonic work of future generations. Schubert's great C major symphony is, in principle, merely an intensification of Beethoven's D major symphony. The absolute physical joy of the work, its variety of musical imagery, its youthfulness, exercise a charm so strong that deep-seated organic weaknesses are readily overlooked.

They are, nevertheless, present, and Beethoven himself must have been aware of it. The carefulness with which he revised his work (to which numerous studies for the finale bear witness) shows that he must have wrestled harder with his raw material than the apparently easy flow of thought in the symphony would suggest. According to Potter, there were three distinct scores apart from the final form, all of which have been lost. Beethoven's self-criticism seems to have been well exercised upon this work, and we may not go far wrong if we attribute his discontent to his knowledge of its organic, as well as of its technical, faults. This discontent must have become acute while he was meditating the next work. Could Beethoven pursue the way which he had struck out for himself in the D major symphony? Would the admixture of traits belonging properly to improvisation, so fruitful in the region of the solo sonata, prove useful also in the great symphonic form? A glance at Schubert's work shows the end of any such development. Beethoven needed another basis upon which to work. In him, fantasy and dream were but the prelude to inner recollection. His very nature, as he ripened, compelled him to clear definition. He dare not rest satisfied with mere luxuriance of ideas, but needed some fixed point of vantage whence he could overlook and marshal them to a definite end. He must not, therefore, rely on the wealth of musical inspiration alone. Besides imaginative emotions, he needed imaginative conceptions from which to work out his plan. In the *Eroica*, Beethoven fights his way through the dream-world of the second symphony, and attains clarity and deliberation of purpose in creation.

The great advance from the second to the third symphony is commonly regarded as a kind of miracle, and the distance between the two works, the importance of the change repre-

sented, is undeniable. It is not, however, incomprehensible.
It arose necessarily in Beethoven's dawning consciousness of his
great destiny as a composer. Certain musical forces were
liberated in him; they had existed previously, but the round
of more or less commonplace activity had prevented them from
unfolding. The more Beethoven developed as man and artist,
the more they struggled for liberty of expression; and at last
the "poetic idea" broke upon the world with an appearance
of catastrophic suddenness. The process was not incomprehensible, but was logically necessary in the Beethoven we know.
He could no longer compose symphonies of the old type. He
longed for a subject into which he could put his very soul, and
being an artist highly sympathetic to the intellectual tendencies
of his time, he fell upon that of personal heroism. His pulse
kept time to that of the age, but it was a chance occurrence which
provided the final impulse. In 1798 General Bernadotte was
in Vienna. Beethoven came to know him as a lover of art, and
he it was who suggested a composition in honour of Consul
Bonaparte. Probably neither Bernadotte nor Beethoven at that
time conceived of anything like the *Eroica* and may have had no
more in mind than a dedication. Nothing was done at the time,
but the idea of a work bearing on Napoleon remained with
Beethoven and for four years it germinated in his mind. At the
moment when his previous stock of ideas was exhausted he found
it ready for use, and made it the basis of a great creative work.

We have seen how the idea of freedom lay at the root of
Beethoven's character and how his development may be traced
in his changing conception of the true meaning of freedom.
Even apart from Bonaparte's world-shaking career, it is probable
that he would first have sought his ideal in a person. He
looked for an actual, historic example of untrammelled, individual will-power. Had he been born a few years later, he
would probably have found what he wanted in past history,
as Goethe in *Götz* and Schiller in *Die Räuber*; but he had the
inestimable advantage of seeing one of the most mighty personalities of modern times in action before him, of observing his
deeds from day to day, and watching their effect upon contemporaries. Beethoven had before his eyes an example of the
strength of the human will, unique of its kind, no phantom of

the imagination, but a living reality. Europe resounded with the thunder of Napoleon's battles, and the free, idealistic buoyancy of the Corsican's fascinating personality appealed to the enthusiastic elements in all nations. Out of the turmoil and confusion of revolution a man had risen who seemed bent on establishing every democratic hope by the strength of his genius and will-power. Beethoven saw in the First Consul that union of autocratic and democratic principles of which he dreamed. The words with which he tore up the dedicatory page of the finished *Eroica* when he heard of Napoleon's proclamation of himself as Emperor are full of the rage and anguish of disillusionment. " He, too, is just like any other man," he cried. " Now he will tread the rights of man under his feet and serve nothing but his own ambition. He wants to stand above all others, to become a tyrant."

Beethoven might tear up the dedication, but the work itself was complete. The touches which make it so lively a picture of a great heroic figure of history remain. The general idea of heroism had been conceived in terms of an individual. Beethoven does not portray philosophical or religious heroism. His hero is a man full of limitless energy, combative, restless, active, employing his power to the full without hesitancy or afterthought. To present this heroism of deed in the symphonic form, to derive four different statements of the heroic will in action from the single underlying concept was the task which Beethoven set himself. He has no story, no life history to tell. He presents the most various possible developments of the heroic character—as a soldier, victorious or defeated, as a bringer of fulfilment—with imaginative freedom. Each movement has an imaginative meaning answering to its form, and the symphony as a whole retains the traditional structure, but the introduction of the " poetic idea " brings about marked changes in the individual movements. The *Funeral March* and the *scherzo* are new and the variation-finale is unusual. The first movement alone retains the traditional sonata character ; but here again the form is reborn through the imagination, a phenomenon almost exceeding in importance the new structure of the other movements.

In the melodic developments, the ground plan and combination

of the various internal parts and groups, the traditional is far
surpassed. The colourism, too, attains a poetic and symbolic
significance which was ever after characteristic of Beethoven's
work.

Blend of tone was not the root idea of Beethoven's method of
orchestral expression. His instrumentation is in the first place
idealistic rather than practical. The sensuous effects of tone
were a secondary consideration with him. He used each colour
as a means of symbolic expression. He personified an instrument, and this personal character remained, even when lost in the
impression produced by the whole. Beethoven's orchestra is
the sum of such individuals, a republic of instruments, and the
different " personalities " are displayed and interact in a fashion
so marvellous and enchanting (the many working together at the
will of one) that the total impression does not absolutely correspond with the requirements of the tone-sense. This difference
between intention and effect increases in Beethoven's later years.
The older he grew, the more profound did his colour symbolism
become, and the greater became the gulf between the perceptions
of his mind's ear and the actual physical sound.

The peculiarities of Beethoven's instrumentation are often
accounted for by reference to his increasing deafness and consequent loss of touch with the actual practice of music. This
explanation seems at first sight enlightening, but it tackles the
problem from a superficial point of view only. If deafness alone
were the basis of the shortcomings in Beethoven's treatment of
the orchestra, how could we account for the existence of such
shortcomings before his hearing was entirely lost ? We know
that the deafness did not progress steadily but grew better or
worse with his general health, and during periods of better
hearing he might have revised his work. Moreover, we know
that during the period covering the composition of the first
eight symphonies, Beethoven was still able to conduct and play
in public. . Since he made no alterations in his work, it must have
been because he thought them unnecessary. The truth is that
he always listened more with the inward than the outward ear.
He used his art as an appeal to the mind, not to the senses. Beethoven's faults of instrumentation are the same as those of his
pianoforte, vocal, and chamber-music, and had organic existence

in his peculiar nature as an artist—not in the mere accident of his deafness. He refused to listen to the complaints of the solo vocalists in the ninth symphony, and he would equally have refused, had his hearing been perfect, to adapt his scores to purely acoustic requirements. With him the idea came first, and by comparison the claims of actuality were nowhere.

Beethoven's model for his individual treatment of instruments was Haydn. Haydn, in contradistinction to Mozart, did not regard the orchestra as a great unit from which the colours of the separate instruments might be prismatically split off. Like Beethoven, he thought of it as an *ensemble* of instruments, as used in chamber-music, a collection of entities. He had, however, extraordinary skill, cultivated to perfection, in subordinating the individual instrument at given moments to the whole. Beethoven lacked Haydn's enforced education in such adroitness. He was more ruthless, and his ruthlessness increased with age. He refused to reckon with given conditions or to allow his intention to be subordinated to them. On all other points he scorned the exigencies of actuality; and why not in this? He enlarged the bounds of orchestral expression not purposely and organically, but as a side issue in the course of the development of the " poetic idea." He did not, indeed, develop the orchestra as a whole, but he individualised its members. In his hands the double-basses ceased to be yoked inevitably with the violoncelli, and in the fourth, fifth, eighth, and ninth symphonies he gave the kettledrums important solo parts. He was the first to use trombones, double-bassoons and piccolos in the symphonic orchestra. He occasionally increased the number in his group of horns. But all these additions to the orchestral palette were made without reference to the colour effect of the whole and were employed only when the colour of the individual instrument could be made to tell effectively. Each instrument received individual treatment and only indirectly contributed to the total impression.

This method of contrasting, but not mixing, instrumental colour naturally led to an increase of expressive capacity in the individual instrument, but it brought with it the dangers of an inexact estimate of the relationships between the colours, and particularly threatened those instruments, such as the trumpets and horns, whose limitations opposed great difficulties from the outset in the way of any increase in their individual significance.   The tone-colours of these instruments, however, had a particular fascination for Beethoven.   The character of his art asked—nay demanded—an increase upon the traditional use of the brass, and he was constantly in danger, when planning his work, of according it an importance which it was technically unable to support.   In this dilemma between idea and fact, he did not sacrifice or modify the idea, but forged ahead with naïve inconsequence.   When his medium became insusceptible of further logical development he would break off short, leaving the imagination of his hearers to carry on the thread.   Forerunners of the modern horn and trumpet—instruments with two ventils—first came in during the second decade of the nineteenth century and were therefore available to Beethoven for his last works only.   Beethoven had not Haydn's capacity for a happy compromise with his medium.   He made the most of the splendid and brilliant tone of the wind, as few did before him ; but the defective technique of these instruments constantly crossed his plans.   It was part of a certain curious contradictoriness in Beethoven's character as an artist—as for example his absolute respect for the traditional range of tone for the violins in an orchestra—that he, who in most matters saw beyond the mere possibilities of the moment, did not grasp the idea of writing the brass parts to correspond with his intention, leaving them confidently to advancing technique for actual fulfilment.

It was only in the treatment of the wood-wind that Beethoven assisted the truly organic, and not merely episodic, development of the symphonic orchestra.   His custom of associating clarinets with the trio of flutes, oboes and bassoons, gave the wood-wind an independence equal to that of the chorus of strings, not only by increase in the number of parts but through the enrichment of the tone-picture.   The clarinet added sensuous warmth and fullness of tone to the thin, pointed tone of the old-fashioned wood-wind trio.   Mozart, during his residence in Mannheim, had already discovered the enlivening power of the clarinet tone, and had used clarinets in the place of oboes in his E flat major symphony, while Haydn used clarinets occasionally in his *Divertimenti* and *Cassations* ; but he was far from the systematic introduction of clarinets into the symphonic orchestra ; they are used in but three of the London symphonies.

Here, again, Beethoven came to fulfil the work of his predecessors, and the effect of this improvement to the orchestra is significant to-day.   He tackled other problems of orchestral expression somewhat inconclusively.   In later years he brought himself to use the " horn-quartet," but not till the ninth symphony.   For the most part, he was content with some compromise which satisfied his momentary purposes.   The result was that he created an orchestra for each occasion, and whereas the early masters have left us numerous works of the same build, each of Beethoven's orchestral compositions is *sui generis*.   The instrumental expression also varies correspondingly from work to work.   In each case it is derived from the particular sphere of thought which gave rise to the composition, the same imaginative impulse underlying the content, form and expression, of the work as a whole.

The first and second symphonies as well as the *Prometheus* music show Beethoven's intention of developing the character of his instrumentation out of the character of the work itself. The fact that, despite beauties of detail, he seldom succeeds in surpassing the orchestral language of Haydn and Mozart is conditioned by the limited content of these three works.   It was otherwise with the *Eroica*.   He had here to portray, both in colour and form, the victorious, combative, robust nature of the hero, and felt the need of vivid, metallic and shining colours. The traditional instrumentation of the " brass " was insufficient. To the customary two horns he added a third, at the same time making a very practical note upon this novelty in the score. He was not, however, satisfied with merely numerical increase. Not only did he want stronger *tutti* colours, but he wanted to use the " brass " to emphasise his main subject, not only by supporting the most important melodic and rhythmic accents but in the expression of the full theme.   In Beethoven's *Eroica* symphony the main thought is to be entrusted to the mighty voice of the brass.   He did not even invent this theme, but borrowed it from Mozart's overture to *Bastien and Bastienne*, transposing it from the gay G major to the more virile E flat major key.

By Beethoven's symbolic use of colour, an idea used by

Mozart to introduce a pastoral play became transformed to an heroic theme. Not only was the "brass," representing extreme power, strengthened in view of the heroic nature of the subject, but the theme was first formulated with an eye to its use, a theme which depended for full significance upon the particular colour of these instruments.

At the opening of the first movement, Beethoven portrays a conflict within the soul of his hero between impetuous forceful activity and pensive resignation. The active side of his nature triumphs. A little before this time, when Beethoven's ear trouble threatened to cripple his creative work, he wrote to Wegeler, "I will take Fate by the throat." The *Eroica* is perhaps the artistic echo of that resolve. The two opposing tendencies are perceptible throughout the movement, crossing each other, pressing upon each other, coming to grips, the resolve to heroic action conquering in the end.

The immediate impression of the piece is one of sudden, almost miraculous, greatness ; but a closer view shows that it is not entirely unconnected with its surroundings. The originality of the work as a whole seems, indeed, to take a secondary place when compared with certain technical audacities, such as the introduction of a new subject into the "exposition part" as a representative of the already exhausted group of the second theme. The vital power of Beethoven's "poetic idea" is shown in the unfolding of an entire movement out of a germ, existing as it were in the title, in the organic connection between the themes, in the unbroken development of the content. A grand and logical sequence, not only of emotion but of thought, is preserved throughout. A process of dove-tailing replaces the old chain technique of new bridge motives. So definite a plan of the whole work could only spring from a clear consciousness of aim, and the possession of an unusually wide outlook gave the thoughts of the musician the spiritual horizon of the poet.

Only the first movement of the *Eroica* has any direct connection with the personality of Bonaparte. The hero's deeds have resulted in victory, the restless will has achieved fulfilment. The scene of the action changes, and with it the person of the hero. Beethoven's friends considered that the death of General Abercromby at the battle of Alexandria on March 21st, 1801, prompted Beethoven to the first sketch of the Dead March ; and studies for it dating from the spring of 1801 seem to confirm this. The first and second movements were certainly begun not earlier than 1803. These dates support the idea that Beethoven did not intend the *Eroica* to be the portrait of any one hero, but that it represents his concept of human heroism as derived from the observation of several different men of heroic stature. How else could the fact be explained that the same hero, who is shown as victor in the first movement, appears in the second movement in defeat and death ? There is no programmatic connection, no story, between the two movements, while the *allegro* and Dead March are entirely independent of each other in content, save for the general theme of heroism which they possess in common.

The *Marcia funèbre* was an interesting symphonic innovation which Beethoven had already introduced in the *adagio* of Op. 26. Yet there are great differences between the two pieces. The first, in A flat minor, is a true march, portraying a mournful and stately funeral train with roll of muffled drums and blare of trumpets. The sonata represents a very striking picture, the symphony a poem inspired by that picture. It is no history of the life of a man, seen from the perspective of the bier, like Wagner's *Götterdämmerung*, but it gives the emotions of a spectator who watches the long train as it approaches from afar and fades again in the distance.

Besides the modelling of the themes, the marvellous art with which the musical ideas are developed, and the steady power with which the tone-poem is carried on to the last note, colourism plays a notable part in the novel effect here attained. The contrast between strings and wind has seldom been so effectively employed as in the passage where the march-theme devolves on the wind, and the mournful accompaniment on the strings. The vision in the maggiore section, the way in which the E flat major melody becomes a march-like accompaniment upon the wind to the strings, bears witness to Beethoven's imaginative audacity. Perhaps most striking of all is the little slurred run for the double-basses, the effect of which contributes largely to the awe-inspiring colourism of the march. This movement forms the counterpart, both imaginatively and as regards musical form,

M

of the first movement—an emotional reaction from the tension of the *allegro*.

Even for Beethoven it could be no light task to add two supplementary symphonic movements to this wonderful presentation of the hero in life and in death. The very nature of the minuet made it difficult to give it imaginative significance in any way comparable to that of the two previous movements. The minuet had formed part of the old dance-suite, and its introduction into the symphony by composers of the schools of Vienna and Mannheim was in reality a compromise between the suite and the symphony, brought about by the strong trend towards folk-music in the South German musician. Within the symphony, the minuet came to be a completion of the first movement, the lively character of which it reproduced in simpler form serving as a bridge-passage from the mood of the slow movement to that of the finale. This inward correspondence between the first and third movements is also clearly marked in nearly all pre-Beethoven symphonies. In his hands the increasing importance of the first movement reacted naturally on the minuet form, freeing it from the stereotyped dance-form and making it the vehicle of fancy. The minuet of the first symphony shows a promising advance in this direction, while that of the second symphony, while maintaining that advance as regards rhythm, is a return to the old model as regards content. The minuet of the third symphony threatens at first to be yet more conventional. The chains of rhythm are, however, soon loosed, and an elusive motive for the strings appears and develops into a restless and rapid theme. A phantasmal dance of tones is interspersed with broad harmonic passages strongly accentuated. A trio follows, opening with a cheerful passage for the horns suggesting a hunting theme, but plaintive string harmonies bring back the mysterious mood of the main movement and lead on to a wild and stirring coda.

Certain thematic resemblances to the first movement, and the fact that the two movements were composed at the same time and later than the rest of the symphony, are grounds scarcely necessary to convince the listener that the same spirit of irresistible activity animates both, though in the first movement shines the light of day and in the third glimmers deepening twilight.

It was, however, a mistake to introduce this movement after the Dead March, thus interrupting the even development of the whole work towards its climax. In two similar cases Beethoven afterwards showed how such an anticlimax might be avoided; in both the ninth symphony and the B flat major sonata, Op. 106, he makes the *scherzo* (which bears the same relation to the main movement as in the *Eroica*) the second movement, and then proceeds to the *adagio*. It may seem impertinent to correct Beethoven, but if we could make up our minds to perform the *Eroica scherzo* before the Dead March, we should be giving it its proper place, a place which Beethoven did not dare to assign to it at that time, having offered his contemporaries enough innovation for one occasion. For us, who would take no exception to this arrangement of movements on theoretical grounds, the *scherzo* would follow as a suitable climax to the first movement, whereas in its present position it is at best an original *intermezzo*.

The inner meaning of the work carries us uninterruptedly from the Dead March to the finale. The importance of the movement has been much disputed and frequently underrated, but Beethoven himself has left us a clue, for the most part disregarded hitherto. This clue is not to be found in any note or explanatory remark, but in the theme whence he developed his cycle of variations. The theme is one of those which seem to have haunted Beethoven for years and which were used by him in a great variety of ways until he at last found a subject upon which he could exhaust their possibilities. The theme which appears in the *Eroica finale* had already been used in the finale of *Prometheus*, in a collection of *contre-danses* for the pianoforte, and again as the subject of the pianoforte variations, Op. 35. Of these three adaptations that in the dances is the least significant; the work was intended as an occasional trifle and Beethoven used the melody which came to hand without scruple. The pianoforte variations are in a different category. Ground plan and working out show clearly that they are in reality a study for the *Eroica finale*, though a study modified to suit the composer's ends as a virtuoso pianist. Here, nevertheless, we are given a hint of the deeper meaning which Beethoven was to find in the theme; for a clue to its original significance we have the score of *Prometheus*. *Prometheus* is full of riddles, the more so that the original text has been lost and that (apart from a few scanty notes by Beethoven) only a rough account of its general intention has been preserved. *Prometheus*, according to the official theatre play-bill, is the tale of " a lofty spirit, who found the men of his day in a state of ignorance, and civilised them by giving them the sciences and arts. Starting from this idea, the present ballet shows us two statues brought to life and made susceptible to all the passions of human life by the power of harmony." Act II is placed in Parnassus and shows the apotheosis of Prometheus, who brings the men created by him to be instructed by Apollo and the Muses, thus endowing them with the blessings of culture. It is natural that the same climax should have occurred to Beethoven when he sought suitable imaginative matter for the finale of the *Eroica*. In this later work, indeed, he was singing the praises rather of human heroism as a whole, than of any one hero. He had created for himself from many models an ideal figure, compact of all powers and virtues. The stimulus afforded by Napoleon was exhausted in the first movement; the person of the hero is changed in the Dead March, and there was no reason why it should not be changed once more and be celebrated as bringer of freedom and knowledge in the finale under the symbol of *Prometheus*.

In his former treatment of the same idea, Beethoven had been limited, partly by the narrow ballet form, partly by his own inability at that time to see all the implications of his wide subject or to treat it exhaustively. Under the inspiration of the idea of a heroic symphony, he now approached his task armed with far greater powers. In the pianoforte variations he had raised his theme from its position as an insignificant dance-tune to the level of a free instrumental poem; he now brought all the resources of orchestral tone-colour to bear upon it and made it the vehicle of his presentation of the heights of heroism. The result was a finale, inferior, perhaps, in intensity of thought and emotional depth to the two preceding main movements, yet technically triumphant and affording a magnificent crown to the whole work.

He used a theme, long associated in his mind with the idea of heroic deeds in the intellectual warfare of mankind, but the connection between the *Eroica* and the *Prometheus* music is not confined to this one theme. The introduction to the finale carries on the thought, portraying Prometheus' descent from heaven with the divine fire which shall vitalise his cold statues of men, in an otherwise inexplicable unison passage with imperious closing chords. A surprising interpolation in G minor paints the fall of the Titans, while through Prometheus' word of power the first statue begins to stir with life. A simple theme (hesitating between the dominant and the tonic) appears, representing the germ of the movement and also the first primitive form of life. The second figure imitates the clumsy, difficult motion of the first. The theme becomes clearer, more definite and conscious, symbolising life's will to form, and suddenly assumes a different aspect; the melody which in the *Prometheus* ballet represented the endowment of man with reason is taken up by the wood-wind above a strong and regular bass theme, intertwined with violin arabesques. A great act of creation seems to take place before our eyes, the creative will calling up an endless multiplicity of forms, till a supernatural triumph of mind is achieved, flooding the universe with light.

It is Beethoven's true *Prometheus* poem which we have here in symphonic form, and for which the ballet and the pianoforte variations were merely preparatory. It may appear somewhat daring to press the analogy between the *Eroica finale* and the legend of Prometheus so far, but has not Beethoven himself invited it by his choice of theme? Is the theme in itself so original and significant that his undoubted affection for it can be justified on purely musical grounds, and could he not have found another with ease had he not intended the connection of ideas to be made? By the use of a theme already known, he did, on the other hand, expose himself to the criticism of those of his hearers who failed to grasp the inner significance of his quotation. It is extremely unlikely that he chose it to save himself trouble, for he attributed great importance to the *Eroica* and would have been unlikely to do anything to diminish its value in his own eyes. The unusual choice of the variation form for the finale is inexplicable apart from its significance as a musical incarnation of the idea of development. Form is here as symbolically used as colour. The theme is peculiarly adapted to the character of the horns, and its values are brought out to perfection by the tone-colour of these instruments.

Beethoven employed three models for his *Eroica*—Napoleon, Abercromby and Prometheus; but he was interested in them not as persons but as types of the strength of man's will, of death's majesty, of creative power; on these great abstractions of all that humanity can be and do, he built his tone-poem.

In the *Eroica*, Beethoven taxed his powers to the uttermost, and even his genius could not readily regain the heights there attained. The next work was not finished till nearly three years later. A number of preliminary studies for symphonies date from the intervening period, but the first one to be worked out was that most sharply opposed in character to the third symphony. It proved, indeed, a counterpart of the *Eroica*, being composed in the cheerful key of B flat major and bearing some resemblance both in form and concept to the D major symphony. The differences are, however, also very striking. A comparison between the second and fourth symphonies shows very clearly how much Beethoven's ripening imaginative grasp had taught his technical musicianship, and from what a height the composer of the *Eroica* looked back upon former work. His labours upon the *Eroica* brought him other fruits besides the completion of that work itself; among them, a fuller consciousness of his own personal greatness, a wider view of a vast realm of imaginative music lying open to him alone. A deep change took place in his mind and spirit. He turned for the moment to lighter matter, but it was with the knowledge that he could impress whatever he touched with his marvellous command of his material.

This absolute self-confidence marked indeed an advance upon the mood of the *Eroica*. The four giant towers of that great building are immensely impressive but we cannot but feel a certain lack of architectural unity in the whole. The work represented a revolution in symphonic form, and it would have been strange if Beethoven could have perfected each detail of the new constitution at once. There is only one other of Beethoven's symphonies in which his struggle with the problems of form is so marked and that is the ninth. In the symphonies from the fourth to the eighth he was engaged in making full

use of the artistic insight he had gained in writing the *Eroica* ;
and at first he could do this better by treating less problematic
material rather than by plunging again into unexplored heights
and depths of thought and emotion. Beethoven accordingly
laid aside his sketches for the C minor symphony, which had
progressed as far as the second movement, and took up some
old studies, dating perhaps from the time of the *Eroica*, and
composed his sentimental and gay B flat major fantasy.

Like the second symphony the fourth opens upon no clearly
marked mood, yet the plan of the introduction in each of these
works is strikingly different. In the earlier work we have an
aimless, fantastic sequence of ideas, in the later, this indecisive-
ness of mood is part of the imaginative scheme of the whole
work. The dreamy and romantic introduction is, however, no
mere traditional device for arousing expectancy, but is based on
the same pensive emotions which animate the *allegro* and there
exercise a restraining effect upon the lively violin theme. The
contrast between joyous excitement and activity and pensive
shy reserve is present in both parts of the main subject. As
with the *Eroica* theme, the main subject of this symphony carries
the germs of its development within itself; and, again as in the
preceding work, the movement is built up upon the two aspects
of the theme. Here the contrast is not important enough to
justify a close, progressive, dramatic development section, and
a group of secondary themes serves rather to display and confirm
the basic mood of quiet gaiety than to emphasise contrasts. For
a time, all elements of strife give way to an idyllic peaceful mood,
but they reassert themselves in the recapitulatory section and
their play becomes almost earnest till, in the coda, joy and peace
are finally enthroned.

The movement is conceived clearly in the romantic vein,
hitherto worked only by the composer in the D major symphony.
The *adagio* is even more distinctly sentimental, and shows
Beethoven in a light so unusual that several attempts have been
made to connect this symphony with some personal adventure.
The " Immortal Beloved " is frequently seen as the source of
this most intimate of all Beethoven's symphonic *adagios* ; but
without pressing for details we may well ascribe the work to
the stimulus of some tense emotion such as inspired the love-

letter, whether aroused by the " Immortal," or some other, beloved. It is an expression of deep, absorbed happiness, and even the interruption of threatening minor tones cannot break the song, Mozart-like in its clear beauty and precision, and truly Beethoven-like in its breadth and depth of emotion.

The plan of the movement resembles that of the *adagio* of the D major symphony in many ways. In both, the tuneful theme is proclaimed first in gentle vibrating tones by the string-quartet (without double-bass) and is then assigned to the wood-wind. In both the construction is that of a free variation on Haydn's model, but the choice and arrangement of subjects are notably more defined and concentrated in the later composition than in the A major *larghetto*. With Haydn, the secondary themes are almost too luxuriant and the significance of the main theme is somewhat lost in consequence; but in the *adagio* of Beethoven's B flat major symphony, the first theme retains its predominance throughout. The cheerful, confident motive of the fourths in the introductory bar takes its place as a subordinate accompanying rhythm to the main melody. The soulful melodious secondary theme for the clarinet aspires to no more than intermediary importance, and the sudden minor change of the theme holds a far more important place in the inner significance of the movement than does the corresponding change in the earlier work. These improvements in technique are all due to Beethoven's imaginative advance, his strict unity of conception, the highly individual character of his themes and the careful economy of construction, despite his overflowing wealth of ideas. In addition to these beauties, exquisite shading of tone, the skill with which the contrasts of strings and wind are utilised, the poetic *soli* for wind instruments and kettle-drums, all work together to produce an atmosphere of deep quiet happiness, which makes this *adagio* Beethoven's most perfect composition in lyrical vein.

The third movement is entitled " Minuet," but this is no more than a title. It is not, indeed (like the corresponding movement in the *Eroica*), a *scherzo*, but it is not a minuet in the traditional manner. The violent alternations, the fury and intensity of emotion, the touch of weird fantasy make it highly characteristic of its composer, a new form, superficially resembling a blend of minuet and *scherzo*. Its connection with the first movement is at once made clear. Here again the theme has two aspects, spontaneous high spirits on the one hand, shadowy mystery on the other. It is drama in a highly compressed form. The " characters " of the theme interact without actual conflict, and the course of the first movement is mirrored without detailed logical arguments in sonata-form. The trio opens peacefully with a song-melody in short 4-bar phrases, followed by a repetition of the *scherzo* motive.

The finale possesses little of that variety of light and shade that characterises the preceding portions. It is full of everyday joyousness and points very clearly to Haydn's London symphony (in B flat major), which served as model for the complete work. The whole movement is based on a rapid semi-quaver theme which hurries with elfish activity through the various groups of strings, accompanied by graceful secondary themes. Near the end there is an *adagio* parody of the main subject, similar to that in the rondo of the G major sonata, op. 31. In short, it is the traditional " cheerful close " of the old form of symphony, although improved and exalted by the force and energy of Beethoven's musical diction.

Regarded apart from its context, this movement would seem no more than a piece of light original humour, but its significance is heightened by its position within the symphonic organism. The course of the work hitherto shows an undercurrent of pensive gravity, melancholy, dreamy depression, but cheerful, even playful thoughts, a desire for the joys of life and action make themselves felt. This conflict with the darker powers is reflected in the first movement and echoed in the third. In the *adagio* these opposites are in some degree reconciled in a romanticism at once cheerful and melancholy. In the finale, the gay and active forces triumph; the opposing powers are reconciled, rather than defeated, through the sense of humour. The conflict is forgotten, and humour dances over hidden precipices. This development with its gay laughing change at the end is, indeed, in the nature of an evasion; but it was a successful one and gave the work a roundness and completeness unattained in Beethoven's earlier symphonies. The success of this masterly work was due to the limitations which the composer deliberately imposed upon his subject. No solution is offered of the grave questions touched on in the first introduction. For the moment these were set aside, soon to be raised again more strongly as the spirit of joyful confidence took charge.

The C minor symphony (No. 5) was begun immediately after the completion of the *Eroica*, and the fact that it was set aside in favour of the fourth symphony suggests that Beethoven felt he had not yet cleared his mind about the scheme of the whole. A study for the finale, which has been preserved, points to a closing movement in 6–8 time in C minor; a first sketch for the slow movement includes a stiffly moving " *andante quasi menuetto*," while the development of the first movement (as originally planned) appears feeble and insipid by comparison with the later version. It is thus clear that the work took on its most distinctive characteristics in the course of Beethoven's protracted struggles with his subject, over the astonishingly long period of some five years. Was the subject-matter commensurably important and difficult to cast into form?

Beethoven himself answered the question when speaking to Schindler and characterised the main theme of the first movement with the words: " Thus Fate knocks at the door." The work deals with the awful powers of Fate and ends with a triumph song of the human will. Underlying the whole is Beethoven's great idea of the freedom of man. While in the *Eroica* he dealt with the struggle for freedom and the blessings of political and intellectual freedom, he pondered upon the great problem of the freedom of the will itself. This subject is touched upon in the B flat major symphony, but in the fifth symphony it reaches the tragic proportions of a serious problem, entwined with the very roots of existence, not to be evaded in the refuge of dreams or the compromise of humour. The struggle is to be to the death, involving not the fate of one ideal hero (as in the *Eroica*) but of all humanity. In the first movement of the *Eroica* the hero wrestles with the limitations and crippling emotionalism of his own being in order that his powers may have full scope, but in the fifth symphony humanity wrestles with all these hindrances expressed in the mysterious idea of Fate.

As in the *Eroica* and the B flat major symphony, the colour of the work is determined by its content. In the fourth symphony Beethoven shows a predilection for solo effects, and by reason of the small range of subject, renounces not only the newly acquired third horn, but also the second flute. In the C minor symphony he employs an entirely new palette. He works for broad effects on a few lines of great power ; vitality informs the entire effort. The work was contemporary with the concert sonatas, and the austere effect of bare unison passages, such as those in the F minor sonata, Op. 57, is not so extensively used in any orchestral work until we come to the ninth symphony. The first few notes show that Beethoven's imagination was making increasing demands upon the resonance of the instruments. His orchestra increases in volume of tone. Consequently he chiefly employs the strings in unison, while his treatment of the wood-wind, particularly in the corner-movements (the first and last), is principally choral. He wants big compact masses of sound and uses solo effects only for the sake of contrast. The " brass " is used in complete groups with all the effect of splendour which is peculiar to it. The naïve idealism of Beethoven's instrumentation is well illustrated here. Whereas the obvious thing would have been to use every possible resource to illustrate the tremendous dynamic displays of force represented in this symphony, he scorned any addition to the group of horns. In the *Eroica*, the horn had been used by him as an important symbol of the presence of the hero. Here, where there is no question of a personal hero, he is content with the traditional complement of instruments, but when, at the finale, he wants to reinforce the volume of sound he uses trombones, which (in his system) symbolise majestic greatness, while in order to make the triumphal character of his close as clear and as forcible as possible, he adds shrill piccolo and booming double-bassoon to the wood-wind.

It will thus be seen that again in the C minor symphony the orchestra was recreated in accordance with the underlying " poetic idea " of the work. We cannot here enter into the details of the wealth of colours employed by the composer in each separate movement. No predecessor recognised and made such splendid use of the mysteriously veiled colours of the bass-strings, and exhibited their grotesque humour as did

Beethoven in the *scherzo* and trio of this symphony. The introduction to the fourth symphony afforded only a vague dream of the eerie world of romance which we enter here.

In the opening, without any introduction in the traditional sense, " Fate knocks at the door," and the resounding blows, twice repeated, awake a tremulous echo in the strings rising to a note of question. At the third summons the nature of the Terrible Guest is no longer in doubt; the scared echoes are roused once more, but this time gather to no questioning dominant chord, but to a strong rhythmic and breathlessly rapid passage broken by short pauses. The horns vigorously take up the opening motive, leading up to an E flat major change, and the challenge of Fate is accepted. The knocking of Fate is heard once more on wind and strings, as though sounding from the two ends of the lists, where the battle is joined and the issue awaited.

The device by which the call and answer to the challenge of Fate are developed from the same motive is a tremendous factor in achieving the unity of the whole movement, and responds to the demand of the subject for a highly concentrated treatment. The composer has an experience to present; not, as in the *Eroica*, a character to portray; and accordingly the repeat loses its recapitulatory character in subordination to the steady progress of the main action leading on to a further stage of development. The " working-out " section which portrays the varying phases of combat and ends amidst the triumphing blows of Fate is followed by a repeat which the addition of an oboe melody makes into a cry of pain. Thereafter the combatants appear to regain courage, but the Fate motive returns with irresistible force, the C major key gives way to C minor and the shadows deepen till the victorious shout of Fate cuts short the last moans of the defeated combatant.

As far as this world is concerned, Fate has conquered; but with the opening of the second movement we are shown another, visionary world, to which the spirit flees from the cruel realities of this life. Rest after conflict is proclaimed, a rest broken by dreams of victory which, though they are but dreams, restore the faith of the vanquished in a future consummation of all his hopes.

There is promise, but as yet no fulfilment, and earth's problems, doubts and questions must be faced once more. At the beginning of the third movement a ghostly solo for the bass-strings closes on an interrogative dominant chord and we find ourselves in yet another world, neither the real nor the ideal, but a place of spirits, half elemental, half infernal. The hammer-strokes of the Fate motive are heard again caught up from the horns by all the other parts. They cloud the moment of hope with doubts and terrible memories. As in darkness that can be felt there follows a nightmare grotesque dance of elemental spirits. The atmosphere is thunderous and oppressive like that of the first movement of the B flat major symphony and like that of the episode before the repeat of the main subject of the first movement of the *Waldstein* sonata. This surpasses anything else which Beethoven has written as an expression of the anguish and oppressive weight of uncertainty. The mood is held almost to the end of the bridge-passage; then confidence in victory suddenly returns and all dark thoughts flee before the final song of triumph.

In the last movement no fewer than four subjects, all alike filled with vigour and the sense of power, succeed each other; but the powers of darkness are not entirely overcome and the eerie notes of the third movement are heard once more. Remembrance of the hopeless conflicts of the past is strong; but faith in victory triumphs and leads on to an inspired *stretto*.

The C minor symphony is unquestionably inferior to the *Eroica* in originality of idea, but surpasses it in compactness of plan and close interconnection of parts. The organic unity achieved shows that Beethoven had here completely mastered his subject, whereas in the *Eroica* he was, as it were, led captive by it. Here, again, he was not afraid of borrowing, and having already made use of Mozart in the *Eroica*, he now takes from him not only the melodic contour of the *scherzo* subject (which is imitated from the finale of Mozart's G minor symphony), but also the second subject of the finale (from the *andante* of Mozart's *Jupiter* symphony). From Haydn—so rich in forms—came the inspiration for the return of the *scherzo* in the finale, which Spohr considered to be, together with the bridge-passage between the two movements, the only idea of genius in the C minor symphony. This adverse criticism of Spohr's is, however, exceptional.   Next to the *Battle* symphony, which was composed later, the C minor symphony was Beethoven's greatest popular triumph, and remains so to this day.   This is clearly due to the nature of the subject, and to the easily comprehensible musical treatment, which in the closing movement borders on the simplicity of folk-music.   *Per aspera ad astra* is not an original theme, but its appeal to the generality of mankind, including the less acute, is all the more certain, and its stages of development, strife, hope, doubt and victory are presented with insight and conviction that make want of understanding or misunderstanding alike impossible.   The French grenadier, who at the opening of the finale cried like one inspired " *C'est l'empereur, vive l'empereur !* " was a living proof that this symphony has a distinct meaning for every imaginative listener.

The work affords another instance of effectiveness following on choice of a tragic subject.   Beethoven here treats of the first and simplest of all tragic problems and he solves it in favour of a " yea-saving " to life.   Once more he dealt with the same theme symphonically in the ninth symphony, where he regards it, not from the point of view of immediate experience, as here, but from that of reminiscent and critical knowledge.   Therein lies the great advance from the C minor to the D minor symphony, a difference deeply marked by the very choice of key in each. Between these two great tragic works lie three great confessions of a joyous world-philosophy, the sixth, seventh and eighth symphonies.

"Ach Gott, do but look upon beautiful Nature and gain strength to face the inevitable calmly," wrote Beethoven to his " Immortal Beloved."   He was himself naturally impatient, even of " the inevitable," and at all periods of his life was wont to express enthusiastic thankfulness for that source of peace. " How glad I am to be able to roam in wood and thicket, among the trees and flowers and rocks.   No one can love the country as I do.   Woods, trees and rock give back the echo that a man longs for."   In such surroundings he could forget the disability which made him dread human society.   " My bad hearing does not trouble me here.   In the country every tree seems to speak to me, saying, ' Holy ! Holy ! '   In the woods there is enchantment which expresses all things—sweet peace of the woods ! "

Nature was for him both friend and priestess. She aroused his deep sense of religion, and his devotion finds stammering expression at Kahlenberg in 1812. " Almighty—in the woods —I am blessed—happy in the woods—every tree has a voice— through Thee, O God, what glory—in such a woodland region— in the hills is rest—peace to serve Thee." Amidst his labours upon Op. 106 at Brühl, near Mödling, he wishes, as often before, for " A little house there, so small that one has but a single room—only a few days in this divine Brühl—longing or demanding freedom or fulfilment." His happiest memories of his work were associated with nature. " When you come to the old ruins," he wrote in 1817 to Frau Streicher, who was staying in Baden, " think that Beethoven often lingered there. As you wander through the mysterious pine woods, think that Beethoven often made poems there, or, as they say, composed."

Various utterances like these, in letters and diaries, give us a very clear idea of landscape as seen by Beethoven. What he most desired and sought in natural beauty was absolute freedom from restraint, finding therein a compensation for the social conventions which irked him. As an enthusiastic disciple of Rousseau, he felt as a blemish any violence done to natural forms. " Sheer art, trimmed up like an old-fashioned crinoline," he said to von Breuning, apropos of a walk in an avenue of the park at Schönbrun, which was clipped according to French taste ; " I am only happy when in the midst of untouched nature." He wanted an unspoiled, but also a peaceful, landscape. He did not care for the great and terrible aspects of nature ; hardly knew them, indeed. The " charming Rhine country " in which he passed his youth, and the pleasant neighbourhood of Vienna which he explored as a man gave him the gratifying and soothing impressions he desired. He knew nothing of the lofty majesty and splendour of the greater aspects of nature and felt no need of them. He loved an idyllic, not a heroic landscape. The composer, who was the first to recognise and express in music the tremendous forces which underlie the thoughts and actions of man, became a dreamer, easily satisfied by the outward aspect of nature.

This way of regarding nature was wholesome for Beethoven as a man, but did not stir the depths of his soul as an artist. He turned to the country for refreshment, not to look for new creative problems. He avoided these almost intentionally. It is hardly possible to doubt that the composer of the *Eroica* and C minor symphonies might have wrested deep secrets from " Nature " and expressed them in his music, had " Nature " been for him a part of life and not a mere means of distraction. Actually, however, he was uninterested in " Nature's " secrets and preferred to regard her as a dispenser of pure pleasures; and, accordingly, in musical representations of the subject, he made no attempt at originality but copied traditional models. He followed the programme of a *Pastoral* symphony, composed by the popular Justin Heinrich Knecht of Stuttgart in 1784, almost word for word; variations from that model were merely of an editorial nature.

Beethoven, in giving his Hymn to Nature the form of a eulogy of simple country life, himself set a limit to the imaginative possibilities of his theme. His fourth and fifth symphonies were emotionally of the " Romantic " school, but his sixth, the *Pastoral*, has absolutely nothing of this. He believed only in the actual and palpable aspect of nature; the subliminal and intermediate world of the Romantic nature-lover was closed to him. He had no feeling for the secret magic of the forest, the fantastic life of rock-formations, the personal character of each tree and flower. Instead, we find in his work a touch of homely pantheism, such as he found expressed in Sturm's *Observations on God's Works in Nature*. The outward aspects of wild nature are linked, sometimes boisterously, sometimes thoughtfully and dreamily, sometimes piously, with the emotional life of the observer, and because the possibilities of such a treatment of the subject are too limited to suffice for an entire symphony, anecdotal episodes are introduced to enliven the picture and carry on the " pastoral " idea. The " jolly concourse of peasants," the " thunderstorm," the " shepherd's song " are all thus introduced after the plan of Knecht's work. They provide Beethoven's work with a formal close, but they have no inward connection with the two foregoing parts, the " stirring of happy emotions upon arrival in the country " or

the " brook scene." The faults of the *Eroica* are re]
and a number of organically disconnected parts are stru...g together, with only a certain outward similarity of subject and a
colour scheme in common to give them the appearance of unity.

Here Beethoven comes down from the heights and adopts a
theme which, both in form and content, involves him with an
already decadent branch of his art. If, in spite of this, the
Pastoral symphony still ranks with the other Beethoven symphonies, it is because of the charm of the programme and the
ease with which it can be understood. Moreover, Beethoven
has succeeded in bringing the individual numbers to an artistic
level so high that the æsthetic failings of the whole are readily
overlooked.

Like almost every great work of Beethoven, the *Pastoral*
constitutes a separate species, with a style, technique and
colourism of its own. He chose a colour-scheme of unusual
charm for this piece, employing wood-wind, two horns and the
strings only, and avoiding all massive accumulations of sound.
The orchestration has a tender, delicate, pastel-like quality, and
the trumpets are omitted until the beginning of the rough
peasant dance. Even in the scenes which require stronger
colour, such as the thunderstorm scene, Beethoven is restrained,
and uses the alto and tenor trombones only. In the closing
movement they are used to provide soft supplementary harmonies.
The piccolo is heard in the thunderstorm scene alone, where
it introduces a lurid streak of colour. The economy of colour
throughout is doubly amazing after the tremendous display and
advance of the C minor symphony.

The development of themes and movements is perhaps even
more singular. Beethoven, who changed from the clearly
outlined periodic formation of the theme in the third and fourth
symphonies to the one-bar basic motive of the fifth, creates, in
the first movement of the *Pastoral*, a very interesting counterpart
to the C minor symphony. In that work, the need for impressive brevity determined the shortness of the chief subject. In
the *Pastoral* the mood is impressionistic, and the quick play of
feeling demands adaptability and pliancy in the material of the
motive. Beethoven here abandons all idea of thematic development, such as he employed in previous works, and contents

N

himself with a loose stringing together of subjects, a broadening stream, without any moment of climax corresponding to that which formed a structural part of his preceding symphonies. He returns to the principles of the D major symphony ; but not, as there, out of weakness and the lack of a strong imaginative basis for his work. In the *Pastoral*, the impressionistic effect is consciously sought and supported by the most carefully considered technique, and is derived from the character of the subject, while the outward appearance of a symphony movement is exquisitely preserved. Apart from the secondary movement, which exhibits a bridge-motive such as had been omitted since the second symphony, and a division into several subjects, as in the fourth, the outward construction is similar to that of the preceding works. Beethoven even retains the organic articulation of the recapitulatory section by the skilful introduction of certain important traits in a new form, but the dramatic contrast of subjects and their strictly logical development is lacking. The subjects appear with unpretentious monotony. The simple outlines are filled in with dynamic colouristic effects whose constant variety emphasises their graceful uniformity.

Even in the first two movements, Beethoven throws off his self-imposed restriction to " expression of feeling, rather than description." Innumerable colouristic effects and much melodic ornamentation in the first movement can only be explained as pictorial representation, while the " brook scene " is tone-painting by virtue of the babbling murmur of its accompaniment, and many details of instrumentation in the variations, quite apart from the " joke " of the bird-song at the close. Such instances are, indeed, merely episodic in the first and second movements, but in regard to the three closing movements, Beethoven's definition cannot possibly be maintained. The music there is pure illustration, as in the *Battle of Vittoria* and kindred works ; and only its strong musical originality lifts the work above the usual level of this type of programme music.

The " jolly concourse of peasants," clothed in rondo form, shows Beethoven's keen power of observation and primitive, blunt humour. The picture is composed in ballet style. The village maidens enter on lightly dancing, hurrying feet, to be followed by the village musicians in festal array, portrayed with all the impudent realism of a Dutch *genre* painter. The fiddles come first, the oboe tries in vain to overtake them, while the bassoon hobbles far behind, heavy and phlegmatic. The clarinets and horns arrive, and very soon the whole guild of musicians is assembled. A heavy march announces the advent of local magnates and an echoing trumpet note gives the signal for the fun to begin. Man and maid join the dance with stampings and joyous shouts. A distant mutter of thunder brings them to a standstill; the couples separate with anxious whisperings, and at a second warning there is a wild rush for shelter, followed immediately by an outbreak of the storm in full force. The flashes of lightning, the howling of the wind, the cries of fear and hurrying footsteps, form a fascinatingly realistic picture. The unresolved dissonances of the bass instruments gives a colour effect of astonishing boldness which not even Berlioz estimated at its true worth.

In order to preserve the absolute realism of his picture Beethoven introduces a more violent return of the thunderstorm after a short and ominous pause. After this, it gradually dies away in the distance, the sun shines out again, and the same motive which painted the anxious scurryings of the crowd at the beginning of the storm returns, in hymn form, as a thanksgiving for troubles overpast. A flute solo, rising in the clear air, leads on to the shepherd's song. A shawm-like clarinet theme is heard answered by the horn upon simultaneous tonic and dominant chords—a characteristic device of Beethoven's to symbolise the meeting of two worlds of feeling. The violins now enter upon a series of tender, almost religiously inspired, variations, whose gracefulness one willingly recognises without losing sight of the fact that Beethoven is here working upon a distinctly lower plane of thought. After the vitality of the dance and thunderstorm episodes, this moralising close is palpably weak. The composer clearly suffers from his programme which excludes the possibility of any strong climax.

In view of Beethoven's earlier borrowings, it would not be surprising if he took some of his motives from Slavonic folktunes; there has been much controversy as to whether the opening theme of the first movement, and a secondary theme in the last, were originally Beethoven's, or whether they were traditional melodies. The many "quotations" in earlier symphonies and quartets make it appear likely that Beethoven borrowed in this work also, and cleverly adapted folk-songs to his subject.

The *Pastoral* marks a further stage of advance in Beethoven's work. In this work he made excellent use of experiences won in the course of the C minor symphony, and although his subject was not novel, nor very happily arranged, it had for him the charm of personal experience. The result was a curious blend of traditional programme-music with Beethoven's own great musical language. The old programme pattern was lifted above its proper sphere and consecrated to classicism by the imaginative genius of a Master.

Hitherto, symphonies had appeared in almost unbroken succession; the *Pastoral* was begun probably before the completion of the C minor symphony and was finished in 1808. A concert on December 22nd, 1808, formed an imposing review of the work of the preceding few years. Two symphonies, the *Choral Fantasia*, the G major pianoforte concerto and parts of the *Mass in C* formed a constellation of new works such as Beethoven was to equal on but two more occasions. After this period of continual composition in the great forms (the opera *Leonora* with its three overtures was part of the same series) there came a pause of several years, given up to various works, not insignificant indeed, but not on the same monumental scale.

The siege of Vienna in 1809 occasioned various outward hindrances to composition, and about the same period negotiations, first with the Court of Cassel, and then with the three princely patrons, forced Beethoven to devote most of his attention to business affairs. In the summer of 1811 he was once more stimulated to do important work, and in 1813 the second of the three great concerts of new works, concerts which play a part in world history, took place. It was a charity concert, and the sensation of the evening was *Wellington's Victory*, but the masterpiece first produced on that evening was the seventh symphony in A major.

The interval of some three years had not been without influence upon Beethoven's symphonic composition. The fifth symphony was the symphonic outcome of the great concerto sonatas, while the *Pastoral* symphony bears witness to Beethoven's revived interest in the artistic interpretation of the small things of common life, after a period of wrestling with great thoughts and emotions. During this period, the smaller, more intimate forms of music appealed to him more than the symphony, and we get not only the chamber music sonatas, but also the most important compositions for instrumental chamber music with pianoforte, the two trios of Op. 70 (1808); the B major trio, Op. 97 (1811); the violin sonata, Op. 96 (1812); the string quartets, Op. 74 (1809) and Op. 95 (1810). Gradually the circle of interest widened once more, but when Beethoven turned to greater work he incorporated the artistic experiences of this period in the ensuing compositions. The whole structure of the A major symphony was thus, from the first, entirely different from that of the earlier symphonies. There is no longer that dualism in the formation of the theme, as in the third and fourth symphonies, where the theme itself carried the germ of the principal movement. The technique of the expression of the motive in the A major symphony points rather to a continuation of the way struck out in the fifth and sixth symphonies, but the new work lacks both the vivid, dramatic and sweeping style of the C minor symphony and the simple representation of feeling, the miniaturist art, of the *Pastoral* idyll.

The differences are not confined to the structure of the several parts, but extend to the arrangement of the form as a whole. There is no cyclic succession, as in the parts of the *Eroica*, no revulsion of emotion based on the conflict of opposites, as in the fourth and fifth symphonies, in which the opening and closing movements, broadly regarded, stand to each other as conflict and reconciliation. Neither does a programmatic thread run through the work as in the *Pastoral* symphony. There is rather a constantly ascending line of interest from the first movement to the last, reaching its climax by its own inherent qualities and without the help of contrast. It represents a single ebullition of temperament, gathering centrifugal power as it is revealed to us by the composer.

That the gulf between this symphony and its predecessors does not consist in the mere eccentricity of the later work, is made plain by a comparison of the seventh with the eighth symphony in F major. The eighth symphony was begun in October 1812, after the completion of the seventh in May of the same year, and it is the only symphonic work which Beethoven may be said to have " dashed off " with little trouble. Despite the speed with which he worked upon it he did not himself value it less than his other symphonies. At the first performance on February 27th, 1814, he was hurt by the coolness of its reception in comparison with that of the A major symphony and declared that it had failed to please because it was " better " than the foregoing work. On another occasion, however, he spoke of the A major symphony as his " most excellent " symphony and called it the " Great " in opposition to the " Little symphony in F," so that one may suppose that he was conscious that he had here achieved two works in his best vein, and of equal value.

A comparison of the first six symphonies with the eighth emphasises differences of the same type as we have remarked in the seventh, and not only are the two works alike in the contrasts they present to earlier work, but they have such direct resemblances to each other that they are plainly two children of the same creative idea. They possess in common an almost cloudless gaiety, rising to wild ecstasy in the seventh and transfigured in the eighth to a loftily humorous outlook on all the vicissitudes of life. The security of joy, possessed (not achieved through conflict as in the fourth symphony) of happiness to which all sorrow seems no more than the shadow of a dream, gave being not only to two new symphonies, but to a new type of symphony. How did Beethoven discover the laws of this new type ?

Constructive principles employed hitherto were useless, since the subject-matter involved the solution of no problems. The new form begins, as it were, where the old left off. There is no question of representing action, portraying character, entering into conflicts or achieving results. All these are taken for granted in the new form and translated from the sphere of intellect and imagination into that of pure perception and feeling. The traditional laws of form, consequently, take the second place as a medium of expression, the first place being taken by the principle of rhythm, derived immediately from the

" poetic idea " and ruling the form in every detail. The power of rhythm makes it possible to present the idea of spiritual cognitions already attained with cumulative force, without the introduction of any new problems.

This brings us very close to Wagner's penetrating intuitive comprehension of the seventh symphony, when he attempted to explain it as the " apotheosis of the dance," not falsely attributing to it a programmatic tendency in the usual sense, but emphasising the high significance of rhythm in the constitution of the form. The eighth symphony may be similarly explained; and if we go a step further upon the way thus opening before us, we shall see that these two works are not symphonies in the same sense as those which come before and after, but rather a culmination of the principle of the suite, a development of the dance; though they have, indeed, nothing in common with the traditional suite, except this all-importance of rhythm as the formative principle. Rhythm is thus made to carry the " poetic idea," and the customary thematic or motival treatment of the symphony gives place to a rhythmic treatment, which preserves the outline of the old form, indeed, but interprets it in terms of free rhythmic development alone. It may be said to be a rebirth of the symphonic form in the spirit of the suite, or better, of the suite in the spirit of the symphony, which takes place in the seventh and eighth symphonies and makes them representative of a hitherto unknown musical species— the unproblematic symphony, unproblematic because it stands above, not below, all problems.

The omission of the slow movement characterises the new type and its place is taken in both these examples by an *allegretto*. Beethoven avoids any approach to emotional pathos. A comparison between these two corresponding movements is enlightening as to the character of the work. Whereas the *allegretto* of the seventh passes like a dream just touched with melancholy, that of the eighth is all dancing happiness. They mark the difference between the two works, which stand in the relation of fierce desire and happy consummation. The A major symphony carries with it a remnant of earth's burden which can only be cast off by a tremendous effort of will, while the F major symphony brings happy tidings of untroubled regions where not so much as an echo of sorrow can ever come.   The seventh represents the climb to the heights, the eighth a happy effortless movement to and fro upon the summit attained.

As a point of departure for this " climb "—if we may thus express the content and drift of the whole symphony under a single concept—Beethoven has created an introduction, surpassing in weight and breadth even the corresponding parts of the second and fourth symphonies and almost attaining the significance of an independent movement.   Gravity and stillness dominate this introduction, suggesting a concentration of force for the coming effort, of force still held in check by the power of quiet and sustained meditation.   If one can speak of contrasts at all in connection with this piece, they are represented by eager, forward-pressing elements on the one hand, and calming, evasive elements upon the other.

There are no sharply defined contrasts here, rather a dance and play of varying moods in the emotional sphere ; but elements out of which contrasts might be developed are nevertheless present.   These sleeping shadows of the subconscious, which in the first movement appear as mere psychological stimuli, now come to the fore and attain independent significance, though their reality never exceeds the reality of dream.   In this region of dreams the first notes of the *allegretto* sound ; the strange A minor six-four chord for the wood-wind and horns, which comes suddenly, like a magic word of power, carrying us to another world, a world of pensive, melancholy dreaming. There are no such gloomy, brooding thoughts as in the mournful introduction to the B flat symphony, nor such restrained passion as in the *largo* of the D major sonata, Op. 10, which Beethoven himself called a presentation of melancholy.   The A minor *allegretto* has not the force of tragedy, but a shadow of sorrow falls and deepens, attains almost threatening dimensions, and fades again into the vague twilight of the dream which gave it being.

This little piece, with its intimate appeal, has been one of the most effective of Beethoven's works since its first performance. It is followed by a *scherzo*, which, like the corresponding movements of the fourth and fifth symphonies, refers back in content to the first movement, and particularly to its introduction.   The contrasts there suggested are here restated, essentially the same but presented in a somewhat more dramatic light. In reality, however, they remain a mere play of psychologic actions and reactions. The main section ends with an interrupted cadence, and a trio melody brings reconcilement. The tune is apparently derived from an Austrian pilgrims' hymn. This middle section is marked by a peaceful and happy mood, and is reminiscent of the corresponding phase of the fourth symphony.

The *scherzo* represents another muster and review of forces; it precipitates no crisis, and attainment is reserved for the finale, a stormy, dithyrambic closing pæon, which soars high above even the great finale of the fifth symphony. With a single abrupt chord, reminiscent of the introduction to the *Eroica*, we are transported to ecstatic regions, and the Leipzig musician, who said that Beethoven must have been drunk when he composed it, had undoubtedly caught something of the music's meaning, though he intended an adverse criticism.

After the fiery intoxication of the seventh symphony a lesser genius would have been temporarily exhausted; Beethoven passes straight on from this bacchic orgy in music to its complement and consummation, the eighth symphony. Here we are established from the first upon the summit of attainment, the long climb, as represented by the seventh symphony, behind us. The eighth symphony stands in much the same relation to the three previous works as does the B flat finale to the foregoing movements of the fourth symphony; except that it is based, not, like this, on evasion, but on an absolutely exhaustive handling of the tragic problems propounded. It is a symphonic rondo, the crown of a ripe philosophy, which sees joyous play and glad activity as the goal of life, as absolute truth. There are clearer depths here than can be fathomed in the chaos of tragedy, purer joys than those of a simple contemplation of nature, sunnier heights than the transport of ecstasy can reveal. This clarity, this purity, this sunshine, this freedom from earthly burdens, this absolute conquest of matter is found through humour, the saving gift of laughter, which rings clear above all questions, all cries of pain, strife or triumph. The F major symphony preaches a speculative wisdom, a Zarathustra philosophy, strong and forceful, absolutely self-convincing, so that we feel it could only be revealed through a very great and exceptional spirit.

Though the work in its finished state appears amazingly simple, and while it was completed in a remarkably short time, it did not, any more than the other symphonies, spring fully grown like Minerva from the forehead of Jove. The first movement, in particular, was subjected to many alterations; the original introduction was rejected, the coda was modified and changed—an almost unheard-of occurrence in Beethoven's work —after the first performance. The closing group of the first version was expanded by no fewer than thirty-four bars, an addition to the structure of the movement which far outdoes in importance the introduction of a new first bar to the *adagio* of the sonata, Op. 106.

The themes in this work show the " periodic formation," which Beethoven had disused after the fifth symphony, while their subdivisions are more clearly defined, more independent and fully worked out than those of the seventh symphony. The subject-matter demands a seemingly archaic technical treatment. Beethoven, indeed, can no longer dispense with the motive as a medium of expression.

The first movement retains traces of a half-jesting discontent, but the second, the *allegretto*, is pure, undisturbed joy, too complete even for the motions of humour. The light and delicate melody of the opening is said to have been derived from a canon by Mälzel, but the *allegretto* is in all probability older than the canon, and the ticking movement of the metronome, despite a certain rhythmic similarity to the accompaniment, can hardly be supposed to have given rise to the theme. This least of Beethoven's *allegretti* is characterised not by the ignorant *naïveté* of the child, but by the simplicity of the man who has come to see in the glad, care-free play of feeling the last word of human wisdom. The piece is full of exquisite, barely definable charm, and is probably the most precious miniature in all symphonic music.

The archaic element, which is marked in the first two movements, becomes predominant in the third—a return to the old minuet which is reproduced to the life with every characteristic trait of easy complacency and dignified gaiety. It is really

Beethoven's first symphonic minuet, for those of the first and fourth symphonies are misnamed. Even this in the eighth symphony is perhaps not perfectly genuine. Every note chuckles secretly with the impish joy of imitation and parody, though an aspect and semblance of grave good faith is preserved. For this very reason, the work seems more old-fashioned than most of the minuets of Mozart and Haydn. Detail after detail vouches for its absolute genuineness, and therein lies the best of the joke.

In the finale the composer abruptly discards the comic mask and abandons make-believe. The laughter of a wholly untroubled spirit, "absolute" humour unconnected with any world of actuality, is here revealed in music. Compared with it Haydn's most exquisite whimsicalities appear clownish and provincial.

Something deeper than the gay mood of an hour is revealed in this intellectual, paradoxical linking-up of every grade and type of humour. The true spirit of music is embodied in laughter. It is not laughter of the eyes, the voice or the mind, but laughter of the emotions; and these emotions are felt to comprehend all that mankind has ever learned through pain and strife, ecstasy and despair, joy and triumph. All wisdom, all folly, every experience of a rich and active life is gathered up and released in this great and holy laughter, in the mirth which lies deeper than reason and philosophy.

Had the eighth symphony been Beethoven's last, his symphonic works would have formed a well-rounded whole, running through the whole gamut of passionate emotion and closing upon a note of surpassing gladness. Apart from the first and second symphonies (which exhibit Beethoven as the technically skilled musician, rather than Beethoven as the imaginative composer), we possess six great poems, complementary to one another. The allegory of the " hero " in the *Eroica* proclaims the mighty deed; the deed itself is seen, in the B flat symphony, as integrant against the disintegrating forces within a single personality, leading up to a joyous, humorous solution ; and, in the succeeding work, in more tragic guise, as the conflict of mankind with Fate.

These three symphonies of conflict are succeeded by three

symphonies of peace, the *Pastoral*—an expression of simple contentment, the seventh—a study in the rising ecstasy of contemplation, and the eighth—a tremendous revelation of temperament, set upon secure heights of glad serenity, forming a perfect culmination to the cycle. The line of development indicated is clearly marked, although it was produced by the natural processes of growth in the artist's soul and not by design. In the eighth symphony, perfect ripeness is attained. No advance on this laughing philosophy would seem possible and, had Beethoven died at that stage, one would probably have opined to-day that symphonic literature had lost nothing by his death. He had actually exhausted the material that life offered, and had composed a series of symphonies like links in a circular chain. Would he now regard the symphonic form as finished for him, and direct his energies elsewhere?

Beethoven seems actually to have had some such thought for a time, and eleven years elapsed between the completion of the eighth and that of the ninth symphonies. In the interval, amongst such works as the last six pianoforte sonatas, the *Diabelli Variations*, the second version of *Leonora*, the *Fidelio* overture, the *Missa solemnis*, and smaller works such as the *Distant Beloved* song-cycle, occur a few studies for another symphony (the earliest, which contains the beginning of the first movement of the ninth symphony, dates back to 1809); but the plan was not seriously taken up till 1817, and Beethoven did not work it out till during and after the completion of the *Mass*.

Where did he find subject-matter for his new work?

The way which had led him from the *Eroica* to the eighth symphony was closed. The stimulus afforded by human experience and translated by Beethoven into the language of art was now exhausted; but there remained the possibility of a comprehensive review, from the high watch-towers of attainment, of all the storms of conscious becoming. Hitherto the problems of life had been faced and solved, one by one, as they appeared; now they were to be regarded and estimated collectively from the angle of philosophic observation. The ninth symphony is thus based on reflection, not on immediate experience, and stands, consequently, outside the circle of the foregoing symphonies. They represent the phases and episodes of life, this the logical sum and conclusion of the whole matter.

In order to attain this standpoint of superiority to experience, the standpoint of the all-knowing observer, Beethoven needed to pass through the works intervening between the eighth and ninth symphonies and thus to cleanse his soul of the last stains of earthly desire and personal passion. The closing movements of the last pianoforte sonatas are a sixfold reflection of this goal, and the *Dona nobis pacem* of the *Mass* is a prayer for peace within and without, for peace, not only with God and man, but with the powers of self. In the struggle for this freedom the idea of a great new work ripened in Beethoven, of a recapitulatory representation of tragedy and its terrors, a proclamation of the resurrection of the spirit to eternal, inexhaustible joys. He descends to realms of darkness from the pure exaltation of his *Mass*, calls up ghosts of the past, and, lifted forever above the grasp of fate, remembers the despairing conflict in which his will once wrestled for earthly joy, before he learned to know its worthlessness. Once more he experiences the change from the adoration of Nature to recognition of the true divine essence ; and now, in the triumph of that knowledge, he raises a mighty hymn in praise of that Power which is stronger than all the fears and sorrows of human life. Joy greets the victor who approaches beatification, and leads him to that Elysium where the limitations of earth are lost and the conqueror of fate finds a happiness far above the petty desires of earth. The dreams of his youth return : " All men shall be brethren," and from *Leonora* comes the echo, " *Wer ein holdes Weib errungen, mische seine Jubel ein* " (Whoever has won a good wife, let him join in our praises).

Broadly regarded, the idea of the work is almost overpoweringly great ; but closer examination shows that the organic unity of the whole is more apparent than real. No single idea runs through it with cumulative force from first to last, as in the preceding six symphonies. It is welded together out of two, or perhaps three great plans, which proceeded simultaneously from Beethoven's workshop. Two of them are plans for symphonies, arising perhaps in that need for twofold expression which marks Beethoven's works as frequently paired, as the third and fourth symphonies, the fifth and sixth, the seventh and eighth. The first of the new pair is described as the *symphony in D*. Studies for it comprise, besides the *scherzo* theme (with the additional fugue, *Ende langsam*) originally designed for the second movement, the present opening of the first movement (probably dating from 1809) and the theme of the closing movement of the A minor string quartet. This symphony later came to be described as the *Symphonie allemande*, probably to distinguish it from its twin which was to be composed for England. We have little documentary information about this second work. There is no word as to its key and no themes which can safely be attributed to it. One remarkable note exists among the studies for the Op. 106 sonata, 1818. "*Adagio cantique* ; sacred song in a symphony in an old mode (*We praise Thee, O God—alleluia*), either to stand alone, or as introduction to a fugue. The whole second symphony to be based, perhaps, on this melody. The singing voices to be introduced in the last piece or in the *adagio*. Orchestral violins, etc., to be increased tenfold in the last piece. Or the *adagio* repeated in a certain melody in the last piece, the singing voices being thereupon introduced little by little. In the *adagio* the text of a Greek myth—*Cantique Ecclesiastique*—in the *allegro*, festival of Bacchus."

Despite the fact that musical sketches are non-existent, or not authenticated, two different plans are clearly discernible. From the first, the *Symphony in D*, is derived the *Finale instromentale*, dating from the summer of 1823. The second provided for a vocal close for a " Symphony in an old mode." It is improbable that Beethoven intended to use the plan thus sketched out for his contemplated tenth symphony. His remarks to Schindler suggest that he had new ideas for that, and that this " second " tenth would not have harked back to plans made at the time of the ninth. Apparently, however, portions of this symphony plan are incorporated in the A minor string quartet, Op. 132. Both the " Thanksgiving for recovery from sickness " and the theme of the finale point to this, though only in certain details. For the rest Beethoven appears to have found other uses. Bearing in mind his notes about an *adagio cantique*, an " *allegro* festival of Bacchus," the repetition of the *adagio* after " certain melodies in the last piece," we are forced to the conclusion that Beethoven blended his two schemes in one. The subject grew under his hand and the ideas were interlaced, the *Symphony in D* and the *Bacchus' festival symphony* each contributing something.

The Greek myth appears to have been sacrificed to effect this union, and it could certainly have found no place in the already concerted plan of the first movement of the *Symphony in D*. At the same time, Beethoven cut out an *Andante moderato alla menuetto* already scored for the work. He did not altogether reject it; but, transposing it from A to D major, he used it as a second subject, and afterwards supplied a new principal theme for the *andante*. The " Greek myth " idea was, however, replaced by another long-cherished plan, a composition for Schiller's ode, *An die Freude* (To Joy). Thus a third idea, independent of the other two, entered the symphony. This subject had long been in Beethoven's mind, as we learn from a letter from Fischenich to Schiller's sister, Charlotte, in 1793. The first sketches bearing upon it date from 1798, and were taken up very seriously in 1811 in connection with the *Birthday Overture*. At that time, Beethoven contemplated a shortening of the text of Schiller's poem. " Extracts, such as ' princes are beggars,' etc., not the whole," he writes in 1812, but the project was laid aside till the need for a suitable close to his dual symphony brought it again to the fore. " *Finale. Freude schöner Götterfunken, Tochter aus Elysium.* The symphony in 4 pieces, of which the second piece may be in 2–4 time, the first in 6–8 major, and the fourth in fugue form." We do not know whether this note, dated 1822, refers to the first or second symphony, but it was later applied to the *Symphonie allemande* " either with variations, to which a chorus is added, or without variations." The fourth piece " in fugue form " is now " the end of the symphony with Turkish music and vocal chorus, 3-time rhythm in the *Gloria*." The course of construction was difficult and complicated and its most important phases only can be indicated here. The introduction of the choir raised as many problems as the structure of the finale and the changes of the melody itself; but Beethoven cast the work in its final form in the autumn of 1823 and finished it in the following winter.

In order to understand the greatness of this symphony, one must bear its origin in mind. Three worlds of thought meet in it; the main movement and *scherzo* of the symphony in D, the *cantique ecclesiastique* of the sister-work modified by the *andante moderato alla menuetto* of the former, and, lastly, in place of the *Bacchus' Festival*, the *Ode to Joy*, linked to the previous movements by quotations rather than developed out of them. It was not the first time that Beethoven attempted to blend separate entities into a homogeneous symphony. The ninth symphony is a rebirth of the *Eroica* type, in which the symphonic form is regarded as a collective organism. The principle of unity of action is disregarded and both scene and characters change. A superfluity of subject matter gives rise to the curious hybrid " symphonic trilogy," whose parts, as in the *Eroica*, are linked together by unity of ideal and construction only.

The similarity of form between the third and ninth symphonies throws into strong relief the difference in treatment of subject-matter. In the *Eroica*, the direct portrayal of a typical character necessitated an equally direct style of art and suggested a dramatic use of the symphonic form. The reminiscent character of the ninth introduces reflective, contemplative elements and suggests a narrative style. The music is not to conjure up life itself, but to evolve a thoughtful memory of life, magnified by the power of an imagination which sees only what is significant and permanent in the past, and to rise from the sphere of personal experience to the universal. Events are not portrayed, but their eternal consequences are illustrated.

The first movement of the ninth symphony, therefore, is not a continuation or expansion of the corresponding movements of the third, fourth or fifth symphonies; it is a concentrated reflection of these earlier battles. Consequently, the main subject is not plainly set forth at first; but, through the power of art, a vision of tragedy is slowly conjured up from a seething cauldron of memories.

Throughout the symphony, to an extent greater than is usually admitted, there are reminiscences of former works; and if these are regarded as emotional echoes, rather than as quotations in the narrower sense, they will be seen as many windows looking out upon that glowing world of memories which is the soul of this symphony. As an instance, one of Beethoven's favourite motives, heard in idyllic guise in the *Pastoral*, heard before that in the *scherzo* of the B flat symphony and, later, in the minuet of the eighth, and also, in the *Egmont* overture, in a passionate and sorrowful transposition to the minor, culminates in its most forceful expression in the suite of the second subject of the first movement of the ninth symphony, where in a chromatic passage for the violins, it declares the pathos of laughter through tears.

The change of approach to his " poetic idea " in this last symphony is shown by the omission of the prescribed repeat of the first part, hitherto retained without exception. The significance which Beethoven elsewhere ascribes to the exposition, because it conceals the germ of the later development, is not missed here, although omitted ; because the creative principle behind this movement is that of dissection and analysis. There *is* no development in the progressive, but only in the argumentative, sense. The main subject gives, at its first appearance, the whole content of the work in imperishable character ; what follows is simply proof and demonstration. The underlying idea reappears at the close practically unchanged ; we are back at our starting point ; we have not progressed as in the other symphonies, but we have plumbed our subject to the depths and scaled its utmost heights.

The novelty of this symphony of contemplation, not of experience, consists in the principle of construction, not by expansion but by analysis of the contents of the subject, and therein lies its interest for later generations. It demands a far more acute psychological exposition of the motive than does the dramatic symphony. Supposing the subject treated to be that of a character, variable in expression but remaining ever the same essentially, the motive becomes a symbolic medium of psychologic processes. The play of thought and emotion is shown without need of the intervention of any spiritual event or experience presented in the guise of motive or theme. The difference is that between programme and programme-less music. In the former, action, indicated in words, opposes thematic characterisation ; in the latter thematic action gives place to an abstract psychological motive.

o

The main course of development, from the first appearance of the chief subject to the moment of inward change at the return of the opening, expressing an almost overwhelming recognition of the power of Fate, thence proceeding to the courageous sadness of the coda and to the pitiless triumph of destiny, thus describes a comprehensive emotional circle, paralleled on the technically musical plane by the details of motival treatment. This is no picture of a struggle with Fate, like the C minor symphony, but a portrayal, without an attempt at rebellion, of Fate itself, and of its terrible domination of the spirit. The soothing and consoling episodes are purely contemplative and serve to throw the character of the basic idea into stronger relief without seeming in any way to oppose it.

In the ninth symphony, the connection of the *scherzo* with the first movement is even clearer than in the other symphonies. This is due, not so much to the immediate formal assimilation of the two movements, which Beethoven had not dared to attempt in the *Eroica* ; it is due to the translation of the basic mood of the principal movement into a ghostly and fantastic region, a translation effected, indeed, in the third, fourth and fifth symphonies, and now rendered more striking by the note-for-note reproduction announced from the introductory bars. After a series of *allegro* and *presto* passages, suggesting burlesque fantastic moods and wild revelry, a rustic melody appears (reminiscent of the trio of the second symphony), suggesting a quieter form of happiness, till, just before the close of the movement, perhaps because it is too early as yet to find lasting peace, it breaks off abruptly, and we get a sudden return to the wild and rapid motive of the *scherzo* opening.

As in the *Eroica* a song in praise of the joy of action immediately follows a dirge ; so here, in the ninth symphony, the *adagio molto e cantabile*, a picture of the deepest and holiest peace, abruptly succeeds the *scherzo*. In both instances, a sudden relaxation of intense effort, a psychological reaction in the composer, is represented, and is felt by the audience as by the composer to have a certain organic inevitability. In the ninth symphony there is no direct continuation of a certain line of thought as in the fifth symphony, but there is fulfilment in the sense that the passionate exhaustion of the first subject is suitably counteracted. In the *Eroica*, sadness follows adoration of free activity ; whereas here a glimpse of the annihilating powers of Fate induces retirement to the consoling and supporting forces of the soul, to religious recollection. The *scherzo* offers not a solution but a bewildering shadow play of consoling or terrifying phantoms. In the *adagio*, the outer world is shut away utterly. A dreamy prelude is followed by one of the most solemn and sacred melodies which Beethoven ever wrote. It was the last part of the work to be composed, later even than the " joy " melody. Prayerfully taken up by the string quartet and echoed by the wood-wind, it rises in fervent exaltation, till, at the moment of holiest contemplation, a new subject emerges, a melody in D major full of yearning, written in the key of " hope " of this work. The two themes of the *adagio* are comparable to the two female figures in Titian's well-known picture, " Earthly and Heavenly Love." A conflict seems to occur between the two, but the religious element predominates. Promises of earth tempt the lonely and prayerful spirit no more. The first subject (now in E flat major) reappears like a herald from on high, but the time of testing is not past. Seductions of earthly delights having failed, there comes a summons to stern combat. For a moment these threaten to break the mood of rapt contemplation, but they cause no more than a momentary shadow. The contemplative mind is closed to all but the supernatural message of a peace more to be desired than all the joys and victories of earthly life.

The *adagio*, with its complete independence as regards train of thought, occupies a curious position between the mutually interdependent first and second movements which precede it, and the finale which follows it. It is made supplementary to the *allegro* and *scherzo* by its confession of a peace unbroken by the storms of life, of a faith in the existence of a purer and better world, in face of a proclamation of the unconquerable might of Fate. The optimistic trend of the movement is based on faith in supernatural regions beyond the reach of the hostile forces which play their part in human life. To give this faith actuality and to make it a weapon against the onslaught of Fate is the task of the last movement. Roused from the depths of religious abstraction mirrored in the close of the *adagio*, the soul is hurled once more into chaotic abysses of passion and doubt. Certain clear concepts gradually emerge. The imaginative use of musical quotations occurs here, with even grander effect than in the fifth symphony. The secret magic formula of the opening, the fast and furious *scherzo*, the *adagio's* lofty message of hope, all offer themselves to the service of this new imaginative effort, and all are rejected in a series of protests from the bass. Sketches for the work give the drift of the text originally planned for this bass recitative. " No, this would remind us of our time of despair," is written after the repeat of the opening of the finale. The first movement is set aside with " Oh no, not this, I want some other kind of delight," and after the *scherzo* theme comes : " This is but jesting—something better and more beautiful." The comment on the *adagio* runs : " This too . . . it is too soft, one must seek something more animated." When at last the " joy " theme resounds from the wood-wind the basses rejoice, " Ah ! this is it. It is found at last—Joy ! "

These naïve, stammering words not only give the content of the bass recitative, but reflect with absolute clearness the conflict through which the composer's ideas had to pass before they were fully formed. Even at this point the conflict is not over ; but a kind of armistice is reached during which the basses and, following these, the other instruments—in order of intensity of colour—from the delicacy of the strings to the splendour of horns and trumpets, intone the " joy " melody. One species of tone alone is lacking and that the most significant, the one for which the melody was originally designed—the human voice. Little by little, the orchestral instruments seem to lose the sense of secure peace in yearning for the human voice ; the song is repeated, restlessly, without climax or close, till suddenly there comes a violent revulsion of mood and the despairing outcries of the introduction are heard anew. At last come the long-awaited words, with a dithyrambic swing, admonishing, promising, " *O Freunde, nicht diese Töne, sondern lasst uns angenehmere anstimmen und freudenvollere* " (" *O brothers, not these cheerless tones, rather let us more delightful ones be singing, fuller of happiness* "). On human lips, the melody at last attains its true significance and, used as a basis of variations, runs through the whole gamut of joyful emotion, from gay festal hymn to wild bacchantic song.

As in the finale of the *Eroica*, the cycle of variations ranges through a world of changing emotions. Tumultuous acclamation of the saving power of joy is restrained as the mind is led to the thought of God, the Creator and Dispenser of joy, who breathed into Man the courage to attempt and to achieve. Now the male voices intone a heroic battle song; an instrumental epilogue supplements it and a strophe of the "joy" song closes the section. The next movement opens in a mood of solemn rapture. Once more the thought of the Godhead, high, inscrutable, enthroned in unapproachable light above the worlds, the Fount of Love, is presented with tremendous weight and power in solemn, marching melody. Ideas of joy and of love are united in the deeply conceived interwoven parts of a double fugue; and the second section ends in prayerful adoration of God, the Father of love and joy. Thanksgiving for the great gift of joy, with a tribute to the omnipotence of love, follow, and on the very summit of absolute, conscious happiness, illuminated peace descends in the ethereal notes of the B major solo-quartet. After this, a giddiness of spiritual intoxication seems to seize the mind, and this greatest of all instrumental songs of life closes with dithyrambic outcry, to echo forever in the hearts of mankind.

One may be inclined to regard the fact that Beethoven's symphonic work ended with the ninth symphony as a special decree of Fate; but from the historic point of view it was mere chance, because studies for a tenth symphony exist and Beethoven's remarks to Schindler leave no room for doubt that it was a serious project. The previous course of events, moreover, afford no reason for supposing that a further development of the symphonic form would have been impossible to Beethoven. On the contrary, it is likely that, setting out from the standpoint of the ninth symphony, he would have created a second cycle of symphonies, bearing the same kind of relation to one another as do the fourth, fifth, sixth, seventh and eighth, starting from the *Eroica*. In the ninth, Beethoven substituted the psychological symphonic epic for the symphonic drama; and why should he not have developed this species as successfully as the former—since his productiveness appeared rather to increase than diminish with age ?

Only one danger appears to have lain in this path of development ; had he followed the trail taken up in the ninth he must quickly have reached the limits of orchestral technique. He must have found the orchestra (as earlier he found the pianoforte) an instrument too poor for the presentation of his thoughts. Here, too, he must have been forced to an abstract type of expression, impossible to translate into terms of actual tone. Even in the ninth symphony, his symbolic use of orchestral colour comes occasionally into such sharp opposition to technical requirements that in practice modifications of the score become necessary. Beethoven, whose sense of tone was becoming increasingly abstract, increasingly foreign to actuality, was further hampered by an orchestra which was particularly behind-hand in the development of the brass, to which instruments he attached increasing importance. In the ninth symphony he used four horns, in the trio of the *scherzo* he employed the trombones, and in the fourth movement he added the piccolo, double bassoons and a strong contingent of percussion-instruments. Yet how primitive were these media, in comparison with the world-embracing ideas which sought expression in form and colour through them !

Instinctive knowledge of this lack may perhaps have led to the choice of the choral finale in the ninth symphony. A close in this form was by no means the only means of bringing the work to a triumphant and victorious end. Of the two possibilities—the choral or instrumental finale—the chorus was the easier for the audience to understand ; but it destroyed, to some extent, the unity of the work. The very words which linked up the thought of the composer with the understanding of the common man dragged down these high concepts from the regions of instrumental expression to the lower sphere of actualities. Beethoven here accepts a process of materialisation in order to explain his ideas. There is no doubt that this treatment of the final part accounts for the popular appeal of the symphony ; but in the history of Beethoven's art with its transcendence of material elements, it represents a retrograde step. It was not even excused by originality or audacity of method ; for not only had Beethoven himself already used the device of the choral finale, in his pianoforte fantasia with orchestra, Op. 80, but lesser contemporaries, such as Peter von Winter and Vincenz Maschek had done likewise. If Czerny's account of the first performance is true, it proves that Beethoven himself then declared that the vocal finale was a mistake, and that he would write a new close for his symphony.

What other solution of the problem of a finale would have been possible? The form which would have answered to the imaginative plan of the work better than a vocal finale and would have crowned the whole tremendous symphonic structure is the fugue, the form through which Beethoven in Op. 106 had expressed the extremest effort of will, the highest spirituality. That the idea of a fugal finale occurred to him is proved by a note, "the fourth movement in the form of a fugue," which is only partly carried out in the double fugue of the chorus.

Why did he abandon the idea of an orchestral counterpart of his pianoforte fugue? He may, perhaps, have felt himself as yet unequal to it. He may have needed the experience acquired through the last string quartets. Does the B flat major fugue, Op. 133, foreshadow the new finale for the symphony?

The inadequacy of the orchestra upon the technical side would certainly not permanently have kept Beethoven from pursuing his own course. As he himself heard tone only in his mind, he came gradually to attribute the same conditions to his audience. The abstract character of his instrumental music is carried to the point of absurdity; and, indeed, approaches the point where music ceases to be tone and exists only as an abstract concept of tone. The ninth symphony presses on to this point; but the finale is like a sudden startled withdrawal to the regions of traditional, well-known musical expression. The question as to whether, in the proposed tenth symphony, he would have pursued the course represented by the first three movements of the ninth and have crossed the border into the land of absolute abstraction is one which his death has left for ever unanswerable. He died, and the life-work thus abruptly broken off, had it come to a perfect close, would not only have wondrously completed the history of a self-evolving artist's nature, but would, at the same time, have afforded a most perfect exposition of the whole æsthetic philosophy of instrumental music.

CHAPTER VI

DRAMATIC WORKS AND OVERTURES

AMONG the many legends for which we have to thank the sentimental and romantic conception of Beethoven is one which
asserts that he was frightened away from operatic work by the
ill success of *Fidelio*. The story is both psychologically improbable and historically false. A single failure of the kind would
be more likely to stimulate than to depress one so vigorous and
supremely self-confident as Beethoven. A glance at his operatic
projects confirms this. Till the last few years of his life he was
keenly interested in the stage and always cherished a desire to
compose opera. That he did so but once was due to the question
of *libretti*. All his life Beethoven sought for a poet who could
write for him a *libretto* to his taste. He never found one, but
the fact that his search was constant and untiring, that again
and again he hoped and attempted, only, warned by his *Fidelio*
experiences, to reject once more, is frequently forgotten. His
many operatic plans are a standing witness to his amazing
tenacity of purpose, despite discouragement.

Beethoven's interest in the theatre is undoubtedly traceable
to youthful impressions. He had played the second violin at
the National Theatre of Bonn for several years, and had thus
acquired not only much practical experience of orchestral music,
but also a wide acquaintance with theatrical matters and with
the operas, musical comedies and melodramas of his time.
Thayer gives us an exact survey of the repertoire of the Bonn
theatre from January 1789 to October 1792. Besides Mozart's
Die Entführung aus dem Serail, *Don Juan* and *Figaro*, we find
Gluck's *Pilgrime von Mekka*, Benda's *Romeo und Julia* and his
famous masterpiece *Ariadne*, Salieri's *Trofonio* and *Axur*, Paësiello's
Barber of Seville, Dittersdorf's *Doktor und Apotheker*, as well
as several musical comedies by Schuster, the prolific Dresden
kapellmeister. Among the playwrights were Grétry, Desaides,

D'Alayrac, Monsigny, Cimarosa, Sacchini, Guglielmi, Sarti, almost all of whom were writers of repute. Most of the popular composers of the day are thus represented; and apart from Gluck's great dramatic works, in which Beethoven appears at no time to have taken much interest, hardly a single contemporary masterpiece is missing.

Ballets included Horschelt's *Pyramus und Thisbe*, and on March 6th, 1791, an old German *Ritterballett* was given and announced as the work of Count Waldstein. Actually Waldstein merely sketched out the action and Beethoven composed the music. Thus Beethoven's career as a composer for the stage opened with two ballets; for his first important work of the kind in Vienna was the music for a " dance-poem," *Die Geschöpfe des Prometheus*, by Vigano.

During the decade which separates these two works, a few theatrical pieces of minor importance appeared. These are two bass arias, *Prüfung des Küssens* and *Mit Mädeln sich vertragen*; a prelude to Umlauf's musical comedy *Die Schöne Schusterin* (probably written in Vienna); *O welch ein Leben*, and *Soll ein Schuh nicht drücken*. Beethoven took lessons in dramatic composition from Salieri at this time but we lack exact information of the duration and nature of these studies. Judging by the few exercises which have survived, he was mainly occupied with learning to use Italian more correctly, and with problems of vocal composition, apparently with the intention of writing Italian opera. A single scene of Italian opera *Ah perfido*, composed about 1795–96, may have been the result—perhaps marks the close—of this course of study. An arietta, *In questa tomba oscura*, composed in 1808 at the suggestion of Mollo the publisher, who engaged sixty-three composers to set the words, is reminiscent of this period.

The performance of *Prometheus* on March 26th, 1801, gave Beethoven a place among the renowned dramatic composers of his day. His fame was well established upon his great instrumental works; but it increased when his oratorio, *The Mount of Olives*, which was several times performed, gave proof of his talent for dramatic vocal composition. Schikaneder, a shrewd man of business who in March 1802 gave *Lodoiska* (an opera by Cherubini, who was at that time unknown in Vienna) at the

Theater an der Wien and made a great success of it, was the first to offer Beethoven a commission to compose an opera. His discovery of Cherubini led to keen competition between the two opera houses of Vienna for the first performance of Cherubini's works. Baron Braun fixed the first night of the *Water-Carrier* at the *Hoftheater* for August 14th, but Schikaneder managed to forestall him by one night. On November 6th *Medea* was given at the *Hoftheater*, and on December 18th Schikaneder announced *Elisa*. His situation, however, became anxious when Baron Braun set out for Paris to discuss with Cherubini in person the composition of a special opera for the *Hoftheater*. Schikaneder decided without loss of time upon a new course. He approached Abt Vogler (at that time staying in Vienna), and Beethoven, whose star was in the ascendant, offering each an honorarium and free lodging in the precincts of the *Theater an der Wien*. In this way the same man, who twelve years earlier had struck a bargain with Mozart and had launched *The Magic Flute*, also gave Beethoven his first commission for operatic work.

It is impossible now to discover what text was proposed. The work was never performed and Schikaneder's star was on the wane. Zitterbarth, the merchant who had financed him, sold the theatre to Baron Braun. The *Hoftheater* and the *Theater an der Wien* were united under a single management, Schikaneder lost his post, and his agreements with Vogler and Beethoven were rendered null. It appears, however, that even before Schikaneder's fall, negotiations for a new opera had been in progress between Beethoven and Baron Braun. Beethoven's connection with the theatre was only temporarily interrupted and his contract with Schikaneder was replaced by another for the composition of *Fidelio*. Beethoven resumed his apartments at the theatre and received his friends there. He worked in private apartments which he rented himself in the *Pasqualatische Haus*, and since he also took lodgings for the summer at Hetzendorf, where in 1805 the greater part of *Fidelio* was composed, he had at that time no less than three residences.

It was after the completion of the *Fidelio* score in the autumn of 1805 that Beethoven's troubles with his first and only opera began. The first three performances on November 20th, 21st and 22nd failed. Yielding to the pressure of friends, Beethoven decided in December on certain alterations, which for the most part took the form of cuts or condensations, more or less well advised. The altered work was performed on March 29th, 1806, and again on April 10th. This time it was better received, but a quarrel between Baron Braun and the composer swallowed such profits as there were. Angry and suspicious, Beethoven demanded the return of the score. He received it, but his connection with the theatre was broken.

Circumstances, however, were unexpectedly favourable to Beethoven. At the close of 1806, Baron Braun found himself obliged to give up the management of the theatre. His place was taken by a board of directors, all men of the highest rank, Prince Lobkowitz, Prince Schwarzenberg, Prince Nikolas Esterhazy and Counts Carl and Nikolas Esterhazy, Lodron, Palffy and Zichy. This change was no sooner made than Beethoven, encouraged by a hint from his friend Prince Lobkowitz, addressed a petition to the " honourable *Kaiserliche, Königliche Hof-Theatral Direktion* " (Imperial and Royal Management of the Court Theatre) asking for the position of composer to the theatre. It is one of the most remarkable documents in Beethoven's history. Beethoven " binds and pledges " himself " to compose yearly at least one big opera, to be chosen by the Honourable Management and the undersigned in consultation, in consideration of which he asks for a fixed yearly salary of 2400 florins as well as the enjoyment, free of charges, of the takings at the third performance of each such opera." He is ready to undertake yet more. He " binds and pledges " himself " to deliver yearly, free of charge, a small operetta, a *divertissement*, choral or occasional work, according to the pleasure of the Honourable Management, but he rests confident that the Honourable Management will raise no objection to allowing him a benefit in the theatre-buildings, at least one day a year in consideration of the said particular works."

Could a musician such as he, whose pleasure in operatic work was permanently embittered by his first ill success, fulfil such a contract? It is possible that the desire for a fixed income may have influenced him to some extent in writing this petition; yet Beethoven, who insists in the opening phrases of the document that his artistic endeavours are untainted by thought of gain, could not have made such a proposition except in good faith. He really believed that he could compose operas, and it is fortunate that the men to whom he addressed himself on the occasion knew him better than he knew himself.   His petition remained officially unanswered, but they sought to make it up to him by private patronage.   Prince Esterhazy commissioned the C major *Mass* and Prince Lobkowitz gave two subscription concerts, for the performance of Beethoven's work only, at his own house.   They took place in the spring of 1807 " before a very select audience, which subscribed very liberally for the benefit of the composer " (*Allgemeine Musikalische Zeitung*).

Had Beethoven been induced to enter this petition solely from a wish for a fixed income, he would, it is clear, have set aside his operatic plans upon failing to secure the appointment he sought, more especially as his other work was now bringing in handsome remuneration.   The fact that he diligently pursued these plans, without any exterior stimulus, and persistently hunted for a suitable subject, proves that he was very much in earnest.   Beethoven's desire to find a suitable text for opera became almost an *idée fixe*.   There was scarcely a literary man of his acquaintance with whom he did not talk over his operatic projects, discussing possible *scenaria* and finally asking for a *libretto*.

At one of the concerts designed by Lobkowitz to compensate Beethoven for the failure of his application to the management of the theatre, the overture to Heinrich Collin's *Coriolanus* was performed for the first time.   This composition strengthened a friendship between the composer and its gifted author, and Collin was the first to have the honour, and endure the martyrdom, of being asked by Beethoven to sketch out a text for an opera.   Eager as he was to find a *libretto*, he was unsparing of work once put into his hands.   There can seldom have been a more critical, more ungrateful, or more undecided composer. He thought nothing of taking a completed text, the fruit of long and detailed discussion, of leaving it lying for years on end, and finally forgetting it altogether.   Collin and Grillparzer particularly must have suffered severely under Beethoven's irresolution, and while the hypochondriac Grillparzer expressed his displeasure merely by half-suppressed complaints and grumblings, Collin and Beethoven came to an open breach.

The first project discussed with Collin was that of an opera after Shakespeare's *Macbeth*. Beethoven was very taken with the idea, and there exists a sketch of a theme in D minor (Beethoven's tragic key) inscribed " Macbeth " and composed probably in 1808. Why was the project never carried out? Was Collin's brother, Matthias, right when he wrote, " Macbeth, which he (Heinrich Collin) also undertook to translate and adapt from Shakespeare's work for Beethoven, was abandoned in the midst of the second act, because it threatened to be too gloomy " ? Years later the *Macbeth* project again received some slight consideration. Anschütz, the actor (the same who was later called upon to speak Grillparzer's elegy at Beethoven's grave), became acquainted with the great composer at Döbling in the summer of 1822. " One day," he writes in his memoirs, " I was walking with him, and the conversation turned on art, music and, finally, upon *Lear* and *Macbeth*. I casually remarked to him that I had often wondered whether he would not illustrate *Macbeth* musically, as a companion piece to the *Egmont* music. The idea seemed to electrify him. He stood as though rooted to the spot, bent upon me a piercing almost demoniacal gaze and answered passionately, " I have already thought about it." The witches, the murder scene, the ghost at the banquet, the visions seen in the cauldron, the sleep-walking scene, Macbeth's ravings and death—it was interesting in the highest degree to watch the play of expression on his face as the thoughts succeeded each other at lightning speed. In a few minutes his mind had run through the whole tragedy. At my next question he turned and hurried away with a hasty salutation. Unfortunately this emotional uproar had no practical result. When, after an interval, I touched upon the subject again, I found that it vexed him and desisted."

Anschütz's story paints in lively colours Beethoven's attitude to most of his operatic projects. A sudden burning enthusiasm, a lightning appreciation of the details most suitable to musical treatment, followed, upon consideration, by doubt, irresolution, annoyance, and finally silence—the sequence was regularly repeated. Collin's second *libretto* suffered the same fate as the first. It was to have been a romantic, fairy opera, *Bradamante*, which Beethoven rejected principally on account of its similarity to Weigl's ballet *Alcina*, brought out in 1798. His objections are interesting, as showing his dislike for the fairy-tale type of opera. " Whatever you do," he writes to Collin, " is sure to be excellent; but as I said to you from the first, I am too well acquainted with the subject of *Alcina*—I remember many scenes from the ballet, *Alcina*, which I find inconvenient, and, more-over, opportunity would be given, especially to hostile critics, to find resemblances both in your work and mine . . . and now, as to the question of magic, I cannot deny that I am prejudiced against that sort of thing, because it so often demands that both emotion and intellect shall be put to sleep—but do as you please about this, I give you my word that if you keep to the subject, just as it is, I will do my part."

Collin appears to have taken Beethoven's protests more seri-ously than his promises. He sent his book to Reichardt, at that time living in Vienna, for composition. When Beethoven heard of this, he did not take offence at the poet's behaviour, but tried to retrieve the *libretto* at the last moment. " Great and incensed Poet," he wrote in November 1808, " drop Reichardt, and take my notes (*Noten*) for your verse, I promise you shall not come to want (*Nöthen*) thereby." Perhaps this uncondi-tional acceptance of the text came too late, and the work was already in Reichardt's hands; for it was the latter who actually composed the opera. The connection between Beethoven and Collin came to an end—for ever, for Collin died on July 28th, 1811. Till then it appears that Beethoven never gave up hope of obtaining a *libretto* from this highly esteemed poet; for in a note of possible librettists he mentions " Kanne, Collin, Werner (particularly for sacred music), Weissenbach and perhaps also Pichler."

Beethoven's dislike of " magic " may account for the fact that he rejected two Indian musical plays offered him by the famous orientalist Hammer-Purgstall. In 1810–11 commissions for the composition of music for Goethe's *Egmont* for Vienna, for Kotzebue's musical play, *The Ruins of Athens*, for the opening of the theatre at Buda-Pest, and also the *King Stephen* brought him into active touch with the stage. During this period he still cherished his operatic plans, his hopes now being set on Paris. On May 20th, 1811, writing to Breitkopf & Härtel, who had apparently suggested some librettist, he says, " What you say about an opera is indeed to be desired, and the management would pay well for it ; but circumstances at the moment are difficult. Nevertheless, when you let me know what the poet asks, I will make enquiries about the matter. I have written to Paris for books, successful melodramas, comedies, etc. (for I will not undertake to collaborate with any poet of this country in an original opera) which I could then have adapted— O poverty of spirit—of purse ! "

A few weeks later he received the book of a melodrama, *The Ruins of Babylon*. It appealed to him, and Friedrich Treitschke, who later adapted *Fidelio*, was willing to make an operatic book out of it. An unexpected incident threatened suddenly to wreck the scheme. A letter dated July 11th, 1811, from Beethoven to the manager of the *Hoftheater* explains the trouble and shows, too, how actively he was already engaged on the new project. " I hear," he writes, " that Scholz the actor wishes to give the melodrama '*Les ruines de Babylone*,' which, as I have already informed you, I hoped to use for an opera, for his ' benefit ' at the *Theater an der Wien* in the near future. I am unable to unravel this tangle ! I presume you know nothing about it ? However that may be, you may rest assured that the melodrama, if given at the *Wieden*, will fill the house four or five times at most—the music to it is very poor stuff—but as an opera it will be a lasting piece of work and will undoubtedly bring incomparably greater profit to your theatre. It is so difficult to find a good book for an opera. During the last weeks I have returned no fewer than twelve, or perhaps more. I have paid money out of my own pocket, yet have been unable to obtain anything of use ; and now, for the sake of an actor's ' benefit,' must I—and I make bold to say it—your theatre also, suffer an injury ? I hope that your better judgment will forbid the actor Scholz to give this melodrama, since I had previously informed you of my intention to make an opera of it. I was so glad to have found this subject, that I told the Archduke and other men of intelligence about it, and they all thought it excellent. I have myself already written to foreign newspapers, telling them to insert the news in their columns, so that no one else should undertake the work. Must I now recall it ? and that on such trivial grounds ? I await, and beg you to let me have, a speedy reply, so that I may know where I am, or else much time will be lost."

The complaint seems to have failed of its purpose, and other operatic plans succeeded those for *The Ruins of Babylon*. In August 1811, Beethoven, while staying at Teplitz, became intimate with a circle of friends, including Rahel, Elise von der Recke, Tiedge and Varnhagen. He immediately renewed his search for an operatic text. This time his choice fell on Varnhagen, believing him capable of satisfying his demands.

Varnhagen in his " *Denkwürdigkeiten* " has left us a vivid picture of the social round among the guests at the Teplitz baths and records, apropos of the mention of Beethoven, how " I came into close contact with him, because of his eager expectation that I might be able to write or adapt a text for him for dramatic composition."

The proposed collaboration with Varnhagen was delayed by the necessity for completing the two works on Kotzebue's words, which Beethoven had already undertaken and which were first performed in February 1812. On this occasion he tried to get an effective book from Kotzebue, who had much experience of the stage. As early as January 1812 he wrote the poet a letter, the flattering tone of which shows his urgent need of the *libretto* for which he asked. " Highly esteemed and highly honoured Sir ! Having written music to your prologue and epilogue for the Hungarians, I could not restrain a lively desire to possess an opera from the hand of so unique a dramatic genius, whether it be romantic, entirely serious, heroic-comic, or sentimental ; in short, I should be delighted to receive any work you might be pleased to send. Frankly I would prefer some great historical subject, especially of the Dark Ages, for example, Attila, etc. ; yet would I thankfully accept, whatever the subject, any offspring of your poet's soul which I can adopt into my musician's soul. Prince Lobkowitz, who asks to be remembered to you, and who now has sole control of opera here, would certainly meet you with an honorarium adequate to your services.

If you do not reject my plea, you will find me lastingly and illimitably grateful to you. Hoping for a favourable and early reply, allow me to call myself your admirer, Ludwig van Beethoven."

This was the first occasion on which Beethoven expressed a definite choice as to the subject of the proposed opera, desiring it to be drawn from ancient history or saga. He seems for a time to have clung to this idea. When Theodor Körner, who by his own account was " plagued perpetually by Beethoven, Weigl and Gyrowetz for texts," sent Beethoven a book, he invited the poet to come and see him and to decide upon some other mythical subject. " Beethoven has approached me about a ' Return of Ulysses.' If Gluck were alive, it would be matter for his Muse," notes the young poet somewhat haughtily.

Körner's death rendered these projects vain; and a prize for operatic texts, offered in the spring of 1812—presumably on Beethoven's behalf—produced no results. For a time he seems to have abandoned his search. His days were fully occupied with the adaptation of *Fidelio*, which was performed in its final state on March 23rd, 1814. At the same period he was also engaged on a few insignificant occasional works for the stage, a closing chorus for Treitschke's musical comedy, *Die gute Nachricht*, a triumphant march for Kuffner's *Tarpeja* (1813), and incidental music, including the funeral march from sonata Op. 26 arranged for the orchestra, to *Leonora Prohaska*, a play by Duncker (1814), which was never performed.

The revision of *Fidelio* brought Beethoven once more into touch with Treitschke, whom he had always admired and who was to have adapted *The Ruins of Babylon* for him for operatic purposes. An original work was now projected. According to the *Sammlung* of January 13th, 1815, Beethoven and Treitschke were considering a work called *Romulus und Remus*. Beethoven confirms the news in a letter to Treitschke, in which he writes, " I intend to write *Romulus* and shall begin within a few days." His remarks to Kotzebue and Körner show that it was just the kind of mythical heroic subject which he wanted; his decision was troubled with no regrets. Strangely enough, the plan fell through, as in the case of *The Ruins of Babylon*, because of a concurrent enterprise. Another operatic composer,

P

Johann Evangelist Fuss, established a prior claim to the subject. It is not surprising that, under these circumstances, Beethoven lost his eagerness for composition. The discouraging episode had an amusing close, for it brought Beethoven a communication from one Dr. Helmuth Winter, in whom, on his own showing, "a very wild and stormy poetic imagination was innate," and who offered him several operatic texts, calculated to "cleave a way to glorious immortality for the musician. If the music of Shakespeare and Schiller inspires you, you must have been born for my poems."

Beethoven seems to have been less interested by Winter's promising offers than by a text by Rudolph von Berge entitled *Bacchus, a great lyrical opera in three acts*, which his boyhood's friend, Amenda, sent him from Courland in March 1815 with a letter, full of exaggerated commendation. Beethoven considered it very seriously. He even made a few notes upon the work, such as " It must be derived from the Bacchus motive," and, elsewhere, " Discords, perhaps not resolved throughout the opera, or quite differently ; not to be thought of in the refined music of these days—the subject must be treated pastorally throughout." These ideas appear to have come to him gradually as he read the poem. The whole project, however, was laid aside in favour of others, and finally forgotten.

Beethoven's attention was now directed to Berlin. *Fidelio* was performed there and proved an unexpected success, Frau Milder-Hauptmann singing in it. On January 6th, 1816, Beethoven wrote the *artiste* a long letter of thanks in which he mentioned fresh plans. " If you would ask Baron de la Motte Fouqué on my behalf to think of a good subject for opera, one that might suit you too, you would do a great service to me and to the German stage. I would like to write exclusively for the Berlin theatre, for I shall never bring off an opera here with these niggardly directors. Answer me soon, as soon as possible, very quickly, as quickly as possible, immediately, and say whether this is practicable." He cannot express his eagerness forcibly enough. " As soon as I have got your answer, I will write also to Baron de la Motte Fouqué. Your influence in Berlin will certainly make it easy for me to write an opera for the Berlin Theatre, with a special rôle for you, and on good terms—only answer me soon, so that I can arrange about my other scribblings."

This attempt to get a commission to write an opera for the Berlin stage was fruitless, and for a time Beethoven desisted in his hunt for a text. The legal case with his nephew's mother, household worries, and finally, some of the great works of the late period, probably kept him too fully occupied. It is also possible that operatic plans dating from this period have been lost. A remarkable entry in the diary for 1820 shows that he had by no means lost his ambition to do work for the stage and was still thinking of it even during the composition of the *Missa solemnis*. He writes, " To compose poetry myself, to copy the metre of the opera, etc., or else a good text-book." When one considers the little sonnet to Bettina, the only known example of Beethoven's poetry, one can scarcely regret that he abandoned the bold project of acting as his own librettist.

Beethoven's plans for opera became less numerous. He grew less enterprising, more mistrustful, and the eagerness with which he at first received a suggested subject quickly gave place to indifference. Anschütz's story of his *Macbeth* proposals belongs to this period and clearly shows Beethoven's increasing disinclination to embark on a big dramatic work. A proposal made by Rochlitz at the instigation of the publishers, Breitkopf & Härtel, met with the same fate. When visiting Beethoven in 1822 Rochlitz wrote down a wish that he would write music for *Faust*, as he had done for *Egmont*. " He read it. ' Ha ! ' cried he, throwing up his hand, ' that would be a piece of work ! That would be worth doing ! ' He went on for a time in this strain, sketched out his ideas immediately, and not at all badly, staring the while at the ceiling with head thrown back. ' But,' he soon began, ' I have been thinking for some time of three other big works. They are well advanced—in my head, you understand. I must get these off my hands first ; two great symphonies, and the other—an oratorio. That will take a long time, and then, you see, for some time back I have found it hard to bring myself to write. I sit and think and think ; I have it, yet I can't get it down on paper. I am afraid of beginning these great works. Once started all goes well '—and so he continued for a long time. So I am left in doubt ; but the idea certainly pleased him and we may hope that he will not lose sight of it."

Like most of these plans, the *Faust* project got no further than this first hasty conception. After an interval of several years *Fidelio* was revived in Vienna and once more brought Beethoven into touch with the theatre. This time it was the management, not the composer, who asked for operatic compositions. An adaptation of *The Ruins of Athens*, by Grillparzer, was considered and several other projects discussed. Count Moritz Lichnowsky made a special effort to keep Beethoven's interest in opera alive. He entered simultaneously into negotiations with the author of the *Ahnfrau* and with the wife of a certain Major Neumann. The latter proposed " a great and beautiful subject " which was " also somewhat romantic," *Alfred the Great*. Neither this proposal, nor a text by Beethoven's friend Friedrich August Kanne, nor an adaptation of the *Weihe des Hauses* under the title of the *Apotheosis in the Temple of Jupiter Ammon*, by the historian, Johann Sporschil, had any result; and a like fate attended negotiations about a text by Schlegel, and about an adaptation of one of Voltaire's tragedies or of *Fiesko*, the outcome of suggestions made by friends to whom Beethoven had spoken of his desire for a subject from antiquity.

With Grillparzer, however, things went a little further. Instead of an adaptation of the *Ruins*, the schemes for two original operas were advanced by Grillparzer, at the suggestion of the directors of the theatre. " Among various subjects for drama," he writes in his memoirs, " which I had marked out for future treatment, were two which seem particularly adapted for opera. One of them had to do with passion in its most extreme manifestations ; but, besides the fact that I knew no woman-singer equal to the principal rôle, I did not wish to give Beethoven occasion, by the seduction of an almost diabolical subject, to go any nearer to the extreme limits of music, which already loomed before him like dangerous abysses."

Despite these anxieties, Grillparzer discussed the plot with Beethoven more than once, and even touched upon matters of detail. The subject was the Bohemian legend of Drahomira, but it was provisionally set aside in favour of a second scheme, the *Märchen von der schönen Melusine*. " I excluded the reflective element as far as possible," writes Grillparzer, " and by giving prominence to the choruses, powerful finales and an almost melodramatic third act, I did my best to suit the peculiarities of the style of Beethoven's last period."

Grillparzer's earlier remark about "the extreme limits of music which loomed like dangerous abysses" is in itself sufficient to raise a doubt as to whether the poet who believed that he was accommodating himself to "the peculiarities of the style of Beethoven's last period" really understood them. His choice of the story of Melusine, which, by his own showing, he did not discuss with Beethoven before submitting it to the management, strengthens the suspicion that he was astray in his judgment of the composer. The text of Melusine is soaked in the "magic" which Beethoven had already objected to in *Brada-mante*, and which appealed to him less and less as he grew older. Thus, *Melusine* suffered the fate of all previous *libretti*. Beethoven considered it, declared himself ready to undertake it, discussed details of treatment at length with the author and, in the end, abandoned this last and most debated of his operatic projects.

Chance may have had something to do with this decision. Schlesinger, a Berlin publisher, came to Vienna about that time, and upon his return spoke of Beethoven's project to the manager, Count Bruhl. Bruhl, who was artistically one of the soundest of Berlin managers, sent the following letter to Beethoven in April 1826. "The music-dealer Schlesinger tells me that you, highly respected Sir, would not be averse to write a German opera for the Berlin Theatre. I am prepared to take up the offer with the greatest willingness, for the theatre which I direct cannot but achieve honour in producing a work specially composed for it by a man who stands so high in the world of art as yourself. Herr Grillparzer's text of ' *Die schöne Melusine*,' of which Herr Schlesinger also spoke to me, seems to me to offer a wealth of matter to an imaginative copmoser. My one doubt is occasioned by the fact that we already possess an opera by Herrn von Fouqué and Hoffmann, which treats of the same story, the well-known and popular *Undine*. On this ground alone, I could have wished that you, Sir, had had some other project in mind which Herr Grillparzer might have worked up;

on this account it would be only with the greatest unwillingness that I would undertake to produce the *Melusine*, otherwise so suitable and charming. I humbly beg you, Sir, to be so kind as to inform me of your view of these circumstances, and to accept the assurance of my particular and most sincere respect."

Apparently Beethoven made no reply to this letter, but there is no doubt that it increased his prejudice against *Melusine*. Kalischer has given a minute account of the tedious negotiations with Grillparzer which lasted some three years. Many interesting remarks were made on both sides, as, for instance, Grillparzer's proposal that each deed of enchantment by Melusine should be accompanied by the same music, and many general discussions upon operatic composition. It got no further than words, however, and among Beethoven's notes and sketches there is not one which can with any certainty be connected with *Melusine*.

With the breakdown of this scheme, the story of Beethoven's operatic plans comes to an end, not many months before his death. Negotiations with Kanne about an adaptation of Goethe's *Claudine* and certain talks with Rellstab about subjects for opera are not to be taken seriously into account. An announcement by Marx that Beethoven intended to compose an Italian opera after Schiller's *Bürgschaft*, for the impresario Barbaja's company when it was playing in Vienna, upon the condition that Weigl was to write the music for the marriage scene in the second act, since he, Beethoven, "had no taste for that form of blessedness," is clearly to be taken as a joke. If Beethoven ever said any such thing (and Schindler disputes it) it must have been one of those somewhat grim jests which he liked to play off upon his associates. He must gradually have realised that a text to suit him was not to be had. He had spared no pains to find one, and there had been no lack of goodwill on the part of librettists, and the total lack of result must be attributed to the impossibility of the task. Beethoven wanted drama and was offered opera. His rejection of every operatic project after *Fidelio* shows that he recognised the inadequacy of this hybrid artistic form ; but the fact that he continued his search so long shows that he was not fully alive to the main differences between opera and the drama which he wanted. His only finished opera, *Fidelio*, affords

further proof of this. Apart from its significance in the history
of musical development it played an important part in Beethoven's
career as a composer, for it led him to the only form of dramatic
music really natural to him, the dramatic overture.

The failure of *Fidelio* is very frequently attributed to the
unfavourable circumstances under which it was first performed
on November 20th, 1805. Can this position be successfully
maintained? It is true that many of Beethoven's friends and
patrons were not in Vienna at the time, and that the audience
consisted largely of French officers; but are we to believe that
this audience condemned the opera out of prejudice against its
unusualness? Were not the French particularly competent
judges of opera and, supposing them not to know German, must
it not have been a favourable circumstance that the original
Leonora was very well known in France?

A study of *Leonora* (as Beethoven wished it to be called), in its
original form, makes one wonder if it could have passed muster
before *any* audience. If it had been better performed before an
audience largely composed of members of Beethoven's circle, it
might with luck have brought him a success due to personal
esteem for its composer; but such success could have been but
momentary. Weaknesses in the work itself, not unfortunate
circumstances, were to blame.

The text of *Leonora* belongs (as the Viennese correspondent to
the Stuttgart *Morgenblatt für gebildete Stände* of April 1807
puts it) to the type of "the 'pain and torment' opera, which
Herr Sonnleithner has introduced to the stage of his country
through the medium of more or less bad translations." Its
contents are characterised as "ingenuous" and it is described
as "a story of the liberation of a prisoner, such as has been the
mode since the appearance of Cherubini's *Water-Carrier*." As
these words show, the "Rettungsstuck" (rescue piece), as Marx
calls it, was no novelty to opera-goers of those days, and, after
being the fashion for a short time, had fallen into discredit. It
was introduced to Viennese audiences in 1802 at the performance of Cherubini's *Water-Carrier*. The author of this much-
admired book, J. N. Bouilly, also wrote *Leonora*. Bouilly had
administered a department near Tours during the Terror, and
the freely adapted subjects which he used in his two most famous

texts, the *Water-Carrier* and *Leonora,* were drawn in substance from incidents within his own experience. In *Leonora* he transferred the scene to Spain. Pierre Gaveaux, composer and singer at the *Théâtre Faydeau* and the first Parisian " Florestan," composed the music for Bouilly's *Leonora.* The work was amazingly successful and the text was translated into German and Italian. The Italian version, which was composed by Ferdinand Paër and performed at Dresden on October 3rd, 1804, was very freely adapted to suit the needs of Italian opera. The German version, the work of Joseph Ferdinand von Sonnleithner, a musical amateur with wide intellectual interests, at that time secretary to the Court Theatre, was closer to the original French. He preserved the songs for the most part as they were, but increased the musical numbers by adaptations of the dialogue, and expanded the first finale (which in Bouilly's version merely introduced the Prisoners' chorus) into a whole scene ; so that the German *Leonora* has eighteen pieces of music in place of the twelve in the French *libretto.*

Sonnleithner was thus able to divide the opera into three acts, a divergence from the original which greatly influenced the fate of the work upon the stage. The action allowed for only one tensely dramatic scene, the struggle between Leonora and Pizarro for Florestan. Through the postponement of this scene to Act III, the exposition became inordinately lengthy and tedious. The first act of Sonnleithner's text had only a few aimless *genre* scenes between Marcelline, Fidelio, Jaquino and Rocco. The second act was enlivened a little by the entry of Pizarro and the chorus of soldiers ; but dramatic contrasts and conflicts were wanting. Not till the Dungeon scene does the composer get a chance of showing why he decided to compose upon the text.

What Beethoven asked of an operatic text was emotional heights and depths on the heroic scale, extraordinary intensity of passion, directed to extremes of wickedness or of virtue and self-sacrifice, the absolute concentration of the characters upon their goal, whether good or evil. His interest was centred upon the strife and passions of the principal figures. He had none of Mozart's endless skill in characterisation, neither did he care for themes of the supernatural or of romantic enchantment, in which, as he complained to Collin, " emotion and intellect must so often be put to sleep." Beethoven's very human art sought to present the problems of human nature on a realistic basis, and the later romantic opera, with its emphasis upon superhuman influences, its substitution of dreamy enchantment for strong emotion, had no appeal for so direct and definite a mind as Beethoven's. He was too manly and vigorous for the sickly magic of romantic poetry, too full of a sense of human responsibility to allow to supernatural powers any decisive influence on human fate, and he regarded the drama as an imaginative intensification of the struggles of real life. For this reason the *Water-Carrier* and the *Vestal* seemed to him the two best texts for opera ; and, failing these, he took a text nearly allied to Cherubini's work, and later sought for mythical subjects, urged on by his longing for such a great, simple and heroic poem as he judged Spontini's *Vestal* to be.

We now see why he chose the text of *Leonora*. Bouilly's book gave Beethoven just what he sought—a realistic plot in which even the arrival of the Minister of State as *deus ex machina* is given a reason and an air of probability. In accordance with Beethoven's religious views, divine providence takes the place of superstition. Each character is under the influence of an emotion which drives him to the extremes of good or ill and typifies some simple human passion, love of freedom, the most exalted faithfulness in the good, and demoniacal vindictiveness in the bad. These contrasts, presented without any attempt at individualisation, as abstract emotional principles, were enough for Beethoven. They gave him opportunity for a presentation of elementary human emotions in music. Concentrating on this idea, he overlooked the inadequacy of the *libretto*, the bad poetry, the superfluity of unimportant episodes, the serious lack of dramatic force.

Beethoven's music could disguise the weakness of the poetry, but not the want of stage technique. With the intention of overcoming this, the work was twice revised, once immediately after the first performance in December 1805, and again on the occasion of fresh rehearsals in the spring of 1814. Otto Jahn, and subsequently Erich Prieger, have summarised the changes made. The alterations in the text are very simple. The second revision, by von Breuning, consisted in a further shortening of the work. He cut down the three acts to two, compressing the first and second into one by leaving out two numbers (the trio " *Ein Mann ist bald genommen* " and the duet " *Um in der Ehe froh zu leben* "), and considerably shortening others. The original third act, likewise considerably cut, thus became the second. Confused by much advice, Beethoven criticised the work too severely, but at that time he was probably too near the original to be able to revise the work organically.

By good fortune, the work did not finally crystallise in this form, for, after the second performance on April 10th, 1806, it was withdrawn owing to a quarrel between the composer and the manager. In 1814, as a result of the impression made by Beethoven's successes during the Congress, three singers of the Kärnthnertor Theatre asked for the score, and Beethoven realised that the work in its shortened form was in reality even less satisfactory than in its dramatically impracticable first condition. By good luck he found a sympathetic collaborator in the secretary of the Theatre, Georg Friedrich Treitschke. The result was a third version, called, against Beethoven's wishes, *Fidelio*. The two-act form was retained, but both acts were worked up to a better climax by a broader treatment of the finales, that in the second act even necessitating a change of scene. The passages experimentally cut out of the first act in the second revision were finally discarded, whereas the preliminary recitative of the great Leonora air was newly written and composed, as also the closing part of the Florestan aria.

Eight years had passed since the previous performance of the work, so that it is not surprising that Beethoven, besides these important alterations, also slightly modified many pieces which remained broadly as before, struck out unnecessary repetitions in the text, simplified passages too instrumentally conceived, and retouched the rhythm and instrumentation. These alterations differed favourably from those made for the second revision, being undertaken for artistic reasons, whereas the latter had merely aimed at shortening the work in performance. Nevertheless Beethoven could not in 1814 think himself back into the emotional and expressional stage of 1805, so that stylistic unevennesses were bound to appear, and the work lost some of its spontaneity. A few points taken at random will show what relationship the various *Leonora* scores bear to one another. A comparison of the *adagio* of the Florestan aria in the two first editions with the same in *Fidelio* emphasises the latter's increased freedom of declamation, its bolder harmonies, while the flow of melody is undoubtedly more naïve and natural in the earlier work. Throughout the score of *Fidelio*, melodic expression is sacrificed to dramatic. The treatment of speech has become more broad and definite. The various settings of the words " *Tödt erst sein Weib* " (" First kill his wife ") exemplify this. In the two first editions they are set to a leap of a third from G to B, in the pianoforte arrangement issued in 1810 from G to B flat accompanied by full orchestra, while in the 1814 version the cry is expanded to a mighty leap of a fifth from E flat to B flat and left to the voice alone. The orchestral portion, too, is enriched by characteristic touches. In the A minor duet in the Dungeon scene, while Rocco and Leonora open the grave, Beethoven has added a bass figure, portraying the rolling back of the stone, while the piece is for the rest almost unchanged.

Artistically, the shortened version bears no comparison with the other two, of which the first excels in freshness and spontaneity, though bound up with a badly arranged text, while the last has the advantage not only of a better *libretto*, but of a closer rendering of the words, a more carefully graduated dynamic and instrumental colour, which compensate for some loss of freshness and artistic unity. As regards dramatic treatment and expression it is a notable advance on the original score.

" This business of the opera is the most tedious in the world. I am dissatisfied with most of it and almost every piece in it is patched. It is a very different matter when one can give oneself up to one's own free reflections or inspiration." We can sympathise with this sigh of Beethoven's, when we follow step by step the story (only outlined here) of his one opera. He speaks with good cause of the " crown of martyrdom," which he won thereby and thanks the faithful Treitschke for having helped him " to save a few valuables from the wreck." It was no empty form of thanks. Beethoven's first *Leonora* would have survived as an admired curiosity in the history of German opera, but the *Fidelio*, thanks to the united efforts of Treitschke and the composer, is a living entity on the stage to-day. The last revision

had the practical result of making the piece " playable," and the
artistic result of intensifying its dramatic forcefulness.

In the history of opera, Beethoven's *Fidelio* must be classified
as a work with some elements of style which point back to the
lyrical opera, others which belong to more ambitious forms of
dramatic music. At that period such a hybrid style was not
uncommon, and, a little earlier, all German opera had taken the
modest form of lyrical opera. Gluck wrote his more important
works for a Parisian audience, and Mozart, who early in his
career attempted to create a German opera in *The Seraglio*, did
not pursue the plan till his last work. Apart from a few early
attempts, such as Holzbauer's *Günther von Schwarzburg*, *The
Magic Flute* was the only work of lasting value that applied the
ripened methods of Italian opera to the German stage. Mozart
attempted to blend something of the German lyrical drama with
the Italian form and Beethoven carried the idea further with
the help of French models, which were of a freer and more
declamatory style than the Italian *cantabile* form. Cherubini's
bourgeois tragedy, too, in contrast to the heroic operas of Gluck
and Spontini, was a stylistic hybrid, employing the couplet, the
chanson, melodrama and dialogue, as well as broadly planned
drama. In a certain sense, the introduction of these smaller
forms was made necessary by the aesthetic character of a type
of opera which was in course of development from the commonplace to the sphere of high tragedy.

Beethoven, accordingly, like his models, incorporated elements
of the lyrical opera in his work. That these spoil the unity of
impression is perhaps due to their length and elaboration, for
even in the third version they occupy a large part of the first
act. Be that as it may, there is no doubt that they are the
product of Beethoven's skilled musicianship rather than of his
imagination, and that the whole force of his personality is not
brought to bear until the second act. These pieces must not,
however, be undervalued. Although they did not fire his
imagination, he made up for want of inspiration by extremely
careful work. Apart from preliminary sketches, no fewer than
three different and complete compositions for Marcelline's aria,
"*O wär ich schon mit dir vereint*," bear witness to the seriousness
with which Beethoven approached work which interested him

but little ; and his effort to get exact expression. But they also show with what difficulty he worked on these songs. The duet, " *Jetzt, Schätzchen, jetzt sind wir allein,*" the two numbers, trio and duet afterwards deleted, and Rocco's *Song of Gold* all deal with the petty world of Marcelline, Jaquino and Rocco, to whose vicissitudes, sorrows and joys Beethoven was unwillingly obliged to turn his attention. He managed to produce some charming and pleasant music even here, but he could not bring to the task the sense of loving participation which an artist should bring to creative work.

From the moment that Leonora appears, we discern a sympathetic change. As Marx has acutely pointed out, her very presence lifts the work to a higher level, the conversation of the other three becomes finer, the range of thought more lofty. At the idea of Leonora, Beethoven's imagination begins to take fire and burns steadily brighter. The quartet canon—one of the most admired numbers in the whole score since its first performance—takes us at a stride into the true sphere of Beethoven's art, while the trio " *Gut Söhnchen, gut,*" with its lively characterisation of the three personalities—Marcelline gentle and anxious, Leonora full of woe yet facing the future with courage, and the kindly, fatherly Rocco—are nearly on the same level of excellence.

The entrance of Pizarro and the soldiers brings a change of mood. Here the librettist has made it very difficult for Beethoven to get his effect. Pizarro is an uninteresting villain ; his meaningless outbursts of rage, the lack of any penetrating conception of his character, are a standing weakness in the scenes where he appears, although Beethoven has made a strong effort to paint the character of the tyrant. The principal key of the Pizarro aria is a forbidding D minor, which with the sinuous violin theme of the opening, the eerie figures for the strings in the middle section, and the diabolically triumphant chords, well portray a villainous outbreak of fury, and grip the hearer despite the deficiencies of the verse.

The succeeding duel between Pizarro and Rocco is more convincing. The contrast between the two characters is strongly brought out by the music—one that of a gentle, vacillating subordinate, the other of an impatient tyrant, sometimes cunning and persuasive, sometimes imperative and overbearing. Beethoven paints the beast-of-prey instincts of such as Pizarro with great vividness in the furtive unison passages of " *Nun eile rasch und munter zu jenem Mann hinunter* " and " *dann werd ich schnell vermummt mich in den Kerker schleichen.*" He follows each turn of thought with exactitude. He hits off Pizarro's pretended probity at the beginning of the duet " *Dir wird ein Glück zuteile* " as explicitly as Rocco's somewhat sentimental emotionalism in " *Verhungernd in den Ketten ertrug er lange Pein.*" It is obvious that Beethoven had no difficulty in entering imaginatively into his characters, but only portentous issues really aroused his interest.

The increasing interest of the work, hitherto gradual, now becomes very marked and the recitative of the great Leonora aria seems to belong rather to the emotional heights of the Dungeon scene than to the introductory first act, and consequently rather overpowers its surroundings. In the original version, its place was occupied by a recitative in E minor ("*Ach, brich noch nicht, du mattes Herz,*" a suppressed cry of pain from the suffering Leonora, but Treitschke's emendation, which is theatrically more effective, brought about drastic changes in the introduction. The wealth of original motives in the great Leonora aria, the variety of instrumental colour, from the stormy figures for the strings, to the " wave-like " motion of the basses and the " rainbows" of the wood-wind, the free treatment of tempos, rhythms and keys, the blend of melody and recitative in song, are clues to what Beethoven's methods might have been, had he attempted another opera. After this powerful exposition the sentimental E major *adagio*, " *Komm Hoffnung*," seems to be a mere bridge passage to the *allegro*, which, with its boldly ascending trumpet theme, its strikingly prominent passage for three horns and a bassoon, attains a heroic level which few but the composer of the *Eroica* could have attempted.

It is the only solo scene for Leonora and undoubtedly the most important in the whole opera, although its position is not particularly well chosen from a dramatic point of view. Treitschke's emendation has somewhat confused the conception of the heroine's character, emphasising heroic, at the expense of feminine, traits. This somewhat previous unmasking of " Fidelio " is in strong contrast with previous scenes, in which both author and musician have portrayed her more simply, and it breaks the unity of the first act. A painfully commonplace dialogue follows, bringing us back to earth after passionate ecstasy and introducing the finale.

It is after this point that Treitschke's most important work begins. In the two previous versions, the chorus with which the scene opens had no connection with the action. Pizarro's entry was not brought about by the prisoners, and his rage was directed against Rocco, because the latter had not fulfilled his command to go to Florestan's dungeon and dig a grave there. The finale ended feebly, both as drama and music, with an address by Pizarro to the watch (represented by the chorus) and distinctly reminiscent of his previous aria in the scene of his wrath.

At the last revision this close was cut out and the finale devised on a new plan. Rocco takes it upon himself to have the cell doors opened, thereby incurring the wrath of Pizarro, who, hearing of the event, hurries up to order the prisoners to be secured once more. By this change, the entry of the prisoners is given a clearer connection with the action, and the composer has an opportunity for a better formal rounding off of the finale ; and the lack of dramatic climaxes—a deficiency which it was impossible at this stage to supply—was compensated, to some extent, by a certain lyrical unity between beginning and end— the prisoners' hopeful acclamations of the sun, and their sub- sequent sorrowful and resigned farewell to the light of day. The other solo scenes take their places between these two choral scenes. Rocco's conversation with Leonora, the brief appearance of Marcelline and Jaquino, who anxiously announce Pizarro's arrival, and the equally brief scene with Pizarro, which acts as a bridge passage to the final chorus of prisoners. As regards both drama and music, the finale hinges on the duet between Rocco and Leonora. Here Beethoven proceeds with the character- isation of Leonora as begun in the canon and continued in the trio, portraying her, not as in the preceding solo scene as a virile and forceful heroine, but as a woman, full of fears and terrors, doubting her own courage up to the last moment, and but slowly and shudderingly bringing herself to accomplish her purpose. Leonora's inspired cry of " *Noch heute* " (To-day !) carries us

immediately to that exalted level upon which the holiest feelings
stand revealed in all their purity. Leonora's joy at the thought
that she dare visit the secret dungeon, her returning realisation
of the difficulties of her task, her transition from triumph to dread,
"*Vielleicht das Grab des Gatten graben*," are most movingly
expressed. The few moments of sunshine are soon darkened.
Minor keys replace the major and a restlessly modulating E flat
major mirrors Leonora's mixed emotions of terror and determination. The very shades of the dungeon seem to be painted
in the music, and not till the quiet close, "*O säumen wir denn
länger nicht*," is a more courageous and self-reliant mood established.

Of the two choruses of prisoners which frame this scene
the first appeared in the original version. The response of the
prisoners, freed for a brief space, to the living light of the sun, the
longing for the fresh air of heaven, is portrayed with most moving
naturalism. A solemn greeting, tinged with sadness, to the
light, from within the narrow walls of the prison court, represents
the faint flicker of hope in the prisoners' breasts at even a glimpse
of the sky.

In the first chorus the prison walls seem to part for a moment,
in the closing chorus to shut in the prisoners once more. Joy
and disappointment, hope and despair are persuasively given
in characteristic intervals. Musical means are more richly
employed than in the former chorus. Solos are added to the
male chorus, in which two female voices seem to blend a
message of comfort and hope with the sorrowful crowd of
prisoners. The two choruses are not especially lofty or intense,
but they serve Beethoven for providing us with yet another
glimpse into the secrets of the human heart.

Despite many beauties, the first act lacks effective unity.
The mixture of relevancies and irrelevancies, the long stretches of
dialogue which connect the musical numbers prevent any single,
decided and evenly developed mood from being established.
Despite certain limitations, the second act is an advance in
dramatic pointedness and unity of mood on the first, and the
composer found the advantage of this. One can see at once that
from a dramatic point of view, Beethoven identifies himself with
his text more here than in the first act, where dramatic develop-

ment is constantly hindered and he is forced to have recourse to conventional operatic usages. In the second act, he is able to give his imagination free rein and seldom does he fall short of the mark. Apart from a new close to Florestan's aria, alterations in the Dungeon scene are but slight, and the new close was made necessary by the arrangement of the finale as a separate scene.

The act opens with a melancholy instrumental passage, Beethoven choosing the F minor key to paint the horrors of the dungeon. The motives are but slightly indicated and some of them recur in Florestan's subsequent aria. The orchestral imagery is darkly poetic, suggesting fear and horror till a consoling B flat major change enters at the words "*Doch gerecht ist Gottes Wille.*" The rattle of chains in Florestan's aria, supplementing the pictures called up by the instrumental motives, is an example of Beethoven's inclination to tone-painting. He thought so highly of the melody of Florestan's aria, with its mingled sorrow and lofty resignation, that he used it to symbolise the lonely prisoner in each of the three first overtures. To-day only a part of the original version is preserved. In 1814 Florestan had, instead of the present sorrowful F minor *andante*, a superficially more effective close. Treitschke has left us what appears to be an account of this particular alteration. " I expressed my opinion," he writes, " that a man almost dead of starvation ought not to be made to sing *bravura*. We considered this and that, and at last, in his opinion, I hit the nail on the head. I wrote words which represent the last flicker of life's flame before its extinction. ("*Und spür ich nicht linde, sanft säuselnde Luft.*") What I now relate will live in my memory for ever. Beethoven came about seven o'clock in the evening. After we had spoken about other things, he asked how the aria was progressing. It was just finished and I handed it to him. He ran up and down the room, muttering and humming as was his wont instead of singing, and flung the pianoforte open. My wife had often begged him to play in vain ; to-day he set the words in front of him and began the most marvellous improvisations of which, unfortunately, no magic could preserve a record. Out of these he seemed to conjure a motive for the aria. The hours flew and Beethoven

Q

continued to improvise. Supper, which he was to share with us, was brought up but he could not be disturbed. At last very late he embraced me, and refusing a meal, hurried home. Next day the superb piece of music was finished."

The date of the *melodrame* which immediately follows Florestan's last raptures is not so certainly known. Sketches for it are found among the first outlines for *Leonora*, but as no absolutely authentic copy of the original version exists and the second does not contain the *melodrame*, while one of the *melodrame* motives is taken from the later *allegro* of the Florestan aria, it would seem that this piece was not complete till 1814. It certainly forms a valuable addition to the score, not only on account of its wealth of pertinent reminiscent themes, but still more because it expresses a mood in music which would be broken by the intrusion of the speaking voice. The entrance from the everyday world into the underworld of the grave is rendered with the utmost realism and at the same time it leads on to one of the chief pieces in the score, the duet in A minor, " *Nur hurtig fort, nur frisch gegraben.*" Here Beethoven makes wonderful use of the eerie tones of the double-bassoon, and the seldom used trombones add a mystic effect to the ghoulish scene. The dull evenness of the accompanying triplets, the mournful motive of the double-basses (without violoncelli) and of the double-bassoons, the icy wind harmonies, the whispering *parlando* of Rocco, all contribute to a picture of tense monotony, to which Leonora's agonised words gradually give dreadful life. Beethoven has grasped the salient points of the situation with incomparable art, the noiseless, apparently monotonous, activity of the two grave-diggers combined with tremendous mental tension, the terror of what the next moment may bring. The contrast between Rocco's anxious activity and Leonora's dawning, heroic resolution, " *Wer du auch seist ich will dich retten,*" is keenly drawn. After the momentary brightening through the C major change, there is a return to the mournful A minor and the scene closes in a ghostly unison of vocal and orchestral parts. Who but Beethoven could have attempted a piece so moving in its apparent simplicity ?

The A major trio which follows does not attain the level of the duet, but this is accounted for by its contents. Beethoven might well have been inspired, by the subject of Florestan's thanks for the succour brought him, to a song of noble and eager gratitude, an effective contrast in its free flowing melody to the constraint of the A minor duet, but there is no greatness of conception in the words, the emotion borders on false pathos, and the piece is inferior by comparison with the neighbouring numbers.

The two closing pieces, the quartet which decides Florestan's fate, and the duet which expresses the triumph of rescuer and rescued, reach a notably higher level. Next to the A minor duet, these are the most important—and intellectually the definitive—portions of the opera, and if Beethoven seems to stand in need of pardon for setting the text of *Leonora*, these three pieces are ample justification. They even reconcile one for the moment to Sonnleithner and incline one to view his many sins and deficiencies in a more favourable light. We have to thank him that the quartet was written; for in the original French the whole scene with Pizarro is spoken.

Beethoven saw that the centre of gravity for the whole work lay here. The scene which kindled his imagination was that which brings face to face the bloodthirsty tyrant, the champion of truth unafraid of death, and the woman who saves her husband and gives death to the murderer. Keeping this goal before him, he follows the vagaries of the librettist undismayed, and arrives here at the heart and soul of the drama, of *his* Leonora drama. Whether the actors in this drama are inspired by heroism, hate or love, they have this in common that the will of each is tested to the uttermost. In this temperamental maelstrom, this clash of opposing forces, Beethoven was in his natural creative element. No psychological analyses of individual character were necessary, but merely the expression of extremes of typical good and evil. The various means by which this is accomplished are very engrossing. While Pizarro's speech is for the most part given in chromatically augmented or diminished intervals, later giving place to abrupt sevenths, Florestan's words are clothed in pure, straightforward major harmonies. Leonora's speech varies greatly according to its significance. When she is speaking to Pizarro it approaches the latter's style in frequency of wide intervals, but becomes harmonically purer and melodically clearer when she addresses Florestan. This dramatic and declamatory treatment of the voice-parts necessitated a thematically independent instrumental part. The descending scale motive with which the piece opens, and which, owing to the use made of it, may be styled the Pizarro motive, the further development of thoughts barely hinted at in the voice-parts, the contrast obtained between different groups of instruments during the dialogue between Pizarro and Leonora, the independent exposition of rhythmic and melodic instrumental motives, all give the orchestra an importance other than merely subsidiary and assign to it a distinct place among the other actors in the drama.

The first part of the quartet is very adroitly developed towards a climax. Three times Pizarro, triumphant, presses in upon Florestan and three times Leonora throws herself between the murderer and his victim. With each of her efforts the tension increases; the action becomes fiercer from the first " *Zurück* " ("Back!") to the second " *Tödt erst sein Weib* " ("First kill his wife!") and the final raising of the pistol. This last brings the climax—the next moment must be decisive.

Here Beethoven relies on a telling realistic effect. Immediately after Leonora's third interruption, a bugle sounds, announcing the advent of the Minister of State. Providence has spoken. A tremendous revulsion of feeling takes place. Excitement roused to fever pitch gives place to paralysed inaction. The flutes and violoncelli announce a prayerful melody, while the voice parts utter boundless thankfulness and suppressed wrath, as it were, muted. A second signal sounds, and the voice of Jaquino, heard from above, breaks the spell which weighs upon the four in the dungeon, and emotional tension finds expression in a broadly reminiscent closing movement rising to a *stretto*-like climax.

Instead of the former dramatic and vivid recitative, a short dialogue now leads over to the jubilant duet which is the second oldest portion of the score. There exists a pianoforte sketch for a trio between Volivia, Sartagones and Porus, " *Nie war ich so froh wie heute, niemals fühlt ich diese Freude.*" In key and time, in melody and details of accompaniment, it agrees almost note for note with the beginning of the *Fidelio* duet and must therefore have been composed before the piece in *Leonora*. In 1803

Beethoven undertook to compose an opera—the text of which is unknown—for Schikaneder. The trio is apparently the sole surviving relic of this unfinished work, the main theme of which was so good that Beethoven adapted it for the *Fidelio* duet. For the sake of the melody he disregards the requirements of metre. The curious doubling of " *namen* " in " *namen—namenlose Freude* " and the unusual accentuation of " *lose* " show how the new words were forced to suit the old melody. The value of the piece is in no way destroyed by these little irregularities. What Beethoven sought to express—joy unbounded, a moment in which all possible wishes find overwhelming fruition—is expressed, and petty corrections of text were rendered unnecessary. The meaning of the words becomes altogether secondary ; they merely carry the vocal and instrumental poetry of the music, which absorbs the feeble lines and infinitely transcends them.

Treitschke insisted that the curtain should fall here, knowing that after such a tremendous hymn of joy, so perfect a climax, a further closing scene could only produce anticlimax. This excellent idea of finishing the work with Leonora's and Florestan's song of freedom was set aside for practical reasons, but Treitschke determined at least to preserve the grand unity of the Dungeon scene and to give independent value to a finale by introducing (in contradistinction to the first two versions) a change of scene and placing the action in an open place before the prison.

In its present form the finale has three main divisions. The first, which was all new work in 1814, comprises the opening chorus " *Heil sei dem Tag* " and the address of the State Minister to the people and the prisoners. The beautiful words newly added here, " *Es grüsst der Bruder seine Brüder, und kann er helfen, hilft er gern* " (A brother greets his brothers, and if he can help them, gladly will he do so !), must have awakened a particularly sympathetic response in Beethoven and his contemporaries. The second division consists of the entrance of Florestan and Leonora, Rocco's declaration, the sentence upon Pizarro and Florestan's liberation, some of the subjects being taken from earlier scores and given in a revised form. The third division has a direct connection with earlier versions. It opens with the oldest piece in the whole opera, the moving *ensemble* in F major, " O

Gott, welch ein Augenblich." Like the theme of the G major duet, this piece, which one would believe to have sprung from the deepest comprehension of the particular situation, was taken from another work, a work, moreover, of Beethoven's youth, the funeral cantata composed in 1790 on the death of Joseph II. Here again Beethoven keeps to the key of the original. The words are markedly different, yet in each case the underlying mood is that of gravity in the face of great events. Beethoven must not be accused of making unscrupulous use of old ideas out of indolence or opportunism, but he had the economy of the artist nature and could not let a good idea of his, however old, perish with forgotten work, but drew it forth at the exactly suitable moment and gave it its due place of honour. One of the most serious and deplorable effects of revision was to give this moving and powerful *ensemble* in abbreviated form only in the *Fidelio* score.

The almost religious mood of this prelude to the closing *ensemble* is followed by Leonora's song of the triumph of married love and faithfulness. This is a shout of jubilation, ever rising to greater heights of ecstasy, and forms an instrumental and vocal companion piece to the finale of the fifth symphony, also in Beethoven's key of victory—C major—which affords a similar sense of irresistible might, of a pressing forward to eternal goals, of the heart-beat of the centuries.

An attempt to estimate the artistic value of *Fidelio* reveals it as a great but unequal piece of work. In many pasages we have Beethoven at his best, but a mingling of various component parts betrays organic weakness and destroys the unity of the whole. The librettist must not alone be blamed for this. The text was far from perfect and unfortunately it failed in just such ways as to emphasize Beethoven's weaknesses as a dramatic composer; but these weaknesses were inherent in his nature. His interest in the situation to be presented was not objective and material, but subjective; and this subjectivity was the measure both of his greatness and of his limitations. Unlike Mozart, or even Cherubini, he had not the gift of entering keenly into all the many small, often petty, details of the outward course of events, and of seeing the eternal in the insignificant and transitory. Beethoven did not possess the true dramatist's gift of vitalising all he touched. With him, artistic interest presupposed human interest; and for this reason—these conclusions are justified by *Fidelio*—whatever other operas he had composed would probably have contained great dramatic scenes but no continuous drama. He instinctively sought to give prominence to what appealed to him, and to arrange his characters in order of ethical worth. Where he lacked real interest he tried to make up for it by care and industry, but he could not escape his own limitations; and the disparity of interest became more obvious the more Beethoven tried to disguise it. It was the subjectivity of his genius which gave him his unique place as a composer of instrumental music, of idealistic imaginative music; but it would always have prevented him from achieving the dramatist's firmly outlined representation of life.

We need, therefore, scarcely regret the failure of subsequent operatic plans. The few small works, apart from *Fidelio*, which Beethoven composed for the stage are, with the exception of the overtures, by no means his best. Of the two ballets, one, the *Ritterballett*, must be classed as unimportant juvenile work; while *Prometheus* has little claim on our regard. Riemann has attempted to analyse the whole score as a cycle of variations, but the rhythmic and harmonic analogies between the different pieces are not marked enough to support this daring theory. Moreover, when Beethoven later on composed variations upon the theme of *Prometheus*, pianoforte variations, Op. 35 and the finale of the *Eroica*, which have so much in common with each other, he did not in any sense go back to the alleged variation form of the ballet music. Rhythmic resemblances between the different pieces may be accounted for by the necessity to suit certain dance steps. The value of the work as a whole, despite a few pretty episodes, is too slight to entitle it to detailed analysis here.

The same may be said of music for occasional poems by Kotzebue, *The Ruins of Athens* and *King Stephen*, both of which were written for the opening of the theatre at Budapest. In spite of later republishing and revision they do not "live." A few numbers from the *Ruins* are still heard in the concert room, the *Overture*, the grotesque *Chorus of Dervishes*, the effective *Turkish March* (the theme for which Beethoven took from the Op. 76 pianoforte variations), and the solemn and formal E flat major *March with Chorus*. Of the score of *King Stephen* consisting likewise of nine numbers, the *Overture* alone is now used. The other numbers need not be regretted. " *Weihe des Hauses* " (written for the opening of the *Josephstädter Theater* in 1822) is merely an adaptation of the *Ruins* with the addition of an overture and closing chorus. Passing over certain slight occasional compositions already mentioned, the only remaining piece of relative value in this branch of music is the music for Goethe's *Egmont*.

This music is established from the first upon a high level by the strength of the poetry. Besides the *Overture* and Klärchen's songs which will be discussed later, the best part of the score is the D minor *larghetto* interlude upon Klärchen's death. It is one of the tenderest of Beethoven's tragic pieces. It is simple, almost bald in expression, telling of the end of a life outwardly insignificant but emotionally rich. The monotonous notes of the horns sound like the beat of a failing pulse, while the hopeless, mournful melody of the oboe ends in stammering phrases and is lost in the dark *pizzicati* of the strings. The colouring is entirely sombre. The wood-wind is used without the flute and the violins keep to a low register. The passing of a soul from the light to the world of shadows is mirrored here without tragic emphasis.

Many attempts have been made to adapt the *Egmont* music for concert purposes, and to unite the several parts by explanatory words. These activities, of which even Goethe approved, have met with little success. The best part of the work, the *Overture*, needs no special means to make it appeal to an audience. Not only the *Egmont* overture, but each of Beethoven's overtures is a magnificent summary of the meaning of the dramatic action to follow. The overture is the part of the score in which Beethoven's dramatic powers find purest and most original expression ; it *is* Beethoven's music-drama, and the rest of the score is merely a commentary and enlargement upon it.

Beethoven was not the first to lift the overture above the level of a mere general introduction, and to establish an intellectual connection between the instrumental prelude and the dramatic action to follow. He only perfected developments which had come down from the masters of the ancient Italian opera-symphonies, through Handel to Gluck and Mozart. What distinguishes Beethoven's work from that of his predecessors is the logic with which he pursues his course throughout. Before him, such references to the action were exceptional and no more than vaguely indicative. Beethoven made connection with the action a matter of principle, and used it for all it was worth. He projected the whole spiritual content of the drama into the overture, even to the extent of making the latter seem superfluous. The one-time prelude lost its introductory character and gradually became an independent instrumental drama, a symphonic concerto overture, separated from the stage.

Beethoven arrived at this stage very rapidly; and of his eleven overtures, only the first two—the *Prometheus* and *Leonora No.* 1 overtures—can be classed as " early work." Both of these have definite connections with the ensuing action, but it is only broadly sketched. Particularly in *Prometheus*, the imagination is given little scope. Beethoven had not at the time so fully assimilated the meaning of *Prometheus* and made it his own as later, when he made it the basis of the finale of the *Eroica*. He therefore confined himself to a mere indication of the most obvious contrasts of the action—the lofty ambition of Prometheus, and the mass of mankind, his followers, led by him to happiness.

It is certainly a remarkable coincidence that, of Beethoven's eleven overtures, no fewer than six are written in C major. Perhaps, however, it is no mere coincidence, for a certain similarity of mood must have caused the frequent choice of the same key by so conscious an artist as Beethoven. C major is Beethoven's key of joy, not of wild jubilation which is expressed in D major, nor of ecstatic transport which is in A major, but of a simple, personal sense of victory and success. Beethoven always choses C major to express stately and majestic ideas, as in *Prometheus*, in the *Birthday Overture*, in the *Weihe des Hauses* and in the three great overtures which followed on *Prometheus*, the three *Leonora* overtures. Here the bright and resonant key of C major stands to him for the idea of freedom. Both the C minor symphony and the opera end in this key, and it forms the basis of the introductory instrumental poems.

There are several opinions as to the chronology of the three overtures to *Leonora* and history has not yet been able to decide the question as to their order. As far as the facts are now known, it appears that Schindler's account that Overture No. 1 (Op. 138) was replaced *before* the first performance, despite Nottebohm's contrary opinion, is true. It seems that it was rejected upon the advice of friends, and with Beethoven's concurrence, as too insignificant. Haslinger got possession of the manuscript, but did not publish it until after Beethoven's death, when he issued it as a business speculation, falsely advertising it as part of the remains. It thus appears that this overture was never performed during Beethoven's lifetime. There are no doubts about the other two C major overtures. No. 2 was played at the first performance in 1805, no. 3 at the revival of the opera in March 1806.

What connects the first *Leonora* overture with *Prometheus* is Beethoven's attempt in both instances to contrast the opening and closing moods of the action with each other in the form of prelude and *allegro*, while the catastrophe presented in the action does not appear in the overture. The richer content and greater range of emotional interest in *Leonora* gave Beethoven an immeasurably stronger imaginative impulse than could *Prometheus*. In the *Leonora* overture, his thoughts circle about the two poles of Leonora's woeful search for her beloved, and his joyful liberation by her endeavours. A dominant, sustained by the strings in unison, provides a solemn opening in all three overtures and is followed by a lengthy and unconcluded prelude. Alternately rising and sinking, the parts appear to avoid a definite subject, till at last the violins, after a recitative passage, introduce a faint sad theme in C minor. The subject, however, is not long maintained and at its close a new vigorously ascending motive is developed. It leads on to a powerful and brilliant *allegro* theme. A plaintive secondary theme is mingled with it, but the main subject takes the lead, and after repeated development becomes more restful, and finally dies out in a G major *cadenza*.

The peace of the *allegro* is suddenly broken by abrupt and urgent unison passages, Joy seems to knock at the prison doors and these spring open groaning on their hinges. Florestan's song is heard, not in A flat major, as in the opera and later overtures, but in the more hopeful E flat major key. It changes to

C major, like a gradually awakening hope of freedom ; and then, in the enthusiastically opening repeat, flows into the main part. The plaintive secondary theme reappears with a striking reminiscence of the beginning, the uncertainty of which is now resolved, and finds its goal. An effective coda with a slowly swelling *crescendo*, as often employed by the Mannheim composers and later by Rossini, brings the piece to a brilliant climax. Beethoven has still one more surprise in store. Immediately before the closing bars the *allegro* theme is given once more, as though in the very exhaustion of too much happiness, and is followed by the proud and vigorous closing chords.

This work certainly fulfils its part as an opera-overture in the ordinary sense of the word. It indicates the course of the action, and reflects the inspiration in which the work arose, without giving away the actual events of the drama. It was not conviction of the worthlessness of this overture that made Beethoven proceed, directly it was finished, to compose another. It is possible that during the work he developed a new theory as to the significance of overtures in general, and the symphonic possibilities of the *Leonora* drama in particular. Just as in the *Prometheus* overture, he first grasped the subject from without and later laid bare the imaginative content of his subject in the finale of the *Eroica*, so here, having finished the first overture, which he autographs as " characteristic," he passes on to deal with the inner meaning of the action. He lost interest in Leonora's personality, her feelings before and after the catastrophe, and concentrated upon the symphonic and dramatic development of the catastrophe itself, which he had passed over in the earlier work, and which he now put in the centre of his picture.

Beethoven overlooked the fact that by thus exhausting the dramatic content of his subject he was rendering the subsequent staging and action of the opera superfluous. He ceased to think of creating a suitable introductory atmosphere by means of his overture, or of its place in the opera as an organic whole. He simply saw before him with increasing clearness an instrumental summary of the opera's scattered dramatic moments. With a tremendous effort of genius he concentrated and presented them with all the force of brevity, unhindered by the technical difficulties of the stage.

With this heightened conception of the meaning of an overture, Op. 138 naturally failed to satisfy the composer, though it
was necessary, in that it prepared the way for the later work.
As an artist, Beethoven worked slowly and intensely, arriving,
by way of a study in traditional style, at the original and deep
conception which gave birth to the second overture.

The Florestan aria forms a connecting link between the three
overtures.   This sad song was employed in the first overture as
a contrast to the two joyous *allegro* portions, and very likely was
the immediate cause of Beethoven's determination to write a
second.   Once the thought of Florestan was introduced into the
overture, the idea of making a more impressive and vivid picture
of the unhappy prisoner, of blending the Leonora prelude and
the Florestan *andante* of Op. 138, already similar in mood, into
a single independent whole must have suggested itself to the
composer.

The structure of the *allegro* arose out of a similar reconstruction
of the prelude.   This had to link up the terrible pictures of the
imprisoned sufferer and the events of the Dungeon scene with
the great turn of fortune and the sound of the trumpet which
brought deliverance.   The usual repeat of the " exposition " is
consequently omitted to avoid any interruption of dramatic
development.   Only the beginning of Florestan's song is once
repeated, like a stammered thanksgiving prayer, immediately
followed by the jubilant coda.

Hitherto the development of Beethoven's form of overture is
easy to understand.   A notable advance has been made from a
mere indication of the basic idea of the action in the *Prometheus*
overture to the more imaginative and vivid presentation of the
same in Op. 138, and to a highly significant summary of the
drama's meaning in the *Leonora* overture, no. 2.   Now, however,
comes a surprise.   Beethoven next writes an overture, which,
while note for note allied to *Leonora* overture no. 2, is an attempt
to combine the conquests achieved in this work with the form of
the earlier overture.   The result is an extraordinary, almost
baroque mixture of the two types of overture represented by
Leonora overtures nos. 1 and 2, giving us *Leonora* overture no. 3,
commonly called the " great " overture.

In order to understand how this work arose, it is essential

to bear in mind the story of the various revisions. The overture suffered the same fate as that of the opera score as a whole—it was shortened in order to suit the public taste. The " great " *Leonora* overture is not, as often supposed, an extension or expansion of ideas dealt with in no. 2. On the contrary, it is a compression and condensation of the older work. So severely is the work reduced that the *adagio* of overture no. 3 consists of but twenty bars, and the *allegro*, up to the entrance of the trumpet solo, of but a hundred bars. So far, the new overture answers to the new opera. Like the latter, it is an abridgment of the older version, achieved by drastic cuts and revised instrumentation.

This, however, does not fully cover the ground of the new version of the overture, which has been more often misunderstood than any other part of the score. The reporter of the *Allgemeine Musikalische Zeitung* described it as consisting of " a very long *adagio*, wandering through every key and succeeded by an *allegro* in C major, which is also undistinguished and cannot bear comparison with other instrumental compositions by Beethoven, such as his overture to the ballet of *Prometheus*, for example." The sequence of ideas in this work, its relation to the action, were not grasped by its first hearers, partly because they did not know the opera, and partly because the free imaginative rendering of the action in music, which Beethoven aimed at in overture no. 2, was strange to them and almost incomprehensible. They could not grasp his free treatment of the formal architecture of an overture. Although Beethoven was little inclined to make concessions, the idea must have dawned upon him that it was useless to hope that his contemporaries as a whole would be able to understand overture no. 2 ; but he would not abandon the dramatic plan of the principal portion—it seemed to him absolutely necessary—and, standing between the demands of the public for a clearly constructed overture on the one hand and his own desire for a more dramatic form on the other, he attempted a compromise which should satisfy both. The first half of the new overture, accordingly, consisted of a shortened presentation of the sequence of ideas in overture no. 2, while in the second half, Beethoven introduced a repetition—superfluous as far as content is concerned but formally correct—of the *allegro* movement. He injured his own work by so doing, for the dramatic sequence of the piece is thereby interrupted. The imaginative thought upon which it is based, and which held it together and gave overture no. 2 its splendid unity and swing, became a secondary consideration. In exchange for this sacrifice, the work gained in symmetry and was made to appear, notwithstanding its connection with the action, more complete and easier to understand as an overture.

The introduction of the repeat of two hundred and fourteen bars caused the new version, which was meant to be an abridgment, to be actually longer than the old and gave it its name of " great." The extension of the coda by rather less than thirty bars is less important. It may have been done with the object of getting a more superficially effective close, for both overture and opera were revised with the idea of making the work more pointed. It would be too much to say that the 1806 score was nothing but a concession to the public, but it was certainly an attempt to get more obvious effects, to fit the unknown into the framework of the known, at the sacrifice of some important innovations.

A comparison of the musical structure of the two overtures will at once make it clear that Beethoven's method of dealing with his material is more suitable and more convincing in the earlier than in the later work. The prelude of overture no. 2 has certain bold and original traits which Beethoven has obliterated in overture no. 3, among them the opening with its pathetic, panting repetition of the two first bars which Beethoven subsequently ran together into a single slowly-dying unison, and the tremendous A flat major chords for the full orchestra which in overture no. 2 are separated by complete pauses, having a more shattering effect than the wind harmonies, which prolong, yet diminish, the emotion aroused in overture no. 3. More striking yet is Beethoven's modification of the B—D flat—B bass intervals in the bridge passage to the *allegro* to an ascending line G—A—B. Overture no. 2 is more robustly, more spontaneously and more grandly conceived than overture no. 3, in which many of the more striking features have been toned down or smoothed out.

The same kind of differences are to be seen in the *allegro*.

The theme in overture no. 2 for the violoncelli, which seems to struggle up from regions of darkness to the light of day, was difficult for these instruments to tackle alone, yet the co-operation of the first violins in the later version destroys the mysterious colour effect. The dynamic and instrumentation of overture no. 3 are more practicable, less abrupt, more artistically balanced, but at the same time the sequence of thought is colder, more objective and—as in the bridge passage to the second subject—less compelling. The altered dynamic deprives this second subject of much of its heroic character. The characteristic minor change of the Florestan theme, which forms the musical basis for the dramatic *dénouement* of the subsequent *allegro*, is omitted. The significant dialogue between strings and wind instruments is altered, as also the powerful C minor intonation of the main subject, which points to the approaching catastrophe, and the wild *fortissimo* passages, just before the rolling unison passages and the trumpet call heard in the distance.

All these very pertinent details, which are worked out with great care in overture no. 2, are barely touched on in no. 3. Up to this point, nevertheless, the two overtures have a certain similarity; for the rest (with the exception of the coda) they are completely different. In no. 2 the first trumpet signal is followed by a short *intermezzo*, the motive of which is derived from the main subject and the Florestan theme in the minor, and expresses the feelings of the rescued, still incredulous of their deliverance. Not till the second fanfare of trumpets do they attain certainty, and, after a long passage of hesitating chords for the strings, interrupted by bassoons and horns, the Florestan melody reappears in C major and leads up to the jubilant coda. In overture no. 3, not only is the fanfare altered to correspond with the new version of the opera, but the answering parts immediately take up the song of thanksgiving (" *Ah, du bist gerettet* ") and repeat it twice in different keys. One may admit the musical effectiveness of the introduction of this solemn melody without shutting one's eyes to the fact that the earlier version, which did not depend on the introduction of a " quotation " (the significance of which is unclear without a knowledge of the text of the opera to follow), had more unity of style and was more dramatically convincing.

It is hardly necessary to point out that Beethoven introduced very imaginative details into the repeat which follows, and so adapted it to the climax which occurs in the drama. The enchanting duet between flutes and bassoons, which may be taken to represent the duet between the rescued lovers, is particularly noteworthy, and the gradual extinction of lights before the *stretto*, which enhances its sudden brilliance, is an exquisite touch. The popularity of overture no. 3 probably depends largely upon this *stretto*, which is, perhaps, the most outwardly brilliant thing in all Beethoven's orchestral music. It is a virtuoso piece for the orchestra; as such its position is assured and it throws the more simple and less obvious overture no. 2 into the shade. All the admonitions of the critics are useless in face of such long-established practice, but it is good to recognise the reasons which have brought this state of things to pass. A right judgment of the two works would accord the adjective " great " rather to overture no. 2 for its grandeur of conception and imaginative originality, than to no. 3, with its additional number of bars.

In the history of Beethoven's development as a composer of overtures, the transition from *Leonora* overture no. 2 to no. 3 signified little more than an outward change, the substitution of epic for drama with the preservation of the most pertinent scenes and dialogue. Nevertheless, this remodelling of the form of immediate experience in terms of expository narrative, prepared the way for a change in Beethoven's attitude as an artist to the overture, and in his manner of handling a dramatic subject. Hitherto the line of development had changed it from a mere sketch of the ideas underlying the opera, or an inducement of an appropriate mood, to an indication of the main contours of the action, as in *Leonora* overture no. 1, and thence to an instrumental representation of the more important moments and scenes of the ensuing drama. From this point, two possible courses lay open, the first implying a retention of the actual scenario of the opera as the basis of the work and, consequently, an overture constructed on programmatic lines. If Beethoven had intended to pursue this course he would never have written *Leonora* overture no. 3; for his energy there is directed, if without complete success, to entire detachment from the scene. Beethoven pursued the second course. He would not commit himself to describing the action as it passes upon the stage; but he drew upon the intellectual common denominator underlying these events. As a musician he did not need the intermediacy of outward action and events which the poet needs for the presentation of his ideas. He went straight to the root of the drama. He recognised the spiritual forces, of which the characters of the poet's text were but speaking symbols, in their "absolute" form, undisguised by symbolism, as the underlying motives of the spirit. The musician, unhampered by the need of offering definite, hard-and-fast concepts, is able to describe the conflicts, victories and defeats of these forces of the spirit with keener concentration than the poet, who has to supply a practically possible plot. He gives in a few minutes the quintessence of a word poem which occupies a whole evening; for his attempts at representation are unhampered by practical considerations. Masks are unnecessary, events superfluous, and only the motion of the soul, the eternal idea behind the drama, is revealed through the musician.

The first uncertain steps towards this consummation were taken in *Leonora* overture no. 3. Here Beethoven attempted to free himself from the compulsion of the scene, although he still used it as a means of presentation. It was but gradually that he learned to burrow so deep that the intermediacy of the scene became wholly superfluous. But circumstances were stated in the briefest possible formula, the overture ceased to be superficially illustrative, and all direct references to the ensuing drama came to be omitted. We are thus brought to the overture to *Coriolanus*.

The fact that the poem upon which Beethoven based this work has been forgotten for a century bears striking witness to the skill with which he compressed the whole content of a full-length tragedy into brief music. The mere name of Coriolanus and the historical events with which we associate it are sufficient to give the clue to Beethoven's tone poem. Reminiscences of Shakespeare's *Coriolanus*, however, throw no light upon it; and for one who has deeply felt and experienced Beethoven's overture they are merely confusing. In order to prevent misleading comparisons with Shakespeare's tragedy and to obviate any interpretation

R

of the overture as a scene between Coriolanus, his mother and his wife, it is well to go back to Collin's work from which Beethoven took his conception of the subject.

As we are told by Collin's brother, Matthias Collin, his drama is not an adaptation of Shakespeare's drama, little known in Germany at that time, but an independent rendering of Plutarch's story. The two poets worked with very different objects. Shakespeare presents the tragedy of a towering personality which " drank hatred of mankind out of the fulness of love," but was prevented from giving expression to hate by the persuasion of love, and, expiating his guilt, died a shameful death, the victim of a petty faction. Collin lacks the wide outlook, the penetrating imagery of Shakespeare. Painstaking, rhetorical pathos is his medium of expression, and his drama is no human or personal tragedy but a philosophic debate, in a stage-setting, as to whether a man may follow his will regardless of pity or circumstance, whether he is free to do what he will with himself, or whether he is bound to society and may not disregard its laws without incurring guilt. Such are the questions which Collin discusses under cover of the story of Coriolanus. The work is a dramatic monologue, the characters, apart from Coriolanus, are mere lay figures, and Coriolanus himself is a passive, reflective personality. His greatness is not exemplified in the action ; it is mutely postulated, and he always acts according to his convictions. No other way is conceivable to him, and it leads to annihilation and suicide. This undeserved tragedy, this conflict between the innate law of a personality and the imposed laws of morality, brings about the downfall of Collin's Coriolanus. Man as an individual is doomed to utter destruction if he cannot and will not bring his own will into accord with the laws governing human society.

This idealistic presentation of the social problem belongs to the late eighteenth century and sounds very didactic to modern ears ; but Beethoven was enough a child of his time to find it enthralling. He felt a lively sympathy for the fearless hero who asserted the rights of his own personality, even to the point of choosing death, who would rather sacrifice life than his free will. As a musician he was able to ignore the moralisings of the play, and particularly the subject of Coriolanus' hatred of his fellow citizens. The philosophic antithesis of aristocratic and social morality, which Collin resolved in a victory for the latter, was transformed by Beethoven into a musical drama of ruthless will-power and emotional feeling. He had already built up one drama upon the same antithesis in the first movement of the *Eroica*. In that work the victory was to will-power, which subdued the rebellious forces of emotion to itself, but it was will-power in its creative aspect. The will of Coriolanus was a will to destruction. In some such light, perhaps, Napoleon appeared to Beethoven in his maturity, not as the power which supports the will, but as that which tears it down and thereby destroys itself. The *Coriolanus* overture is a negative of the *Eroica*, the light parts appearing dark, and the dark, light.

The *Coriolanus* overture is far shorter than the *Leonora* overture, but the reason for this is easily understood. Once Beethoven had determined to hold aloof from any direct representation of the scene, and to confine himself to the motive forces underlying the drama, he could omit all detail from his musical exposition, but he no longer needed to omit the repeat as in *Leonora* overture no. 2. Now that this repeat no longer broke in on a sequence of images, since he was working independently of these, he could use it to advantage to enhance the imaginative force of his work as in the great symphonies. The *Coriolanus* overture is frankly a new departure without the concessions still present in *Leonora* no. 3.

Not only the form but the handling of the orchestra show that the composer was working on a new principle. The instrumental texture is less richly woven. The style is so concise and compact as to seem almost consciously an attempt to be archaic. The strings are given the chief burden of carrying the subject; the wind instruments (usually treated as a chorus) are employed to bring out the most important accents; and the structure of the subject itself is simple and lends its character to the whole work. This simplicity may be partly accounted for by the unusualness of the matter; but it would not be thinkable in this form apart from Beethoven's new conception of the character of an overture.

Beethoven's overture to Goethe's *Egmont* bears a certain similarity to his *Coriolanus* overture, being at once its counterpart and its opposite. The sharp contrast between the two works lies in the matter of which they treat. In *Coriolanus* there are no tensely dramatic moments and no sudden revolutions of fortune; the fate of Coriolanus is sealed from the opening notes. The tragedy of *Egmont*, as Beethoven understood it, is entirely different. He deliberately excluded from the overture all thought of the details, which he later elaborated so lovingly in the score, and here again he confined himself to the underlying spiritual forces in which the drama arose. Beethoven's Egmont is no fond lover, forgetting political cares in the caresses and endearments of his mistress, but the personification of a suffering and oppressed people. His death is the death, not of a mere individual, but of all lovers of freedom; and his triumph is the triumph, not of a heroic champion, but of all the oppressed. Beethoven's Egmont has no individual traits and is simply the symbol of humanity under the heel of brutal tyranny which, though defeated in this world, is crowned with glory through death.

The *Egmont* overture has thus a loftier basis than the *Coriolanus* overture. On the one hand servitude, suffering and death; on the other freedom, triumph and immortality—these form the introduction and coda, the two poles between which Beethoven's drama of *Egmont* is unfolded. The introduction has an interesting counterpart in an earlier work of Beethoven, the prelude to the second act of *Fidelio*. The outward connections between the two are unmistakable. Both are in F minor (used in these two orchestral pieces only); both open with broad, gloomy chords; both come to a consoling D flat major change. Unmistakable, too, is the underlying spiritual affinity of these works, the picture of sufferers languishing under brutal tyranny, the atmosphere of the dungeon and the grave.

For the rest, the content and meaning of the two works demanded considerable differences in the working out. The *Fidelio* prelude is intended to be more illustrative, and upon closer comparison it looks like a preliminary sketch for the introduction to the overture, which enters more deeply and imaginatively into its subject, and at the same time carries within itself the seeds of subsequent *allegro* themes. The threatening, oppressive opening chords reappear later in shortened rhythms, which make them sound more fierce and imperative as a secondary " tyrant " theme. The *allegro* theme is built up out of the trustful, reassuring D flat major melody of the violins, which, after a minor change, becomes urgent, passionate and proudly rebellious.

In contrast to the simplicity of the *Coriolanus* overture, the sequence of poetic and musical ideas is extraordinarily delicate with a wealth of significant detail. The clearly contrasted and combined " tyrant " and " hero " subjects in the bass and upper parts of the introduction, and the brilliant development of these ideas in the *allegro* are not the only remarkable features. The overture hints at several of the most important musical interludes. The tender E flat major theme for the wood-wind, which returns a mild answer at the first entrance of the dominating secondary theme, occurs again three times in the course of the drama. It first appears in the epilogue to the scene between Oranien and Egmont, in which the cautious Oranien tries to persuade Egmont to flee. Next, as though confirming Oranien's prophecy, it is heard immediately after Egmont's arrest, and finally, it occurs in the D minor *larghetto* on the death of Klärchen. The repeated use of this subject excludes any theory of a merely chance coincidence with the overture. The theme, which appears in the overture in *allegro* time, in the interludes as *larghetto*, seems to point to a fateful trait in Egmont's character, the levity which, despite all warnings, led him to disregard the dangerous purposes of his enemies. This very levity, however, which brings about Egmont's fall, is at the same time the cause of the charm which his knightly personality exerts over others ; and it is thus a particularly brilliant piece of imaginative reasoning, which leads Beethoven to introduce it again in sorrowful violin *pizzicati* at Klärchen's death, like a fleeting memory of that endearing yet fatal quality.

The way in which the thematic dialogue of the overture is managed can hardly be praised enough. The alternately hopeful, beseeching and defiant replies to the relentless, menacing secondary theme lead up to that terrible moment when, after the appearance of the brutal " tyrant " theme, a single sword-stroke seems to silence replies for ever and plunge all in blackest night ; but from the mysterious darkness of the wood-wind harmonies ascends a shining song of thanksgiving for victory. It is but a vision, and is therefore presented, not in Beethoven's realistic key of joy, C major, but in F major ; but it so pulses with the unutterable delights of freedom that all fear of death, all the crippling circumstances of actual life, vanish before the supernatural ecstasies of this vision of the future.

The *Egmont* overture was Beethoven's last tragic work of the kind. The spiritual change which he underwent about this time and which led him to the joyous heights of the eighth symphony may account for his abandonment of tragic subjects in the region of overture also. The works which follow show Beethoven's hand clearly enough, but small trace of his spirit. These are the two overtures to the *Ruins of Athens* and *King Stephen* composed in 1811. They are mere potpourris of motives from the musical plays for which they were written, and have no deeper significance. Nevertheless they fulfil their object as effective " occasional " overtures, and Beethoven himself found the right word when he called the overture to the *Ruins of Athens* a " little recreation piece." He was, however, unwise enough to sell these two pieces, together with an overture in C major, op. 115, as original compositions to the London Philharmonic Society for seventy-five guineas. His business connection with England was considerably injured by this transaction, which was neither decent nor honest. Not only were Londoners disappointed that Beethoven had not sent work specially composed for the Society, but the pieces themselves were adjudged unworthy of Beethoven and after one or two rehearsals were laid aside.

It is less easy to justify the condemnation of the third overture of the three, Op. 115, by his irritated London critics, than of the first two. The autograph note " in the first vintage month (October) 1814, in the evening, on the name-day of our Kaiser " has caused the piece to be nicknamed the *Birthday Overture* (" *Namensfeier-Ouverture* "), but the contents do not justify the title any more than another name tacked on to the work, to Beethoven's amazement, soon after its appearance, " *La chasse*." The object of the piece is best described by Beethoven in a note upon the first sketch, " Overture for any occasion—or for use at a concert." Here he touches on the idea of a concert overture, very unusual in his day. Moreover, he considered for a long time whether he would not finish the piece with a choral movement,

" *Freude schöner Götterfunken*," and expressly described it on the title-page as " *gedichtet*," that is " written in poetry " by himself. It may be that he was merely trying to replace the foreign word " *komponiert*," which he disliked, by a German equivalent; but he may have had the idea of actually writing his own text, since he was here beholden to no previously prepared subject.

This second explanation is not improbable. Beethoven wanted to emphasise his intellectual independence in the conception of this overture. As a " tone-poem " the work, though vastly superior to the two " occasional " overtures which preceded it, does not come up to earlier works of the kind. Although the motives and instrumentation of the lively *allegro* are so charming and original, and the introduction so solemn and impressive, Beethoven expressed the same ideas far more forcefully and loftily eight years later in the " *Weihe des Hauses*." Overture Op. 115 may almost be regarded as a study for the later composition. It occupies, therefore, a middle status among Beethoven's works, greater than the lesser compositions, but not comparable with the really great.

Contemporary with it and of very similar artistic value is the *Fidelio* overture in E major, composed on the occasion of the revival of the opera in 1814. It was probably intended to add to the attractions of the opera by a new overture; but this plan came to nothing as Beethoven did not finish it in time. He probably felt no particular inner compulsion to the work. Like the *Birthday* overture, it has the general, festal and joyous character of a concert overture. The effervescent main motive is reminiscent of the *Quoniam* of the second *Mass*, and the sentimental, reserved *adagio*, which reappears at the beginning of the coda, is like a gentle echo of Leonora's *Hope* aria. Originally Beethoven intended the work to be a direct thematic reference to the first *Leonora* overture no. 1, which was at that time quite unknown, but he abandoned the project. He produced a fiery and impetuous *allegro*, which had no suggestion of the struggles and sorrows which go to make up the drama. It is clear that the work was intended to be a prelude and no more; that Beethoven had definitely turned his back upon the dramatic overture, and was aiming at a form which should achieve the musical presentment of a single thought, omitting everything reminiscent of the action.

He proposed during his later years to write an overture of the same type upon the name of Bach,* but though he made several studies for it the work was never completed. His last overture was the " *Weihe des Hauses* " (" Blessing of the House "), written in 1822, which has been grossly underestimated and has been performed rather for its suitability to certain occasions than for its own sake. It is, however, the end and crown of Beethoven's overture compositions. It marks the attainment of fresh heights beyond the *Egmont* overture and shows us what Beethoven's idea as to the meaning of overture came to be in riper years.

The opening of the Joseph Theatre in Vienna was the occasion of Beethoven's writing this exceptionally solemn and spiritual piece of music. It opens with splendid and majestic chords suggestive of a great triumphal arch. The wood-wind announce a solemn pacing melody which swells into a lofty, festal anthem, such as we find in Beethoven's work alone. A blare of trumpets and roll of kettle-drums is heard, and we seem to see a princely train enter the new and lofty halls—not the poor building of the Joseph Theatre, but some great palace of Beethoven's imagination. The scene becomes increasingly brilliant. Strings and wind alternate, doubtfully at first, as though in a timid attempt to break through the solemnity and ceremony of the entrance. A lively vigorous theme appears, gathering assurance as it proceeds, till in the *allegro* it is fully displayed in a powerful fugue. The great procession loses its rigid and stately grouping, as though its members were exploring, each for himself, the delights of the new palace, till, reassembling, they join in a chorus of praise.

In this *allegro* is to be found the most important orchestral expression of the later Beethoven's love of the fugue. The strength and intensity, the skill with which the parts are dispersed and reassembled, the wealth and variety of imagery in this piece, provide such an example of Beethoven's handling of the orchestral fugue that the non-completion of the fugal finale of the ninth symphony becomes a matter of bitter regret. The

* In German B = B flat, H = B natural.

wonderful way in which Beethoven, in this overture, reflects the
joy of possession, the increasing delight in an accomplished work,
renders negligible the particular petty occasion for which he
wrote.   It is a perfect expression of the joy of a creator in his
creation, the pride of one who, having built a glorious temple,
can invite mankind to enter and to celebrate its feasts at the altars.
It is an apotheosis, at once secular and religious, of the priestly
quality of the artist.   The " *Weihe des Hauses* " is a reincarnation,
through the spirit of Beethoven, of Mozart's overture to *The
Magic Flute*.

Beethoven's course as a composer of overtures and other
dramatic music is a very curious one.   He set out to write opera
but ended with so undramatic a work as the overture, Op. 124.
Amazing as this result may seem, it was but the logical consequence of the general development of Beethoven's genius.   In
his dramatic, as in his other work, his tendency was ever to
abstractions, a tendency which lay at the root of every modification
of opinion and practice which took place in him.   He began with
the most materialistic dramatic form, actual presentation upon
the stage ; but even here he characteristically avoided the
individual and particular aspect of things, judging them rather
by their underlying ethical values.   He never, in composition,
followed the details of the plot closely and exhaustively.   He was
not a simple, but a critical observer of the world.   He began to
weigh and measure, where he was expected merely to accept and
illustrate.   Only those aspects of life which answered to his
very exacting demands aroused his real interest.   It thus came
about that he withdrew those figures in the drama whom he really
loved from amidst the confusion of petty events and expressed
them in the overture, the first type of scenic, dramatic overture.
Here again his abstract tendency created a difference.   What
interested Beethoven most was not the personal, the human, the
sum of small particular characteristics which form an individual,
but the idea incarnate in some heroic figure.   Gradually he
isolated this idea from the individual who symbolised it, and
expressed it in the form of the symphonic, dramatic overture.
In time he lost interest in the dramatic conflicts between these
idealised representatives of the action, scorned the effects to be
had from contrasts, abandoned the symphonic treatment with

its opposing themes, and made the closing thought of the whole the single basis of his work.

This brings the wheel full circle. With the achievement of this actionless type of overture as represented by the *Fidelio* overture, the *Namensfeier* overture and the " *Weihe des Hauses*," Beethoven is back again in principle to the *Prometheus* overture, which also arose out of the closing mood of the work. But the approximation is merely apparent. Beethoven did not experience and wrestle with his many different views of dramatic music in vain. He was now able to give no mere outward indication of the closing mood of a work, but the ethical quintessence of the whole action, as he had experienced it. He found his way through the drama, and beyond the drama, to heights whence he could view the essence of things, where the material fell away, and his discerning spirit could find the underlying and informative idea.

CHAPTER VII

VOCAL WORKS

WHEN Cherubini heard Beethoven's *Fidelio* at Vienna in 1805, he judged from the way in which the singing-parts were handled that the composer had had little experience in vocal scores hitherto. He accordingly sent to Paris for a theory of vocal music, as taught at the Paris Conservatoire, and presented Beethoven with it. Beethoven received it with thanks and kept it carefully, with a German translation, till the end of his life. It is doubtful, however, whether he derived such benefit from its study, as Cherubini hoped. Most critics of Beethoven's vocal scores have concurred with Cherubini in the belief that Beethoven did not understand composition for the human voice, a belief which has gradually become so well established, that many take it as a recognised and indisputable fact. A few choral passages, in very troublesome registers, in the ninth symphony and in the great *Mass*, and a few difficult solo-parts in the same works are cited as examples. It is seldom asked whether Beethoven made these demands upon the singer from want of experience in vocal music, or for some quite different reason. The simple statement that he demanded the same kind of achievements from the voice as from orchestral instruments, and consequently wrote unsingable parts, is usually accepted. Do the facts corroborate this? Must the critic of Beethoven's vocal music generously overlook what are certainly shortcomings, judged by the rules of vocal technique, in consideration of his greatness in other fields of his art? Or are the shortcomings rather in the critic himself, who, perhaps, takes too superficial a view of the composer's whole attitude to vocal music, and believes that it is to be summarily accounted for by reference to his methods of instrumental composition?

" I let myself be guided by song; I tried to write as flowingly as possible, and I am ready to answer for my work at the tribunal of sound judgment and good taste," wrote Beethoven in a text-book for the Archduke Rudolph. In his youth he had every opportunity of forming his style on good singing, and through his work as organist in the church at Bonn and as second violin in the orchestra at the theatre there which brought him into touch with experienced singers, he must have obtained a fairly exact knowledge of the human voice and of the best way to use it. Such influences must have had some effect, even upon a man of average gifts; much more upon Beethoven, who was naturally a very keen observer, with a very exceptional *flair* for self-education. His earliest song-compositions show that he did make use of these advantages. Many of them date from the Bonn period, among them the *Elegie auf den Tod eines Pudels*, which, like the later *Busslied*, is striking for its expressive-ness and suitability to the voice. The majority of the eight songs, published in Vienna as Op. 52, probably belong to the Bonn period. The cantatas, on the death of Joseph II and on the accession of Leopold II, were composed in Beethoven's native city; and in both of these pieces, as well as in a few lesser songs, a grasp of the effective use of the possibilities of the voice is unmistakable. It is the technical facility with which the twenty-year-old composer uses his material which makes these works remarkable, and not their artistic worth. Apart from the opening chorus and the F major aria with chorus in the memorial cantata (later used in the second *Fidelio* finale), the vocal compositions of the Bonn period have little inherent significance. The songs are treated by verses, and are confined to the general characterisation of a mood ; but they are thoroughly and pleasingly " singable "—as much so as the aforementioned portions of an operetta, probably composed in Vienna.

Both the facts of Beethoven's life, and the works composed at that period, show that, while in Bonn, Beethoven assimilated experience in the handling of vocal parts, but when he arrived in Vienna he clearly felt the need of systematising and supple-menting his hitherto self-acquired knowledge under the direction of a master of musical technique. He took lessons, not only from Haydn, Schenk and Albrechtsberger, but also from Salieri, in dramatic composition. Exercises done for this master prove that Beethoven's object was to get experience in the treatment of the voice and to become acquainted with Italian texts; the course was a preparation for the composition of Italian opera. Solo-scenes with orchestra, "*Ah perfido*" (1796), "*Primo amore piacer del ciel*," and the trio "*Tremate, empi tremate*" (1801), are clearly based on these studies; while a number of songs in the Italian style for one or more voices, mostly unaccompanied, were very likely actually composed during the lessons, or perhaps as preparatory exercises. A later fruit was the arietta "*In questa tomba oscura*," written in 1807 at the instigation of a publisher. This piece has a tang of theatrical pathos, notably in the emphatic "*Ah perfido*," and proves how easily Beethoven was able to adopt this particular style of composition, when he wished. Occasional transcription of phrases of vocal music by famous masters appear in his sketch-books, showing how constantly he strove to improve his knowledge of the capacities of the human voice. He studied the technical bases of vocal music, just as he took lessons from the best virtuosos of his day in order to get immediate personal experience of each instrument.

It is thus perfectly clear that Beethoven did not lack knowledge of the voice; and that he could, if he wished, have written as "singable" music as any before or after him. Why did he not do so? "Does he imagine that I think of his wretched fiddle when the spirit is upon me?" he said once to Schuppanzigh, when the latter complained of a difficult violin passage. The words are a clue to Beethoven's attitude to the rules and technique of vocal music. They were but the foundation on which he built his ideas. When, particularly in later years, his score was occasionally impracticable, it was not because of the composer's ignorance or wilful misuse of his material, but because of the absolute insufficiency of that material for the expression of his tremendous thoughts. Beethoven, himself a pianist, frequently overstepped the bounds of possibility in his pianoforte works, and in the same way he would not allow his experience and practical knowledge to hamper his demands upon the voice-parts, but used that knowledge merely as a point of departure whence he could further develop his style according to the law of his being. As regards the pianoforte, advancing technique for a time kept pace with the increasing demands of the composer, but vocal music remains always much the same.

The possibilities of choral singing have indeed increased, but the soloist is faced with the same difficulties as when the first singers of the solo-parts in the ninth symphony in vain assailed the composer with proposals for alterations.

The real basis of the difficulty under discussion lies not in Beethoven's ignorance of the rules of vocal music, but in the insufficiency of the human organ as the mediator of Beethoven's thought; and, furthermore, in the inseparable connection of the sung note and the word.

As a dramatic composer Beethoven did his utmost to rid himself of the fettering word and attain free instrumental expression.   He was an artist who tended ever more to abstractions; and words, bound up as they are with the world of conceptions and images, were a hindrance to be thrown off, a cocoon to be broken through, so that the spiritual essence of things might be perceived.   This effort to transcend words contradicted the very nature of song, particularly of the solo-song, the song pure and simple.   For the development of the song, a composer was needed who would not, like Beethoven, try to annihilate or transcend words, but would, on the contrary, attempt the most plastic possible exposition, the most lively interpretation of the text in music.   A genuine absorption in the details of the visible world and a spiritualisation, through music, of life in all its forms are as necessary to the song-writer as to the dramatic composer, for the good of his art; and it was just this self-abandonment to exterior influences, this adaptability and plasticity, which was utterly foreign to Beethoven's nature.   He was only inspired as an artist where as a man he was truly interested.   His vocal works thus bear the stamp of his greatness and also of his curious one-sidedness.   This one-sidedness, which confined him to a single opera, made his emotional range as a song-writer very narrow.

It was not only his abstract bent which caused Beethoven to go astray when but half-way to the goal in this branch of music, in order to follow his personal inclinations.   Closely connected with this love of abstractions was a lack of the power of observing the myriad bright forms, the thousand delicate charms of the world about him.   The *Pastoral* symphony shows that his outlook on the world was that of one who merely seeks relief for his feelings

in his surroundings. He did not see Nature with the eye of
the artist, but with that of the simple, artistically untrained man.
This curious innocence of gaze, this lack of that delicate per-
ceptiveness and sensibility, through which the romantic breathed
the soul of enchantment into all things, separates Beethoven
markedly from the later great masters of song. Modern song
composition subsists and develops, by virtue of this romantic
attitude to life ; for the romantic, through his strongly sensuous
mode of perception, opened new and inexhaustible resources to
the art of song, which at the time of Mozart and Haydn was
a confined province of music ; and it was the romantic who
made it once more an independent branch of the art.

Beethoven was not inspired to follow that road. His strenuous
idealism stood in stark contrast to the emotional sensuousness of
the romantic. He expressed not the image of things seen, but
the effect of that seeing upon his mind. He saw the whole
world of appearances as he saw nature and the countryside in
the *Pastoral* symphony. It was never the object, but merely
the scaffolding of his artistic exposition. This explains the
true meaning of the phrase " more an expression of feeling than
a picture," which is so often misunderstood. Beethoven was a
true son of the eighteenth century in his manner of overlooking
the individual artistic value of objects, and of translating all
exterior impressions into terms of purely human emotional
values. The highly intellectualised character of Beethoven's
art, however, when exercised on the poetic plane, gave rise to
work which, though it was far removed in spirit from late
romantic song, far surpassed anything previously achieved in
that *genre*. From being merely a pleasant family pastime, the
song acquired full concert value ; and this we owe to Beethoven,
who appeared as the harbinger of a generation of great song
composers.

Beethoven's earliest important song was " *Adelaide*," after
Matthisson's words, composed about 1796. The work is vital
and effective even to-day ; but it was followed by no other
notable secular songs till 1803–10, during which period—
shortly before and during his friendship with Bettina—Beethoven
composed a great many songs, using Goethe's words almost
exclusively. Three songs of Op. 83 (" *Trocknet nicht*," " *Was*

zieht mir das Herz," " *Kleine Blumen, kleine Blätter* "),* a four-fold composition, " *Nur wer die Sehnsucht kennt*," the four chief of the six songs of Op. 75 (" *Kennst du das Land*," " *Herz mein Herz, was soll das geben ?* " " *Es war einmal ein König*," and " *Gretels Warnung* "),† belong to this period. All of them, together with the *Klärchen* songs composed shortly afterwards, show Beethoven's lively interest in Goethe's poetry. The flow of song then ceased for a time, till in 1816, after the publication of a few insignificant pieces and a second setting of Tiedge's " *An die Hoffnung*," came Beethoven's chief song-work, " *An die ferne Geliebte* " (" To the distant Beloved "), a song-cycle in six parts. Afterwards Beethoven abandoned this branch of composition, except for a very few small songs, written for a newspaper or upon some other chance occasion. In the song-cycle, Beethoven had perhaps said all he had to say as a song writer.

Beethoven's whole lyric output might almost be regarded as a series of variations upon the " *An die ferne Geliebte* " theme. Its central thought is mirrored in pathetic and sentimental guise in " *Adelaide* "; the songs from Goethe sound a sometimes passionate, sometimes hopeful, note of yearning; while in " *An die Hoffnung* " and the song-cycle, idealistic pathos and urgent desire are lost in a manly, grave and noble content. In all these songs, there is expressed a longing as for some far-distant star, whose light inspires the youth, and lifts the man above the storms of passion to still contemplation. We find a conception of love, like that of Michelangelo in the Vittoria Colonna, without a touch of sexuality, a desire which seems not even to hope for fulfilment, and sees the object of longing as far removed as the heavens. If Beethoven's letter to the " Immortal Beloved " must be somehow related to his works, it can only be through this song, unique as it is in its kind. The letter is a comment from Beethoven's own life upon his songs, and expresses in words the same feelings of an unquenchable, more than earthly, passion of longing.

---

* " Tears of love "; " Longing "; " With a flowered ribbon " in the Augener complete edition of Beethoven's sixty-seven songs.

† " Knows't thou the land "; " New love, new life "; " Song of the Flea " and " Peggy's Warning."

Regarded as pieces of music, the songs from Op. 46 to Op. 98 show stylistic differences arising out of differences of text. " *Adelaide* " is archaic in diction and metre, and is planned formally upon the old aria scheme, which had hitherto been the accepted pattern for solo-songs on the grand scale. The noble pathos of the melody, the swinging, even rhythms, the characteristic harmony, answers to the style of the early instrumental work at its best. It is true that the words are not so forcefully treated as in later work; there are occasional attempts to illustrate the text; but melodic expression holds first place and the declamatory treatment of the voice arises out of it. In the Goethe songs, the music is more delicately moulded to the words, and in the two first pieces of Op. 75, " *Kennst du das Land* " and " *Herz, mein Herz* " (a Beethoven study in Cherubini's manner), and in the three songs of Op. 83, the words are made the natural fulcrum of the melody. An attempt to compose according to the particular intention of a poet, and not merely in the general mood indicated by the subject of the poem, is very notable in four settings of Goethe's " *Nur wer die Sehnsucht kennt* " (" Who knows what longings are?"), which were all published at the same time.

The two *Klärchen* songs, which also appeared at this date, have a more ambitious orchestral accompaniment, in accordance with a more exigent subject. Hitherto Beethoven had written no accompaniments of independent significance. His pianoforte accompaniments to songs, with few exceptions, had done no more than give simple support to the singer, while the introductory and closing passages had served as preludes and cadences, but no more. The *Klärchen* songs, with their wealth of orchestral detail, are thus a notable advance, which later works followed up. If one compares the setting of Tiedge's " *Hoffnung*," finished in 1815, with the first sketch for this work dating from about 1804, not only does the newly added introductory recitative with its quartet-like accompaniment seem a notable enrichment of the work, but the vocal part itself is more varied, freer and grander in expression than the earlier version, which seems insignificant and stiff beside it. The accompaniment is a refinement upon the simple supporting chords of the first state. It is true that Beethoven still confines himself to a direction marked out by

s

the voice part, but a rich and varied life unfolds itself in the shelter of the protecting line of the song-melody. Changes of emotion, rise and fall of excitement, alternate pauses and precipitancy of thought, are clearly painted in changing rhythmic images.

A treatment of the accompaniment, depending principally on variety of rhythmic figuration without the aid of independent motives, is still the rule in the song-cycle, Op. 98. It is the first great song-cycle in the history of German song and shows a wonderful variety of expression. The songs follow each other in organic sequence; words and music interact, changing with the swiftly changing moods of the lonely lover, and the unity of the last song and the first completes the circle in exquisite accord with the spiritual state portrayed. The work opens with a pensive, heartfelt greeting to the beloved woman, a growing longing for the peace of the valley, till the mysterious C major change, whereby the melody appears in the pianoforte part like a *Fata Morgana*, while the voice-part maintains a single note in dreamy forgetfulness; then clouds and brooks are charged with the lover's message. Each of these four closely connected songs is in its way so deep an expression of the love emotion, that they have for all time set the standard for this type of idealistic, enthusiastic lyricism. The "*May Song*," with the joyous trills and cuckoo's cry of its bridge passage, is fully joined to the minor close with its pastoral bass and note of sorrowful resignation. The song of self-dedication, with its twilight vision of bliss, brings us back to the lonely thoughts and serious mood of the opening once more.

All Beethoven's songs cannot, of course, be linked up with the theme of the "*Ferne Geliebte*"; but, with few exceptions, such as the roughly humorous "Song of the Flea" in *Faust*, he has done his best work in this vein; and when he leaves the emotional region thus marked out for him, his work becomes entertainment rather than art, and is strongly "dated."

Of the remaining solo-songs, only one group calls for special remark, six sacred songs, the words by Gellert, published in 1803. They are of a devotional and meditative nature and are entitled "*Bitten*," "*Die Liebe des Nächsten*," "*Vom Tode*," "*Die Ehre Gottes aus der Natur*," "*Gottes Macht und Vorsehung*,"

" *Busslied.*" Beethoven here strikes a note of solemn majesty ; the " *Busslied,*" with its two parts showing contrition and hope in God in striking contrast, forms an effective musical close to the series. In these lyrics, for the first time, he found a poetic stimulus to his religious instincts, though he could not give them full expression ; for this neither Gellert's words nor a solo-voice could suffice. He did not work in this vein again till he began the great choral works.

Beethoven's activity as a song-composer was thus comparatively circumscribed ; he lacked the inward equipment to reconstruct the form organically. His numerous arrangements of foreign folk-songs can be given no high place in the tale of his work. Beethoven had not, like Herder, a sociological and psychological interest in such work ; neither did he feel the glamour of distance and the unknown, the delight in colour and strange scenes, which later captivated the romantics. He was led to the subject for purely practical reasons, such as the sound financial offers of the Edinburgh publisher, George Thomson, who was issuing a comprehensive series of Irish, Scottish and Welsh songs. His plan was to get well-known musicians to arrange certain melodies, to which he afterwards supplied suitable verse. His first bargains were struck with Pleyel, Kozeluch and Haydn ; in 1803 he approached Beethoven and obtained his services after long negotiations. Beethoven was to provide a pianoforte accompaniment, an *ad libitum* violin and violoncello part, a prelude and a postlude. Exquisite workmanship here and there shows that Beethoven came to take a very great interest in this work, which he originally undertook in a commercial spirit. " The Scottish songs show how unconventionally the unusual melody can be harmonised," he said, delighted with the interest of his work, and he forthwith made plans for the arrangement of the songs of other nations in the same manner. Thomson, however, would have nothing to do with these projects, and Beethoven's collection of Portuguese, Spanish, Italian, Russian and other songs were later published by Schlesinger. Between 1809 and 1823 he finished no less than 164 such settings, of which about 120 were published in Thomson's collection. This work led to no lasting revival of folk-music, for Beethoven's arrangements of the songs robbed them of their specifically national character and resulted in an inorganic blend of folk-song with international, cultured music. The demand for Thomson's collection soon ceased, but Beethoven gained artistically through the undertaking. His conceptions were enlarged and enriched, and the stimulus thus received is very evident in the variations for pianoforte and flute, or violin *ad libitum*, which appeared between 1818 and 1820 and show a sensitive application to instrumental music of ideas acquired from the songs. His contact with folk-music is shown in other work of the period. From the Op. 59 quartets to the *Pastoral* and A major symphonies and the trio of the ninth symphony, we catch echoes of foreign folk-tune, which go to prove that Beethoven's art has a real reference to the folk-song, and that it could be brought within his emotional range.

Beethoven's work as a song-composer in later years was, however, not confined to "arrangements." As a lyrical composer, indeed, his work ended with the song-cycle. He turned instead to the composition of canons. "I make them as a poet makes epigrams," he said—giving us a remarkably complete characterisation of his own form of canon composition. Beethoven's canon is not a "round" composed for social occasions. It is a leaf from an album, a snapshot, sometimes a pointedly humorous, or pensive crystallisation of a momentary mood, a farewell, a welcome, a New Year's or birthday greeting, a joke on personalities, a proverb. Very often Beethoven wrote the short text himself; occasionally he made use of well-known quotations or quaint sayings. No less than some forty such pieces are known, of which more than two-thirds must be attributed to Beethoven's last ten years. These epigrammatic canons are markedly different from former pieces of the same type, such as the canon in *Fidelio* which develops to a lyrical *ensemble*; in the latter, the form expressed a poetic situation very finely, the boding fears of four persons finding the same musical expression. In the later canons, on the contrary, even in those of serious content, the chief charm lies in the intellectual witty form and pithy compactness. They show the play of a choice mind, expressing in this close-knit aphoristic form, its view of life and man, from its own exalted angle.

With the canon—the "*Kreisfluchtstück*," as the word was

humorously Germanised in Beethoven's circle—Beethoven's work as a song-composer ends. It was the humorous reverse side, as it were, of the lyric emotion, for which he soon found the solo-song too small a vehicle. Instead of the representation of an emotional state, he gives us a commentary upon things which life brought to his notice, and which clamoured for expression, but which were yet too insignificant to afford material for great work. Nevertheless, as the studies for the canons prove, he did not produce even these *minutiæ* carelessly, but gave serious effort and thought to them, as to his other works.

The canons fill up what is wanting in Beethoven's lyrical work, as a confession of his attitude to mankind and to the world. The lyrics are an artistic representation of his attitude to woman and to religion ; the canons show his relation to other aspects of the exterior world. In the former we see reserved and reverend love-emotion, an ethical view of the self; in the latter, true friendship, good-fellowship, a rough sense of humour, para-doxical high spirits. The songs are a comparatively insig-nificant part of Beethoven's work, but as a personal document they have great interest. They give immediate impressions of events, thoughts and feelings, which in the rest of Beethoven's compositions go through a process of dissolution and admixture before they emerge as works of art. They mirror his attitude to life from the emotional sentiment (almost sentimentality) of the " *Adelaide* " period to the intellectual aphorisms of the canons, whose colder art portrays a mere spectator's interest in the things of the material world.

In contrast to the confessional value of the solo-songs, the smaller choral works arose almost exclusively in outward circum-stance. We have already spoken of the cantatas composed in Bonn on the death of Joseph II and the accession of Leopold II ; these were followed in 1814 by a similar work upon the occasion of the Congress of Vienna, " *Der glorreiche Augenblick* " (" The Glorious Moment "), which, without being actually inferior work, offers no new material to the critic. The " *Elegische Gesang* " (" *An die verklärte Gemahlin meines Freundes Pasqualati* ") also composed in 1814, is more interesting. Here Beethoven has achieved a work of the most moving and simple piety, within a small frame and with the simplest materials—four voices and a string-quartet. Its kinship with the *andante* of the B flat major trio of Op. 97 points to an underlying similarity of mood in the two works. Besides this *Elegie*, a few small vocal pieces, the convivial *Bundeslied*, the devotional *Opferlied* (set four times), and the slight *Lobkowitz Cantata*, written for birthday celebrations, may be mentioned. Certain choruses, written as incidental music for plays, have no independent significance.

Beethoven's little cantata upon Goethe's " *Meeresstille und glückliche Fahrt* " (" Fair sea and prosperous voyage ") is one of his most successful *genre* pieces. His approach to his subject is very different from that of Mendelssohn, who later composed a charming instrumental landscape upon the programmatic basis of these verses. He follows the poet's words very closely, both choral and instrumental music being vigorously and intuitively illustrative. The absolute quietude of the opening, the oppressive stillness of the air, and the " immensity " of ocean are convincingly portrayed. The bridge-passage to the *allegro* is equally apt, suggesting the first breath of the breeze, the gentle impact of rippling waves, the rending of the mists and the brightening heavens with their promise of good fortune. The sighing of the wind is given in a gentle, fluttering motive, a jubilant *crescendo* of all the parts picturing the rising hopes of the sailors as they draw towards land. According to a few slight preliminary sketches, this piece would appear to have been composed in November 1815, probably as a special " attraction " for a concert conducted by Beethoven on December 25th in aid of the city hospital. He had shortly before been granted the freedom of the city of Vienna, and it is possible that the concert as a whole, and " *Meeresstille* " in particular, may have been his expression of gratitude to the citizens. On the same evening another work, the *Birthday Overture*, Op. 115, was performed for the first time, while for the last item of the programme, Beethoven chose one of his early pieces, the dramatic cantata, " *Christus am Olberg* " (" Mount of Olives ").

This work, now almost forgotten, was probably composed between 1799 and 1801. Like the *Prometheus* overture and the first symphony, its success was immediate and extraordinary, and helped to establish Beethoven's reputation as a composer. After the first performance in Vienna, it was given no less than four times within a year, and as late as 1825, Holz writes in one of the conversation note-books that "the *Christus* has hitherto always drawn a full house." In later years, Beethoven himself had no great opinion of the work; and when in 1811 he sent it to Breitkopf and Härtel's for publication he wrote: "If there is anything remarkable about this oratorio, it is the fact that it is my first and earliest work of the kind, that it was written in a fortnight in the midst of continual tumult, anxiety and trouble (my brother was mortally ill at the time). . . . If I were to write an oratorio nowadays it would certainly be done very differently." Beethoven emphasises the hurried nature of the work in yet another letter, where he relates how the text "was written by me, with the poet, in a period of fourteen days," and that "the poet was musical, had written much for music, and I was able to talk it over with him constantly."

The poet was Franz Xaver Huber, the author of Winter's "*Unterbrochene Opferfest*" and other operatic books popular in those days. The hasty completion of the *Christus*, as of the *Meeresstille*, suggests that it was written for a particular object, and had to be ready by a certain date, probably for a concert on April 5th, 1803, at which both this work and the second symphony were first performed. Beethoven's remarks as to the time expended must not be taken literally; for most of the work upon the *Christus* was done in 1800 and 1801, and he probably refers rather to the final "polishing" of his work than to its conception and working-out.

The *Christus* paid even more heavily than the *Prometheus* for its early success by speedy neglect. It is one of those works which it is vain to attempt to revive, because the exploitation of a religious subject, that of the Passion, for *bravuras* and operatic *ensembles* offends our taste. Furthermore the artistic value of the score is unequal. The second part of the work, the subject of which is Christ taken prisoner, was designated "comic" by Rochlitz, a tasteful and intelligent contemporary of Beethoven. Beethoven, indeed, protested against this judgment, but time has confirmed it. On the other hand, the instrumental prelude to the solo-scene of the Saviour wrestling alone in prayer is very interesting. The key—that of E flat minor—is striking, being a key seldom used by Beethoven. The mysterious *crescendo* chords of the trombones, horns and bassoons remind one of the opening subject of the D minor sonata, Op. 31 ; both works seem to have fatalistic significance. A melancholy E flat minor unison of strings, muted in the upper registers, follows. Threatening calls from the horns, a *sforzati* outcry, *tremoli* portray the spiritual agonies of Gethsemane, but they are the pains of a merely human, though noble sufferer ; there is no touch of supernatural grandeur in the work. Beethoven, however, attains the most extraordinary perfection of spiritual expression here, as soon as he is able to follow his own imagination unhindered by the text. The first recitative of Jesus, thematically connected with the introduction, preserves for a short time the mood there suggested, while the announcement of the Angel, in powerful chords on the trombones and solemn orchestral harmonies, is not wanting in a certain exalted pathos.

After the Jesus aria the piece loses interest. A modern audience remains unmoved by a Saviour singing tenor arias, a Seraph who, supported by a four-part angel choir, indulges in *coloraturas*. There remain a few good episodes, such as the recitative of the Seraph announcing the will of God, details from the subsequent duet and the recitative of Jesus, " *Willkommen, Tod,*" but with these the artistic value of the piece is exhausted. The chorus of approaching soldiers and terrified disciples, Peter's boastful bass recitative, the trio (the Angel, Jesus and Peter) with its reminiscences of the first finale to *Fidelio* (Pizarro and the soldiers) have no more than historical interest. The pompous closing chorus of angels achieves no more than conventional, superficial solemnity. On the whole the *Christus* deserves its present scant reputation. It is one of those works in which Beethoven sacrificed to the spirit of his age, and received his reward in public success, very useful to him at the time.

Beethoven projected several oratorios in later years. Among others which he seriously considered as texts were Collin's *Zerstörung Jerusalems*, Bernard's *Sieg des Kreuzes*, Kuffner's *Elemente* and *Saul*. These plans for oratorios, however, seem to have been even less spontaneous than those for opera ; the idea of making money lay behind them all. It is unlikely that Beethoven could have done really great work in the didactic, moralising oratorio, so much in fashion in his day. A text, such as that of the *Christus* and allied works, in which things divine were translated into terms of things human, were diminished in order to be made comprehensible, could never give him scope for the expression of his religious perceptions. On the contrary, he needed a text which should exclude everything personal in the narrower sense of the term, which should be free of actual occurrences in order that the deeper significance of symbolic action might become apparent. No poet could have provided him with a text thus free from incidental superficiality even if he had definitely rejected such texts as were fashionable in his day. The form of the dramatic epic was as inadequate for his purpose as that of the lyric. Beethoven's religious sense needed to express itself as a pure confession of faith, free of conventional forms and glosses. He could find such a basis upon which to work (if he did not intend to do without words altogether) only in a single form, hallowed by centuries of use to enshrine the most solemn act of the Church, the Mass.

Beethoven composed two such works, each bearing witness to his inner life, his personal apprehension of God, his attitude towards problems of belief, yet differing so widely from each other that they may be described as the two poles of Beethoven's faith. They bear much the same relationship to each other as do the fifth and ninth symphonies, in which tragic works immediate experience and reflective cognition of the power of Faith are contrasted. The first of the two *Masses* rests on a basis of naïve acceptance of ecclesiastical dogma ; the second is the memorial of a subjective, critical religion.

This explains why the later work has been neglected in favour of the earlier. The one opens a window upon a new world, the other mirrors the old ; but it also reflects the soul of Beethoven which, even when it is in a world of conventional conceptions, is never less than musically and poetically original. The *Mass in C*, composed in 1807 at the instigation of Prince Esterhazy, is a work not of Beethoven's youth, but of his prime. It is contemporaneous with other great poems in C major, *Leonora* and the fifth symphony, and expresses in the region of sacred music the joyful and victorious mood of these two works. An atmosphere of simple piety pervades the *Mass;* no inner disunion, no brooding doubt, no unsatisfied thirst for knowledge, finds expression here; but Beethoven shows us how genius can re-create, even when not overstepping the bounds of commonly accepted ideas. The *Mass in C* is a confession of the composer's faith, and is at the same time liturgically practicable; it expresses a great artist's confident belief, at a time when he was one in thought and feeling with the spiritual " powers that be " of his period.

Beethoven had few possible models for his work at his disposal. He was little acquainted with music before that of the preceding generation, of which none could have served him as a copy. In this instance, indeed, he was self-limited to an uncritical interpretation of the text; but Beethoven's general attitude towards vocal music made it certain that his work would be very different from that of any of his immediate predecessors. These aimed at a clear presentment of subject, a pleasing musical drapery of the text, and sought to make it easy to understand by bringing it within the ordinary run of human emotion; whereas Beethoven, on the other hand, emphasised the significant idea behind the words of the Mass. He had a great desire to oppose the increasingly worldly music of the period by a style answering truly to the symbolic acts of the Mass. He wanted not merely to present, but to expound, the sense of each phrase in imaginative music, to lay bare the underlying thought.

He knew himself how far he was departing from traditional treatment. " As to my *Mass*—although in general I dislike saying much about myself "—he wrote to Breitkopf and Härtel on June 8th, 1808, " I believe, nevertheless, that I have treated the text as it has seldom been treated before." This peculiar method was not due to a conscious striving after originality; it was the immediate expression of his nature which led him here, as elsewhere, to try to get to the heart of things. Although, by comparison with the cyclic structure of the *Mass in D*, the work seems to-day simple and ordinary enough, it startled contemporaries by its novel treatment of the text and consequent modifications of style and construction. Prince Esterhazy's reputed remark after the first performance on September 13th, 1807, " But, my dear Beethoven, what have you done this time ? " (if true), goes to show how puzzling Beethoven's church music must have been to an audience accustomed to very different work. The three-part plan of the *Kyrie*, the free, almost conversational contrast of choral and solo parts, the imaginative modelling of the separate clauses of the *Gloria* and *Credo*, the elaboration of the *Benedictus* at the expense of a solemn, tender yet brief *Sanctus*, the passionate, anguished *Agnus Dei*, with the significant reference in the *Dona nobis pacem* to the imploring theme of the *Kyrie*, were thought particularly startling. These divergences from tradition show Beethoven's independent and individual grasp of his subject in the *Mass in C*. Most of them recur in the later *Mass in D*; on a far greater scale, indeed, but clearly deriving from the earlier work.

The second *Mass* was produced ten years after the first, though from 1814 and onwards motives occur which were later employed in the *Missa solemnis*. The plan of the work was clearly formulated in 1817 and 1818, when Beethoven began to work upon it with the idea of producing it at the enthronement of the Arch duke Rudolph as Archbishop of Olmütz. As it grew under his hands, this practical object faded more and more into the background. The score was not complete till 1825, when Beethoven asked subscriptions of fifty ducats from various European courts, from big musical societies and patrons of music. Ten copies were bought from him personally. After much tedious bargaining with several prominent publishers, the work passed into the hands of Schott of Mayence. Only three movements of the *Mass* were ever performed in Beethoven's presence —at a concert on May 7th, 1824, when the ninth symphony was given for the first time. During his lifetime it was given in full but once, and then at St. Petersburg at the instigation of Prince Galitzin, who commissioned the last string quartet. The whole *Mass* was first produced on German soil at Warnsdorf (Lausitz) by the cantor, J. V. Richter, in 1830. After its performance in 1844 at a Rhenish musical festival, conducted by Heinrich Dorn, it gradually won itself a place on the concert platform.

On the concert platform, but not in the church. Therein lies the most striking difference between the *Missa solemnis* and its predecessor in C major. The earlier work appeals to a devout congregation assembled to worship. In the *Great Mass* all consideration for, all immediate reference to, ritual is abandoned.

The tremendous length of the individual sections, and the consequent duration of the work as a whole, would make an accompanying ecclesiastical ceremony seem a mere insignificant interruption, transferring the centre of balance from the service to the music. The composition has far outgrown the original idea of an artistic elucidation of the priest's words. The tremendous spiritual tension which it imposes upon performers and hearers demands a greater resonance, a wider outlook, a more vital and richer concept than the church of a particular creed, compelling the thought to follow a definite course, can afford. Beethoven breaks through the walls which divide the church from the world; his church extends to the limits of his vision; his altar is the heart of the universe, and he will suffer no dogmatic limitations. "From the heart—may it find its way to the heart again," he writes above the *Kyrie*, and thereby tells us to what audience he is speaking—to all those whose hearts are capable of receiving what he was capable of perceiving. Thereby he tells us of the place for which he writes—every place where confession of faith which rises from the depths of the spirit can find an echo.

The character of the *Mass in D* is unecclesiastical in the highest sense; its conscious abandonment of the usual form arose in the application of the same idea which had made Beethoven's symphonies so exceptional, to the region of religious music. As a composer of symphonies, Beethoven had aimed at a greater comprehensiveness than his predecessors, abandoning the narrow circles of polite society for the democratic concert-hall; and in the same way he composed his *Mass* for a wider congregation than that of the official church. His symphonies, the expression of the struggles of man towards self-realisation, had already consecrated the newly evolved public concert, and it would be no profanation if the *Mass* were to be played in the same building. This *Mass*, indeed, took no account of liturgic customs; it was, from the artistic point of view, a logical pursuance of the path struck out in the symphonies. It was the summary of Beethoven's world philosophy hitherto, the coping-stone of his eight-symphony edifice, the standpoint from which he could look back and take that comprehensive view of life which he further embodied in the great ninth symphony.

The difference between these two great and almost contemporaneous works—the *Mass* and the ninth symphony—lies in the fact that the former represents the conquest of new and hitherto unexplored ground, while the latter is retrospective. These new conquests were perhaps the result of knowledge and experience acquired by the artist during the composition of the eight symphonies, yet the application of such knowledge (which found its purest worldly expression in the unclouded gaiety of the eighth symphony) to questions of transcendental philosophy was both audacious and new. Only the outward form, words, plan and structure were borrowed from the ecclesiastical Mass ; inwardly the work is the appropriate link between the eighth and ninth symphonies—a " sacred " symphony with solo and choruses, answering to the " secular " which immediately followed it.

Not only the symphonies, but all Beethoven's previous works, may be regarded as preparatory for this great work. One must have some conception of Beethoven's marvellous illumination of thought and feeling, both as man and artist, at this time, of every detail of evidence of the tremendous processes of spiritual purification and germination which preceded the year 1818, in order to realise how, in the course of years, the spiritual preliminary conditions for this great and final confession of faith had been organically developed. The springs of Beethoven's being, which had hitherto produced each its own broad river, now flowed together. In the eighth symphony he had explored the symphonic region to its bounds, in the song-cycle composed in 1816 he had exhausted secular song as he understood it, in the quartets, Op. 74 and 95, and the trios, Op. 70 and 97, he had attained a point beyond which the further development of chamber-music seemed almost impossible, in dramatic music he had achieved the *Birthday Overture* (a preliminary study to the future " *Weihe des Hauses* "), while, as regards the sonata, in the *Hammerklavier* sonata, Op. 106, the last great work before the *Mass*, a region of metaphysical music was disclosed.

All these achievements were now to be co-ordinated and new heights attained. The possibility of attaining them was suggested to Beethoven when his artistic capacities were fructified by religious concepts. Long before, after the second symphony, the idea of personal heroism had opened new ways before him,

and setting out with this in his mind he had been able to present
the rich material offered him by life in a variety of forms, and to
fight his way through to even higher conceptions of that ideal of
freedom and heroism.   That battle was now over ; he had come
to an understanding with his world ; he now sought an understanding with his God.   Thus the matter of his art, which
seemed exhausted, was renewed, and the battle began once more,
this time to be fought out with the powers of his own soul.   The
prelude to this new warfare was the B flat major sonata, but it
came first to full expression in the *Mass*.   Beethoven's new
material was the poetry of transcendental idealism.   He abandons
such symbols from the visible world as he had used in the *Eroica*
and succeeding works, and turns towards the invisible, the
divine. • It was the thought-world of the *Mass* which opened
these regions to him.   He took its words in a purely poetical
sense, its use as a form of divine service being, as it were, accidental.   His imagination was weary of the problems of life; it
drank in the atmosphere of the words of the *Mass*, drawing
therefrom strength for further journeying.   In this way, by
means of the words of a traditional form of prayer, Beethoven
gained entrance to a new world of images and forms, and the
Mass became the second great turning-point of his art, as the
Eroica had been the first.   The third symphony embodies the
" poetic idea " to which Beethoven was groping in preceding
works ;   the *Mass* presents   the   same   idea, transfigured and
spiritualised.   Freedom, personal, social and ethical, is consecrated and raised to heights where every activity, even of an
apparently earthly kind, is flooded with unearthly light.

The *Mass* thus grew out of an artist's striving for spiritual
perfection.   The exhaustion of the worldly material of his art
prompted the yearning, the necessity, for a transcendental knowledge ;   but it was *words* which provided the starting-point for
these new regions.

This connection with words, with a more clumsy world of
thought—as in the closing movement of the ninth symphony—
may at first sight appear a retrogression from instrumental freedom, yet in the case of the *Mass* the text provided stimuli which
were absolutely necessary to the further development of Beethoven's music ;   without their fructifying effect, the later works

would have been as unthinkable as the unprogrammatic symphonies without the *Eroica*. Moreover, the Latin of the *Mass*, with its powerful diction and fine imagery, with the strong metaphysical significance of its concepts, gave him opportunities in plenty to dissolve the substance of the words in sound, to refine upon the coarse garment till it became a perfumed and transparent veil able to clothe the musical expression exquisitely, without extinguishing or overloading it.

Beethoven's treatment of the text, however, free and imaginative, unceremonious and touched with little conventional respect, as it appears, could only spring from a deeply religious spirit. He borrows not only the words of the Christian rite; he makes use of their imaginative stimulus; not only as a musician, but as a thinker, he enters into that crisis where, if anywhere, some definite attitude towards the problems of belief is forced upon a man and becomes a condition of further spiritual growth. For Beethoven the crisis results in a joyful, confident yea-saying to the essentials of the Christian faith. As surely as the *Mass* is a most exalted memorial of perfected understanding between a man and his God, so surely does this understanding rest on a Christian philosophy of life. Not only does it begin with this, but ends with it also. The personal element is only to be found in the method of presentation and peculiar type of demonstration. We cannot value the *Mass* aright, remarkable alike in the history of its composer, and as an artistic embodiment of the great truths of the faith, until we see it as an exposition of Christian teaching by the power of the poetic imagination.

The Christian character of the work is particularly marked in the two first movements—the *Kyrie* and the *Gloria*. They are the most objective portions of the score and are free from disputatious and critical elements. They spring from the composer's deep contemplation of the glory of God and are little more than an attempt to mirror that vision. The *Kyrie* re-echoes the immediate impression of this glimpse of Divine Majesty, whereas the *Gloria* shows the same picture in motion, the sequence of divine events, the glory of eternal life. The composer takes the simplest concept of the Christian philosophy—God as King of all worlds, enthroned in glory—and makes it the centre of his picture. The work is subjective rather in its imaginative variety and mutability, in its richness of colour, in its vigorous line, in short, in the strength and originality of the presentation, than in any critical penetration of the text itself.   These two opening movements fix, once for all, the sense and significance of that which is to be presented.   Beethoven is still subservient to his text, being merely a mediator of established data.   He approaches his subject as a believer with no doubts as to the being and the power of God ; and this sure and confident piety forms the imaginative basis of the two first movements.

The *Kyrie* at once strikes the note of greatness and majesty, of the infinite repose and changelessness of God amidst the ebb and flow of creation.   Choruses seem to represent angelic choirs singing praises before the Throne, while solo voices utter the prayers of mankind, imploring mercy.   The Angelic choir takes up the cry of " *Eleison*," lifting it to mystic heights, and the vision of God's majesty gives place to that of God the Son, as Mediator and pitiful Saviour.   The chorus no longer represents the angelic host, but the mass of humanity, timidly echoing the prayers of its leaders, as symbolised in the solo voices.   The Beatific Vision returns for a moment, as if in earnest of pardon, and the movement closes in humble adoration.   As the *Kyrie* speaks of God, incomprehensible, immutable, enthroned *above* the universe, so the *Gloria* speaks of Him as creative activity *in* the universe.   The *Kyrie* reiterates a single impression ; the *Gloria* is full of diversity, though welded into an artistic unity. It is a marvellous achievement, in which Beethoven follows every turn of words, yet without losing his vision of the whole. He does this, as regards external structure, by avoiding such closed forms as would commit him to a definite musical theme, and by substituting a free declamatory expression of the idea, malleable and sensitive to every turn of word or thought.   Yet he preserves the unity of the whole by his treatment of motive, using one, very sharply defined and very short, very adaptable and susceptible to modulation without loss of character.   It is the climax of a technique of expression which he had been developing since the fifth symphony.

In the *Gloria*, Beethoven presents the old faith, illuminating all with the light of his genius, even shedding fresh light on certain points, yet, in the main, content to illustrate, to describe.

He approaches the *Credo* in a different spirit; the object of his expository art is no longer outside, but within himself; he must confess his own individual attitude to the things he has hitherto described.

When the task of composing for the *Credo* was undertaken by one whose views coincided with the axioms of dogma, or by one, such as Bach, who had sufficient greatness of mind to find the common basis of Christianity beneath the outward differences of sects, it could be musically treated in much the same way as the *Kyrie* or the *Gloria* ; the more difficult doctrinal portions were kept in the background, while clauses more comprehensible to the mind, and more amenable to musical treatment, were brought to the fore and made the bases of the whole work. Neither an attitude of naïve faith nor a concentration upon musically easier clauses was possible for Beethoven. The light of his imagination was turned most upon the hidden meaning of the most difficult portions of his text. The problem of unity in diversity was here even greater than in the *Gloria*, while the composer had set a higher goal before him—a deep interpretation of meaning. Had he been a poet in words he would have written, perhaps, a new " Creed of Life "; as a musician he took the words handed down to him, but used them only as the scaffolding for his building.

The main foundation support of this building is the tremendous opening *Credo* theme, an unshakable, confident affirmation of belief. Beethoven used the same idea later in the Protestant " *Gott ist eine feste Burg*." It is solemn but unecclesiastical, and non-liturgical in the accustomed sense. It has not the ring of a dogma pronounced by the priest. This theme—expressing man's faith in a divine creative Hero—dominates the opening movement to *omnia facta sunt*.

This opening is a confession of the Creator's holiness and power. The middle movement shows that holiness and power in action, while the goal of that action is portrayed in the close. The *Credo* has thus a poetic symphonic plan ; its diversity conforms to a logical unity.

The diversity is particularly marked in the middle movement (*Qui propter nos homines* to *cuius regni non erit finis*), which possesses more musical beauties, and is also more emotionally

T

" effective," than the more abstract first and closing movements. The emphasis is upon the story of the Incarnate life as a story of heroism, and, at the end, the Lord appears as seated on His Throne, not, as in the corresponding part of the *Gloria*, in immutable majesty, but as a warrior triumphant.

Once more the *Credo* is heard, not this time as an affirmation of faith in the Being of God, but in His mighty acts. The finale of this " Divine Heroic Symphony " reaches its climax in the *Et vitam venturi*. In the *Eroica* the hero wins culture for humanity as the fruit of his life and death; but here the prize is life everlasting.

The expression of this metaphysical idea of life is the greatest work of the ageing Master—one of the greatest and noblest works of art in all Christendom. It is perhaps the climax of the whole tremendous *Missa solemnis*. The spirit of the *Gloria* might conceivably have been expressed by some painter of great genius, that of the first two parts of the *Credo* by a poet, but this last part is possible to music alone.

Much of this section offers great practical difficulties to the performers. Its demands on the human voice are extreme, and justice cannot be done to the music as a whole, except in very favourable circumstances and under a very able conductor. It is one of those works in which Beethoven wrestles with the limitations imposed by matter. Some ideas inexpressible in colour, can find expression in musical sound, but for others the way seems barred even here; they demand, perhaps, some new form of art. Much of Beethoven's work arouses such speculations. Is it by mere chance that his three most exalted and metaphysical works, the last movement of the Op. 106 sonata, the original finale of the quartet Op. 130 and the *Credo* finale in the *Great Mass*, are fugues in B flat major ?

In the course of musical development since Beethoven's day, roads have been struck out which avoid this sharp antithesis of the ideal and the actual; but these three works represent the highest achievements of his art, mountain-peaks piercing the clouds, symbolising the greatness of a will which strove beyond the border of human possibility and was thus doomed to unfulfilment.

With the *Sanctus*, Beethoven returns to the valleys. The

tension of rapt contemplation of the Divine Hero is released in purely human emotion, a personal expression of the effect of the great experience. The *Sanctus* becomes not, as with Bach, a hymn to the Highest, but an intimate expression of deep inward emotion, of silent recollection. The instrumental colour of the whole is wonderfully still and solemn, and the jubilant outbreaks of the *Pleni sunt cæli* and *Hosanna*, to which Beethoven was constrained by the text, somewhat disturb the unity of the work.

The *Benedictus* opens upon a note of intense devotion, for only to the devout can the vision of God's Messenger be vouchsafed. The Vision breaks, is acclaimed, fades, and the *Agnus Dei* is a cry for heavenly guidance from those still left to wander in earth's darkness. The culmination of the *Agnus Dei* is the *dona nobis pacem*, a prayer for peace in the soul and amongst men. Fears of judgment arise, but are soothed by the message of Divine peace, expressed in a majestic fugue, the theme of which is borrowed, apparently knowingly, from Handel's *Hallelujah Chorus*. Once more the clamorous fears of the heart find expression in a cry for help, once more comes the reassurance of pardon and peace; and the whole work closes in a mood of solemn exaltation and power.

A survey of the whole course of the *Mass* makes it clear that its four outstanding features are the *Gloria* finale (*In gloria Dei patris, Amen*), the *Credo* fugue (*Et vitam venturi*), the *Benedictus* and the *Dona*. They show the artistic goals which Beethoven had in view, the profit which he got from his work upon the *Mass*, and point to the several courses along which his work subsequently developed. These all branch off from the *Dona*. As he grew older, the composer thought less of victory than of the peace which victory brings. "*Dona nobis pacem*," a prayer for inward and outward peace, now became the goal of all his work. The struggles which necessarily preceded the "peace," and which were but shortly indicated in the *Dona*, were now to be expressed at greater length. The most immediate and most powerful presentation of such a struggle is given in the first movement of the ninth symphony, of which the two orchestral *intermezzi* of the *Dona* are a slight sketch. The tragic first movement thus springs from the *Dona*, and the *Gloria* is a model for the finale of the ninth symphony.

The two intermediate movements, however, the *Credo* fugue and *Benedictus*, indicate Beethoven's exalted spiritual attitude towards the material with which he had to deal. The finale of the *Credo*, expressing faith in a life of the spirit, timeless and endless, and the *Benedictus*, faith in the wonder of divine revelation, are the Alpha and Omega of Beethoven's creed. They make his attitude towards religious questions perfectly clear. This attitude was a blend of critical thought with convinced faith. This faith is stated in the *Kyrie* and *Gloria*, it is vindicated and confirmed in the *Credo*, illumined and transfigured in the mystic holy light of the *Sanctus*, while its application to life is begun in the *Agnus Dei* and carried on in subsequent works.

Thus the *Mass*, though apparently a divergence from the main stream of Beethoven's work, is seen to be an organic part of it. It sprang from both human and artistic necessity in the composer, from the need of fresh imaginative stimulus, and from the desire to grapple with the problems of belief; and thus it contributed to the composer's life as man and artist. When Beethoven began the *Mass* in his forty-eighth year, he was ripe enough to conceive of religious subject-matter for his art, not as the antithesis, but as the natural and necessary continuation of the secular. Yet his creative spirit was too restless to remain satisfied with this tremendous attempt to grapple with religious problems. From the heights which he had attained, he looked back upon the course of his life and began the great summary and reckoning which opens with the ninth symphony and closes with the last string quartets.

CHAPTER VIII

CHAMBER MUSIC

BEETHOVEN lived and wrote during a period of change both in the social standing and business opportunities of the composer of music. Hitherto the cultivation of the art and the support of the artist had been exclusively in the hands of princes, noblemen or other rulers; the artist was committed to their service. Very occasionally some particularly prominent musician was able to attain a certain independence as virtuoso and teacher, but the *composer* was obliged to work under the ægis of a patron. Mozart's tragic end proves how hard it was, even for so prolific a composer as he, to fight his way to independence. Mozart, however, made the attempt, and so did Haydn during his later years, but Beethoven was the first to make a determined effort to preserve his independence from his youth—that is, from his arrival in Vienna at twenty-two years of age. Circumstances were at first even less favourable to him than to Mozart or Haydn. Mozart could rely on a certain income from lessons and lectures as well as on payments for his operas, while Haydn received furthermore a fixed salary as kapellmeister to Prince Esterhazy, but Beethoven was obliged from the first to depend on the price of his compositions as a principal source of income. In the early years of his life in Vienna he gave lessons, but apart from the fact that he did not wish to be dependent on such work, his increasing deafness soon made this impossible, and in later years the Archduke Rudolph remained, for friendly reasons, Beethoven's sole pupil.

He could hardly regard money made by concerts as a reliable source of income. The concerts were few and irregular; they supplemented his resources occasionally, but he held them chiefly with the object of making his works known. For his works he lived, for their sake he strove to preserve his independence, and upon them he depended for his principal support.

It is, in the circumstances, a remarkable thing that Beethoven actually succeeded in marketing his compositions and thereby avoided the personal servitude to which the musician had hitherto been condemned.

The pension granted to Beethoven in 1809, upon the sole condition that he should be domiciled in some Austrian town, gave him almost unlimited personal freedom, but the monetary depreciation following the finance patent rendered it insufficient to lift him above the fear of want. He had still, therefore, to seek other sources of income and, following the practice of his day, he asked payment in return for the dedication of a work. The patron who made such a payment customarily received not only the honour of the dedication, but also the right to sole possession of the dedicated work for a year or some such period. Dedication, accordingly, was no mere appeal to the generosity of a rich music-lover, but represented a business transaction.

Beethoven did not always adhere to this custom, but dedicated many of his works to friends from whom he neither expected, nor would have accepted, any payment. Other dedications, such as that of the ninth symphony to King Frederick William III, were made in the hope of obtaining a decoration. Beethoven clearly did not regard dedication as a regular source of income and he seldom had recourse to the system of asking subscriptions for proposed works. He only did this at all extensively in the case of the *Missa solemnis*, which brought him in ten subscriptions amounting to five hundred ducats, as well as a fee of one thousand *gulden* from the publisher.

Publishers' fees were his most important and most reliable source of income. The unpleasant taste of mendicancy, of speculation upon the generosity of an aristocratic patron (impossible to dissociate from the custom of dedications), necessarily brought discredit upon it in the end, particularly as the increase of the business of publishing provided a new market for the artist. The princely patron gave place to the publisher as intermediary between artist and public. The wider that public became, the more its interest in the artist's thought increased, the surer could he be of the acceptance of his works by the publisher and the greater the sums he could command. Increasing competition between publishers still further improved the artist's position.

Beethoven dealt not only with the long-established firm of Breitkopf & Härtel of Leipzig, but with many new firms which sprang up in his time, such as, among others, Schott of Mainz (1773), Artaria (1780) and Cappi (1796) of Vienna, Simrock (1790) of Bonn, Hofmeister & Kühnel (1800) of Leipzig (taken over by Peters in 1814), Mollo (1800) of Vienna, and Schlesinger (1800) of Berlin.

This change of conditions was extraordinarily favourable to Beethoven at the beginning of his career. New publishers needed new works, and his compositions were greatly in demand by the public even when they were adversely criticised. As early as 1800 Beethoven wrote to Wegeler : " My compositions are bringing me in a good deal of money, and I may say that I have more orders, almost, than I can possibly fulfil. I have six, seven or more publishers competing for my work ; they do not bargain with me ; I demand and they pay."

This is a glowing picture, but circumstances remained almost equally favourable all his life. Very occasionally he got comparatively poor terms for some one of the greater works, as *The Mount of Olives*, and the *Mass in C major*. He usually had numerous offers even for works which were expensive to publish and promised no wide sale, and it is a remarkable fact that the *Missa* —so difficult to perform—was applied for by almost every publisher of repute in Germany, while the four last quartets, though outside the range of most players, fetched at once eighty ducats. As Kretzschmar says, Beethoven was the first musician to live to see his scores in print. The possession of works by Beethoven gradually became a mark of distinction for a publisher, and even the works for which little success was to be expected were bought and displayed as advertisements.

Yet more important than the sense of personal independence which Beethoven thus obtained was the liberty to choose the type of music he would write. After the Bonn period he was absolutely free to compose what and how he wished, to follow the promptings of his genius without reference to any other will. It is true indeed that, apart from certain " occasional " works which need not be considered here, he did, sometimes, write " to order," or upon some other outward prompting (the *Missa solemnis*, planned for the enthronement of Archduke Rudolph as Archbishop of Olmütz, and the three first of the last great quartets, commissioned by Prince Galitzin, are examples) but it would be a mistake to deduce from this that he was dependent on chances of this kind. He took them when they suited him, but he was never obliged to work for money in a degrading sense, although in discontented mood he sometimes complained that this was so. Such complaints were mere ebullitions of temperament and are not to be taken literally. Actually Beethoven's own will was supreme in the matter of composition, and when the interior impulse was lacking neither flattering promises nor advance payments in cash (such as he received from the Viennese Society of Musical Amateurs for an oratorio, *The Victory of the Cross*, which he never even began) could persuade him to work.

Since, therefore, Beethoven's works proceed direct from an untrammelled creative will, the question as to what were the laws governing that creative impulse is one to which we may hope to find an answer. What is the explanation of the close proximity at some periods of widely different works, of the complete neglect, at other times, of some particular branch of music ?

The sequence of Beethoven's symphonies, from the *Eroica* to the B flat major, from this to the C minor and so on to the ninth, is a logical sequence, and, in the same way, his work as a whole will be found to have been governed by certain laws, independent of chance. The classification of Beethoven's works under groups, symphonies, dramatic works, etc. shows the ripening of the composer's mind, the steady expansion of his range of thought and emotion, in each idiom. Since the composition of a symphony, for example, rests upon very different premises, both as regards matter and treatment, from a pianoforte sonata, this separation of the works as a whole into groups has certain obvious advantages ; the delicate threads which link work to work within each group could not otherwise be recognised and studied ; but the functional unity thus discerned in each group presupposes a like organic unity, a like logical development, in the works regarded as a whole.

The groups hitherto considered cannot, however, be taken as representative of that whole, for each covered but a period, more or less lengthy, of the composer's working life. The majority of the pianoforte works date from before 1810, the later sonatas

appearing at long intervals till 1823, when Beethoven said farewell to the pianoforte.   The picture afforded by the symphonies
leaves yet more blanks to be filled in.   From the first to the
eighth they cover his thirtieth to his forty-second year ; of earlier
years they tell us nothing, and of later the ninth symphony alone
gives us a highly significant though by no means exhaustive
summary.   The dramatic works and songs are quite inadequate
for this purpose.   The opera and the two *Masses* mark certain
culminating points in his career, but give no general impression
apart from their connection with other works, while the smaller
choral works, songs and overtures are merely scattered among
other compositions and, by themselves, mark no clear line of
direction.

One group remains, a type of music which Beethoven practised
steadily throughout his life, which represents every phase of his
development and expresses his personality from the beginning
of his career to the moment when death brought his work to
an end.   Every current in his life's flow, every change in his
outlook upon the ends or the means of art, is reflected in his
chamber music ; all that he strove for, all that he attained is
mirrored here.

The position occupied by chamber music in Beethoven's
work shows the exceeding importance which he attributed to
it.   On the pianoforte he did pioneer work, discovered new
ways, dared innovations, for which he found the light, mobile
and plastic form of improvisation especially advantageous.   The
symphonies, on the contrary, massive, simple, sculpturesque in
tone and architectonic in form, define and comprehensively
formulate his conclusions.   The chamber music works occupy
a midway position between these two opposites.   The form is
less free and mobile than that of the solo sonata ; needing the
co-operation of at least two performers, it cannot respond to
changes of mood with the freedom of the instrumental monologue,
but demands conscious mutual adaptability from two or more
minds.   On the other hand, it allows for a freer expression of
individual personality than the orchestra, which, being the
musical counterpart of the mass of humanity, aims principally
at mass effects and attains artistic perfection in so far as the
individual subordinates himself to a wider unity.

Chamber music attempts a synthesis of these two other types of music—the freedom of the individual within a community founded on mutual understanding, neither anarchy nor complete subordination, but a reasonable independence with limitations justified and freely accepted by the self, a republican unity, in short, composed not of slaves but of men of strong and self-reliant character. Beethoven perceived the necessity of attaining this ideal of chamber music the more clearly, as in the course of his career he brought out the element of improvisation in the solo sonata, while, on the other hand, emphasising the massive, symphonic-character of orchestral work. He sought to strike a balance between these opposites, to use the conquests while avoiding the one-sidedness of each.

Regarded from this view-point the whole of Beethoven's chamber music appears as a ceaseless struggle to reconcile improvisation with symphonic expression, sometimes inclining towards the one, sometimes to the other, and at last finding the desired mean. The process by which this consummation was achieved was, however, a very lengthy one. In other branches of music Beethoven found his tone material, at least, ready to his hand. He was himself a master of pianoforte technique, while the constituent parts of an orchestra were already well established and were altered by him only in a very few instances. In chamber music, on the contrary, so many patterns offered that the mere choice among them made considerable demands upon time and energy. Every instrument in use in his day served both for orchestral and chamber music, offering a vast number of possible combinations. Beethoven had first to select his media and explore their several possibilities. His work may be classified under the heads of chamber music for wind instruments (occasionally supported by pianoforte or strings), chamber music for pianoforte and strings, and chamber music for strings alone. He began to cultivate these three species almost contemporaneously and had done work in all three before his arrival in Vienna. Gradually, however, a selection was made which shows an orderly course of development. The first group—music for wind instruments—closes with the year 1800, the septet and the horn sonata being the two last compositions of the kind. When they were finished Beethoven's interest in the group was exhausted;

he never returned to it and used wind instruments for orchestral music only.

His interest in the second group—music for pianoforte and strings—lasted longer. Its chief charm for Beethoven lay in the opportunity it gave for his own participation as a pianist, and his partiality diminished with his diminishing capacity for performance, as in the case of his solo pianoforte works; the two groups began to suffer neglect almost simultaneously. The B flat major trio, Op. 97, written in 1811, was followed by only two violoncello sonatas, Op. 102 (1815) and a small B flat trio of but a single movement. The trio variations upon Müller's theme, *Ich bin der Schneider Kakadu*, composed in 1823, despite its piquant charm, marks no real revival of a lost interest, but is merely a faint echo of serious work done earlier in this vein.

One type of chamber music, and one only, retained Beethoven's keen interest to the last—music for stringed instruments alone. He did not immediately find a combination which could give him lasting satisfaction. He began with trios and at last arrived, by way of the quintet, at the quartet. The first works of this group date from 1800 (the year which saw the last of the chamber music for wind instruments), and with them begins Beethoven's greatest path of achievement, the way which leads from the six quartets of Op. 18 up to the five last which represent the coping-stone of his whole life's work. Everything he wrote, everything he experienced or achieved, is expressed in this series of works. Chamber music for strings alone is, indeed, the very heart and kernel of Beethoven's creative work, around which the rest is grouped, supplementing, explaining, confirming. His life is there faithfully mirrored, not in the " diary " form of the sonata improvisations, not in the monumental style of his symphonic works, but with absolute intellectual clarity, independent of the sensuous appeal of personal virtuosity or of the compelling force of great orchestral tone masses, and limited to the outwardly inornate form of a " conversation " between four " individuals " of equal standing and privileges.

As Beethoven approached this goal he several times declared his discontent with the *first* group. Speaking of the septet to Holz, he remarked that there was, of course, feeling in it, but little art, and, writing to Breitkopf & Härtel of the sextet for two clarinets, two horns and two bassoons (now known as Op. 71) he said, " The sextet belongs to my earlier work and was, moreover, written in a single night—there is nothing more to be said but that it is the work of an author who has done at least a few better things—yet for many people these are best."

Mature artists very frequently speak slightingly of their youthful efforts because they measure them by the scale of later achievements, and Beethoven fell into this mistake. His depreciation of the sextet, Op. 71, and of the septet is not justified. " Feeling " is indeed predominant, but it constitutes the peculiar charm of these two works. Also, despite Beethoven's words, they are by no means lacking in art. He probably referred to the development of idea, the strictly logical motival exposition upon which, in later years, his work was based. The art displayed in these works for wind instruments is, indeed, limited, but it is so perforce since the tone material admits neither of the expression of especially significant ideas nor of very penetrating analysis. The art with which Beethoven exploits and exhausts the means at his disposal, the way he suits the emotion to the spirit of his instruments, recognises their tone-character and obtains the most exquisite effects, actually by means of their technical deficiencies, is the more amazing. Granted that too much need not be expected of music for wind instruments and that, consequently, comparisons with other forms of music are immaterial, still these compositions must be allowed a very real place in Beethoven's work as part of the organic whole.

In works for wind instruments Beethoven frankly enters the realm of music as social entertainment. Apart from pianoforte compositions written for his own use as a virtuoso, such work undoubtedly lay nearest to his hand, affording him the best chance of hearing his music performed and of getting his name as a composer known. The Elector Max Franz liked wind instrument *ensembles* and was entertained at table by a small orchestra consisting of two oboes, two clarinets, two horns and two bassoons. Beethoven probably wrote his two earliest compositions for this combination, a *rondino* and *octet* (published posthumously as Op. 103). At the beginning of his residence in Vienna he arranged it as a quintet for strings and published it in this guise in 1796 as Op. 4. The arrangement varies considerably from the original and shows a more refined taste and a better appreciation of the finer effects, but the general character of the work, the outlines of the themes and the plan of the whole is so suitable for a wind *ensemble* that the original has the advantage, despite the later improvements.

As in all works of this genre, Beethoven uses the key of E flat major as best adapted to make the most of the good points of wind instruments. The gay and jovial character of this work has no hint of the heroic significance which Beethoven was later to lend to that key, and it is highly suitable to the kind of occasion for which it was written. The first movement presents a constant play of emotional moods, alternately headlong and restrained ; its vigorous close brings an end, indeed, but no decision. In the *andante* a delicate and tender idyll is developed in the interchange of oboe and bassoon. The pensive and reflective elements of the first movement are here transformed to dreamy meditation and, touched by a few passing shadows, the movement finds a peaceful close upon a duet for the two solo instruments. The lively character of the minuet is prophetic of the Beethoven *scherzo* to come, and restates the play of cheerful and pensive emotional contrasts presented in the opening *allegro*. In the finale the happy mood which underlies the work naturally triumphs.

The *rondino*, written for the same combination of instruments, is near, although not equal, in value to the *octet*. The theme resembles that of the second *Fidelio* finale, " *Heil sei dem Tag*." The work is decked out with all kinds of pretty instrumental effects, of which the echo on the horns at the close was apparently the pride of the young composer's heart, but its one-movement form seems uninteresting to us to-day and it fulfilled its destiny when it was performed at the Elector's dinner-table. A sextet for a string quartet and two horns, published in 1819 as Op. 81*b* but composed probably in 1795, calls for no special remark. It is really a *duo* for the horns with string accompaniment. Of its three movements—*allegro*, *adagio* and *rondo*—the second stands out because of a grave, almost solemn melody, which, nevertheless, fails of full expressiveness, owing to the limitations of the leading instruments.

A few similar two- and three-part compositions date from about the same period; three duos for clarinet and bassoon, a trio for two oboes and cor anglais, published as Op. 87, variations upon Mozart's *La ci darem* for the same combination of instruments, and a flute duet " for my friend Degenhart, from L. v. Beethoven, 1792, August 23rd, 12 o'clock at night." As the inscription shows, this was an occasional work, possibly the last piece composed in Bonn. Three duos for clarinet and bassoon, probably written in Bonn, may also have been occasioned by Beethoven's friendship for two musicians. The skill with which he manages to be entertaining and stimulating despite the limitation to two parts and the small inherent charm in the tone of the instruments is simply astonishing. The first two pieces have three movements, the slow movements being distinguished for graceful feeling, while the variation and other movement of the third duo are nowise lacking in pretty and delicate characteristics.

Still finer is a trio for two oboes and cor anglais, a broadly designed work in four movements which arouses regrets that the present age seems to have lost the capacity for appreciating works of this type. The piece possesses very considerable artistic values which are lost in any adaptation which dispenses with the delicate crystalline tones of the oboes, to which the cor anglais provides the necessary depth and shading. The *adagio* in particular is one of the most sensitive of Beethoven's earlier compositions, while the minuet, the graceful trio and the long-drawn-out first movement, are perfect miniatures and the effective finale would undoubtedly be acclaimed to-day. Compositions of this kind make us sadly regret an age of musical culture fine enough to produce such perfect works of art despite material limitations.

The same high level is maintained in the sextet, Op. 71, which Beethoven recommended so coldly to Breitkopf & Härtel. It was probably an " occasional " work written very quickly, though hardly in a " single night " as Beethoven asserts. Opening with solemn expectant E flat major harmonies, a gay interplay of motives is soon introduced, passing from instrument to instrument so that each may display its peculiar quality. The *adagio* is the gem of the work, perhaps of all music for wind instruments alone. A simple and graceful melody given out by the bassoon is repeated by the clarinets and passes through a series of changes, ever simple yet fresh and interesting, to a happy close. The minuet is of the *scherzo* variety. The other four instruments follow the lead of the horns till they come to the trio, which they carry through without them; all six instruments unite joyously in the main section and die away one by one to the marching rhythm of the rondo-like close in which the principal rôle falls to the first clarinet.

These works show a comprehensive knowledge of the possibilities of wind instruments, and the idea occurred to Beethoven, naturally enough, to associate the pianoforte with the wind *ensemble* and so exercise his powers as composer and performer simultaneously. Plunged in the interest of the attempt, the question as to whether the combination could lead to really great art would be set aside. Among Beethoven's earliest works of the Bonn period is a G major trio for pianoforte, flute and bassoon and a sonata for pianoforte and flute. Of more value is an E flat major quintet, Op. 16, for pianoforte, oboe, clarinet, horn and bassoon, reminiscent both in form and orchestration of Mozart's E flat major quintet. The score, which consists of three movements, is lavish in ideas. A wealth of natural feeling fills the energetic *allegro*, the melodious *andante* and turbulent closing *rondo*, surpassing all previous works of this type.

Beethoven probably also wrote the Op. 11 trio for clarinet, violoncello and pianoforte, and the horn sonata, Op. 17, for his own use as pianist. The last-named work arose in this way. Wenzel Stich, a horn player who had become famous under the name of Giovanni Punto, came from Munich to Vienna early in 1800 and speedily struck up a friendship with Beethoven, who promised him a sonata for his concert, which was to be held on April 18th. "The concert, including this sonata, was advertised," Ferdinand Ries writes, "but the sonata had not been begun. The day before the performance Beethoven set to work and the sonata was ready for the concert." We can scarcely accept this literally, but it is probable that the work was composed at high speed. The content is not highly significant but the feeling is genuine, the music is clear and well constructed and by no means unworthy of the master in his twenty-ninth year. Within the limitations imposed he makes the very most of his material.

The trio in B flat major, Op. 11, for pianoforte, clarinet or violin and 'cello, probably composed in 1798, has much in common with the Op. 1 trios. The part assigned to the clarinet, however, imposed limitations which make the work seem simpler than the earlier trios. This difference greatly pleased contemporary critics, who, for the most part, found Beethoven's early works too scholarly and difficult. "This trio," says the *Allgemeine Musikalische Zeitung* in 1799, "is by no means easy in parts, but it runs more flowingly than much of the composer's other work and produces an excellent *ensemble* effect with pianoforte and clavier accompaniment. If the composer, with his unusual grasp of harmony, his love of the graver movements, would aim at natural rather than strained and *recherché* composition, he would set good work before the public, such as would throw into the shade the stale, hurdy-gurdy tunes of many a more talked-of musician."

The fact that even in this simple work Beethoven was admonished to be "natural" shows how hard his colleagues found it to reconcile themselves to his new form of expression. In the first movement of the trio there are, indeed, certain surprising harmonic changes, such as the opening of the second subject in D major following immediately upon the strong F major close of the preceding section, or the abrupt alternation of one-bar periods in A minor and F major in the course of the second subject, but apart from such details the work offers no difficulties to understanding. As was inevitable with this combination of instruments, the pianoforte takes the lead, neither clarinet nor violoncello attempting equality. They play a part, however, in the thematic development, which is notably delicate and intricate, showing the influence of the preceding pianoforte trio with strings. On the whole, emotional outweighs formative strength; the melodic charm of the themes has to make up for deficient logic, and the effective treatment of the pianoforte for the comparative insignificance of the accompanying instruments. The two following movements are less serious in tone than the first, the *adagio* melody echoing the minuet theme of sonatina Op. 49, and hinting at the coming septet, while the finale consists in variations upon a theme from Weigl's opera, *The Corsair*, developed with great charm. The variations in the closing section of the trio are, however, unsatisfactory, and we can well believe Czerny's statement that Beethoven wrote them at the special request of the clarinet player (perhaps the famous Beer), and that he was displeased with the work and intended to re-write it.

In his works for wind instruments and pianoforte Beethoven had now exhausted all the possibilities, taking into consideration the technical development of the wind in his day. In his quintet, Op. 16, he had contrasted the two groups—pianoforte and string quartet—giving them equal rights. In the Op. 11 trio he had assigned the leading rôle to the pianoforte, the other instruments supporting it and producing very graceful tone effects. In the Op. 17 sonata he undertook once more a blend of pianoforte and horn, but the wind instruments were unable to keep pace with the composer's increasing demands. No wind instrument had the capacity which Beethoven required from the pianoforte in the solo sonatas, Op. 13 and 14. Had he continued with this type of composition he must either have given his own instrument absolute leadership, with the wind as a mere accompaniment, or he must have kept the pianoforte upon a lower plane. Neither course being practicable for him, he abandoned this branch of music, and the horn sonata was his last great work of the kind.

There remained the possibility of improving the expressive range of an *ensemble* of wind instruments by the co-operation of strings. Beethoven experimented in this direction with the Op. 71 sextet, but since he assigned the leadership to the horns and used the strings merely as accompaniment, the advantages of mixed orchestration were not forthcoming in that work. To get an evenly developed *ensemble* it was necessary to give equal rights to the two groups, strings and wind. The violin needed the partnership of some wind instrument allied to it in significance of tone and technical flexibility, and the clarinet was best adapted to the purpose. The viola and violoncello stood in similar relation to the horn and bassoon, while the double bass afforded a secure harmonious basis for the whole. Such an arrangement favoured the just and even development of the capacity of each instrument, besides affording opportunity for contrasted choral effects of strings and wind or for their union into a single, almost orchestral, tone-picture.

U

This was the combination which Beethoven chose for his ripest and also his final work in this genre, the Op. 20 septet. Its enthusiastic reception shows how closely this particular work suited contemporary taste. Whenever the talk turned on Beethoven's best work, even in the later part of his career, when he had found his way into so different a creative *milieu* that he himself was scarce able to appreciate its qualities, the septet was always mentioned. Among all the works which Beethoven wrote before 1800, scarcely one is so filled with the gay courage, the pride of life that expressed his youth, as this number. The enforced limitation of expression to the strictest simplicity, the few possible emotional shades, the need for restriction in plan and development which in general is the disadvantage of a wind *ensemble*, is actually serviceable to Beethoven here, while the advantages of the combination, the manifold tone effects, the sensuous charm of the union of various instruments, are so strikingly emphasised that the enthusiasm of any audience at any period was, is, and will remain very natural.

In a happy moment of inspiration Beethoven united the results of all his previous struggles with the art of *ensemble*. The whole is planned in the form of a suite. A slow prelude leads up to an *allegro con brio*, surpassing in wealth and charm of ideas even the first movement of the Op. 16 quintet, and suggesting a lively and pleasant conversation. The *adagio cantabile* remains in the same intellectual sphere, only exchanging sentimental meditation for gay activity. The easy swaying minuet leads back from the dream realms of the *adagio* to the busy life of the first movement. Beethoven had used the theme of this movement several times previously, in a different melodic shape in the *adagio* of the clarinet trio, Op. 11, and, transposed into G major, in the minuet of the Op. 49 sonatina, but not till now did he bring out all its comfortable, almost complacent humour, its robust cheerfulness. The following trio is one of the most delightful things in Beethoven's work and many years later found a grand echo in the trio of the eighth symphony. There are three further sections, a variation section upon a pleasant B flat major theme, a spirited *scherzo* with a splendid melody for the 'cello in the trio, and an impetuous *finale-presto* which wells up from a solemn, mournful *andante* ranging to heights of almost passionate joyousness. The content of this movement, and indeed of the whole work, is distinguished less by originality of thought or feeling than by the power and certitude with which Beethoven adopts and makes his own a branch of music long cultivated by others, his still youthful genius exercising itself first upon the less demanding problems of his art.

That Beethoven's chamber music for wind instruments was but preparatory for his orchestral work, that it was symphony in miniature, is proved by the fact that he abandoned it as soon as he found his powers equal to the greater task and that the compositions for wind instruments came to an end as the symphonies began to appear. The concert of April 2nd, 1800, was at once an end and a beginning; an end of his apprenticeship in the technique of orchestral media, of which he was now absolute master and which, with the aid of a wealth of emotional power, he raised to its utmost capacity in the septet. From this height he surveyed the kingdom upon which he was now to enter, and the first symphony may be said to have grown up under the protective shadow of the septet. Had his artistic aim been merely to clothe changing emotions in graceful musical form he would doubtless have cultivated both symphonic and solo wind instrument music together, but he was striving for an art which should represent more than vague emotionalism, which should show a logical sequence of conscious thought and become a vehicle of spiritual and intellectual experience. Wind instruments by themselves were insufficient for these purposes; their independence had to be sacrificed that they might serve a greater organism, the orchestra, within which their good points could be effective, while their deficiencies could be covered by the other instruments. From this point of view it is not at all surprising that Beethoven wrote no symphony before his thirtieth year, or that he wrote no chamber music for wind instruments after it. The two groups are in reality one, the former leading on naturally to the latter. Beethoven later felt and criticised the lack of " art," as he understood the term, in the earlier group, that " art " which came to ripeness in the first symphony.

The wind instrument compositions were studies in the traditional manner for the symphonies. Beethoven's chamber music, as he subsequently conceived it, was singularly traditionless, being the most complete expression of the master's individuality.   This new chamber music was not derived from Beethoven's music for wind instruments (which issued in the symphonies), neither was it directly connected with the string quartets of Haydn or Mozart; it originated, like all Beethoven's work, in pianoforte music.

The pianoforte was Beethoven's pioneer instrument. He made his earliest innovations under cover of pianoforte improvisations, but it was a far cry from the fluid form of improvisation to the massive architecture of the symphony.   Beethoven made chamber music with pianoforte a bridge between the two. The result was an extraordinary change in the position of the pianoforte with regard to this branch of music.   Originally the pianoforte in *ensemble* had been used to supply an accompaniment, a background, but no more.   Later improvements in technique gave it greater expressive capacity than that of most other instruments and the position was then reversed; there was some danger that the pianoforte would dominate the situation entirely and force other instruments into the background.   This was particularly likely to happen when wind or strings were used as closed groups in contrast to the pianoforte.   This double chorus system was adopted by Beethoven in his first *ensembles*, the three quartets for pianoforte, violin, viola and violoncello, composed in 1785.

In the story of Beethoven's artistic development the pianoforte quartets occupy an intermediate position between his early attempts, interesting and talented, yet not in themselves of great value, and his first youthful masterpieces.   They are more original than the sonatas dedicated two years earlier to the Elector, but they retain signs of immaturity.   Beethoven's own opinion may be deduced from the fact that he never published them but used certain themes from them in later work.   It is matter for regret that a grave and dreamy F sharp minor *andante* from the D major quartet was not so used, for it was well worth Beethoven's later and better treatment.   The second of these three works, that in E flat major, is of greater intrinsic value than its fellows.   The form is distinctive, consisting of two movements (instead of the traditional three as in the C major and D major quartets), a passionate *allegro con spirito* in E flat minor, preceded by an *adagio* prelude in E flat major, and an independent variation movement. The second theme of the *allegro* points to the coming *Pathétique*, and in many details of treatment the work is a first example of that piercing and illuminating expressiveness which came to perfection in the pianoforte sonata, Op. 13. In the variation movement the different aspects of the theme at the opening and close show the exquisitely developed tone sense, and the fertile imagination of the fourteen-year-old composer.

In later years Beethoven never returned to the pianoforte quartet. His early experiments taught him that one of the three string instruments (usually the viola) was superfluous, or could only be admitted at the expense of the pianoforte part. There was even less room for the viola than under the old " double choir " arrangement, when the pianoforte *ensemble* came to be conceived as a republic of equally important instruments. In such a republic the pianoforte, with its marked individuality, tended to obtain undue predominance, and to counteract this it was necessary to associate with it other instruments of strong individuality. Wind instruments and viola were rejected, leaving the violin and violoncello, both capable of holding their own with the pianoforte, and the only two instruments which permanently claimed Beethoven's interest for solo parts outside orchestral work. Most of his chamber music with pianoforte (after the Bonn quartets) consists of trios for pianoforte, violin and violoncello and duos for pianoforte with one or other of these instruments.

The first trio for pianoforte, violin and violoncello in E flat major was probably composed in Bonn. It consists of *allegro*, *scherzo* and *rondo*, and the absence of a slow movement accords with the cheerful mood which predominates in the work. The contents of this composition have no special originality, but the ably-handled interplay of major and minor changes, the delicate bridge passage to the recapitulation in the first movement, the effective use of tone contrasts, the piquant rhythm of the *scherzo* and the charming alternations of *staccato* and *legato* phrases in the *rondo* are matters of considerable though superficial interest. It appears that Beethoven originally intended this trio for publication with others as Op. 1, but changed his mind and suppressed it. This may appear harsh in view of the many charming qualities of the work, but a glance at the three compositions of Op. 1 as it now stands justifies Beethoven's decision. These three pieces are the first which lift him above mediocrity and which astonished contemporaries as not merely talented, but assured and mature expressions of his capacity.

As with the pianoforte sonatas published shortly afterwards as Op. 2, the date of composition of these trios is uncertain; they were certainly well known in Vienna for some time before their publication in 1795. Beethoven probably brought with him studies—or even early completed versions—of them when he left Bonn, but it is clear that the Viennese period had a marked effect on both manner and matter of the finished works.

The opening movement of the trio in E flat major is of the Bonn period as regards thematic material. The motive of trumpet-like ascending chords with which it begins is paralleled in earlier works, but the way is new in which the composer spins out his energetic subject to an eight-bar theme and makes the motival structure of the whole correspond with a logical emotional sequence. The whole movement is, nevertheless, built rather upon the display of a series of charming tone-images than upon the desire to convey a particular thought. The same may be said of the first movement of the second trio, in G major, an *adagio* in which the composer improvises freely upon the leading subject of the *allegro*, thus linking the content of the two movements. As was to be expected from the G major key, the mood of the piece is cheerful. Beethoven's distribution of themes and motives among his three instruments, the different treatment he accords to the strong, restful, occasionally sentimental tone of the violoncello on the one hand and to the vivacious pianoforte and violin on the other, the distinction he makes between the string instruments with their greater warmth of tone and the pianoforte with its greater range and fluency, are very remarkable.

Two similar closing *rondi* correspond with these two spirited opening movements, a merry mood predominating in both, but the two middle movements are of far greater interest and importance. The other movements are distinguished by delicacy of workmanship, a motival development and texture hitherto unheard of, but in the two *scherzi* the strength and wealth of

Beethoven's mind is for the first time clearly discernible. The introduction of the *scherzo*—here ventured for the first time— lends the trio an almost symphonic aspect. In content these two *scherzi* surpass not only all Beethoven's previous work of the kind but also the *scherzi* of the later pianoforte sonata, Op. 2. The possibilities of announcing a single short subject alternately upon three different tone-registers may be the reason for Beethoven's greater success in the *scherzi* of the trios than in those of the Op. 2 sonatas.

In the trios, as in the sonatas, the composer puts his best into the slow movements.   The A flat major *adagio* of the first trio has a spirituality and gravity unknown heretofore in the piano- forte *ensemble*.   Although the pianoforte assumes the leadership here, the two string instruments do not come far short of it in importance, and the whole is an enchanting "song for three voices."   The slow movement of the G major trio, a " *largo con espressione* " in E major, is even finer.   It is one of those bitter- sweet pieces such as occur in Beethoven's early work only, and of which the *larghetto* of the second symphony is the supreme example.   Here, in the trio, the instruments seem to compete in beauty and warmth of tone, and the themes from first to last breathe an atmosphere of peace and joy in which life's struggles and pangs have no existence, or exist only as the faintest passing shadows.

" Beethoven's three trios were first heard by the musical world at one of Prince Lichnowsky's *soirées*," writes Ries. " Nearly all the foremost artists and amateurs were invited, among them Haydn, whose opinion was awaited with intense interest. (The trios were played and caused an immediate sensation.   Haydn said many pleasant things about them but advised Beethoven not to publish the third in C minor.   This much offended Beethoven, who thought it the best of the three (and, indeed, it is the most popular nowadays and creates the greatest impression).) He took Haydn's remark very ill and got it into his head that Haydn was envious and jealous of him and determined to be his enemy.   I must say that when Beethoven spoke to me of all this, I believed but little of it.   I accordingly took occasion to question Haydn himself.   His answer con- firmed Bethoven's statement in so far as he said that he would not have thought that this trio would be so quickly and easily understood or so favourably received by the public.''

Haydn's known straightforwardness and integrity make it highly unlikely that he was envious or jealous of Beethoven, but it is, on the contrary, very probable that the C minor trio shocked him and that he thought its publication imprudent. Something " unrestrained " in Beethoven's personality, which Goethe noticed in later years, and noted with mild disapproval, appeared here for the first time in a work technically mature and planned on the grand scale and might well fill Haydn with astonishment and apprehension.   He was sixty years of age, and overlooked the fact that with Beethoven a new generation had grown up which would feel the charm of this wild expression of naked emotions, this rebellion against traditional bounds and limitations.   Haydn saw the signs of intellectual immaturity in this exposure of the intimacies of the soul, something offensive to his taste and habit of thought. (For Beethoven, on the contrary, the C minor trio meant the first decisive blow struck for the new kingdom which was to be his own.) It shows, in contrast to the rounded smoothness of the E flat major and G major trios, a condition of spiritual ferment, but this very condition of ferment was of more importance to Beethoven's future development than the clearer but less original rest and security of the other two works.

In the C minor trio the first and last movements are the most interesting.   The first movement is dominated partly by violent and partly by melancholy emotion, followed by a pensive and almost monotonously peaceful *andante cantabile* ending in a gently melancholy *coda*.   The troublous emotions thus aroused dominate the minuet, although gay and humorous flashes appear in the first bridging movement and in the C major trio.   The ideas suggested by the first movement come to full expression in the *finale prestissimo*, which presents a highly characteristic turmoil of emotional excitement—a picture of Orestes pursued by the Furies—but peace is attained at the close.

The Op. 1 trios, published in 1795, were followed in 1808—thirteen years later—by two Op. 70 trios, Beethoven's next works of the kind.   During these intervening years the piano was of tremendous importance to the composer as an instrument allow-

ing free improvisation, and perhaps for this reason he was dis-
inclined to employ it in combinations. When occasionally he
did so employ it, under pressure of circumstance, as in the very
second-rate clarinet trio, Op. 11 of 1798, it is clear that he had to
flog his fancy and consequently fell far short of the standard of
the Op. 1 trios. He much preferred string *ensembles*, which
provided him with an æsthetic basis quite other than that of
pianoforte music. While still in Bonn he composed a trio in
E flat major for strings, published in 1797. A year after the
publication of the Op. 1 trios he produced a quintet, Op. 4, a
rearrangement of the wind octet, Op. 103. Two serenades, Op. 8
and 25, three string trios, Op. 9 (published in 1798), and the
three first quartets, Op. 18 (published in 1800), mark the growth
of a predominant interest in stringed instruments, an interest
which Beethoven maintained for ever afterwards.

During the next thirteen years the pianoforte ceased to have
any part in Beethoven's chamber music, but although its future
was bound up with the fact that it was the composer's instrument
of improvisation, he did, as a virtuoso, employ it from time to
time as a concert instrument in duo sonatas for pianoforte and
violin or violoncello. The marked difference between these
works and the chamber music proper is highly interesting. The
latter aims at the exclusion of virtuosity as an end in itself, while
the duo sonatas make a point of preserving it, and their whole
structure shows an unmistakable trend to the form of the double-
concerto without orchestral accompaniment. The incidents of
their composition, so far as they are known, show that they were
designed for particular concerts given by Beethoven's fellow-
musicians. The horn sonata, Op. 17, which belongs essentially
to this group, was composed at the request of the virtuoso Punto
for his appearance in Vienna. The two violoncello sonatas, Op. 5,
were composed during Beethoven's visit to Berlin in 1796 for
dedication to King Frederick William II, himself a violoncellist,
and for performance by the violoncellist Duport, then also in
Berlin. The A major sonata, Op. 47, was written for the violinist
Bridgetower, the G major sonata, Op. 96, for the violinist Pierre
Rode, who visited Vienna in 1812, and for the Archduke
Rudolph. It is probable that the other duo sonatas are of similar
origin, and the works for pianoforte and violin, with the single

exception of Op. 96, were composed between 1798 and 1803, when Beethoven the virtuoso had many opportunities of giving concerts with violinists. The violoncello sonatas, Op. 102, were composed in the summer of 1803, while Linke, 'cellist of the Rasumovsky quartet, was staying with the Countess Erdödy at Jedlersee, and Beethoven, then in Baden, was a frequent visitor to the house. Existing sketches for a violoncello "pastoral" sonata date from this year.

External circumstances had probably more to do with the production of the duo sonatas than with any other works of Beethoven, and, indeed, it is highly unlikely that he would have composed so many works of this nature from inner compulsion. The necessity to balance imaginative and structural elements, giving full value to the character of each instrument and allowing a display of virtuosity from each performer, demanded from the first a spirit of compromise which made high poetic flights impossible. The ten violin sonatas in particular are examples of the concert piece, aiming principally at brilliant outward effect. In the three first works, sonatas in D major, A major, E flat major, dedicated to Salieri, the demands upon the performer are comparatively modest, though they are greater than in Mozart's duo sonatas. They are fresh, inventive, tuneful and easily understood music, while certain movements, such as the variations *andante* of the D major sonata and the solemn C major *adagio* of the E flat major sonata are expressive as only Beethoven can be in work of this kind. In the melancholy A minor *andante* of the second sonata the tone contrasts of the two instruments are exquisitely employed. The Op. 12 sonatas, indeed, contain beauties which are by no means to be despised, while comparison with the *Pathétique* sonata, Op. 13 (which immediately followed them), emphasises the grace with which they conform to the taste of the time and to the capacity of the amateurs for whom they were designed. The fact that they were nevertheless sharply attacked in the *Allgemeine Musikalische Zeitung* need not surprise us in view of the hostility of the critics to Beethoven's work as a whole at that time.

The next works of the kind, the A minor sonata, Op. 23, and F major sonata, Op. 24, are more important, the first being a notable advance in originality of musical expression, while the second has, by the grace and charm of its themes, won a high place of favour among works of this description—the " *Frühlings-Sonata.*" It is interesting to notice how the choice of key settles the main character of these compositions ; in the second the quiet and happy F major at once strikes a note of contentment and ease, while melancholy passion is expressed in the first in A minor, a key comparatively seldom employed by Beethoven and used elsewhere but once (in the quartet Op. 132) as the basic key of an entire work.

The closely allied works, Op. 23 and 24, were immediately followed by the three trios in A major, C minor and G major of Op. 30, dedicated to the Emperor of Russia. Here again the key determines the character of the work. A major and G major keys (representing a half-demonstrative, half-pensive gaiety) were used by Beethoven several times in violin sonatas without full exploration of their emotional possibilities, but here, within the necessary limitations of the violin duo, there is a notable advance on earlier works. Technical demands are higher and the type of the obligato double concerto becomes more marked, while in the slow movement an effort after a more sensuously pleasing effect makes itself felt. Pieces such as the D major *adagio* of the A major sonata, the *tempo di minuetto ma molto moderato e grazioso* passage in E flat major in the G major sonata with its trio melody, partly reminiscent of Haydn, partly prophetic of the A flat major sonata, Op. 110, are among the most attractive which Beethoven has composed. The best of the three sonatas of Op. 30 is that in C minor, pathetic in character, as is to be expected from the choice of key and allied to Beethoven's other works in C minor in emotional content. There is, however, no logical development of the subject, as in other works, but rather a stringing together of ideas in different shades of tone-colour, the unity of the whole being temperamental rather than logical.

The next sonata, the ninth, for pianoforte and violin in A major, is inferior to the C minor sonata in imaginative power, but is the more popular work because of its somewhat virtuoso brilliance, and this is commonly considered the best of Beethoven's duo sonatas. This estimate is justified in so far as the A major sonata represents the purest type of concerto duo ; it is a favourite with performers because honours are equally divided between the two instruments.   Moreover, the piece bears the name of the most famous violinist of the time, Rudolph Kreutzer, to whom it was dedicated after Beethoven's quarrel with the mulatto Bridgetower, for whom it was originally intended and with whom Beethoven first performed it.   It is Beethoven's third violin sonata in A major, or rather, since the first movement, with the exception of the introduction, is in the minor, the second in A minor, and certain details recall a previous A minor piece, Op. 23. In the Kreutzer sonata the slow introduction is an innovation, the violin announcing a solemn *adagio* theme which is repeated under a bold harmonic change by the pianoforte.   A vigorous and passionate *presto* proceeds, after a plaintive *adagio* change, to a stormy close.   In this movement the poetic element is predominant, but the two following movements are entirely given up to virtuosity.   In the variations movement a simple melody is decorated with every device of virtuosity, while the finale, resembling a tarantella and originally designed for the A major sonata, Op. 30, is one of Beethoven's most outwardly brilliant pieces and affords a fine exhibition of temperament.

With the A major sonata, Op. 47, Beethoven reached his destined goal as regards the duo sonata form, and it was mere accident—the arrival of the violinist Rode in Vienna in 1812— which induced him to turn once again to a form of which he was already beginning to be weary and to compose the G major sonata, Op. 96.   The style of the work shows clearly that he attempted a compromise between the appointed task of writing a pleasing and effective piece for performance, and the need to follow his own changed mentality, which rendered a solution on the old lines impossible.   The piece is the most carefully worked out and most finished of Beethoven's violin sonatas, but the art applied is too exquisite for its purpose and the G major sonata was in practice neglected, like the eighth symphony, to which it bears some resemblance in its range of joyous emotion.

Of Beethoven's ten violin sonatas, the seventh, ninth and tenth are the most striking; the seventh is the most emotional and has the best " swing," the ninth is richest in superficial effects, the tenth is the most imaginative and the most musically perfect.   Not one, however, can compare with the contemporary solo sonatas for the pianoforte; their main interest arises out of the skill with which the virtuoso element is combined with the sonata character.

The five violoncello sonatas are on the whole more successful. In contrast to the rapid succession of violin sonatas, their composition lasted over a much longer period of time, between 1796 and 1815 ; they show a wider range of thought and richer variety of form. The violoncello is better adapted as a solo instrument for chamber music duets than the violin ; its noble tenor tone and virile, earnest yet adaptable and sympathetic character surpass for this purpose the coquetry and bravura of the violin and substitute simple cantabile for firework effects.

This explains the deeper inner significance of violoncello sonatas, Op. 5, composed in 1796, as compared with violin sonatas, Op. 12, composed later. The emotional earnestness and structural grandeur of the opening movements of these two pieces are surprising. The fact that neither the G minor nor the F major sonatas has held its due place in general estimation is attributable to the weakness of the finales of both. In particular the commonplace dance-like *allegro-rondo* of the G minor sonata forms a poor anti-climax to the emotional intensity of the opening. Till that time, violoncello sonatas with elaborate pianoforte parts had not been written, and this may account in some degree for the somewhat careless composition of these two finales. Beethoven appears to have been satisfied to emphasise the sonata-like character of the new duos in the opening movements and to have confined himself in the *rondi* to giving the performers room for technical display.

Beethoven produced no similar work till twelve years later, in his sonata in A major for pianoforte and violoncello, Op. 69. We do not know what led him to undertake this work, but it was probably written for a particular occasion. Its general character is quiet and dignified, the emotional expression inclining neither towards passion nor sentimentality. The *scherzo* theme in ascending syncopated rhythms is one of the most charming specimens of its kind and leads on to a trio which strikingly recalls that of the A major symphony. Beethoven has lavished musical ideas on the work with a prodigal hand, particularly in the *adagio*, which is rich in beauties.

Two more duos for pianoforte and violoncello remain to be

mentioned, works of an almost baroque character, whose dry musical exterior conceals an imaginative impulse which reaches out boldly beyond the limits of conventional expression. They may be regarded as distinct attempts to overcome the concerto style of the duo sonata and to give it the character of an intimate dialogue. The pains expended on the attempt, however, serve only to prove that the duo sonata is unworthy of the proposed dignity. What these two pieces gained in range of thought and expression they lost by the sacrifice of outward graces indispensable to the form. In result they are hybrids; as regards theory and content they are the most important of Beethoven's works in the region of chamber music for two instruments, but in practice they miss the effectiveness of previous works through want of the necessary apparel of sensuous musical charm. By intention the two works are a most interesting translation of the " fantasia sonata " in terms of chamber music for more than one instrument. The C major sonata is actually designated as a " free sonata " by Beethoven in manuscript. Psychologically the work bears a striking similarity to the A major sonata, Op. 101, begun at the same time but not completed till the following year. The C major duo, however, lacks the immediate appeal, the melodic charm of the pianoforte sonata, and appears somewhat dry and poor by comparison. The second sonata of Op. 102, that in D major, develops on the usual formal arrangement of *allegro* and *adagio*, followed immediately by the closing movement, in the form of a fugue. In contrast to the C major sonata, which begins in dreamy emotion and moves gradually towards a restrained gaiety, the D major sonata opens with headstrong determination and energy, an exhibition of will-power, then passes through a phase of tenderness and melancholy in the adagio " *con molto sentimento d'affetto*," and returns to a mood of exalted confidence in the fugue. A somewhat similar train of thought characterises an earlier work, the first of two trios, Op. 70, for pianoforte, violin and violoncello, composed in 1808. The two pieces are alike in key and arrangement and vary only in detail; but while the trio has not the hard tone and difficult melodic changes or the stiffness of expression of the sonata, it lacks the possibility of climax contained in the fugal *finale*. The first and last movements of the trio are not very richly elaborated and are really mere introduction and epilogue to the *largo assai ed espressivo*, one of the most wonderful expositions of melancholy in all Beethoven's work. It has a mystic character which has given the whole trio the nickname of the " *Geister-trio*," " Ghost Trio," and it may be by no mere chance that the first studies for this *largo* are found on the same sheet of paper which contains the sketch in D minor for *Macbeth*.

From certain letters of the time it would seem that Beethoven originally intended the D major trio, and that in E flat major which appears under the same opus number, for pianoforte sonatas. If this conjecture be correct (the letters are not perfectly clear on the point) these trios in their original form would have bridged the wide interval between the concerto sonatas— the last of which, Op. 57, was composed in 1806—and the two-movement sonatas, Op. 78 and 79, and would have considerably shortened the three years' pause in solo compositions for the pianoforte. The conjecture is supported by internal evidence, particularly by the structure of the E flat major trio. Its delicate transitions of mood and almost idyllic, gay, emotional character point towards the coming pianoforte works. On the other hand, it is far less compressed and is of the four-movement form, disused by Beethoven in pianoforte composition after the E flat major sonata, Op. 31, which appeared in 1802, and which was the last of the great concerto sonatas. By a reversal of the process of development Beethoven returned once again to the lesser form in a work analogous in construction to the pianoforte sonata. The E flat major sonata and the trio of Op. 70 are linked in other respects than identity of key and number of movements. They possess one striking similarity; despite their four parts, both works lack a slow movement. In each instance the composer sought to avoid the interruption of a cheerful train of thought by sadness or emotionalism.

Beethoven's Op. 70 trios mark a new era in pianoforte composition, an era closed by the B flat major trio, Op. 97, written in 1811. This work bears all the marks of his happiest period— the period in which the " C minor " troubles of his early manhood had been overcome and the " D minor " problems of late years had not yet presented themselves—but at this date he had lost his inclination for the genre and miniature work which also marks this period, and he was once more strongly impelled to the great forms. The impulse to symphonic work, dormant from 1808, was reviving, and during the time of transition (from the period of the Goethe songs to the first studies for the seventh symphony) the B flat major trio was composed. In emotional content it partly recalls the preceding period, but its strength of form and melodic luxuriance point forward to a date when lyrical inspiration gave way to monumental. It also marks the last stage at which it was possible for Beethoven to make the pianoforte the centre of a chamber music *ensemble*. A short B flat major trio in one movement dating from 1812 was written merely for the amusement of a child (Maximiliane von Brentano), and a sketch for an F minor trio begun in 1816 remained unfinished. The last of the series was the violoncello sonata, Op. 102, written in 1815. Beethoven wrote but one more composition for a trio of instruments, a cycle of variations upon " *Ich bin der Schneider Kakadu*," a theme by the popular composer Wenzel Müller. In earlier years he wrote variations for pianoforte and violoncello and for pianoforte and violin upon themes from Mozart and Handel; also, during the Bonn period, a cycle of trio variations, published later as Op. 44, upon a theme of his own in E flat major. These pieces were written for amateurs at the request of publishers and call for no special notice, but the *Kakadu* variations are on a different level. They form a companion piece on a smaller scale to the *Diabelli* variations, and though they lack the deep humorous insight and vast range of the latter, they are full of charming enthusiasm and keenness, with witty surprises and delicate sarcastic changes in store for the hearer.

A survey of Beethoven's chamber music works with pianoforte as a whole shows it as partly preparatory, partly supplementary, to the solo works. The two groups must be taken together in forming any comprehensive estimate of Beethoven's pianoforte work. While the Bonn quartets represent the next stage, of development after the boyish sonatas dedicated to the Elector and the early Viennese works, the Op. 1 trios prepare the way for the subsequent solo sonatas. After this, trio composition is suspended for a time and a period of concerto sonatas for violoncello and violin sets in, closing temporarily with the

Kreutzer sonata, Op. 47, in 1803, when the virtuoso impulse revived strongly in Beethoven and impelled him to the composition of the great concerto sonatas. After the broad fresco style of this period the Op. 70 trios lead on to works of the two-movement sonata type, while the B flat major trio of 1811 once more attempts expansion towards symphonic form. The C major sonata, Op. 102, for violoncello and pianoforte points unmistakably to the great A major sonata, Op. 101, and the fugue of the D major sonata is prophetic of Op. 106. Finally, during the last years we have the *Kakadu* variations, a miniature of the *Diabelli* variations, which bring the chamber music for pianoforte and strings to a close.

Although these works thus form an organic whole with the solo pianoforte compositions, they are neither so numerous as the latter nor, collectively, of such high poetic value. Beethoven's most ambitious attempt in chamber music with pianoforte is the early C minor trio, Op. 1, and the very fact that he composed no similar work for thirteen years shows that the pianoforte trio as a form of music had no charms for him during the most important years of his development. The line of spiritual descent from the C minor trio (as pianoforte music sank into the background) must be traced through the chamber music for strings alone, which gradually claimed the master's interest to the complete exclusion of other forms of chamber music. The cessation of his own activities as a pianist may have contributed to this state of affairs, but since loss of hearing did not prevent him from writing solo sonatas in later years, the real cause of his abandonment of the trio must lie deeper. Beethoven must have recognised that the pianoforte was unsuitable for chamber music, especially for that ideal of chamber music to which his spirit aspired as an expression of absolute abstraction in music, detached as far as thinkable from the material aspects of tone.

This urge to abstraction underlies each several branch of Beethoven's music and gives momentum to all his development. In the region of solo pianoforte music it led him at last to compose works almost unrealisable in actual tone works, which make their appeal to a purely mental sense of tone-values. In symphonic work it found expression in indifference to the actual impression produced by certain combinations of sound, in

x

idealistic instrumentation, and, above all, in choice of poetic subject. In the drama this urge led him from opera to dramatic overture and thence to the actionless concert overture. It conditioned his curious attitude to vocal music, prevented him from cultivating the song on lines which admitted further development, and led him to overlook the technical limitations of the human voice. Its influence on his work taken as a whole was to lead him to reject those branches of music which were least capable of becoming vehicles for transcendental ideas, and it impelled him to a kind of inspired *résumé* or repetition of thoughts already expressed at the end of each of the stages into which the course of his development naturally falls. Two different lines of advance may be traced in his work : the first consists in a gradual rejection of the more material forms of his art and culminates in the great quartets of the last period ; the second, running laterally, shows his various periods as it were in section, the results of the experience of each period in abstract form. Thus all the activities of the years before 1800 culminate in the Op. 9 trios and Op. 18 quartets. The period of the great concertos is crowned by the three Op. 59 quartets of 1806. The Op. 74 and 95 quartets sum up in themselves all the spiritual tendencies of the year 1809–1810, and the five last great works express the impulses which went to form the later pianoforte sonatas, the *Masses* and the ninth symphony.

The quartets are thus seen to reveal the quintessence of the other works of each period, and the manner in which this is presented in music is surpassing in delicacy and perfection. The obstacles with which the composer's will had to contend in other branches of music, and which forced him either to submit to the limitations of his material or to write work impossible of performance, are non-existent here. The mechanical imperfections of the pianoforte, of the orchestra, or the human voice, have no counterpart in the string quartet, a group of instruments perfectly united yet perfectly individualised. It is a combination in which the most exacting reformer could suggest no improvement. Despite their independence, the homophonous character of the instruments adapts them for mutual support and fulfilment. In chamber music for pianoforte and strings the underlying principle is that of tone contrast, but in the string *ensemble* there is similarity of tone underlying individuality. Hence the characteristic double effect of the string *ensemble*—unknown to any other combination of instruments—obtained from a unity of tone which can yet be analysed into several distinct tone individualities. In combination they represent a greater range of tone than is obtainable from the pianoforte and they allow an independent treatment of the parts impossible on the keyboard. They possess the pianoforte capacity for *cantabile* with far greater flexibility. They have almost the force of the orchestra, for they comprise the most important part of the orchestra. They lack indeed orchestral diversity of colour, they have not the register capacity of the pianoforte tone, or the sensuous warmth of the singing voice, and they are dependent on the art of light and shade, but, for the musician with a bent to abstraction, this constitutes the chief charm of the string *ensemble*. He wishes to avoid the sensuous charms of other means of expression ; his thoughts are too airy and fine to bear the weight of the garments of tone in its more material aspects, and he seeks to weave a vesture as transparent and ethereal as the ideas themselves. For this purpose the string *ensemble* is peculiarly adapted, and from the moment that Beethoven first realised this he chose this branch of music to summarise his intellectual conquests stage by stage, and to concentrate therein all the rays of his spirit at the end of his creative life.

An often-quoted extract from Wegeler tells of the probable beginning of Beethoven's active interest in composition for strings alone. Speaking of the musical Fridays at Prince Lichnowsky's house, where so many of Beethoven's works were first performed and where the magnificent Lichnowsky quartet was always at his disposal for chamber music, he says : " Here Beethoven first played to the veteran Haydn three sonatas dedicated to him. Here, in 1795, Count Appony commissioned Beethoven, for a named sum of money, to compose a quartet, of which he had hitherto composed none. The Count said he did not wish to retain the quartet for himself for six months before publication, as was the custom, nor did he demand its dedication to himself, etc., etc. After I had many times reminded Beethoven of this commission he set to work twice upon it, producing at the first attempt a great violin trio (Op. 3) and at the second a violin quintet (Op. 4)."

Wegeler's story contradicts the known history of the two works named by him. The Op. 4 quintet is a rearrangement of a wind octet and is not to be counted as an original work by Beethoven. Similarly the trio is not the result of an attempt at a quartet in 1795, for Beethoven brought it with him from Bonn, as Thayer relates, and could have done no more than revise it at this time. The history of his next works for strings also contradicts Wegeler's report. The Op. 3 string trio was followed in 1797 by a *Serenade*, also for three stringed instruments, and in 1798 by a series of three trios for violin, viola and violoncello. It thus appears that Beethoven felt no immediate attraction to the quartet. He had already given proof of his amazing skill in three-part instrumental music in the Op. 87 trio for two oboes and cor anglais, and in his variations on Mozart's *La ci darem* for the same instruments. The first group of Beethoven's chamber music consists, therefore, of Op. 3, 8 and 9, five works in all, now almost forgotten, together with the companion piece to Op. 8, the graceful *Serenade*, Op. 25, for flute, violin and viola. With the exception of the last-named work, in which the inclusion of the flute imposed certain limitations, these trios are not only examples of Beethoven's work in its maturity, but in many ways surpass the Op. 18 quartets, and it is due to the superficiality of a too hurried and restless musical culture that works of such importance should have been so long neglected.

The first of these trios, Op. 3 in E flat major, begun during the Bonn period, bears outwardly the character of a *divertimento* and is divided into an *allegro*, an *andante*, a first minuet, an *adagio*, a second minuet and a *finale*. The underlying character of the work is one of measured cheerfulness, and, indeed, moderation is the keynote throughout the development of the work. In the *Serenade*, Op. 8, on the contrary, Beethoven gives rein to his sense of humour, his untroubled, sunny delight in existence. The form of this work, answering to its character, is slighter than that of the preceding trio. Its chief charm lies in the grace and ease of the themes and the pleasing skill with which they are arranged.

The *Serenade*, Op. 8, is a clever piece of work and very perfect in form, while the instruments are ably and effectively handled in Op. 3, but both works are surpassed in the three Op. 9 trios, which represent the best that Beethoven had to express in this branch of his art. The words of the dedication of these pieces to the Russian Count Browne, " *au premier Mécène de sa Muse la Meilleure de ses œuvres,*" prove that Beethoven was well aware of their excellence. His description of them as " the best of his works " was much more than a figure of speech. None of his previously published works equalled them in gravity, in logic, in mastery of form and matter. They bear all the characteristic marks of Beethoven's great work for strings, the absolute intellectual clarity, the firmness of structure, the sure poetic touch. There is, indeed, a strong symphonic element in these trios. It is frequently mentioned as a remarkable fact that Beethoven wrote no symphony before his thirtieth year, but it should not be forgotten that his symphonic bent was displayed much earlier in two directions—in his love of dabbling in orchestral colour as displayed in the works for wind instruments, and in his tendency to symphonic structure in the " colourless " yet intellectually weightier string trios. Of these three trios the first, in G major, is perhaps composed on the grandest scale. The second, in D major, is by comparison less imposing, and though full of ideas, imaginatively and delicately worked out, and structurally sound, it yet suggests carefully calculated entertainment. In the third, the C minor trio, the note of earnestness and genuine feeling is once more unmistakable; it contains one of the most beautiful and tuneful of all Beethoven's *adagio* movements.

The Op. 9 trios for strings were published in 1798, and on April 2nd, 1800, the first symphony was performed for the first time. In the same year the B flat major sonata, Op. 22, the closing work of the first great series of pianoforte compositions, was written and the first performance of the septet took place. The date marks a change in Beethoven's style of composition. His interest in the lesser branches of instrumental music declined and he felt the need for a co-ordination of the various means of musical expression hitherto cultivated singly, an impulse to combine in a single work the imaginative logic of the string trios, the colour of the wind *ensembles*, and the symphonic variety of the four-movement sonata-form. He felt that in the separate cultivation of these forms there was little more of lasting value to be attained. Consequently at the moment when he turned to the symphony he abandoned the string trio and wind *ensemble*, although the fantasia-sonata still offered a future to pianoforte composition and Op. 26 and 27 were in course of preparation. Thus three great tendencies were brought together in the symphony and were never afterwards disunited. The date of the first performance of the first symphony marks the end of all those types of chamber music cultivated by Beethoven hitherto, with the single exception of the concerto pianoforte *ensemble*.

External circumstances also combined to arouse Beethoven's interest in the string quartet. Lichnowsky's musical mornings, the prevailing interest in chamber music, the great quartets of Haydn and Mozart and, above all, Beethoven's personal acquaintance with the much-admired composer of quartets, Emanuel Aloys Förster, must have contributed to hasten the inevitable transition. At the turn of the century and before his thirtieth year, Beethoven had so mastered and developed the three branches of his art that he was able to use them as effective bases of all his future creative work. The fantasia-sonata became the most flexible form of improvisation, the symphony the greatest expression of the architectonic impulse, and the quartet the purest vehicle of abstract musical thought.

The Op. 18 quartets were published in two numbers, each containing three works, but they did not appear in the order of their composition. As, however, no particular line of development can be traced within the cycle of quartets the order is immaterial. A version of the F major quartet, differing in some respects from the final form, was completed in 1799. In this earlier version Beethoven presented it to his friend Amenda, but a year later he wrote : " Do not pass on to others the quartet as you have it. I have altered it considerably, having but just learned to compose quartets aright, as you will see when I send it to you." A comparison of the details of the two versions shows that the revision tended to a freer, more soloistic treatment of the accompanying parts, a clearer individualisation of the violoncello part and greater tonal delicacy in the *ensemble* effects; alterations, in fact, that wider experience, or the counsel of some old hand, such as Förster, would be likely to suggest. The main idea of the composition, however, remains unchanged. This is no disadvantage, for the fresh *naïveté* of the content, the unassuming clarity of structure are great charms, and more would have been lost than gained by over-meticulous revision. As the work stands it is gratifying to the performer and offers pleasant not over-difficult problems to the listener, and shows the skill of the composer in handling the quartet instruments, among which the violin is still given the most prominent place. We possess a poetic exposition of the second movement in Beethoven's own words as related by Amenda to Wiedemann. " When Beethoven had finished his well-known quartet in F major he played the glorious *adagio* to his friend and asked him what it suggested to him. ' It suggested a lover's parting,' said Amenda. ' Well,' replied Beethoven, ' the tomb scene in *Romeo and Juliet* was in my mind.' " The story seems to be confirmed by the discovery of a study, never executed, entitled *Les derniers soupirs,* but whether Amenda's anecdote be true or not, this *adagio affettuoso ed appassionato* is a most moving song of sorrow such as only Beethoven could accomplish when he turned to the grave D minor key. The work closes, however, on a triumphant note.

The next quartet, in G major, is less variable in mood. The work is exceedingly graceful, and its nickname, the " Compliment Quartet," well describes the character of the main subject, and indeed indicates the tone of the whole work, despite a somewhat graver second movement.

Gaiety also characterises the quartet in D major, as is to be expected from the choice of key, though a pensive and sentimental strain is woven into the work, and the *andante* in B flat major is definitely lyrical.

The A major quartet, the earliest composed of the second collection, is a perfect type of the concerto quartet. The minuet, which here occupies the position of second movement, is one of the few of Beethoven's movements so named, which is actually a minuet. The *andante cantabile* which follows is a wonderful example of Beethoven's skill in preserving and exploiting the individual character of his instruments, both separately and in unison.

A virtuoso and concerto-like element is strong in the B flat major quartet. In feeling, the work broadly resembles the B flat major sonata composed about the same time. The prevailing mood is one of cheerfulness and the *scherzo* is a glorious piece of musicianly humour. Reaction from these high spirits is represented in the " *la malinconia* " passage ; the work, however, reaches a joyous close.

The fact that Beethoven wrote five of his first six quartets in the major indicates his need for the expression of joyful and gay thoughts at that period. It is noteworthy that we possess no studies for the quartet in C minor. This rather suggests that it was separated from the others by time as well as by the character of its contents. It may be, as Riemann supposes, a revision of some older composition now lost. Apart, however, from any definite evidence of an earlier date, it seems more likely that the C minor quartet is the latest composed of the Op. 18 group, a supplementary work to the C minor sonatas, Op. 10 and 13, the C minor pianoforte trio, Op. 1, and the C minor string trio, Op. 9. With these may also be associated the C minor pianoforte concerto, the C minor duo, Op. 30, for pianoforte and violin, and even the C minor symphony, sketched as early as 1804, and the overture to *Coriolanus*. This almost unbroken succession of different kinds of works in C minor, taken together with the fact that Beethoven scarcely used that key after the completion of the *Coriolanus* overture and of the C minor symphony (1808), suggests that some common idea underlies them all. This idea found perfect expression in the two great orchestral poems and appeared no more in Beethoven's works till a much later period, when, in the Op. 111 sonata of 1821–22, it is once more presented, clothed in the garment of a far riper philosophy and worked out to an entirely different solution. It is quite justifiable to speak of a " C minor problem " dominating the tragic works of Beethoven's youth and early manhood, which later gives place to " F minor " and " D minor problems."

The subject of this early work in C minor is the search for life's first great object of contest. There is a sense of gnawing inner dissatisfaction, a desire to meet and overcome difficulties, the spur of ambition and the longing for victory. These emotions, being subjective, require an intimate and psychological form of musical expression. The C minor sonatas and chamber music works represent not an actual conflict with the powers of fate, but an attempt to realise and understand the existence of such powers and their significance for the increasingly self-conscious personality. And since there is no actual conflict there is also no result; whence it comes that each of these works, among them the C minor quartet, has an inconclusive ending; they die away either in passionate restlessness or in a dim visionary premonition of victories not yet attained.

Among the Op. 18 quartets the C minor quartet with its mournful earnestness stands as sole witness of an outlook on life, a restless dissatisfaction, the very opposite of the cheerful sense of concord with the world and mankind expressed in the other five. Within the group the C minor quartet has no companion piece, but such a work exists in the string quintet, Op. 29, the first and last example of Beethoven's use of this form in original composition. The choice of key is remarkable. Beethoven's works in C major hitherto were the sonata, Op. 2 iii, the pianoforte quartet in C major, the trio for two oboes and cor anglais, and the pianoforte concerto, Op. 15. Apart from the wind trio these are among Beethoven's least important juvenile works. The beginning of his distinguished work in C major is the first symphony composed in 1799–1800. This was followed by the overture to *Prometheus*, the Op. 29 quintet and the *Waldstein* sonata, Op. 53 (1804), after which comes a succession of great works in C major, the three *Leonora* overtures, the C major quartet, Op. 59, and the first *Mass*. After this the C major mood disappears for a time to reappear later spasmodically in the violoncello sonata, Op. 102, the overtures, Op. 115 and 124, and the *Diabelli* variations. This gradually growing preference for, and subsequent neglect of, a particular key is in itself interesting, but special significance attaches to it when we come to comparisons with the series of C minor works. Such a comparison shows that Beethoven cultivated the keys of C major and C minor contemporaneously till he united them, and explored to the depths the characteristics of both, in the fifth symphony, completed in 1808. The contrasts which Beethoven here obtains within a single work, and which he used again later in the Op. 111 sonata, are to be found in the earlier compositions, where pairs of works in C major and C minor respectively are complementary. They are not so closely interconnected as the separate movements of the symphony and of the sonata, but they nevertheless mirror inwardly allied conceptions, leading to painful emotions in the C minor works and to joy in the C major.

A psychological affinity of this kind clearly exists between the C minor quartet, which bears no relationship to the other members of the Op. 18 group, and the C major string quintet, Op. 29. A mood of deep earnestness is common to each, but whereas the quartet is full of passionate excitement, the quintet suggests exalted repose; the opening movement of the quintet, indeed, might be played immediately after the close of the C minor quartet, so clearly does it confirm and develop the "major" mood, barely attained and shortly stated at the end of that work.

Besides Op. 29 and a quintet fugue in D major, Op. 137, composed in 1817, apparently as an exercise, two other string quintets exist. Each bears an opus number, but nevertheless they are mere arrangements of earlier works. The Op. 4 quintet is an arrangement, with some alterations and considerable improvements in structure and technique, of the octet for wind instruments. Beethoven probably intended in this case to make use of a piece of unpublished work and to improve upon it by translating it into terms of other tone-values. The Op. 104 quintet, on the contrary, owes its origin to chance. In 1817 some person unknown sent Beethoven a quintet arrangement of the C minor trio, Op. 1. Beethoven disliked the version and immediately set to work and completed a new arrangement, adding the following humorous note: "A terzett arranged as a three-part quintet by Herr Gutwillen ('good-will'), cleared up and changed from the mere semblance of five parts to the real possession of five parts and raised from utter destitution to a condition of some reputation by Herr Wohlwollen ('wish-well') on August 14th, 1817. N.B.—The original three-part quintet score has been offered up as a

solemn burnt-offering to the gods of the under-world." This
arrangement differs in detail from the original, but there are
no important changes. Other arrangements by Beethoven are
the setting of the D major symphony as a pianoforte trio and
the arrangement of the E major sonata, Op. 14, as a quartet in
F major. Later on he refused to undertake work of this kind,
and the Op. 104 quintet, as we have seen, was the result of a
whim. A weak arrangement by some other person induced
Beethoven to set the Op. 133 quartet fugue for the pianoforte,
but the work had no charm for him, nor did he attain the
exquisite skill therein of Johann Sebastian Bach or Liszt. The
particular garment of sound was always absolutely settled for
Beethoven by the poetic idea for which he sought expression,
and he regarded "arrangements" as mere concessions to the
public or the publishers.

Moreover, this absolute dependence of the form of expression
upon the underlying idea ruled Beethoven's choice of the
various branches of composition. No general desire for change
directed his interest to chamber music for strings only; he
chose it because it was, at a certain period, the perfect medium
for his ideas. After the completion of the Op. 8 and 9 trios,
the Op. 18 quartets and the Op. 4 and 29 quintets, his interest
in this branch of music suffered eclipse for more than four years,
that is, from the publication of the quintet in 1801 to the beginning of the first of the Op. 59 *Rasumowsky* quartets on May 26th,
1806. What is the explanation of this remarkable fact?

By the end of the century Beethoven had struck out all the
three main lines of future development, the fantasia-sonata in
the region of the sonata, the great symphonic style for orchestral
work, and a highly abstract and philosophical type of chamber
music. Progress in chamber music, however, since it summarised his experience, postulated progress in the other branches,
and these, at the moment, were but on the threshold of a new
stage of development. The chamber music hitherto answered
to the style of the first symphony and the fantasia-sonatas, and
new ground had first to be won and held on these lines before
a basis for fresh chamber music works could be found. On
the symphonic side this basis was eventually afforded by the
Eroica, with its conscious recognition of the force of the poetic

idea, and by the *Leonora* overtures, while in the region of the
sonata it was supplied by the increased prominence of concerto
elements, and the consequent change of style in the solo sonatas
up to Op. 57 and the duo sonatas up to Op. 47.   While these
important changes were taking place the composer was also
drawing fresh experience from the composition of his opera
Leonora, so that a threefold stream contributed to the next great
chamber music works, the three symphonic concerto quartets
of Op. 59.

The first of these quartets, that in F major, moves, emotionally,
from a quiet consciousness of power to a fantastic and excited
display of activity, thence to sorrowful plaints and, finally, to
a sense of vigorous well-being.   The two companion works
are like it and each possesses a " yea-saying " close, but rests
on different psychological premises and pursues a different
course of development.   These are simple in the C major
quartet and more complicated in the E minor, in accordance
with the choice of key.   Beethoven's E minor compositions,
indeed, are amongst the most delicately felt and exquisitely
shaded of his works.   In these quartets he introduces Russian
melodies—perhaps in compliment to the Russian Count Rasumowsky, who commissioned the work—but quite apart from
this circumstance the use of folk-song is appropriate, both in
the cheerful rough humour of the F major finale and in the
E minor trio.

These E major and E minor quartets are founded on conflict
and contrast, acute and violent in the first, subtle and subjective in the second, but the following C major quartet has
quite another basis.   It is entirely free from problems and
forms a reconciling close to the group of which it is the final
number.   During a time of wrestling with the problems of
new form, Beethoven had replaced the minuet by the light-
hearted *scherzo*—which was his peculiar creation—but, with his
problem solved, he returns in this work to a minuet, which
he well names *menuetto grazioso*.   This does not, however,
retain the old-fashioned, pleasant minuet character throughout.
The mask falls and Beethoven's characteristic humour, deep
and packed with the reality and meaning of life, attained by
conquest—not by evasion—of life's tragic problems, breaks

through. The closing fugue of the C major quartet ranks with the greatest of Beethoven's works. Intellect and imagination are here so mingled that it is difficult to know which takes the lead, while form and content are assimilated each to each by *the* musician who felt, thought and dreamed in tone. Here Beethoven reached an eminence so commanding that for the moment further advance seemed impossible, and he accordingly turned aside for a time to other branches of his art.

It has been shown that the three Op. 59 quartets are not merely accidentally associated, but that they have spiritual affinity. The closing movements of all three strike the same note of victory and each work marks an advance on the preceding; they are all three embodiments of a single poetic idea, variously presented, each time with increasing perfection. Exterior conflicts are first portrayed, then interior problems, while in the last of the three the strife of opposites becomes a thing of the past, and only a memory of past battles varies the final song of enduring triumph. The illuminated and transfigured soul speaks in the last of these quartets as in the eighth symphony, and the resemblances between these works are not due to chance. They, however, serve to emphasise the difference between the Beethoven of 1806 and the Beethoven of 1812. The composer of the C major quartet has not yet learned the last secrets of laughter; he is still the victor rather than the philosopher. Triumph, indeed, is the underlying motive of the third, fourth and, above all, the fifth symphonies, and it is of these works that the Op. 59 quartets are an abstract and epitome. This central idea of triumph gives rise to the monumental style of the *Rasumowsky* quartets and impels to a mighty display of force. The finale of the C minor symphony, finished in 1808, represents the extreme of this line of development. It is an idea which strains the form of the string quartet to the uttermost, and the result is a series of works of a majesty and expressive power such as no one before Beethoven had dreamed of obtaining from four string instruments. This was the victory won in the *Rasumowsky* quartets, but Beethoven realised that there are greater things than conquest and triumph and that, these accomplished, the way at last lay open for the free development of his own personality. Formerly that personality had yearned for strife as a means of testing its own powers; now the strife was over and in quietness he had learned to know himself. Now follows the great period of peace in his creative work, culminating in the seventh and eighth symphonies. The two-movement sonata also appears, with a return to the use of the pianoforte in chamber music. In his struggle with Fate, Beethoven's idyllic instinct was aroused, and while he worked on the C minor symphony the *Pastoral* was germinating. The mood of victory led him on to delight in little things and also to a joyous consciousness of his own indomitable personality. He had fulfilled his prophetic boast, " I will take Fate by the throat," and while we admire the courage of the words, the strength which translated them into action is even more admirable. Knowledge of power together with a capacity for delight in the idyllic side of life were the fruits of the years of conflict, of the period which gave birth to the great compositions in praise of personal heroism. E flat major, Beethoven's " heroic " key, indicates the basic mood of the works of 1808 and 1809. The series opens with the E flat major trio, Op. 70, and includes the great E flat major pianoforte concerto and culminates in the E flat major quartet, Op. 74.

There are several points of resemblance, both external and internal, between the E flat major quartet and that in C major. Each expresses a glad sense of power, but in the later work the idea is more fully developed and established with greater wealth of detail. The spiritual roots of the C major quartets are to be sought in the two preceding quartets in F major and E minor, so that a detailed introduction was superfluous. The E flat major quartet, on the other hand, has no close connection with any other work and consequently needs an introduction to explain clearly the premises on which the work is based. The subject is the victory of a sheer delight in creative power over a restless search for fresh knowledge, and here the artistic expression is so finished and absolute that once more a phase in Beethoven's development as man and artist is rounded off and brought to a close.

Now the battle with Fate has been fought to a finish, the C minor phantoms have been exorcised, and the victorious composer has awakened afresh to the joy of creation, but the inward triumph was not yet complete and he had still to reach that state of illumination—represented in the eighth symphony—whence he could smile on calamity and observe life's comedy with great-hearted gaiety. In the winter of 1809 to 1810 Beethoven's greatest orchestral work in F minor—the *Egmont* overture—appeared. It portrayed a victorious hero who bought victory at the price of the annihilation of his personality. The need to recognise the reverse side of victory and the sacrifices it may demand clamoured in his soul for artistic expression, and formed a pessimistic commentary on the mood of triumphant rejoicing. At the moment when Beethoven had fought out his battle, when he could look back on all the stages of the contest and taste the fruits of victory, he became most intensely aware of what it had cost him. The result of this mood of combined retrospection and introspection was the F minor quartet *Serioso*, Op. 95, composed in October 1810, thus preceding the seventh and eighth symphonies. The autographed title, which did not appear in the printed edition, shows that the composer sought no happy solution of his problem. The powers of darkness which he conjures up here have no longer full power over him, and he can therefore deal with them imaginatively as a subject for artistic exposition. *Serioso* is a title, like the *Pathétique* applied to Op. 13, which implies that the composer is consciously assuming a mask, a mask which in Op. 95 he himself discards at the last. By a most surprising change at the close of the work the spirit of laughter takes charge and is hailed as the solution of life's problems, and the way now lies clear to the eighth symphony.

The manuscript of the *Serioso* quartet bears the date " 1810, in the month of October," written in Beethoven's own hand; the next great quartet, in E flat major, Op. 127, was not finished till about January 1825, after the completion of the ninth symphony in the spring of the preceding year. This leaves an interval of fourteen years, a far longer gap than is to be found in any other one branch of Beethoven's composition. These intervening years saw the production of the three last symphonies, the six last sonatas together with other works for the pianoforte, the *Fidelio* overture, the *Name-day* overture, the " *Weihe des*

Hauses," the last pianoforte duets and trios, and Beethoven's principal vocal works, solo and choral, the *Song Cycle* and the *Great Mass*. The creative impulse was thus active in all branches, putting forth works of the first importance, with the sole exception of the string quartet. Not so much as a single sketch or study dating from these years has come down to us. When Beethoven was staying in Linz in 1812 he wrote, at the request of the cathedral kapellmeister, three *equale* for four trombones, a slight work, afterwards performed at his funeral. Studies for a string quintet and a quintet fugue in D major date from 1817, but Beethoven's interest in the string quartet seemed to have disappeared entirely. In a letter of 1822 to the publisher Peters of Leipzig there is mention of a quartet which Peters " would soon receive," but no studies for Op. 127 earlier than those of 1824 are known to exist. Whether there be such or not, it is certain that the composition of the quartet was not undertaken seriously till the *Mass* was complete and the ninth symphony nearly so. After the long silence Beethoven took up the quartet with tremendous enthusiasm, almost as though he wished to make up for lost time. From the spring of 1824 till the end of 1826, when mortal illness put a stop to all activities, he devoted himself solely to quartet composition. Five works resulted, differing completely from former quartets in both the scale and complexity of their structure, while no serious comparison can be made between them and other contemporary works, which were all of an " occasional " character, slight pianoforte pieces, canons, etc. How can we account for this striking change, following upon fourteen years' neglect of this branch of music, or explain the following three years' exclusive concentration upon it ?

Circumstances may have had something to do with the revival of Beethoven's interest in the quartet. In November 1822, Prince Nicholas Galitzin, an intelligent admirer of Beethoven's work, asked the composer if he were willing to undertake a commission for three quartets, while in the spring of 1823 Ignaz Schuppanzigh, leader of the Lichnowsky (later the Rasumowsky) Quartet, returned from a seven years' absence in Russia and began to give quartet concerts. These events may have influenced Beethoven, but we know from the letter to Peters that the idea of composing a new quartet was in his mind before the arrival of Galitzin's letter or the return of Schuppanzigh, and we must seek some deeper cause for the revival of this creative impulse which had lain dormant for fourteen years.

The cause is perhaps to be found in a change in Beethoven's artistic emotions and ideas. The desire to exhibit an exact and precise account of the great turning-points in Beethoven's life and to correlate them with the phases of his spiritual development as a composer has led to various classifications of " periods " and " styles." Anton Schindler's biography is based on a purely chronological division of the life into three periods, the first ending in 1800, the second in 1814, while all later compositions are classed together as of the third period. This is simplicity itself—the works are grouped as belonging to youth, early and late manhood—but it takes no account of the peculiarities of Beethoven's development. In *Beethoven et ses trois styles*, Wilhelm von Lenz attempts a more interesting approach to the question. He retains the threefold division, but marks his boundaries at Op. 20 and Op. 100, characterising the first style as " traditional," the second as " personal " and the third as " intensely personal " or " qualitative." It is a fault of both classifications that the changes from one period to the next are made to appear sudden and intentional, whereas in reality the changes were gradual and unpremeditated; many passages of the so-called " last period " might to all appearance have belonged to an earlier stage, while details of earlier compositions are occasionally prophetic of a future development of style. It is a thankless task to look for clear boundary lines, and any such attempt tends to break up the unity of the works as a whole and to obscure the fact that they were the expression of a gradually unfolding, gradually ripening personality.

Liszt was convinced of the triviality, if not of the positive harmfulness, of this method of classification by periods and styles when he wrote his well-known letter to Lenz on the subject. He suggested, as a substitute for Lenz's three styles, a division of the works into two categories, " la première celle où la forme traditionelle et convenue contient et régit la pensée du maître, et la seconde, celle ou la pensée étend, brise, recrée

Y

et façonne au gré de ses besoins et de ses inspirations la forme et le style." *

In this definition Liszt purposely avoids making a boundary line and satisfies himself with a phrase, generally accepted as clever, which bears little relation to the facts. Apart from a few " occasional " works, Beethoven wrote nothing in which the idea was slave to the form. Here and there a work may appear to us conventional, either wholly or in detail, but this is not due to subordination of the idea to the form. In such cases the conventional form is part of the underlying concept on which the work is based and means that the composer has been thinking conventionally (according to our standards), not that he has submitted to any exterior compulsion. The contrast between form and idea on which Liszt's theory is based does not, in fact, exist in Beethoven's work, which represents a ceaseless process of assimilation of form to idea, the idea, as in every true work of art, being always the primary and actively creative element, the form the secondary and receptive element. The first part of Liszt's definition is, therefore, meaningless, but the second finely expresses the formative might of the poetic idea, which ruled no " second period " merely, but the whole of Beethoven's creative life.

Beethoven once told Schindler that he thought of expressing in words the poetic idea underlying each of his compositions; had he carried this out it would have been easy to trace his development by the changing subjects of his work. As it is, apart from a very few programmatic works, we are left without such signposts and can only come to know the poetic idea by study of the musical form. The results attained by the student will differ according to his idea of what is involved in the concept " form." If by form is understood principally the technical structure of a work, details of melodic, harmonic and rhythmic expression, a long process of refinement, a continuous conscious striving for more poetic and intellectual musical expression will be noticed. The long-drawn-out melodic and thematic phrases

---

* " In the first of which, traditional and conventional form circumscribes and directs the master's thought, while in the second, the thought first strains and breaks, then recreates and fashions form and style to express its own needs and inspirations."

of early years either receive characteristic motival articulation or they are shortened and become tersely formulated motives. The picturesqueness of these motives becomes greatly intensified. Pregnant and effective use is made of the symbolic suggestion of rising or falling passages, wide and short intervals, motives which circle about a note and motives which repeat a note again and again. The composer's brain is constantly at work absorbing knowledge as material on and in which the imagination can work. Every interval has its particular significance, and it is the very wealth of purposeful melodic images, and the constant development and modification of the underlying thought that has given the later works the reputation of being hard to understand.

These processes, traced in melodic form, take place in rhythm and harmony also. Choice of a particular key sets the basic mood of a whole work, and each passing change of key connotes the composer's imaginative associations with that key. Thus each modulation of a movement, a period, or a theme is based on poetic intention and brings with it associations of ideas which it would take years of close psychological study to analyse. A glance at the opening harmonies of Beethoven's works, a moment's consideration of their significance, is sufficient to show the inexhaustible emotional suggestiveness of harmonic effects and the wide influence which he attributed to them. The rhythmic element, too, steadily increased in significance. Rhythmic expansion and contraction, combinations of unequal rhythm in the different parts and rhythmic emotional effects of all kinds are employed with ever-increasing purpose and definition. When one considers what further resources Beethoven possessed in dynamic and phrasing, it seems hardly surprising that many students are now directing their attention to these and endeavouring to fix the boundaries of the several styles by reference to the technique of expression.

Despite the interest of these researches, however, it must never be forgotten that all these details, which together represent the architecture of music, are of secondary importance in the expression of the poetic idea. Melody, harmony, rhythm, dynamic and phrasing appear in very similar guise in all works of the same period, and it is the tone-form in which they are

clothed which gives difference of effect; it is this which corresponds most clearly and intimately with the content and character of a composition, this which first embodies the poetic
idea and determines all the other elements of form and structure.
These tone-forms afford the real clue to the ideas which stirred
in the composer. They do not succeed or replace each other
in order of time, but, appearing simultaneously, display the
poetic idea underlying each phase of the composer's life under
the tone symbolism of three separate styles, that of the sonata
improvisation, that of the monumental symphony, and that of
the abstract quartet. Each of these styles reveals a different
stream of spiritual tendency in the soul of the composer. His
development can best be traced in his changing activities within
each of these three great branches of composition.

Regarded from this view-point the year 1800 is seen to mark
a turning-point in Beethoven's work, a point at which he first
came to full self-consciousness and adopted the fantasia-sonata,
the symphony, and the quartet as the three great means of
revealing the contrasts of his own nature. Pioneer work is
done in the fantasia-sonata, which expresses hitherto vaguely-
felt emotional conflicts in terms of clear imaginative thought
and leads up to the *Eroica*. The symphony now takes the
lead and maintains the line of advance from the *Eroica* to the
lofty eighth symphony. The sonatas and quartets of this
period have certain symphonic and concerto-like characteristics.
They are supplementary to the symphonies and give symphonic
expression to such ideas as are outside the scope of the orchestral
symphony. The pianoforte now resumes its task of striking
out new paths, but since it is no longer a question of winning
and establishing a poetic consciousness, but of conquering an
entirely new imaginative kingdom, the pianoforte sonata is
unequal to the whole task and the composer seeks fresh stimuli
in the region of vocal music, in the inspiration of the word.
During the period of the symphonic style, opera, and the
dramatic programmatic overture (which was opera in crystallised form), opened up for Beethoven the possibility of new
imaginative premises. Secular and, still more, sacred music,
gave him, through the sung word, an impulse (culminating in
the *Great Mass*, which stands in solitary grandeur among

Beethoven's works) which led to the expansion of the capacity of instrumental expression. Reborn in the *Great Mass*, the poetic idea entered on a new life in the three forms of sonata, symphony and quartet. Once again the sonata took the lead, Beethoven mastering the new elements of expression through the medium of free, subjective, improvisation. Again the leadership passed from the sonata to the symphony and the new instrumental speech was translated into the symphonic style. This time, however, the symphony did not maintain its dominance. A group of quartets followed, not, like earlier quartets, a supplement to, or new rendering of, symphonic ideas in a more delicate musical idiom, but as an expression of the quintessence of the human and artistic knowledge of the composer. The last creative period is that of the quartet style, pure and simple.

April 2nd, 1800, is a day marked in history as that on which a Beethoven symphony was publicly performed for the first time, but March 6th, 1825, is a date of no less interest. On that day the first of the five great quartets was performed for the first time by Ignaz Schuppanzigh, Karl Holz, Franz Weiss and Joseph Linke, " the great Master's execrable 'cellist," as he signed himself when, shortly before the performance, Beethoven sent round a humorous note running: " Friends! Herewith each man receives his part and it is hereby enjoined that each one solemnly pledges himself on his honour to do his best, to distinguish himself and mutually to outdo all the others. Everyone who has to do with the subject referred to, must sign this."

The performance opened a new series of Schuppanzigh's subscription concerts and was thus advertised in the *Bäuerles Theaterzeitung* of March 3rd, 1825: " The first of these concerts is to be held on March 6th and will be honoured by an entirely new and masterly quartet of Beethoven's composition. This work (still in manuscript) should afford all the more pleasure to all lovers of fine music, as it is the only quartet which the celebrated composer has written for fifteen years." Alfred Ebert gives an account of the concert. Schuppanzigh, who despite constant pressure only received the work a very short time before the date of the concert, was hardly equal to the difficult task. " The result of the performance was the open agreement of all present, both professionals and amateurs, that they had understood little or nothing of the course of the work. Clouds seemed to be gathering about this youngest star of Beethoven's creative genius, when a true friend of art arranged for a new performance of the quartet by the above-named gentlemen, the position of first violin being taken by Herr Professor Böhm, who, in the interval, had played the new quartet before a small and select company of experts with great *éclat*. This professor now performed the marvellous quartet twice on the same evening, before the same very numerous assembly of artists and critics to the entire satisfaction of all; the threatening clouds vanished, and the magnificent work of art shone forth in all its blinding glory."

The newspaper correspondent's rhapsody was no mere rhetorical figure; the public enthusiasm is proved by the fact that the quartet was six times performed within the next few months. A false idea has gained credence that Beethoven's works during the last few years were undervalued by the Vienna of his day. On the contrary, the success of the quartet amounted almost to a sensation; it can have been no puny generation, as Hermann Kretzschmar remarks, which was thus able to accept and appreciate Beethoven's works in their novelty.

The E flat major quartet is, indeed, simple and in its main lines easy to understand compared with its successors. It is Beethoven's second quartet in E flat major and has much in common with the earlier work. The " harp " quartet, Op. 74, marked the close of a period of strife and expressed the re-awakening of the spirit of sheer delight in creation, while the E flat major quartet, Op. 127, also represents a summoning up of the forces of personality, a statement of a new attitude towards life and its problems. The work opens with a proud and stately prelude in E flat major, a proclamation of indomitable will-power, triumphant after many past conflicts. It does more than usher in a single new quartet; it is, in fact, the portal to the whole artistic kingdom of Beethoven's last years. As, long before, in the Op. 74 quartet, a mood of joy in creation follows, but there is a wide difference between the Beethoven of 1807 and the Beethoven of 1824. In the earlier work he had been content with clever playful variations, a simple witty song theme. Here it is the mystery of artistic conception which concerns him and we are reminded of the *Benedictus* of the *Mass*. In a series of marvellous variations he attempts to embody and set forth the revelation which has been granted to his seeking soul. After certain lively passages, the mood of deep earnestness returns and a simple and touching epilogue closes the movement. The subsequent *scherzo*, with its alternations of wild, almost rough humour and eeriness, is something of a riddle. It is the richest in content and the most prolix of Beethoven's quartet *scherzi*, and may represent a last uprush of the powers of darkness before they succumb finally to the spirit of joy. The finale takes up the word where the third movement has abandoned it. The whole movement has the character of a march. A spirit of indestructible happiness dominates it. Some adventurer from the heavens seems to visit the earth he has left, with tidings of gladness, to return to his home in the heavens once more.

The first studies for the next two works in A minor and B flat major were begun immediately after the conclusion of the E flat major quartet, but a serious illness, diagnosed as inflammation of the bowels, interrupted the work, which was resumed during Beethoven's sojourn in Baden at the beginning of May. The content of the A minor quartet shows that the work was not merely interrupted but considerably altered as a result of Beethoven's illness.

It should be remembered while considering this work, Op. 132, that its opus number does not correspond with its date of completion; it was actually finished before Op. 130 and 131. The three works arose almost simultaneously. Studies for the B flat major quartet were begun almost at the same time as those for the A minor quartet; the latter was finished at the latest in August 1825, the former in September or October. While Beethoven was still working on the B flat major quartet he began studies for the C sharp minor quartet, which he worked upon till about July 1826; the work was not in the hands of the publisher, Schott, till September. The A minor, B flat major and C sharp minor quartets thus form a triptych, differing markedly from the preceding E flat major quartet and the succeeding F major quartet. The F major quartet, op. 135, was not begun till July 1826, by which time the C sharp minor quartet was finished save for a few details. The five quartets thus fall into three groups, the introductory Op. 127, the closely associated Op. 132, 130 and 131, and the final op. 135.

In the E flat major quartet Beethoven had retained the usual four-movement sonata form, but in the three following works there is a tendency to increase the number of movements and to adopt elements associated with the suite. The A minor quartet possessed five, the B flat major quartet six, and the C sharp minor quartet seven movements. This is the more curious in that in Op. 135 Beethoven returns to the four-movement structure, and the movements themselves are shorter and less discursive than those of the central group of quartets. The close connection between these works is shown by the fact that Beethoven interchanged movements amongst them, as for example, the G major *tedesca* of Op. 130, which was originally written in A major and intended for the A minor quartet.

The most remarkable testimony to the organic connection between these three quartets—a witness hitherto seldom recognised or fully appreciated—is the thematic bond which undoubtedly exists between them. It must be remembered that for any critical æsthetic valuation of the B flat major quartet the original version with the fugue as closing movement, not the later version with a final rondo, should be reviewed. Nottebohm has shown that the fugue theme of Op. 130 and the opening theme of the A minor quartet are contemporaneous and closely associated, and he believes that " there can scarcely be a doubt that Beethoven drew from studies for the fugue theme the motive of four long notes with which he opens the first movement of the A minor quartet and which he uses again later in that work. The fugue studies thus served a double purpose."

The purpose served was, as a matter of fact, not double but threefold. This theme formed not only the main subject of the first movement of Op. 132 and the fugue subject of Op. 130 (now Op. 133), but by a change from ascending sixths to descending thirds it became the principal theme of the first and, reversed, of the last movement of Op. 131. It is the leading idea of the whole group of Beethoven's three greatest quartets, and recognition of the fact throws new light on the composer's train of thought.

Nottebohm's statement needs correction in one other respect. The motive of which he speaks (consisting not of tones but of semitones) not only opens the first movement of the A minor quartet and is used again later, but, as close study will show, is, in reality, the main theme of the movement, the musical germ of the whole. It appears first in the opening *assai sostenuto* as a mysterious prophecy: G sharp—A—F—E. Presently, in its threatening ascending form and reversed as F—E—G sharp—A, it assumes the character of an unalterable edict of Fate; and how changed has Beethoven's conception of that edict become since the days of the C minor symphony! There it sounded as an insistent relentless challenge; in the F minor quartet it had a ring of devilish spite; here it is the mysterious voice of an oracle speaking of things beyond reach of thought. As such it floods and interpenetrates the whole movement, and the A minor theme, usually taken as the main subject, is merely a plaintive antiphon. Thus regarded the movement ceases to appear broken or erratic and is seen for what it is—a splendid imaginative hymn to Fate, conceived not as destructive but as a constructive character-moulding force, the whole expressed in a remarkable, perfect and close-knit form. The close of the movement suggests to the hearer Dürer's *Knight, Death and the Devil*; it is an apotheosis of ethical heroism, a restrained, unpretentious heroism, without so much as a single pathetic gesture.

It is more than probable that reminiscences of the first movement played a part in determining the themes of the subsequent scherzo-like *allegro ma non troppo*; both the characteristic G sharp—A of the opening bar and the five-beat violin theme (suggesting the plaintive antiphon) are explicable thus. The complexity of thought characteristic of the quartet style, which is full of hidden and, at the first glance, apparently chance associations, supports such a theory. If we accept it, the A major *scherzo* appears as a translation of the *allegro* theme into the language of a more sprightly emotional mood. A folk-dance melody follows, not rough, as in the earlier *thème russe*, but pleasant and graceful. The subsequent country waltz is known to be derived from a collection of *Deutschen* (German country-dances) used by Beethoven in the 'nineties for a ball at the Assembly Rooms. Here rhythm and emphasis are changed, and a mood of dreamy reminiscence is suggested. The mood is interrupted by a return of the "Fate" motive of the first movement, a remarkable *intermezzo* which cuts across the peaceful course of the *scherzo*, bringing back the terrible earnestness of the first movement. The gayer mood triumphs, however, and the movement ends in perfect inner peace.

It is not known whether Beethoven sketched this movement before or after his illness, but the finale was undoubtedly planned earlier. There are no studies for the *adagio*, which suggests that Beethoven may originally have intended the present finale to follow the *scherzo* immediately ; if this were so, the A minor quartet, as, probably, the F major quartet, was at first planned without an *adagio*. No studies for the *adagio* dating before Beethoven's illness have been found ; the *adagio* as we have it bears the inscription, "Devout thanksgiving to God for recovery from sickness ; in the Lydian mode," and was clearly planned after his recovery. Emotions aroused by that illness, thoughts about death, expressed jokingly in the canon, "*Doktor, sperrt das Tor dem Tod*," undoubtedly led to the introduction of this *adagio*, either not originally planned or at any rate not in this form.

The idea of a song of praise in the old modes occurs in symphonic studies of 1818, but was abandoned in favour of other plans. A personal experience now recalled it. "Recovery" is to be understood not merely in the narrower sense of physical convalescence, but as victory, by the grace of God, over the assaults of Fate. Seen thus, the *adagio*, despite its later genesis, fits in organically with the train of thought underlying the A minor quartet. The movement opens with a prayer to which the answer comes in a fresh upspringing of the joy of life. The sick man restored in body and soul turns to face the world again with renewed courage, with zest and confidence, and this is expressed in a brisk marching melody. The period of unbroken joy cannot be long and he soon finds

the conflict for which he is fresh armed.   An *allegro appassionato*
in A minor presents the image of a swimmer, battling with the
waves, surmounting one only to encounter another, till his
powers are exhausted, a type of the endless hostility of the
elements.   Help, however, comes at last from without, a great
promise, filling the soul with hope and dwarfing all the agonies
of life.   An indescribable sense of bliss, not ecstatic as in the
seventh symphony, not humorous as in the eighth, but passionless and perfect, dominates the close.   It is the mood of which
Bettina von Arnim makes Beethoven speak when he declares
that he has no fears for the future of his music, " for whoever
really understands it must become free of all the misery which
others bear about with them."

It is significant, not only for the history but also for the
content and matter of the B flat major quartet, that the theme of
its closing movement is twin to the opening theme of the A minor
quartet ; the idea from which the first sets out forms the culminating point of the second, a reversal in the case of the B flat
major quartet of the usual course of development.   Elsewhere
the finale represents the unknown goal to which the earlier
movements tend and is developed out of them ; but in the B flat
major quartet the subject of the finale is fixed from the first,
and the earlier sections have to work to it.   The fact that the
centre of gravity is thus placed in the fugal finale affects the
relationship of the other movements to each other.   They do
not stand in direct sequence, nor do they represent a continuous
line of development ; each from a different view-point relates
directly to the close.

This idea once grasped, the fantasia-like sequence of movements and kaleidoscopic changes of mood are easy to understand.   The sonata-like first movement, the *scherzo-presto*
in B flat minor, the D flat major andante, the *danza tedesca*
in G major and the *cavatina* in E flat major, form a suite,
almost a pot-pourri, of movements without any close psychological interconnection.   Our theory, however, explains this
fact and also the lack of any imaginative centre of gravity before
the fugue ; each movement is merely episodic inasmuch as
it prepares for the finale.   Even the opening movement, which
usually gives clearest expression to the poetic idea underlying

a work, proclaiming, as it were, the " argument," here affords no hint of what is to come. Every one of these movements, including the finale, can be regarded as a work in itself without detriment to the effect. The final fugue, however, mighty in form and in range of thought, gathers up all the parts in itself and makes a unity of the work, portraying the changing aspects of life as revelations of a single creative will which is seen in unveiled majesty at the close.

The first movement is compact of energy, the second and third of fantasy, sometimes dark, sometimes sunny, the fourth of unclouded happiness, while the fifth, the *cavatina* (of which Beethoven said to Holz, " Never did music of mine make so deep an impression upon me, even the remembrance of the emotions it aroused always costs me a tear "), expresses intense religious fervour. Each is a deep and characteristic expression of the composer's personality, but a bond of spiritual union is lacking till it is supplied by the finale, the great quartet fugue which was later published separately as Op. 133. The theme of the movement appeared, in the A minor quartet, as Destiny calling mankind to action. The conqueror of Fate sees Fate no longer as inimical, but as the only way to greatness. Fate's command, once felt as bitter and fiercely resisted, is now heard as the message of freedom and blends at last with the personal will which once strove against it. This union of the will with the behest of Fate, this reconciliation of implacable law with personal freedom, clamoured for artistic expression. The ideas of Freedom and of Necessity are blended by Beethoven in his fugue, upon which he wrote, " *Tantôt libre, tantôt recherché.*" The inscription is more than a note on form ; it is the poetic " programme " of the movement, indicating the reconciliation of the two great opposites of Freedom and Necessity which here finds symbolic expression.

As the studies show, the subject of the fugue is closely allied to the main theme of the A minor quartet, but it is not absolutely similar. The brooding minor character of Op. 132 is replaced by the more energetic major. The small ascending sixth is magnified to a clear-cut diminished seventh. The theme does not begin with a dissonant seventh interval but with a powerful key-note. These alterations give a greater, more heroic turn to the theme. A short prelude, described as an *overture*, affords a fantasia-like summary of the three sections of the movement. It begins with an energetic first exposition of the " Fate " theme of the fugue. There follows a tender, dreamy G flat major episode, suggesting the self-consecration of the will of the combatant, while the "Fate" theme loses its inimical aspect and is freely and joyfully accepted by the will. Thereto follows the third great phase of the movement, an exposition of the " Will " theme leading on to an expression of world-embracing might. Through a defiant *allegro molto con brio* in ⁶⁄₈ time it proceeds to a joyful and confident *meno mosso e moderato* in ³⁄₄, with a vigorous repetition of the G flat major theme, rising unbroken to a *stretta* apotheosis. The work is one of compelling, almost overwhelming greatness ; it is above comparisons save, perhaps, with two other fugues in B flat major, the finale of Op. 106 and the *Et vitam venturi* of the *Mass*. Even Beethoven could climb no higher ; he returns to the world of normal, glad emotions and concepts by way of the C sharp minor quartet and the F major quartet, a way which would perhaps have led on to a new C major quintet had he lived. But he brings with him the great illumination to which he attained in the B flat major finale ; the great " Fate and Will " motive, at first a speculative creed, is herein applied to life and action and is found to be a word of support and power.

In its fresh application it appears in altered guise. The ascending sixths and sevenths are replaced by descending thirds, emphasised by a marked *sforzato*, while the opening seventh is robbed of its dissonant effect by a preparatory fifth. Treatment of the melody, transposition from B flat major to C sharp and the substitution of *adagio* for *allegro* tempo make the theme appear as a contrast to that of the final subject of the B flat major quartet. On the other hand, the form in both cases is a fugue. The two works are alike architecturally, but in the C sharp minor prelude the theme is reversed, the composer, who in the former work had made thereof wings to carry him to the heights, thus symbolising a return to life from the transcendental regions of the B flat major fugue.

The idea of a reawakening to the joy of life is expressed both in the general plan and in the particular sequence of the

succeeding movements.   In contrast to the kaleidoscopic changes
presented by the movements of the B flat major quartet, those of
the C sharp minor quartet represent a steadily ascending line.
Even external interruption by pauses between the individual
movements is avoided.   This close unity prepares the way for a
return to the four-movement form.   The C sharp minor quartet,
indeed, possesses seven separately numbered movements, but
closer observation shows that the division is purely external.   The
last movement but one, no. 6, is a slow introduction to the
finale, the *presto*, no. 5, stands for the *scherzo*, and the recitative-
like introduction, no. 3, leads up to the variations *andante*,
no. 4, so that nos. 3—7 taken together, represent slow
movement, *scherzo* and *finale*.   It is only the first movement,
consisting of an *adagio-fugue* in C sharp minor and an *allegro
molto vivace* in D major, which departs from the traditional
order of the quartet.   In this movement the poetic idea of
the whole work is proclaimed.   The return to life, to joyful
thought and emotion, an *incarnatus est* in the human rather
than in the religious sense, is presented in each section of
this twofold movement, the first representing the mystical
rebirth, a return from the world of visions and dreams to
the world of reality, the second, the homophonous D major
section, confirming and giving actuality to the new-won hope
in life.

It is one of the beauties of the C sharp minor quartet that
moments of hesitation, of reflection, if not altogether absent, are
confined to short *intermezzi*, short connecting movements
numbered separately, which, since the main line of development
ascends steadily throughout the work, are merely bridge-passages
from the emotional sphere of one main movement to that of the
next.   The movement numbered as third, which leads from the
opening movement to the variations-*andante*, bears the character
of a recitative.   The soul, newly returned to human life, seems
to ask the question, " What next ? ", to seek and to find new
tasks.   The variations-*andante* is a song of joy followed by a
high-spirited *scherzo* in the form of a march-like *presto* movement
in E major.   These two movements present a vision of life with
all its delightful possibilities ; with the close of the *presto* the
desire for active participation is once more fully aroused.   The

powerful closing chord of the E major *scherzo* is followed by a G sharp unison, thrice repeated, which seems to ask, " What am I to do in this world ? " Passivity gradually gives place to activity. After a pensive and hesitating passage a finale-*allegro* plunges us once more into the maelstrom of active life. The same musical thought which represented the return to life reappears in the introductory fugue, the third changed to a sixth as before in the A minor quartet, to symbolise action. This second C sharp minor theme is in reality a transformation of that which preceded it and, consequently, of the main theme of the work. As if to dispel all doubts on this point, a third subject, C sharp—B sharp—A—G sharp, appears with a rhythmic continuation resembling the fugue theme. Both the intention and the meaning of these transformations are plain. The amazing expressiveness and versatility of this musical subject are now displayed. It appears in ever-varying forms, sometimes barely reminiscent of the original, till in the *coda*, at the moment of greatest tension, it becomes a choral-like hymn of victory. The spirit of man, illuminated through the anguish of moral conflict and assured of the unity of Will and of Fate, of Freedom and Necessity, returns once more to earth. The same idea which supported it in the A minor quartet and carried it to dizzy heights in the B flat major fugue now leads it back to face life anew. The three great quartets thus form a tremendous imaginative musical triptych ; the prophet ascends to the mountain top, sees his God face to face and returns to his people with the tables of the law which is written and established for all eternity.

Like the F major symphony, Op. 93, the F major quartet, Op. 135, stands at the close of a phase of development and possesses the peace of a goal attained. It lacks moments of great spiritual tension, of wild excitement over deep questions and problems. These having been exhausted in preceding works are merely subjects of imaginative reminiscence. The form accords with this intentional limitation of the subject matter. There is a return to the four-movement quartet type, and the individual movements are not on so great a scale as those of the preceding works. The F major is in the nature of an epilogue, a retrospective " The poet speaks."

The results of this retrospection in 1826 naturally differed from those of 1812. High-spirited laughter is no longer accepted as the final wisdom. Wherefore the humour of this quartet has not the elfishness, levitation or vibrating tempo of the eighth symphony. An earnest mood prevails and the work is inspired more by reflection than by gaiety.

It is believed that Beethoven first intended to write the F major quartet in three movements. It is not known whether the *lento assai, cantante e tranquillo* is the movement which he introduced later, but it is clear that the course of the work up to that movement, with its alternate moods of pensiveness and gaiety, required a supplement or contrast of deeper emotion, and therefore the short D flat major *lento* is organically sound. This movement is devout and religious in tone and reflects the mystic faith of the composer, a vision from which he can scarce turn his eyes to the things of earth.

From this world of quiet ecstasy he is called back to reality by the noise of battle. Over the finale Beethoven writes, "*Der schwer gefasste Entschluss*" (implying determination made and held in face of difficulty), while he inscribes the opening *grave* theme "*Muss es sein?*" (Must it be so?), and the *allegro* theme "*Es muss sein*" (It must). There are many stories which connect these words with incidents of Beethoven's life, but, true or false, they do not affect the spiritual verities here revealed. The contrast designed is psychological; it is the conflict between visionary quietism and disciplined activity. "Stern resolution" is required even though it be soul-wrenching, for a return from dreams of peace to that creative activity which is man's destiny. In the finale Beethoven asks a question of life and, as answer, proclaims the gospel of the Deed.

In the finale, Op. 135, the gospel of action is posited, the "stern resolve" is made, but the works of that gospel and the fruit of that resolve were yet to be embodied. Now the "Will to Life" is supreme. Where will it lead? Death cut short the answer to this question; but we have a hint or premonition of what it might have been, in the B flat major *rondo*, which replaces the fugue as finale of the B flat major quartet as we now have it and is the last work completed by Beethoven. Apart from the pressure of the publisher, Artaria, and other friends, it would be profoundly interesting to know why Beethoven cut out the final fugue of Op. 130 (which is the very heart of the whole work), and to learn what mental or emotional process led him to substitute a cheerful close. In performance the wonderful work was found too long and too exacting. The B flat minor *scherzo* and *danza tedesca* were encored at the first performance on March 21st, 1826, but the public, though respectful, could make nothing of the fugue. Beethoven composed a new final movement which was not (like the fugue) a summary and epitome of the preceding movements, but was merely *en suite*, another gem in the multi-coloured ornament. He could not have conceived this finale when he composed the B flat major quartet, but the intervening F major quartet had reawakened in him a spirit of mirth and he wrote the new *finale* by way of humorous, perhaps ironic, contrast to the fugue. What did publishers, performers and public care about heights and depths ? What they wanted was a gay close ; let them have it. The result was a piece of diabolic humour, irony and sarcasm, unexampled in music. The composer would show his hearers, since they wished to dance, what he understood by dancing. Like the demon fiddler of the old legend, he plays to the bewitched assembly till dancing becomes a torture and the musician's fiendish laughter mingles with the notes of his fiddle. Faster, faster whirls the dance, more intricate grow the steps as the fiddler wills, till at last, tired of his magic, he sounds the closing chord, and just when his mastery is at its highest, when all inimical powers are subject to his spell, at the climax of wisdom and artistic greatness, another Player steals behind him. The fiddle falls from his hand. The play is out ; the song is sung.

Compared with the works of other musicians of the first rank, Beethoven's compositions are few in number and restricted in kind ; a glance at the collected works of Bach, Handel, Haydn and of the short-lived Mozart and Schubert confirms this. But to deduce that Beethoven was therefore less creatively fertile would be wrong. The explanation lies in the peculiar nature of his genius as an artist. He was first a thinker and a poet, and secondarily a musician. He never subordinated his ideas to the limitations of tone or of his craft. His whole work is ever a struggle of idea with tone-material, which material he made for

z

ever more adaptable, more expressive as a vehicle of thought. It is this process, with its many difficulties, which accounts for Beethoven's slow development and the comparative fewness of his works. The thought-infused nature of his art and the type of problem which he chose for artistic treatment demanded evolution and continuous refinement of style. This book is an attempt to lay bare these intricacies, arguing back from the musical expression in which the composer embodied them. It attempts to present the idea of *freedom* as the basis of all his inspiration and to follow in his works his changing presentment of freedom as a political and cultural, a personal, a religious, and finally as an ethical concept. By this means it is possible to give Beethoven his place in the history of human development. He has expressed the thought of Kant, Schiller and their compeers, and the struggles of the revolutionary epoch, in terms of music. His philosophic attitude conditioned his position as the greatest of all instrumental composers in musical history. The world of abstract thought which clamoured in him for expression demanded a correspondingly pure and absolute form of musical revelation. The great epoch of idealism and classicism in Germany found its most perfect artistic expression in his idealistic instrumental music, not depending on any connection with the sung or spoken word.

Regarded from this aspect, Beethoven's art might appear to be a product and expression of the cultural ideas of his period, but it is, of course, rooted in the remoter past. The impulse towards abstraction which is the driving force behind his work is ever discoverable as the motive force in the history of musical development. What else is instrumental music but an abstraction, attained through the liberation of music from vocalism, and thus an extension of the range of musical expression? And is not music, vocal or instrumental (apprehensible as it is by the ear only), a finer vehicle of art than any means which depend on visual images? In visual art, painting is an abstraction of sculpture, which in turn derives from a concentration of architecture into a single entity in three dimensions. From architectonic form to figure sculpture, each in three dimensions, to the two dimensional painting, from the visible surface to invisible sound, from the sung word to abstract instrumental tone, and, within instrumental music, from the simplest dance to the expression of the deepest philosophy—these advances represent, not indeed the historical, but the æsthetic line of development, by which artistic impulse has travelled from the most obvious and corporeal to the most transcendental and spiritual forms. The fact that chronologically these forms co-exist is not incompatible with the theory of their æsthetic sequence. The impulse to abstraction governs not only the means of presentation but also the choice of ideas to be presented and the manner in which these conceptions are expressed. That the impulse to abstraction does, in fact, dominate the whole history of art is proved by a comparison of the sequence of religious cults therein expressed ; for, in the last resort, all art is the symbolic expression of belief. The " religion " of Beethoven's day was the ethical system of Kant. This ethical system is at the back of Beethoven's music, and it was the effort to express the philosophic concepts involved which carried his music so far into the region of abstraction. Where, we must ask ourselves, does this line of development tend ? Beethoven adventured to the limits of abstract musical exposition. What task remained for his successors ? Were all possibilities of further progress exhausted, and had the history of music reached its close ?

It seems as if Nature herself were bent on proving the inexhaustible possibilities of that aspect of creative activity which we call art, when she chose for the apparently limitless genius of Beethoven his date in the history of musical art. When Beethoven was composing his last quartets, the Schubert songs and instrumental works and the operas of Weber and Spohr were coming to birth. In 1826 Mendelssohn wrote the *Midsummer Night's Dream* overture, and shortly after Beethoven's death Berlioz completed the *Sinfonie Fantastique* in Paris. The three channels along which the creative stream was henceforth to flow, song, opera, and programme music, were thus already indicated. Beethoven's instrumental music opened the way along which these three types were to attain perfection. It was by means of " the word " that they became partakers of Beethoven's artistic conquests, and discovery of the full artistic significance of " the word " was the outcome of the Romantic Movement.

A period of high abstraction was followed by a reaction towards the sensuous in musical expression. The ethical creeds and precepts of Beethoven's era were superseded by a period of frank delight in aspects of the material world. The artistic world as a whole passed through a phase, which in a measure had occurred more than once in Beethoven's career. For he had returned to "the word" again and again for refreshment and renewal of inspiration, e.g. in opera, in the programmatic title, and in sacred or secular lyric, and had therein found new stimuli for instrumental work. His successors attempted to revitalise instrumental music by like contact with "the word." In the intellectual life of the day the romantic outlook dispossessed classical idealism and favoured an inclination to the sensuous in music. From connection with "the word" and with the concept implied thereby, sprang the three great types of music already enumerated. The first, represented by Schubert, Mendelssohn, Schumann and Brahms, centred in the song, and carried stimuli derived therefrom into the region of instrumental expression—as strikingly exemplified in Mendelssohn's title, *Songs without Words*. Closely connected with the song composers is the group of programme-music writers, hailing from France; these were led by Berlioz and Liszt, who elevated the older forms of programme-music to higher importance on the lines of Beethoven's dramatic overtures. The third group, the musical dramatist, of which Richard Wagner is the greatest representative and final example, made use of the stimulating power of "the word" combined with the appeal of visible action.

Romantic lyricism, romantic programme-music and romantic music-drama are the three great streams of music which emerged from the seeming *impasse* in instrumental music brought about by Beethoven's impulse to abstraction. His abstractions were sensualised but they were also humanised. The romantic age saw itself in Beethoven and called him a "Romantic." To-day, in our effort to overpass the romantic movement, it is needful to view his work on a more spiritual plane. No one generation can conceive and express an adequate exposition of his works; that is neither necessary nor desirable; but the spirit in which each successive generation regards the great artists of the past is the measure of its own creative strength or weakness, of the direction of its ideas, of its intellectual and spiritual dependence or originality.

Ludwig van Beethoven bears the hall-mark of supreme creative genius in that many-sidedness, that infinite variety which affords ever-fresh matter for inquiry and ever gives forth new flashes of illumination as succeeding generations seek to explore the mystery of his being.

APPENDIX I

Year.	Month and Day.	Event.
1712	Dec. 23rd	Louis van Beethoven, son of Adelard van Beethoven, a tailor, baptised at Antwerp.
1733	March	Louis van Beethoven appointed Court musician (bass-singer) to the Elector Clement Augustus at Bonn.
	Sept. 7th	Louis van Beethoven married Maria Josepha Poll; Van den Eeden, a Court musician, acted as witness.
1739?		Birth of Johann van Beethoven, third child of the marriage.
1752		Johann van Beethoven appointed to the Electoral choir.
1761	July 16th	Louis van Beethoven appointed Kapellmeister to the Elector Max Friedrich, at the same time retaining his post as singer.
1764	April 24th	Johann van Beethoven appointed Court musician, with a yearly salary of one hundred *thalers*.
1767	Nov. 12th	Johann van Beethoven married Maria Magdalena (born Dec. 19th, 1746), daughter of Kewerich, the Elector's personal cook, widow of Laym, formerly a valet, of Ehrenbreitstein.
1769	April 2nd	Ludwig Maria van Beethoven, first child of the marriage, baptised. Died six days later.
1770	Dec. 17th	Ludwig van Beethoven, second child, baptised at St. Remigius', Bonn.
1773	Dec. 24th	Death of Kapellmeister Louis van Beethoven.
1774	April 8th	Kaspar Anton van Beethoven baptised.
	Aug. 17th	Stephan von Breuning born.
1775	Sept. 30th	Death of Maria Josepha, widow of Kapellmeister van Beethoven.
1776	Oct. 2nd	Nicholas Johann van Beethoven baptised.
1778	March 26th	First public appearance of Ludwig van Beethoven, " aged six," at Cologne.
		Music lessons under Van den Eeden.
1779		Music lessons under Tobias Friedrich Pfeiffer (pianoforte).
	Oct.	Christian Gottlob Neefe (born Feb. 5th, 1748, died Jan. 26th, 1798) came to Bonn.

Year.	Month and Day.	Event.
1780/1		Music lessons under Franz Georg Rovantini (violin and viola).
		Music lessons under Willibald Koch, a Franciscan, (organ) ?
1781	Oct. *or* Nov.	Beethoven went by ship to Rotterdam, with his mother.
1782	June 20th	Neefe accompanied the Electoral household to Munster. Beethoven deputised for him as organist.
		Became acquainted with Franz Gerhard Wegeler (born Aug. 22nd, 1765, died May 7th, 1848) and, through him, with the von Breunings.
		Publication by Götz, in Mannheim of *Variations upon a March by Dressler* for the pianoforte, composed by "*un jeune amateur, Louis van Beethoven, agé de dix ans.*"
1783	March 2nd	Beethoven mentioned in an article by Neefe for Cramer's *Magazin der Musik.*
		Beethoven deputised for Neefe as cembalist in the orchestra.
		Three pianoforte sonatas, dedicated to the Elector Max Freidrich, "made by Ludwig van Beethoven aged eleven years," published at Speyer by Bossler.
1784	Feb. 15th	Beethoven applied for the post of Assistant Court Organist.
	April 15th	Death of the Elector Max Friedrich. Accession of Maximilian Franz (born Dec. 8th, 1756), youngest son of the Empress Maria Theresia.
	June 25th	Issue of Revised Pay List. Beethoven cited as organist, with yearly salary of 150 *gulden.*
1787	Spring	Beethoven went to Vienna and returned to Bonn early in July.
	July 17th	Death of Beethoven's mother, from phthisis.
1788	June 17th	Ferdinand Ernst Gabriel, Count Waldstein (born March 24th, 1762, died Aug. 29th, 1823), initiated into the Teutonic Order at Bonn.
1789	Nov. 20th	In response to Beethoven's petition, the Elector ordered that half his father's salary, amounting to 100 *thalers*, should, in future, be paid to Ludwig for the education of his younger brothers, and that the father should leave Bonn.
		Beethoven employed as viola-player at the theatre.
1790	Feb. 20th	Death of the Emperor Joseph II of Austria. Beethoven composed a funeral cantata, also a cantata upon the coronation of Leopold II.
	Dec. 25th	Haydn passed through Bonn on his way to London.
1791	March 6th	Beethoven's music for a *Ritterballet* performed by members of the Bonn aristocracy at the Bonn Assembly Rooms, Count Waldstein being named as composer.

Year.	Month and Day.	Event.
1791	Sept. 18th– Oct. 20th	Chapter of the Teutonic Order held by Max Franz at Mergentheim. Beethoven accompanied the Royal choir thither, and met Abt Sterkel, the pianist, in Aschaffenburg.
1792	July	Haydn passed through Bonn on his return from London to Vienna and heard one of two cantatas composed by Beethoven in 1790.
	Nov. 2nd or 3rd	Beethoven left Bonn.
	Nov. 10th	Beethoven arrived in Vienna. Lodged with Strauss in the Alservorstadt, first in an attic, later in ground floor apartments.
	Dec. 18th	Death of Johann van Beethoven, Ludwig's father, in Bonn.
1793		Beethoven studied under Haydn till end of 1793.
	Aug.	Beethoven studied under Johann Schenk, composer of the *Village Barber*, till May 1794.
1794	Jan.	Beethoven studied under Johann Georg Albrechtsberger, till about April 1795, and under Salieri till 1802.
		Beethoven lodged in the household of Prince Karl Lichnowsky, Alserstrasse, 45.
1795		Beethoven made an offer of marriage to Magdalena Willmann, the singer (?).
	March 29th	First public appearance in Vienna at the *Burgtheater*, at concert in aid of widows of members of the *Tonkünstlergesellschaft* (Society of Musicians). Played pianoforte concerto in B flat major, op. 19. Removed to the Ogylyischen Haus in the Kreuzgasse; later to Metastasiogasse, no. 35.
	May 9th, 13th, 16th	Notice in *Wiener Zeitung* (*Vienna News*) asking subscriptions for " three great trios by Ludwig van Beethoven " op. 1 (Publisher, Artaria & Co.).
	Nov. 22nd	Ball of the *Society of Plastic Arts* at the Assembly Rooms. Dance-music written by Beethoven and Süssmayer. (Previously by Hadyn, Kozeluck, Dittersdorf and Eybler.)
	Dec. 18th	At Haydn's concert in the Assembly Rooms, at which the three *London Symphonies* were performed in Vienna for the first time, Beethoven played a pianoforte concerto composed by himself.
		In the course of the year Beethoven's brothers, Karl and Johann, came to Vienna.
1796	Jan. 8th	Beethoven played a pianoforte concerto at a concert given at the Assembly Rooms by Bolla, the singer

Year.	Month and Day.	Event.
1796	Feb.	Beethoven went (with Prince Lichnowsky's suite?) to Prague and thence to Dresden (?) and Leipzig (?) and Berlin. On June 21st and 28th he played before the Berlin Academy of Song.
	Summer	Journeys to Pressburg (?) and Buda-Pesth (?).
1797	April 6th	First performance, at Schuppanzigh's concert, of quintet, op. 16.
1798	Feb. 5th	General Bernadotte entered Vienna.
1799		Beethoven entered into contests of skill with Josef Wölffl, and became acquainted with Johann Baptist Cramer (born Feb. 24th, 1771, died April 16th, 1858) and with Domenico Dragonetti, doublebass player (born April 7th, 1763, died April 16th, 1846). Lodged in Tiefen Graben, Greinersches Haus, no. 235.
1800	April 2nd	Beethoven's first concert at the Court Theatre. First performance of the first symphony, the septet and a pianoforte concerto (C major?), played by himself.
	April 18th	Beethoven appeared at a concert given by Punto (Johann Stich), a virtuoso on the horn. First performance of sonata for horn, op. 17.
		Contest of skill with Daniel Steibelt, at the house of Count Fries.
	Summer	Beethoven at Unterdöbling. Prince Lichnowsky granted Beethoven a yearly salary of 600 *gulden* and shortly afterwards, it appears, gave him a valuable set of Italian quartet instruments.
	June 29th	Beethoven wrote to Wegeler about his ear trouble (1801?).
1801	Jan. 30th	Beethoven played horn sonata with Punto at a charity concert arranged by Frau von Frank at the Assembly Rooms.
		Beethoven lodged in Seilerstätte, Hamberger Haus.
	March 26th	First performance of the historical and allegorical ballet, *The Men of Prometheus*, by Salvatore Vigano, music by Beethoven, at the Court Theatre.
	Summer	Beethoven in Hetzendorf (?).
	July 6th, 7th	Letter to the "Immortal Beloved."
	July 26th	Death of the Elector Max Franz at Hetzendorf.
		Beethoven's friends Stephan von Breuning, Anton Reicha, and Ferdinand Ries (1784–1838), son of Franz Ries the violinist of Bonn, came to Vienna.
		Ferdinand Ries and Karl Czerny (1791–1857) took pianoforte lessons from Beethoven.
1802	Summer	Beethoven in Heiligenstadt.
	Oct. 6th, 10th	The Heiligenstadt Will.
	Late autumn	Beethoven in Vienna. Lodged in Petersplatz.

Year.	Month and Day.	Event.
1803	April 5th	Concert at the *Theater an der Wien.* First performance of the *Mount of Olives*, the second symphony and the pianoforte concerto in C minor. The first symphony also performed. Takings—1800 *gulden.*
	May 24th (?)	Concert given by Beethoven and the violinist G. A. P. Bridgetower. First performance of the A major sonata (Kreutzer Sonata), op. 47, for pianoforte and violin.
	May and July	Beethoven and von Breuning lodged together in the " Red House." Quarrel with von Breuning. Illness of Beethoven.
	June 29th	Notice in the *Zeitung für die elegante Welt* that Beethoven was to write an opera for Schikaneder (*Theater an der Wien*). Beethoven assigned rooms at the theatre.
	Summer	Beethoven in Baden and Döbling, Hofzeile, 4 (*Eroica-Haus*).
	Oct. 5th	Correspondence opened with the publisher George Thomson of Edinburgh.
	Nov. 2nd	Letter to the painter Macco. " There are times in a man's life that have to be endured somehow."
1804	Feb. 11th	Baron Braun took over the *Theater an der Wien.* Beethoven's operatic projects consequently fell through. Shortly afterwards, Beethoven undertook to compose *Fidelio.*
	Spring	Clementi in Vienna.
	May 20th	Napoleon proclaimed Emperor.
	June, July, Aug. (?)	Private performances of the *Eroica* by Prince Lobkowitz's orchestra in the presence of Prince Louis Ferdinand of Prussia.
	Autumn	Beethoven lodged in the Pasqualatischen Haus, Mölkerbastei.
1805	Jan. (?)	Performance of the *Eroica* at a private concert given by the bankers, Würth and Fellner, Franz Clement being the first violin.
	April 7th	First public performance of the *Eroica* (" Symphony in D minor ") at Franz Clement's concert.
	June–Sept.	Beethoven at Hetzendorf, engaged on *Fidelio.*
	July	Beethoven met Sonnleithner, Cherubini and Vogler.
	Nov. 13th	Vienna besieged by the French.
	Nov. 20th, 21st, 22nd	Performance of *Fidelio* at the *Theater an der Wien* (Overture no. 2).
1806	March 29th and April 10th	Performances of *Fidelio* (Second version with Overture no. 2).
	May 25th	Beethoven's brother Karl, revenue official, married Johanna Reiss in Vienna.

Year.	Month and Day.	Event.
1806	May 26th	First string quartet of op. 59 begun.
	Sept. 4th	Birth of Karl van Beethoven, son of Karl Kaspar. (Died April 13th, 1858.)
	Oct.	Beethoven visited Prince Lichnowsky at his estate near Troppau in Schlesig. Quarrel with Lichnowsky.
	Dec. 23rd	First performance of the violin concerto by Franz Clement at his concert in the *Theater an der Wien*.
1807	Jan. (?)	Beethoven applied to the management for the post of composer to the theatre.
	March	Two subscription-concerts at Prince Lobkowitz's palace. First, second and third symphonies, also fourth symphony for the first time, the *Coriolanus* overture and pianoforte concerto in G.
	April 20th	Beethoven signed a contract, selling Clementi, for the sum of £200, the copyright in Great Britain of the following works:—Quartets op. 59; fourth symphony; *Coriolanus* overture; pianoforte concerto in G major; violin concerto in D (also arranged for pianoforte).
	May–July	Beethoven in Baden.
	July–Sept.	Beethoven in Heiligenstadt.
	Sept. 13th	First performance of *Mass in C* in Eisenstadt.
	Winter	Institution of " Amateur Concerts " in Vienna; held first in the "Mehlgrube" Rooms, then in the University Hall, where Beethoven conducted many of his own works.
1808	March 27th	Grand performance of the " *Creation* " before Haydn, Beethoven, and many other renowned musicians.
	Spring	Beethoven suffered from a disease of the fingers and underwent an operation on the nails.
	Summer	Beethoven in Heiligenstadt, returning during the autumn to Vienna, Krugerstrasse, 1074.
	End of Oct.	Beethoven received, through Count Truchsess-Waldburg, an invitation to become Kapellmeister to King Jerome of Cassel.
	Nov. 24th	Johann Friedrich Reichardt, " Kapellmeister of Hesse-Cassell," came to Vienna.
	Dec. 22nd	Beethoven gave a concert at the *Theater an der Wien*. First performance of fifth and sixth symphonies and of the *Choral Fantasia*. The *Gloria* and *Sanctus* of the *Mass in C*, pianoforte concerto in G, a free *Fantasia* for the pianoforte, and the *Ah perfido* were also performed.
1809	Feb. 26th	Archduke Rudolph and Princes Lobkowitz and Kinsky guaranteed Beethoven a salary of 4000 *gulden*.
	May 10th– end of June	Vienna besieged and occupied by the French.

Year.	Month and Day.	Event.
1809	May 31st	Death of Joseph Haydn.
	Aug.	Beethoven in Baden; later in Vienna, Walfischgasse.
	Sept. 8th	Charity Concert at the Theatre. Beethoven conducted the *Eroica*.
	December	Beethoven ill.
1810	April	Proposal of marriage to Therese Malfatti (?). Beethoven lodged in the Pasqualatische Haus.
	May	Bettina von Arnim in Vienna.
	May 24th	First performance of music to Goethe's *Egmont*.
	Summer	Beethoven in Baden. First performance of pianoforte concerto in E flat at the *Gewandhaus*, Leipzig, late in the year.
1811	March 15th	New finance patent came into force. Beethoven's salary reduced to 1360 *gulden* = 952 *thalers*.
	April 12th	Beethoven wrote to Goethe telling him about the *Egmont* music.
	Aug. 1st	Beethoven came to Teplitz, where he met Varnhagen-Rahel, Tiedge, Elise von der Recke, Amalie Sebald.
	Sept.	Beethoven left Teplitz to visit Prince Lichnowsky at Troppau. Performance there of the *Mass in C*. Return to Vienna. Prince Lobkowitz's affairs placed in the hands of guardians. Payments to Beethoven ceased from Sept 1st, 1811, till April 1815.
1812	Feb. 9th, 10th, 11th	Performances of the *Ruins of Athens* and *King Stephan* at the opening of the theatre at Buda-Pesth.
	Feb. 12th	Carl Czerny played the pianoforte concerto in E flat for the first time in Vienna.
	July 7th	Beethoven at Teplitz.
	July 17th	Beethoven's letter to little Emily.
	July 19th–23rd	Meeting between Beethoven and Goethe.
	July 27th	Beethoven went to Carlsbad.
	Aug. 6th	Beethoven and Polledro, the violinist, got up a concert in aid of the town of Baden, near Vienna, which had been burned down. Sonata for pianoforte and violin and improvisations.
	Aug. 8th	Beethoven went to Franzensbad, returning *via* Carlsbad (Sept. 7th), to Teplitz.
	Sept. 16th	Beethoven at Teplitz where he met the Brentanos, and Amalie Sebald, with whom he corresponded.
	Oct. 5th	Beethoven visited his brother Johann at Linz. Played and improvised at a private concert given by Count Dönhoff.
	Nov. 2nd	Prince Ferdinand Kinsky (born 1781) died at Prague. Payments to Beethoven ceased till March 31st, 1815.

Year.	Month and Day.	Event.
1811	Nov. 8th	Johann van Beethoven married Therese Obermeyer, against Ludwig's advice. Ludwig returned to Vienna.
	Dec.	Pierre Rode, the violinist, came to Vienna.
	Dec. 29th	Rode and the Archduke Rudolph played the newly-composed sonata for pianoforte and violin, op. 96.
1813	End of April	Seventh and eighth symphonies rehearsed before Archduke. Proposed concert did not take place.
	May 27th	Beethoven went to Baden and remained there, with a few short absences, till middle of Sept., when he returned to Vienna.
	June 21st	Wellington's victory at Vittoria.
	Dec. 8th	Concert in the University Hall. First performance of seventh symphony and *Wellington's Victory*. Two marches by Dussek and Pleyel performed on Mälzel's mechanical trumpeter.
	Dec. 12th	Second performance. (Both performances for benefit of the wounded from the battle of Hanau.)
1814	Jan. 2nd	Beethoven's first exclusive concert. At the Grand Ballroom. The *Battle* symphony, parts of the *Ruins of Athens* and seventh symphony.
	Feb. 27th	Second concert of Beethoven's work only. First performance of eighth symphony, also seventh symphony, *Battle* symphony and trio, *Tremate*.
	March 16th and 17th	Mälzel performed *Battle* symphony at Munich.
	April 11th	Beethoven, at Schuppanzigh's concert, played for the first time the op. 97 trio, and again, several weeks later, with Schuppanzigh at Prater. Last public appearance as a performer of chamber-music.
	April	Became acquainted with Anton Schindler (born 1796, died 1864).
		Lodged in the Bartensteinschen Haus, Mölkerbastei no. 94.
	April 15th	Death of Prince Lichnowsky (born 1773).
	May 23rd	First performance of *Fidelio* (third version) with an old overture. Beethoven conducted, assisted by Umlauf.
	May 26th	Performance of *Fidelio* with the newly-composed E major overture.
	July 18th	*Fidelio* performed as a " benefit " for Beethoven.
	Summer	Beethoven in Baden. Returned to Vienna in September.
	Sept. 26th	*Fidelio* performed in the presence of the kings assembled for the Congress.
	Nov. 21st	*Fidelio* given for the first time in Prague, conducted by Carl Maria von Weber.

Year.	Month and Day.	Event.
1814	Nov. 29th	Beethoven concert in the Ballroom. Seventh symphony, *Battle* symphony, and, for the first time, the *Glorious Moment* cantata.
	Dec. 2nd	Repetition of the concert of Nov. 29th.
	Dec. 25th	Second repetition of the same concert for charitable purposes.
	Dec. 31st	The Palais Rasumowsky burnt down.
1815	Jan. 25th	Concert by royal command in the *Rittersaal* of the Castle. Beethoven accompanied the canon from *Fidelio* and *Adelaide*. Audience with the Empress Elizabeth of Russia, at which he presented her with a *Polonaise*, op. 89, composed for her. Received 150 ducats for the *Alexander* (violin) sonata, op. 30.
	Jan.	Agreement reached with Kinsky's heirs and with Lobkowitz. Beethoven lodged in Seilerstätte, 1055/1056.
	Summer	Beethoven in Baden and Döbling. Returned to Vienna in the middle of October.
	Oct. 11th	First performance of *Fidelio* in Berlin.
	Nov. 15th	Death of Beethoven's brother Karl, in Vienna.
	Nov. 16th	The Viennese authorities granted Beethoven the freedom of the city and freedom from taxes.
	Dec. 25th	Charity concert for the funds of the City Hospital. First performances of the *Name-day Overture*, op. 115, the cantata, *Meeresstille und glückliche Fahrt*. Also *The Mount of Olives*.
1816	Jan. 19th	Beethoven undertook the guardianship of his nephew Karl.
	Feb. 2nd	Karl put to school under Giannatasio del Rio. The Schuppanzigh Quartet dissolved. Schuppanzigh went to Russia, Linke, the violoncellist, to Croatia, Weiss, the viola-player, remained in Vienna. Hummel left Vienna.
	End July– Sept.	Beethoven in Baden. Karl visited him there after a successful operation for rupture.
	Winter	Beethoven conducted the seventh symphony at a concert for the St. Mark's Hospital. Anselm Hüttenbrenner met Beethoven. Beethoven fell ill ("Inflammatory catarrh") in the course of the winter and remained so till the following spring. Czerny gave Karl pianoforte lessons.
	Dec. 16th	Death of Prince Josef Franz Lobkowitz (born 1772).
1817	April	Beethoven left the Seilerstätte Haus and moved to the Vorstadt Landstrasse.
	May 2nd	Sudden death of Wenzel Krumpholz, the violinist. Beethoven composed the Monks' song for *Wilhelm Tell*.

Year.	Month and Day.	Event.
1817	May	Beethoven went to Heiligenstadt and stayed at Pfarrplatz no. 2. Left in June for Nussdorf, where he stayed till end of September. Visited by Potter, the London conductor, Heinrich Marschner, Marie Pachler-Koschak a pianist of Graz, and Christoph Kuffner, the poet.
		Beethoven rented a house in the Gärtnerstrasse (no. 26, the "*Haus zum grünen Baum*").
		The law-suit with Mälzel concluded by agreement.
	Dec. 25th	Beethoven conducted the eighth symphony at a concert for the City Hospital, in the Ball-Room.
1818	Jan.	Beethoven brought Karl home from Giannatasio's school.
	Feb. 3rd	Beethoven thanked Thomas Broadwood of London for a pianoforte just received.
	May 19th	Beethoven went to Mödling with Karl and lodged in the Hafnerhaus.
		Karl sent to school under Pastor Fröhlich. Expelled by him after a month. Received private tuition for entrance examination to Gymnasium in Vienna.
	Sept.	Karl's mother sued Beethoven at law. Her suit dismissed. Beethoven returned to the Gärtnerstrasse, Vienna.
	Dec. 3rd	Karl, who was attending the Gymnasium, ran away from Beethoven to his mother. Brought back by the police, and sent by Beethoven once more to Giannatasio's school.
	Dec. 10th	Karl's mother again sued Beethoven.
	Dec. 18th	The suit referred to the Municipal Council. Beethoven brought Karl home.
1819	Jan. 7	Beethoven summoned to appear before the Council. Karl placed in Joseph Kudlich's school.
	Jan. 17th	Beethoven conducted the seventh symphony at a charity concert.
	March 15th	Beethoven elected Honorary Member of the Laibach Philharmonic Society.
	End of March	Beethoven surrendered his guardianship. Undertaken by Councillor von Tuscher.
		Karl to be placed at the *Institute von Sailer*, at Landshut.
	May 7th	Karl refused a passport.
	May 12th	Beethoven at Mödling. Giannatasio refused to receive Karl, who was placed under Joseph Blöchlinger.
	July 5th	Tuscher surrendered his guardianship. Beethoven resumed it.
	Aug. 2	Johann van Beethoven bought an estate, "Wasserhof," near Gneixendorf. Beethoven intended to buy a house at Mödling.

Year.	Month and Day.	Event.
1819	Sept. 14th	Meeting with Zelter, and, later, with Friedrich Schneider.
	Sept. 17th	The Council deprived Beethoven of the guardianship of Karl and assigned it to his mother, jointly with Leopold Nussböck, official sequestrator.
	End of Oct.	Beethoven returned to Vienna from Mödling. Lodged in the Josephstädter Glacis.
	Oct. 31st	Beethoven protested against the decision of the Council. Advocate Dr. Bach.
	Dec. 20th	The Council dismissed Beethoven's case. Beethoven applied to the Court of Appeal.
		Beginning of the " Conversation Note-Books." Schindler became more intimate with Beethoven.
1820	March 18th	Beethoven made a written offer of the second *Mass* to Simrock of Bonn.
	March 23rd	Letter to E. T. A. Hoffmann of Berlin.
	April 8th	The Court of Appeal decided in Beethoven's favour. The mother to have no power of guardianship. Hofrat Peters, tutor to the Lobkowitz children, appointed co-guardian with Beethoven. Karl's mother's appeal to the Emperor was dismissed.
	May	Beethoven in Mödling, Achsenaugasse.
	End of Oct.	Beethoven back in Vienna, Vorstadt Landstrasse, Haupstrasse, 244 (" *im grossen Haus der Augustiner* ").
		Beethoven fell ill of " a rheum " during the winter.
	Dec.	A series of sacred concerts, instituted by Franz Xaver Gebauer (first held in the Mehlgrube Hall, later in the Hall in the Herrngasse), where Beethoven's works were several times indifferently performed.
1821	Summer	Beethoven lived at Unterdöbling, going in September to Baden (*Rathausgasse*). July–August, ill with jaundice. In October returned to Vienna, Landstrasse.
	Autumn	Beethoven arrested as a tramp on account of his ragged appearance and consigned to the lock-up (1822 ?).
1822	Jan. 1st	Beethoven elected honorary member of the Steiermärk Music Society.
		Business negotiations about the *Mass* with Simrock, Schlesinger, Artaria, Diabelli, Steiner, Peters.
		Increased intimacy with his brother Johann, who advanced him money.
	April 13th	First performance of Rossini's *Zelmira* in Vienna. Beethoven visited Rossini.
	May–July	Beethoven at Oberdöbling, Alleegasse 115. Returned to Vienna, late in July, to new lodgings in the Kothgasse.
	May 24th– Aug. 2nd	Friedrich Rochlitz in Vienna. Visited Beethoven.

A A

Year.	Month and Day.	Event.
1822	Sept. 1st	Beethoven in Baden.
	Oct. 3rd	The Josephstädter Theatre opened with the *Weihe des Hauses* overture. Beethoven at the pianoforte with Kapellmeister Franz Gläser and Schindler as conductor.
	Nov. 3rd	Performance of the *Gratulationsmenuett* for Hensler, manager of the Josephstädter Theatre.
	Nov. 3rd	*Fidelio* performed, after a three years' interval, at the Kärntnerthor Theatre with Wilhelmine Schröder (-Devrient) in the principal rôle. Beethoven had to cease conducting during the dress-rehearsal.
	Nov. 9th	Prince Nicholas Galitzin wrote from St. Petersburg commissioning three string quartets.
1823	Jan. 25th	Beethoven accepted Galitzin's suggestion, asking 50 ducats for each quartet.
	Feb. 8th	Beethoven wrote to Goethe, asking him to get the Archduke of Weimar to buy a subscription copy of the *Mass*. At the same time, he wrote to Zelter and, later, to Cherubini, Schelble (Frankfort St. Cecilia Society), Prince Galitzin, The Emperor of Russia, the Kings of Sweden, Denmark, Naples, England, Prussia, France, Bavaria and Saxony, the Archdukes of Hesse-Darmstadt and Tuscany, the Elector of Hesse-Nassau and Prince Radziwill. Ten copies were ordered at 50 ducats apiece.
	Feb. 23rd	Count Dietrichstein suggested, through Count Moritz Lichnowsky, that Beethoven should compose a *Mass* on the Reutter pattern, for the Emperor. Beethoven planned a *Mass* in C minor. Sold one bank-share to settle most pressing debts.
	March 19th	Beethoven handed the Archduke Rudolph a copy of the *Mass* score.
	April 13th	Franz Liszt, Czerny's pupil, gave a concert at the Ball-Room. Beethoven present (?).
	April (?)	Grillparzer visited Beethoven, after sending the text of *Melusina*.
	April 29th	First performance of *Fidelio* in Dresden. Wilhelmina Schröder (-Devrient) singing, Carl Maria von Weber conducting. Profit of 40 ducats.
	May 4th	Schuppanzigh gave a concert to celebrate his return from Russia. His quartet began to meet again from May 14th, with Holz, Weiss and Linke.
	May 17th	Beethoven in Hetzendorf at Baron Müller-Pronay's villa. Suffered from eye-trouble and abdominal complaints.
		Wrote to a number of newspaper editors about his election in 1822 to an honorary degree in the Swedish Academy of Arts.

Year.	Month and Day.	Event.
1823	Aug. 13th	Beethoven left Hetzendorf for Baden.
		Karl passed the "leaving" examination at Blöcklinger's school and was to attend the University. Beethoven had him to stay with him at Baden.
	Oct. 5th	Carl Maria von Weber visited Beethoven at Baden. Also Maria Pachler-Koschak.
	End of Oct.	Beethoven back in Vienna at Ungargasse, no. 323, Vorstadt Landstrasse. His nephew lived with him and attended the University. "Frau Schnaps" kept house.
	Oct. 25th	First performance of *Euryanthe* in Vienna. Beethoven not present.
1824	Jan. 8th	Beethoven helped Karl's mother by forgiving her the sum due from her for her son's education. Eye-trouble persisted till March.
	Feb. 20th	Louis XVIII of France presented Beethoven with a gold-medal for his *Mass*.
	Feb.	Viennese music-lovers petitioned Beethoven to have his new works performed in Vienna.
	April 6th	First performance of the *Missa solemnis* in St. Petersburg at the instigation of Prince Galitzin.
	May 7th	Concert in the Kärtnerther Theatre. Overture, *Weihe des Hauses*, three hymns from the *Missa solemnis*, ninth symphony. Umlauf conducted. Gross takings 2200 *gulden*. Net profit 420 *gulden*.
	May 23rd	Repetition of the concert at the Ball Room. Overture, ninth symphony, *Kyrie* from the *Mass*, trio "*Tremate*" and aria, "*Di tanti palpiti*" by Rossini. Deficit. Beethoven guaranteed 500 *gulden*.
	May	After the concerts, Beethoven withdrew to Penzing, no. 43; but, because people stared through the windows, he went to Gutenbrunn near Baden, where he stayed from July to November.
		Corresponded about the *Mass* with Probst (Leipzig) and Schott (Mayence).
	July 19th	The publisher Schott obtained the *Mass* (1000 *gulden*), the ninth symphony (600 *gulden*) and quartet op. 127 (50 ducats).
	Sept.	Stumpff, a harp-maker of London, visited Beethoven at Baden.
		Andreas Streicher discussed plans for a Collected Edition.
	Nov.	Beethoven returned to Vienna. Lodged in Johannesgasse, no. 969. He was asked to leave, as being too noisy a lodger. Moved to Krugerstrasse, 767.
	Dec. 20th	Charles Neate asked Beethoven, in the name of the

Year.	Month and Day.	Event.
		Philharmonic Society, to visit London, under a guarantee of 300 guineas.
1825	Jan. 15th	Beethoven answered Neate, demanding another 100 guineas for the journey. His demand was refused.
	March 6th	First performance of quartet op. 127 by Schuppanzigh, Holz, Weiss and Linke. It was badly performed and was ill-received. At Beethoven's request, Joseph Böhm performed it on March 23rd, when it was received with enthusiasm.
		Carl Holz, public officer and violinist (1798–1858) became intimate with Beethoven.
	Mid April to May	Beethoven seriously ill (" inflammation of bowels "). Rellstab visited Beethoven. Sent poems which Schubert later set to music.
	May 6th (*circa*)	Karl left the University at Easter and began to attend the Polytechnic. Vice-principal Reisser undertook co-guardianship with Beethoven. Karl lodged with Schlemmer, an official, when Beethoven went to stay at Gutenbrunn near Baden. Karl took to ill company. Beethoven had on this account to journey constantly to Vienna from Baden, and became very anxious and annoyed. Johann took a hand in the affair to Beethoven's annoyance. He refused Johann's invitation to Gneixendorf.
	May 23rd	Ninth symphony performed at the Lower Rhine Musical Festival at Aachen; conductor Ferdinand Ries. The *scherzo* was omitted and the *adagio* shortened.
	Sept. 2nd	Beethoven visited at Baden by Haslinger, Holz, Sellner the oboe-player, Graf the pianoforte-maker, and Friedrich Kuhlau. Beethoven in riotously high spirits.
	Sept. 9th	Private first performance of quartet op. 132 by Schuppanzigh's Quartet at the " Wild Man " inn at Prater. There were present, Beethoven, the publisher Moritz Schlesinger from Paris, the conductor Sir George Smart of London, Carl Czerny and Karl van Beethoven. Schlesinger acquired the work for 80 ducats.
	Sept. 11th	At the same place a big private society of musicians and musical amateurs performed trios, op. 70 and op. 97 and quartet op. 132. Beethoven conducted at the pianoforte and afterwards improvised.
		Shortly afterwards, Karl disappeared for a time, to Beethoven's great perturbation.
	Oct. 15th (?)	Beethoven took rooms in the Schwarzspanierhaus. Frequent intercourse with Stephan von Breuning and his family.

Year.	Month and Day.	Event.
1825	Nov. 6th	Public performance of quartet op. 132 at a concert given by Linke, the 'cellist, at the Music Society's room "*Unter den Tuchlauben*." Enthusiastic reception. Trio op. 97 also played.
	Nov. 13th	Schuppanzigh's concert. Trio op. 70 in D major.
	Nov. 20th	Schuppanzigh's concert. Quartet op. 132. At these concerts, many of Beethoven's works were performed; during the following year, second and third symphonies, the *Choral Fantasia*, quartet in F major op. 18, E flat major trio, and the septet.
	Nov. 29th	Beethoven proposed for honorary membership of the Society of Music-lovers, in Vienna.
1826	End Jan.	Beethoven taken ill. Eye-trouble; pains in the back; gout. Remained unwell till March.
	Feb. 6th	Letter to Abt Stadler about Mozart's *Requiem*.
	March 21st	Public performance by Schuppanzigh of quartet op. 130 with fugue. The second and fourth movements were encored. Artaria bought the quartet for 80 ducats.
	April	Hofrat Kuffner visited Beethoven and discussed oratorios, *The Elements* and *Saul*.
	April 6th	Letter from the manager, Count Brühl, about an opera for Berlin. Friedrich Wieck visited Beethoven; also Schubert (?). Plans to visit Ischl and Gastein in the summer.
		Trouble with Karl, who, in rebellious mood, complained that he was a prisoner. Violent scenes. Johann acted as peace-maker.
	July 30th	Karl attempted suicide in the Rauhenstein ruins at Helenental, apparently on account of debts. He was taken to his mother and then, in charge of the police, to the hospital, where he was visited by a priest. On his recovery, several plans were proposed; finally it was settled he should join Stuttersheim's Regiment at Iglau.
	Sept. 29th	Beethoven took Karl to Gneixendorf to complete his convalescence. Beethoven fell ill. Signs of dropsy.
		80 ducats received from Schott for quartet op. 131 despatched to him in August.
	Oct. 30th	Beethoven sent Schlesinger quartet op. 135, for which he received 80 ducats.
	Nov. 25th	From King Frederic William of Prussia, to whom he had dedicated the ninth symphony, Beethoven received a diamond ring instead of the wished-for Order.
	Nov. 25th	Artaria paid Beethoven 15 ducats for the later-composed finale to quartet op. 130.

Year.	Month and Day.	Event.
1826	Dec. 2nd	Beethoven returned to Vienna seriously ill.
	Dec. 5th	Dr. Wawruch visited Beethoven after Drs. Braunhofer and Staudenheimer had given up the case. Pneumonia (?).
	Dec. 10th	Johann came to Vienna. Conferred with Artaria. Several works performed.
	Dec. 14th	Stumpff sent an *édition-de-luxe* of Handel's works from London (40 vols.).
		Von Breuning visited Field-Marshal Stuttersheim with Karl, and provided him with equipment, assisted by Johann.
	Dec. 19th	Jenger came from Graz, bringing a letter from Maria Pachler-Koschak.
		Gerhard von Breuning constantly with Beethoven.
	Dec. 20th	First operation.
1827	Jan. 2nd	Karl departed to join his regiment at Iglau.
	Jan. 3rd	Beethoven made his Will.
	Jan. 8th	Second operation. Malfatti took charge of affairs. Visits from Haslinger, Bernard, Dolezalek, Piringer, Streicher and Nanette Schechner.
	Feb. 2nd	Third operation.
		Wegeler wrote from Bonn.
	Feb. 8th	Beethoven wrote to thank Stumpff and to ask for monetary assistance.
	Feb. 17th	Beethoven answered Wegeler's letter.
	Feb. 22nd	Beethoven wrote to Smart and Moscheles in London, asking for assistance from the London Philharmonic Society. At the same time he wrote to Schott, asking for wine.
	Feb. 27th	Fourth operation.
	March 1st	Stumpff wrote to say that the required assistance had been granted.
	March 6th	Beethoven wrote again to Smart and on the 14th to Moscheles, as he had received no answer from London.
		Pasqualati, Breuning and Streicher kept Beethoven supplied with delicacies and wine.
	March 8th	Hummel and Hiller visited Beethoven.
	March 13th	Hummel visited him again.
	March 18th	Beethoven wrote to thank Moscheles.
	March 23rd	Hummel, with his wife, visited Beethoven. Also Franz Schubert (?). Last dispositions added to Will. (" *Plaudite amici, comoedia finita est* ").
	March 24th	Beethoven received the Last Sacrament. Last signature for Schott (quartet op. 131). At midday a present of wine arrived from Schott.
		Towards evening Beethoven became unconscious.

Year.	Month and Day.	Event.
1827	March 26th	Beethoven died about 5 o'clock in the evening during a thunderstorm. Only Hüttenbrenner was present.
	March 27th	Post-mortem examination made.
	March 28th	Dannhauser took a death-mask.
	March 29th	Funeral at 3 o'clock in the afternoon. Service in the courtyard of the Schwarzspanierhaus and afterwards in the parish church in Alserstrasse. From there to Währinger cemetery. Grillparzer's funeral oration spoken at the grave by Anschütz, the actor.
	May 5th	Beethoven's household effects sold by auction.
	June 4th	Death of Stephan von Breuning.
	Nov. 5th	Auction of Beethoven's literary remains. Fetched total sum of 9885 *gulden*.
1863	Oct. 13th	First exhumation. Scientific examination of the skull. Reburial in the same grave.
1888	June 21st	Second exhumation. Reburial in the principal cemetery of Vienna.

Year.	Works for Pf. only.	Concertos and Concert pieces with Orchestra.	Symphonies.	Dramatic Works, Marches and Dances for Orchestra
1782	9 Variations on a March by Dressler. Two-part fugue in D for organ.			
1783	3 Sonatas, dedicated to the Elector, in E flat, F mi., and D.			
1784	Rondo in A major.	Pf. concerto in E flat (only the pf. part is now in existence).		
1785			Study for a symphony in C mi. (Theme from the 2nd pf. quartet).	
1787	Prelude in F. mi. (pub. 1805).			
1789	preludes in all keys (pub. 1803 as op. 39).			

II

BEETHOVEN'S WORKS

Vocal Works.	Chamber Music.		
	Wind Instruments and various.	Pf. and Strings.	Strings only.
Song:—" *Schilderung eines Mädchens.*"			
Song :—" *An einen Säugling.*"			
		3 quartets in C, E flat and D for pf., vn., viola & 'cello.	
	Trio, pf., flute & bassoon.		

Year.	Works for Pf. only.	Concertos and Concert pieces with Orchestra.	Symphonies.	Dramatic Works, Marches and Dances for Orchestra.
1790	24 variations in D upon Righini's "*Venni amore*"	Pf. concerto in D (?) (only one movement now exists).		
1791				Music for a German *Ritter-ballett*.
1792	13 variations in A upon Dittersdorf's "*Es war einmal ein alter Mann*." Variations in C and F mi. for 2 pfs., on a theme by Waldstein (both works pub. in 1794). Fragment of a sonata in C and F mi. to Eleonore von Breuning (sent in 1796). 2 sonatinas in G and F.	Fragment of a vn. concerto in C.		
1795	3 sonatas in F mi., A and C, op. 2 (pub. 1796).	Pf. concerto no. 2 in B flat, op. 19 (first version).		12 German dances. 12 minuets.

Vocal Works.	Chamber Music.		
	Wind Instruments and various.	Pf. and Strings.	Strings only.
Cantata on the death of Joseph II, for solo, chorus and orchestra. Cantata on the "Accession of Leopold II to the Imperial Throne." 2 bass arias with orchestra :" *Prüfung des Küssens*" and "*Mit Mädeln sich vertragen.*"			
Songs, op. 52 (pub. 1805) : — " *Urians Reise um die Welt*," "*Feuerfarbe.*" Also :—"*Ich, der mit flatterndem Sinn*," "*An Minna*," "*Erhebt das Glas*," "*Elegie auf dem Tod eines Pudels*," "*Klage*," "*Punschlied*," "*Wer ist ein freier Mann*," "*Mann strebt die Flamme zu verhehlen.*"	Octet in E flat, op. 103, for 2 oboes, 2 clar., 2 bassoons, 2 horns. Rondino in E flat. Fl. duet in G. 3 duos in C, F and B flat for clar. & bassoon. Sonata for pf. & fl. (?). Duo for a musical box.	Trio in E flat for pf., vn. & 'cello. 14 variations in E flat upon an original theme for pf., vn. & 'cello, op. 44. 12 variations in F mi. upon Mozart's "*Se vuol ballare*" for pf. & vn.	Trio in E flat, op. 3 (?), for vn., viola & 'cello (pub. 1797).
	Trio in C, op. 87, 2 oboes & cor anglais.	3 trios in E flat, G, and C mi., op. 1 (begun in Bonn ?	

Year.	Works for Pf. only.	Concertos and Concert pieces with Orchestra.	Symphonies.	Dramatic Works, Marches and Dances for Orchestra.
1795	6 variations in G "*Nel car più non mi sento.*" 9 variations in A "*Quant' è più bello!*" 12 variations in C "*Menuett à la Vigano.*"			
1796	Sonata in D, op. 6, 2 pfs. Sonata in E flat, op. 7. 2 sonatinas in G and G mi., op. 49 (?) (pub. 1805). Rondo in C, op. 51 i. 2 *Bagatelles* in C mi and C. *Allegretto* in C mi.			
1797	12 variations in A on a "*Dance Russe,*" from ballet "*Das Waldmädchen.*" 3 sonatas in C mi., F and D, op. 10, and 6 variations on a Swiss Song.	Arrangement of pf. concerto no. 2 in B flat, op. 19.		

Vocal Works.	Chamber Music.		
	Wind Instruments and various.	Pf. and Strings.	Strings only.
Adelaide, op. 46 (pub. 1797). " *Opferlied* " (Matthisson). " *Seufzer eines Ungeliebten* " and " *Gegenliebe* " (variations, theme from *Choral Fantasia*). 2 songs for Umlauf's " *Schöne Schusterin* " : (1) " *O welch ein Leben* " (Tenor), (2) *Soll ein Schuh nicht drücken* " (Soprano). Scene, with orch. :— " *Ah perfido*." Farewell song to citizens of Vienna.	Variations upon Mozart's " *La ci darem*," 2 oboes & cor anglais. Sextet in E flat, 2 vns., viola, 'cello & 2 horns, op. 81b (pub. 1819). Sonatina and *Adagio* in F mi., mandoline & cymbals (?).	pub. 1795). 6 German dances, pf. & vn.	
	Sextet in E flat, op. 71, 2 clar., 2 bassoons, 2 horns (pub. 1810). Fragment of quintet, oboe, 3 horns, bassoon (?). Quintet in E flat, op. 16, pf., oboe, clar., horn, bassoon (pub. 1801).	2 sonatas in F and G mi., op. 5, pf. & 'cello. 12 variations in G for pf. & 'cello upon march from " *Judas Maccabeus*."	Quintet in E flat, op. 4, 2 vns., 2 violas, 'cello (arrangement of octet, op. 103). Duet for viola & 'cello (" with 2 obbligato monocles.")
Austrian Battle Song.	Serenade in D, op. 25, for fl., vn., viola (?), (pub. 1802). Trio in B flat, op. 11, pf., clar. & 'cello.		Serenade in D, op. 8, for vn., viola & 'cello. 3 trios in G, D and C mi., op. 9, for vn., viola & 'cello.

12 variations in F,

Year.	Works for Pf. only.	Concertos and Concert pieces with Orchestra.	Symphonies.	Dramatic Works, Marches and Dances for Orchestra.
1797	*Sonate pathètique* in C mi., op. 13 (pub. 1799).	Composition of pf. concerto no. 1 in C, op. 15. Rondo in B flat for pf. & orch.		
	2 sonatas in E and G, op. 14 (?pub. 1799). Variations in C on Grétry's " *Une fièvre brûlante.*" 10 variations in B flat on Salieri's " *La stessa, la stessissima.*" 7 variations in F on Winter's " *Kind willst du ruhig schlafen.*"		1st symphony in C, op. 21 (pub. 1801).	
1799	8 variations in F on Süssmayr's " *Tändeln und scherzen.*"			
1800	Sonata in B flat, op. 22. 6 variations in D, 2 pfs., on original theme " *Ich denke dein.*"	Pf. concerto no. 3 in C mi., op. 37.		
1801	Sonata in A flat, op. 26. Rondo in G, op. 51 ii. 2 sonatas in E flat and C sharp mi., op. 27. Sonata in D, op. 28.			Music for ballet " *The Men of Prometheus,*" op. 43. 12 *Contredances,* 2 vns. & bass (pub. 1802 ?).

Vocal Works.	Chamber Music.		
	Wind Instruments and various.	Pf. and Strings.	Strings only.
		op. 66, pf. & 'cello, on Mozart's "*Ein mädchen oder Weibchen.*"	
		3 sonatas in D, A, E flat, op. 12, pf. & vn.	
	Septet in E flat, op. 20, for clar., horn, bassoon, vn., viola, 'cello & double-bass. Sonata in F, op. 17, for pf. & horn.		6 quartets in F, G, D, C mi., A, B, op. 18, 2 vns., viola, 'cello (pub. in 2 numbers, 1800–1801).
		Sonata in A mi., op. 23, pf. & vn. Sonata in F, op. 24, pf. & vn. 7 variations in E flat for pf. & 'cello on Mozart's "*Bei Männern, welche liebe fühlen.*"	Quintet in C, op. 29, 2 vns., 2 violas & 'cello.

Year.	Works for Pf. only.	Concertos and Concert pieces with Orchestra.	Symphonies.	Dramatic Works, Marches and Dances for Orchestra.
1802	2 sonatas in G and D mi., op. 31. *Bagatelles*, op. 33. 6 variations in F, op. 34, on original theme. 15 variations in G on an original theme. 15 variations with fugue in E flat, op. 35, on a theme from *Prometheus*. 3 marches in C, E flat and D, op. 45, 2 pfs. Sonata in E flat, op. 31 iii (pub. 1804).	Romance in G, op. 40, for vn. & orch. Romance in F, op. 50, for vn. & orch.	2nd symphony in D, op. 36 (pub. 1804).	6 country dances, 2 vns. & bass.
1803	7 country dances.		3rd symphony in E flat, op. 55 (pub. 1806).	Opera begun for Schickaneder.
1804	Sonata in C, op. 53. *Andante favori* in F. Sonata in F, op. 54 (pub. 1806). Sonata in F mi., op. 57. Study, written in 1806 (pub. in 1807). 7 variations in D upon " *Rule Britannia.*"	Triple-concerto in C, op. 56, pf., vn., 'cello. Study.		*Fidelio* (*Leonora*), op. 72. *Leonora* overture no. 1 in C, op. 138, and *Leonora* no. 2 in C (pf. arrangement pub. 1810).
1805		Triple-concerto in C,		

Vocal Works.	Chamber Music.		
	Wind Instruments and various.	Pf. and Strings.	Strings only.
Canon :—" *Ein anderes ist das erste Jahr*," " *Lob auf den Dicken* " for 2 voices & chorus. Oratorio " *Christus am Olberge*," op. 85 (pub. 1811). 2nd setting of Matthisson's "*Opferlied*."		3 sonatas in A, C mi. & G, op. 30, pf. & vn. Rondo in G, pf. & vn. (?).	Quartet in F after sonata in E (pub. as op. 14 i).
6 Gellert songs, op. 48. Song " *Das Gluck der Freundschaft*," op. 88.		Sonata in A, op. 47, pf. & vn.	
Song " *An die Hoffnung* " (*Tiedge*), first setting. Song " *Der Wachtelschlag*."			

Year.	Works for Pf. only.	Concertos and Concert pieces with Orchestra.	Symphonies.	Dramatic Works, Marches and Dances for Orchestra.
		op. 56, finished (pub. 1807).		
1806	32 variations in C mi. on original theme.	Pf. concerto no. 4 in G, op. 58. Vn. concerto in D, op. 61.	4th symphony in B flat, op. 60 (pub. (1808).	*Leonora* overture no. 3 in C (pub. 1810).
1807		Violin-concerto arranged as a pianoforte concerto.	5th symphony in C mi., op. 67 (pub. 1809). 6th symphony in F, op. 68 ("*Pastoral*") (pub. 1809).	Overture to Collin's *Coriolanu.* in C mi., op. 62 12 *schottishes*, 2 vns. & bass.
1808		Fantasia in C., op. 80, pf. chorus and orch.		
1809	6 variations in D, op. 76, on original theme. *Fantasia*, op. 77. Sonata in F sharp mi., op. 78. Sonata in G, op. 79. Sonata in E flat, op. 81a (" *Das Lebewohl* ").	Pf. concerto in E flat, op. 73.		2 military marches in F.

| Vocal Works. | Chamber Music. | | |
	Wind Instruments and various.	Pf. and Strings.	Strings only.
Song:—"*Empfindungen bei Lydiens Untreue.*"			3 quartets in F, E mi. and C, op. 59.
Mass in C, op. 86, soli, chorus & orch. (pub. 1812). Ariette. " *In questa tomba.*" 3rd setting of Matthisson's " *Opferlied.*"			
4 settings for Goethe's " *Nur wer die Sehnsucht kennt.*"		Sonata in A major, pf. & 'cello, op. 69. 2 trios in D, and E flat, op. 70, pf., vn. & 'cello.	
Songs :—" *Ich denke dein* " (Matthisson). 4 songs from Goethe, op. 75 :—" *Kennst du das Land* "; " *Herz mein Herz* "; " *Flohlied* " (from *Faust*) ; " *Gretels Warnung.*" " *Die laute Klage* " (Herder). " *Lied aus der Ferne* " (Reissig). Settings of Scottish, Irish and Welsh songs for Thomson begun.			Quartet in E flat, op. 74.

Year.	Works for Pf. only.	Concertos and Concert pieces with Orchestra.	Symphonies.	Dramatic Works, Marches and Dances for Orchestra.
1809				Oct. 1809–May 1810, music for Goethe's *Egmont*, op. 84.
1810	Pf. piece in A mi. "*Für Elise.*"			*Schottische. Polonaise.* March in C. (All for military band).
1811			7th symphony in A, op. 92 (till May 1812, pub. 1816). 8th symphony in F, op. 93 (till Oct. 1812, pub. 1816).	Music for Kotzebue's plays *The Ruins of Athens* and *King Stephen.*
1812				
1813			"*Wellington's Victory*" (*Battle Symphony*), op. 91. Triumphant march in C for "*Tarpeja.*"	
1814	Polonaise in C, op. 89. Sonata in E mi., mi., op. 90 (Aug. 16th).			*Fidelio* overture in E. *Birthday Overture* in C, op. 115. Music for *Leonora Prohaska.*

Vocal Works.	Chamber Music.		
	Wind Instruments and various.	Pf. and Strings.	Strings only.
3 songs from Goethe, op. 83 :—" *Trocknet nicht*," " *Was zieht mir das Herz*," " *Kleine Blumen, kleine Blätter*," " *An den fernen Geliebten*," " *Der Zufriedene* " (Reissig).			Quartet in F mi., op. 95.
Song :—" *An die Geliebte* " (Stoll). 4 *ariettes* and a duet, op. 82.		Trio in B flat, op. 97, for pf., vn. & 'cello.	
Canon on Mälzel's " *Tata*." 2 songs from Reissig, " *Welch ein wunderbares Leben*," " *Der Frühling entblühet*." Canon " *Kurz ist der Schmerz* " (1st version. " *Höre, die Nachtigall singt* " (Herder).	3 *Equale* for 4 trombones.	Little trio in B flat for pf., vn. & 'cello. Sonata in G, op. 96 for pf. & vn.	
Cantata, " *Der Glorreiche Augenblick*." Trio, " *Tremate, empi :* " (sketched 1801–1802). Trio, 2 tenors and bass, " *Die stunde schlägt*."			

Year.	Works for Pf. only.	Concertos and Concert pieces with Orchestra.	Symphonies.	Dramatic Works, Marches and Dances for Orchestra.
1814				
1815		Studies for pf. concerto in D.	Studies for Symphony in B mi.	
1816	Sonata in A, op. 101.			March for a grand parade of the Watch.

Vocal Works.	Chamber Music.		
	Wind Instruments and various.	Pf. and Strings.	Strings only.

Vocal Works.	Wind Instruments and various.	Pf. and Strings.	Strings only.
Elegies, op. 118: Chorus "Germania," "Ihr weisen Gründer." Cantata, sopr., 2 tenors, basses & pf., for Bertolini. Songs, "Bardengeist," "Merkenstein" (twice set). 2 songs from Reissig: "Die stille Nacht umdunkelt," "Ich zieh ins Feld." Canon, "Kurz ist das Schmerz" (2nd version). Canon, "Freundschaft ist der Quelle." 1st Vol. of Scottish songs publ.			
Cantata, "Meeresstille und glückliche Fahrt," op. 112. Chorus, "Es ist vollbracht." "An die Hoffnung" (Tiedge), op. 94 (2nd setting). "Der mann von Wort" (Kleinschmid), op. 99.		2 sonatas in C and D, op. 102, pf. & 'cello.	
Song-cycle, op. 98 (Jeitteles). Lobkowitz cantata. Song "Wo blüht das Blümchen."		Studies for trio in F mi.	

Year.	Works for Pf. only.	Concertos and Concert pieces with Orchestra.	Symphonies.	Dramatic Works, Marches and Dances for Orchestra.
1816				
1817				
1818	Sonata in B flat, op. 106, "*Dernière pensée musicale.*"			
1819				11 Mödling dances (?).
1820	Sonata in E, op. 109.			
1821	Sonata in A flat, op. 110.			
1822	Sonata in C mi., op. 111 (Jan. 13th). "*Bagatelles*," op. 119.			Overture in C, op. 124. Closing chorus to *Weihe des Hauses.* Studies for overture on B-A-C-H (till 1825).
1823	33 variations in C on waltz by Diabelli. "*Bagatelles*," op. 126. 6 *schottisches.* *Rondo capriccioso* in G major, "*A fuss about a lost*		9th symphony in D mi., op. 125 (pub. 1826).	

Vocal Works.	Chamber Music.		
	Wind Instruments and various.	Pf. and Strings.	Strings only.
Canons, " *Gluck zum neuen Jahr*," and " *Das Schweigen und das Reden.*"			
Monks' song from *William Tell*.			Quintet fugue in D, op. 137, for 2 vns., 2 violas, 'cello.
Songs, " *Nord oder Süd*," " *Ruf vom Berge.*"			Quintet, op. 104. Arrangement of Trio in C mi., op. 1.
Song, " *Lösch aus mein Licht.*"			
Song, " *Auf Freunde, singt dem Gott der Ehe.*"		6 varied themes for pf. with fl. or vn. *ad lib.*	
Canon, " *Hol Euch der Teufel.*"		10 varied themes for same combination.	
Canon, " *Glaube und hoffe.*"			
Canon, " *Seine kaiserliche Hoheit.*"			
Canon, " *Auf einem, welcher Hoffmann geheissen.*"			
Song, " *Wenn die Sonne nieder sinkt.*"			
" *Gedenke mein.*"			
2 Canons, " *St. Petrus war ein Fels*" & " *St. Bernadus war ein Sankt.*"			
Canon, " *O Tobias Haslinger.*"		*Adagio* and 10 variations in G, op. 121a, pf., vn. & 'cello on Müller's " *Ich bin der Schneider Kakadu*" (pub. 1824).	
Song, " *Ich war bei Chloe ganz allein*" (sketched 1798).			
Opferlied (Matthisson), 4th setting for solo, chor. & orch., op. 121b.			

Year.	Works for Pf. only.	Concertos and Concert pieces with Orchestra.	Symphonies.	Dramatic Works, Marches and Dances for Orchestra.
1823	*penny*" (pub. 1828).			
1824	Little Waltz in E flat.			
1825	Little Waltz in D. *Schottische* in E flat.			
1826	" Ludwig van Beethoven's Last musical Thought " in C (pub. after his death by Diabelli). An arrangement of a proposed string quintet (?).		Studies for a 10th Symphony.	

Vocal Works.	Chamber Music.		
	Wind Instruments and various.	Pf. and Strings.	Strings only.
Bundeslied, op. 122. Canon, "*Gedenket heute an Baden.*" Provisional close to *Missa solemnis*, op. 123 (pub. 1827). Study for *Mass* in C sharp mi. Leaf from an album : "*Der edle Mensch.*" Canon, "*Edel sei der Mensch.*" "*Te solo adoro.*"			
Italian song-fragment. Canon, "*Schwenke Dich.*" Canon, "*Gott ist eine feste Burg.*"			Quartet in E flat major, op. 127.
Canons, "*Bester Herr Graf, Sie sind ein Schaf,*" "*Das Schöne zu dem Guten,*" "*Doktor, sperrt das Tor dem Tod,*" "*Si non per portas,*" "*Kühl nicht, lau nicht,*" "*Ars longa, vita brevis,*" "*Freu dich des Lebens.*"			Quartet in A mi., op. 132. Quartet in B flat, op. 130.
Canon, "*Es muss sein.*" "*Wir irren allesamt, nur jeder irret anders.*"			Quartet in C sharp mi., op. 131. Quartet in F, op. 135. *Finale* for quartet in B flat, op. 130.

INDEX OF NAMES

ABERCROMBY, General, 160, 166

d'Alayrac, composer, 201

Albrechtsberger, Johann Georg, 18, 19, 139, 252, 345

Alexander I., Emperor of Russia, 299, 354

Alexandria, 160

Allgemeine Musikalische Zeitung, 87, 151, 204, 237, 289, 298

Amenda, Karl, 20, 47, 210, 310, 311

Anschütz, Heinrich, actor, 205, 359

Antwerp, 343

Appony, Count, 307

Aristotle, 54

Arnim, Bettina von, 27, 46, 49, 211, 255, 331, 349

Artaria, Mathias, publisher, 279, 336, 345, 353, 357, 358

Aschaffenberg, 17, 345

Augsburg, 85

Bach, Dr. J. B., barrister, 353

—— Johann Sebastian, 9, 19, 65, 71, 81, 85, 148, 149, 248, 273, 275, 315, 337, 376

—— Philip Emanuel, 84, 101

Baden, 43, 175, 298, 327, 347, 348, 349, 350, 351, 353, 354, 355, 356

Barbaja, impresario, 214

Bäuerles Theaterzeitung, 325

Beer, Joseph, clarinet player, 289

Beethoven, Caspar Anton Carl van (brother), 5, 13, 20, 29, 30, 31, 343, 345, 347, 348, 351

—— Heinrich Adelard van (great-grandfather), 343

—— Johann van (father), 4, 6, 7, 8, 13, 14, 18, 343, 345

—— Johanna van (sister-in-law), 31, 32, 347, 352, 353, 355, 357

—— Karl van (nephew), 29, 30, 31, 32, 36, 37, 57, 58, 348, 351, 352, 353, 355, 356, 357, 358

—— Louis van (grandfather), 4, 5, 7, 343

—— Ludwig, Maria van (brother), 5, 343

—— Maria Josepha (grandmother), 343

—— Maria Magdalena van (mother), 4, 5, 6, 13, 15, 343, 344

Beethoven, Nicolas Johann van (brother), 5, 13, 30, 31, 86, 343, 345, 349, 353, 356, 357, 358

Benda, Georg, 200

Berger, Rudolph von, 210

Berlin, 20, 43, 49, 86, 210, 211, 279, 297, 346, 353

Berlioz, Hector, 179, 339, 340

Bernadotte, General, 154, 346

Bernard, Karl, 264, 358

Bertolini, physician, 25, 375

Bigot, Marie, 25, 49

Blöchlinger, Joseph, 352, 355

Böhm, Joseph, 326, 356

Bolla, Mme., singer, 345

Bonn, 3, 8, 9, 11, 12, 13, 14, 15, 16, 17, 20, 41, 47, 48, 83, 84, 85, 94, 95, 120, 200, 252, 261, 279, 287, 297, 304, 308, 343, 345, 346, 353, 358, 363

Bossler, publisher, 344

Bouilly, J. N., 215, 216, 217

Brahms, 144, 340

Braun, Baron, 24, 202, 203, 347

Braunhofer, physician, 358

Breitkopf and Härtel, publishers, 54, 117, 207, 211, 263, 266, 279, 283, 286

Brentano, Antonie von, 27, 49, 349

—— Franz von, 27, 349

—— Maximiliane von, 27, 49, 304, 349

Breuning, Herr Hofrat von, 10

—— Christopher von, 10, 47, 344

—— Eleonore von, 10, 47, 49, 95, 344, 362

—— Frau Helene von, 10, 14, 15, 47, 49, 344

—— Gerhard von, 40, 344, 358

—— Lenz von, 10, 20, 47, 344

—— Stephan von, 10, 20, 33, 34, 37, 42, 47, 175, 217, 343, 344, 346, 347, 356, 358, 359

Bridgetower, G. A., 23, 297, 300, 347

Broadwood, Thomas, 36, 86, 352

Browne, Count, 20, 309

Brühl, Count, 213, 357

—— near Vienna, 175

Brunswick, Count Franz, 46, 47, 137

—— Countess Therese, 49, 50

Buda-Pesth, 206, 231, 346

Bülow, Hans von, 136, 140, 142
Bürger, G. A., 125

Cappi, publisher, 279
Carlsbad, 43, 349
Cassel, 25, 26, 180, 348
Cherubini, 87, 201, 202, 215, 217, 220, 230, 251, 257, 347, 354
Chopin, Frederick, 144
Cimarosa, 201
Clement Augustus, Elector, 343
Clement, Franz, 347, 348
Clementi, Muzio, 85, 101, 111, 347, 348
Collin, Heinrich von, 204, 205, 206, 216, 242, 243, 264
—— Matthias von, 205, 242, 370
Cologne, 7, 8, 12, 343
Courland, 210
Cramer, Johann Baptist, 106, 111, 346
Cramer's Magazin der Musik, 9, 344
Czerny, Karl, 90, 92, 115, 116, 125, 199, 289, 346, 349, 351, 354, 356

Dannhauser, Johann, 41, 359
Degenhart, flute-player, 286
Desaides, 200
Diabelli, Anton, 32, 142, 143, 304, 305, 353, 376, 378
Dietrich, Anton, 41
Dietrichstein, Count, 354
Dittersdorf, 65, 200, 345
Döbling, near Vienna, 43, 347, 351
Dolezalek, 358
Domanowecz, Zmeskall von, 20, 33, 47, 133
Dönhoff, Count, 349
Dorn, Heinrich, 267
Dragonetti, Domenico, 28, 346
Dresden, 20, 200, 216, 346
Dressler, composer, 94, 344, 360
Duncker, 209
Duport, Jean, violoncellist, 297
Dürer, Albrecht, 329
Dussek, Johann Ladislaus, 350

Ebert, Alfred, 325
Edinburgh, 24, 259, 347
Eeden, van den, 7, 9, 343
Ehrenbreitstein, 4, 343
Eisenstadt, 24, 348
Elizabeth, Empress of Russia, 29, 351
England, 28, 29, 44, 48, 86, 246
Eppinger, Heinrich, 20
Erard, 86
Erdödy, Countess, 25, 49, 298
Ertmann, Baroness Dorothea von, 25, 49
Esterhazy, Count Karl, 203
—— Count Nicolas, 203
—— Prince Nicolas, 24, 203, 204, 265, 266
—— Prince Nicolas Joseph, 277
Eybler, Joseph von, 21, 345

Fellner, banker, 347
Fichte, 71
Fischenich, 191
Flittner, Friederike, 8
Förster, Emanuel Aloys, 310
Frank, Frau Christine von, 346
Franzenbad, 43, 349
Frederick William II., 297, 357
—— III., 278
Fries, Count, 346
Frohlich, pastor, 352
Fuss, Johann Evangelist, 210

Gabrielli, Giovanni, 74
Galitzin, Prince, 32, 267, 280, 320, 321, 354, 355
Gaveaux, Pierre, 216
Gebauer, Franz Xaver, 353
Gelinek, Abt, 19, 84
Gellert, 258, 259, 369
Gläser, Franz, 354
Gleichenstein, Baron Ignaz von, 20, 47
Gluck, 75, 200, 209, 220, 233
Gneixendorf, 30, 36, 42, 352, 356, 357
Goethe, 29, 46, 54, 71, 154, 232, 243, 255, 256, 257, 262, 304, 348, 354, 371, 372, 373
Götz, publisher, 344
Graf, pianoforte-maker, 86, 356
Graz, 33, 45, 352, 358
Grétry, 117, 200, 366
Grillparzer, 32, 56, 63, 204, 205, 212, 213, 214, 354, 359
Grossman, Frau, 11
Grossmann, Herr, 8
Guglielmi, 201
Guicciardi, Countess Guilietta, 49, 50, 51
Gutenbrunn, near Vienna, 356
Gyrowetz, Adalbert, 21, 209

Hammer-Purgstall, Joseph, 55, 206
Handel, 19, 36, 67, 233, 275, 304, 337, 358
Häring, violinist, 20
Haslinger, Tobias, 52, 234, 356, 358, 377
Haydn, Joseph, 17, 18, 21, 27, 55, 71, 75, 81, 113, 130, 146, 147, 148, 157, 158, 159, 168, 169, 173, 187, 252, 255, 259, 277, 292, 295, 296, 310, 337, 344, 345, 348, 349
Heiligenstadt, 23, 43, 346, 348, 352
Heller, singer, 12
Hensler, theatrical manager, 354
Herder, 259, 371, 373
Hetzendorf, 17, 39, 43, 346, 347, 354, 355
Hiller, Ferdinand, 33, 358
—— Johann Adam, 9
Hirsch, Karl, 139

Höfel, Blasius, 41
Hoffmann, E. T. A., 213, 353
Hofmeister and Kühnel, publishers, 104, 279
Holland, 43, 83
Holz, Karl, 34, 48, 135, 263, 283, 325, 332, 354, 356
Holzbauer, Ignaz, 220
Homer, 54
Horace, 54
Horschelt, composer, 201
Huber, Franz Xaver, 263
Humboldt, Alexander von, 71
Hummel, Johann, 20, 28, 87, 111, 351, 358
Hüttenbrenner, Anselm, 33, 37, 351, 359

Iglau, 37, 357, 358
Italy, 44

Jahn, Otto, 217
Jedlersee, 298
Jeitteles, 375
Jenger, 358
Jerome, King of Westphalia, 25, 348
Joseph II., Emperor, 11, 230, 252, 261, 344, 363
Junker, 83

Kahlenberg, 175
Kalischer, Alfred Christlieb, 214
Kanne, August, 63, 206, 212, 214
Kant, Emanuel, 54, 71, 72, 338, 339
Kewerich, 343
Kiesewetter, Hofrat von, 20
Kinsky, Prince, 26, 29, 348, 349, 351
Klein, Franz, 41
Kleinschmid, F. A., 375
Kloeber, August von, 41, 42
Klopstock, 54, 63
Knecht, Justin Heinrich, 176
Koch, Willibald, Fra., 7, 344
Körner, Theodore, 125, 209
Kotzebue, 27, 206, 208, 209, 231, 372
Kozeluch, Leopold Anton, 259, 345
Kraft, Anton, 22
—— Nicolas, 22
Krebs, Johann Ludwig, 65
Krems, 36
Kretschmar, Hermann, 279, 326
Kreutzer, Rudolph, 23, 300
Krumpholz, Wenzel, 20, 115, 351
Kudlich, Joseph, 352
Kuffner, Christoph, 56, 63, 209, 264, 352, 357
Kuhlau, Friedrich, 356
Kuhnau, Johann, 65

Lachner, Franz, 33
Laibach, 352

Landshut, 352
Laym, valet, 4, 343
Leipzig, 9, 20, 125, 185, 279, 320, 346, 355
Lenz, Wilhelm von, 140, 321
Leopold II, 252, 261, 344, 353, 363
Letronne, Louis, 41, 42
Lichnowsky, Prince, 20, 21, 22, 25, 39, 86, 295, 307, 310, 320, 345, 346, 348, 349, 350
Lichnowsky, Count Moritz, 20, 212, 354
Liechtenstein, Prince, 20
Linke, Joseph, violoncellist, 298, 325, 351, 354, 356, 357
Linz, 320, 349
Lipavski, pianist, 84
Liszt, Franz, 33, 143, 144, 315, 321, 322, 340, 354
Lobkowitz, Prince, 22, 26, 29, 203, 204, 208, 262, 347, 348, 349, 351, 353, 375
Lodron, Count, 203
London, 17, 36, 45, 246, 344, 345, 355, 356, 358
Louis XVIII of France, 355
Louis Ferdinand, of Prussia, Prince, 39, 347
Luchesi, Andrea, 11
Lyser, Johann Peter, 40

Macco, Alexander, 347
Mähler, Willibrord, 41
Malfatti, Dr. von, physician, 25, 358
Malfatti, Therese, 50, 349
Mälzel, Johann, Nepomuk, 28, 186, 350, 352, 373
Mannheim, 8, 9, 75, 94, 158, 162, 235, 344
Maria Theresa, Empress of Austria, 11, 344
Marschner, Heinrich, 33, 352
Marx, A. B., 214
Maschek, Vincenz, 199
Matthisson, Friedrich von, 54, 255, 365, 369, 371, 377
Maximilian Franz, Elector of Cologne, 11, 12, 14, 15, 16, 17, 18, 285, 286, 344, 345, 346
Maximilian Friedrich, Elector of Cologne, 6, 8, 11, 12, 16, 94, 120, 304, 343, 344, 360
Mayseder, Joseph, 28
Mendelssohn, 144, 262, 339, 340
Mergentheim, 17, 83, 345
Meyerbeer, 28
Michelangelo, 109, 256
Milder-Hauptmann, Anna, 210
Mödling, near Vienna, 43, 137, 175, 352, 353, 376
Mollo, publisher, 201, 279
Monsigny, Pierre Alexandre, 201

Morgenblatt für gebildete Stände, 215
Moscheles, Ignaz, 28, 101, 358
Motte-Fouqué, Baron de la, 210, 213
Mozart, Leopold, 65
—— Wolfgang Amadeus, 3, 7, 9, 13, 19, 20, 21, 71, 75, 81, 83, 84, 87, 88, 101, 106, 121, 123, 146, 147, 148, 149, 157, 158, 159, 160, 168, 173, 187, 200, 202, 216, 220, 230, 233, 249, 255, 277, 286, 287, 292, 298, 304, 310, 337, 357, 363, 365, 367
Müller, Wenzel, 32, 283, 304, 377
Munich, 287, 350
Münster, 9, 16, 17, 344

Napoleon, 72, 154, 155, 160, 164, 166, 243, 347
Neate, Charles, 29, 355, 356
Neefe, Christian Gottlob, 8, 9, 10, 11, 12, 62, 84, 94, 343, 344
Neumann, Frau, 212
Nottebohm, Gustav, 18, 95, 113, 234, 328, 329
Nussböck, Leopold, 353
Nussdorf, near Vienna, 352

Obermeyer, Therese, 350
Oliva, Franz, 34
Olmütz, 32, 266
Opitz, actor, 8
Ovid, 54, 65

Pachler-Koschak, Marie, 33, 49, 352, 355, 358
Paër, Ferdinand, 106, 216
Paësiello, Giovanni, 200
Palffy, Count, 203
Paris, 86, 207, 251, 356
Pasqualati, Baron, 202, 261, 358
Penzing, near Vienna, 355
Peters, Councillor, 353
—— publisher, 279, 320, 321, 353
Pfeiffer, Friedrich Tobias, 7, 343
Philharmonic Society, London, 36, 246, 355, 358
Pichler, poet, 206
Piringer, Ferdinand, 358
Plato, 54
Pleyel, Ignaz Joseph, 87, 259, 350
Plutarch, 54
Poll, Maria Josepha, *see* Beethoven
Polledro, Giovanni Battista, 349
Potter, Cyprian, 153, 352
Prague, 20, 43, 101, 346, 349, 350, Prater, 350
Pressburg, 346
Prieger, Erich, 217
Probst, publisher, 355
Pronay, Baron, 39, 354
Punto, Giovanni, *see* Stich

Rahel (Varnhagen), 27, 208, 349
Rasumowsky, Count, 24, 130, 298, 316, 320, 351
Recke, Elise von der, 27, 208, 349
Reicha, Anton, 16, 346
—— Joseph, 16, 20
Reichardt, Johann Friedrich, 85, 206
Reinecke, Karl, 143
Reiss, Johanna, *see* Beethoven
Reisser, 356
Reissig, C. L., 371, 372, 375
Rellstab, Ludwig, 33, 214, 356
Richter, J. V., 267
Riemann, Hugo, 231
Ries, Ferdinand, 13, 48, 50, 88, 89, 93, 287, 295, 346, 356
—— Franz, 13, 346
Righini, Vincenzo, 117, 362
Rio, Giannatasio del, 351, 352
Rochlitz, Johann Friedrich, 33, 41, 211, 263, 353
Röckel, Joseph, 25
Rode, Pierre, 27, 297, 300, 350
Romberg, Andreas, 16, 28, 87
Romberg, Bernhard, 16
Rotterdam, 344
Rossini, 33, 235, 353, 355
Rousseau, Jean Jacques, 66, 175
Rovantini, Francis George, 7, 344
Rudolph, Archduke, 26, 27, 32, 121, 128, 207, 252, 267, 277, 279, 297, 348, 350, 354

Sacchini, 201
Sailer, schoolmaster, 352
St. Petersburg, 267, 354
Salieri, 18, 21, 28, 117, 200, 201, 252, 298, 345, 366
Salzburg, 3
Sarti, Giuseppe, 201
Schechner, Nanette, 358
Schelble, 354
Schenk, Johann, 18, 252, 345
Schikaneder, Emanuel, 22, 23, 24, 201, 202, 229, 347, 368
Schiller, 25, 46, 54, 55, 71, 85, 154, 191, 210, 214, 338
Schiller, Charlotte, 191
Schimon, Ferdinand, 41, 42
Schindler, Anton, 34, 37, 48, 50, 51, 56, 99, 137, 170, 190, 197, 214, 234, 321, 322, 350, 353, 354
Schlegel, 212
Schlemmer, 356
Schlesinger, Martin, publisher, 213, 259, 279, 353, 357
—— Moritz, publisher, 356
Schleswig, 25, 348
Schneider, Friedrich, 353
Scholz, actor, 207

Schönbrun, 175
Schott and Sons, 36, 266, 279, 327, 355, 357, 358
Schröder-Devrient, Wilhelmina, 354
Schubart, 63
Schubert, Franz, 33, 46, 153, 337, 339, 340, 356, 357, 358
Schumann, Robert, 142, 144, 340
Schuppanzigh, Ignaz, 20, 22, 28, 33, 253, 320, 321, 325, 346, 350, 351, 354, 356, 357
Schuster, Joseph, 200
Schwarzenberg, Prince, 20, 203
" Schwarzspanierhaus," 33, 34, 86
Scott, Sir Walter, 54
Sebald, Amalie, 27, 49, 349
Sellner, oboe-player, 356
Seume, 54
Seyfried, Ignaz von, 25
Shakespeare, William, 64, 205, 210, 241, 242
Sicily, 44
Simroch, Nicolas, 279, 353
Sina, violinist, 22
Smart, Sir George, 29, 356, 358
Sonnleithner, J. F. von, 215, 216, 227, 347
Speyer, 6, 344
Spinoza, 71
Spohr, 28, 173, 174, 339
Spontini, 217, 220
Sporschil, Johann, 212
Stadler, Abt., 357
Staudenheimer, physician, 358
Steibelt, Daniel, 19, 88, 346
Stein, Andreas, 85
—— Freiherr von, 71
—— Nanette (late Streicher), 25, 49, 85, 175
Steiner, publisher, 353
Sterkel, Abbé, 17, 345
Stich, Wenzel ("Punto"), 287, 297, 346
Stieler, 41
Stoll, poet, 373
Streicher, Andreas, 25, 49, 85, 355, 358
—— Nanette (née Stein), 25, 49, 85, 175, 358
Streicher's Magazine, 41
Stumpff, harp-maker, 36, 42, 355, 358
Sturm, writer, 54, 177
Stuttersheim, 357, 358
Stuttgart, 176
Süssmayr, 117, 345, 366
Swedish Academy, 56
Swieten, van, 19

Teplitz, 27, 43, 49, 208, 349
Thayer, A. W., 9, 30, 308
Thomson, George, 24, 259, 260, 347, 371
Tiedge, 27, 54, 208, 256, 257, 349, 369
Titian, 195
Tomaczek, 87
Treitschke, Georg Friedrich, 29, 207, 209, 218, 219, 222, 223, 225, 229
Troppau, 25, 348, 349
Truchsess-Waldburg, Count, 348
Tuscher, Councillor von, 352

Umlauf, Ignaz, 201, 350, 355
Unterdöbling, 346, 353
Unzelmann, see Flittner

Varnhagen von Ense, 27, 208, 349
Varena, Hofrat, 45
Vigano, Salvatore, 22, 201, 346
Vittoria, 28, 350
Vogler, Abt, 23, 65, 111, 202, 347
Voltaire, 212

Wagner, Richard, 50, 161, 183, 340
Waldstein, Count, 15, 16, 19, 83, 85, 118, 201, 344, 362
Warnsdorf, 267
Wawruch, physician, 358
Weber, Carl Maria von, 33, 144, 339, 350, 354, 355
—— Dionys, 101
Wegeler, Franz Gerhard, 10, 14, 20, 39, 47, 48, 54, 160, 279, 307, 308, 344, 346, 358
Weigl, Joseph, 21, 117, 206, 209, 214, 288
Weiss, Franz, 22, 325, 351, 354, 356
Weissenbach, Dr. Aloys, 29, 206
Wellington, Duke of, 28, 350
Werner, 206
Wiech, Friedrich, 357
Wiedemann, 311
Willmann, Magdalena, 20, 49, 50, 345
Winter, Helmuth, 210
—— Peter von, 199, 263
Wölffl, Joseph, 19, 84, 87, 111, 346
Würth, banker, 347

Xenophon, 54

Zelter, Karl and Friedrich, 33, 353, 354
Zichy, Count, 203
Zitterbarth, merchant, 202
Zmeskall, see Domanowecz.

INDEX OF WORKS

"*Adelaida*," song, op. 46, 22, 29, 255, 256, 257, 261, 351, 365
" *Ah perfido* " (*scena*), 201, 253, 348, 365
Alexander sonatas, *see* Sonatas for pf. and vn., op. 30
Alfred the Great, proposed opera, 212
Allegretto in C minor for pf., 364
" *An den fernen Geliebten*," song, 373
" *An die ferne Geliebte*," song-cycle, op. 98, 188, 256, 258, 269, 320, 375
" *An die Geliebte*," song, 373
" *An die Hoffnung*," song, op. 94. ii, 256, 257, 369, 375
" *An einen Säugling*," song, 361
" *An Minna*," song, 363
Andante favori in F major, *see* Sonatas for pf., op. 53
Ariettas, four, op. 82, 373
Arrangements :
of 2nd symphony as trio for pf., vn., and 'cello, 315
of op. 61 for pf., 122, 123, 348, 370
of op. 14. i (pf. sonata) as quartet, 315
of trio, op. 1, in C minor as quintet, op. 104, 314, 377
of op. 133 for pf., 315
of Scottish, Irish, and Welsh melodies, 259, 260, 371, 375
of octet, op. 103, as quintet, 365
of Portuguese, Spanish, and Italian songs, 259, 260
" *Ars longa, vita brevis*," canon, 379
" *Auf einen, welcher Hoffmann geheissen*," canon, 377
" *Auf, Freunde, singt dem Gott der Ehe*," song, 377
Austrian Battle Song, 365

B–A–C–H (studies for an overture), 32, 248, 376
Bacchus, proposed opera, 210
Bagatelles :
op. 33, 95, 96, 368
op. 119, 141, 376
op. 126, 141, 376
in C mi., 364
in C major, 364
" *Bardengeist*," song, 375
Battle of Vittoria, see *Battle* symphony

Battle symphony, 29, 65, 66, 129, 174, 178, 180, 350, 351, 372
" *Bernardus war ein Sankt*," canon, 377
" *Bester Herr Graf*," canon, 379
Birthday Overture, see *Name-day* overture
" *Bitten*," song, op. 48, 258
" *Blessing of the House*," see *Weihe des Hauses*
Bradamante, proposed opera, 206, 213
Bundeslied, song, op. 122, 262, 379
Busslied, song, op. 48, 252, 259

Canons, Beethoven's, 260, 261
Cantatas :
on death of Joseph II, 230, 252, 344, 363
on accession of Leopold II, 252, 344, 363
for Bertolini, 375
" *Der glorreiche Augenblick*," 29, 261, 351, 373
for Pasqualati, op. 118, 261, 262, 375
for Lobhowitz, 262, 375
" *Meeresstille und glückliche Fahrt*," op. 112, 29, 262, 351, 375
Choral symphony, *see* Symphonies No. 9
Christus am Olberg, see *Mount of Olives*
Concerto for pf., vn. and 'cello in C, op. 56, 24, 120, 141, 368, 370
Concertos for pf. and orch. :
in E flat (fragment), 120, 360
in D (fragment), 120, 362
op. 15 in C, 120, 346, 366
op. 19 in B flat, 120, 345, 362
op. 37 in C mi., 121, 312, 347, 366
op. 58 in G, 24, 121, 122, 123, 124, 180, 348, 370
op. 73 in E flat, 121–124, 125, 318, 349, 370
in D (study for), 125, 374
Concertos for vn. and orch. :
in C (fragment), 362
op. 61 in D, 24, 121–124, 348, 370
op. 61 in D arranged for pf., 122, 123, 348, 370
Congratulatory minuet, 32
Contre-dances, 12, 366
Coriolanus, overture, op. 62, 66, 69, 72, 140, 204, 241–243, 244, 312, 348, 370

Country dances (7) for pf., 368
Country dances (6) for two violins and
    doublebass, 368

" Das Schöne zu dem Guten," canon, 379
" Das Schweigen und das Reden," canon,
    377
" Der edle Mensch," 379
Der Frühling erblühet, song, 373
" Der Mann von Wort," song, op. 99,
    375
" Der Wachtelschlag," song, 369
" Der Zufriedene," song, 373
" Dernière pensée musicale," see Sonatas
    for pf. op. 106
Dervishes, Chorus of, from King Stephen,
    231
Diabelli variations, see variations for pf.
Die gute Nachricht, closing chorus for,
    209
" Die Ehre Gottes aus der Natur," song,
    op. 48, 258
" Die laute Klage," song, 371
" Die liebe des Nächsten," song, op. 48,
    256
" Die stille Nacht umdunkelt," song, 375
" Die Stunde schlägt," terzet (vocal), 373
" Distant Beloved, The," see " An die
    ferne Geliebte "
" Doktor, sperrt das Tor dem Tod,"
    canon, 331, 379
Drahomira, proposed opera, 212
Duet for viola and 'cello, 365
—— for flutes in G, 286, 363
Duet, vocal, op. 82, 373
Duos (3) for clar. and bassoon, 286, 363
—— for a musical box, 363

" Edel sei der Mensch," canon, 379
Egmont, incidental music and overture
    for, op. 84, 66, 69, 70, 75, 193, 206,
    232, 244–246, 319, 349, 372
" Ein anderes ist das erste Jahr," canon,
    369
Elegie auf dem Tod eines Pudels, song, op.
    52, 252, 363
" Elegische Gesang an die verklärte
    Gemahlin meines Freundes Pas-
    qualati," see Cantatas
Elemente, Die (proposed oratorio), 32,
    264, 357
" Empfindungen bei Lydiens. untreue,"
    song, 371
Equales, 3, for 4 trombones, 320, 373
" Erhebt das Glas," song, 363
Eroica symphony, see Symphonies, op.55
" Es ist vollbracht," chorus, 375
" Es muss sein," canon, 379
" Es war einmal ein König," song, op. 75,
    256

Fantasia for pf., op. 77 in G, 90, 91, 37
    choral, for pf., orch., and choir, op.
    80 in C, 124, 125, 180, 199, 348, 357,
    365, 370
Farewell Song to the Burgers of Vienna,
    365
Faust, proposed music for, 211, 212
Faust, " Song of the Flea," from, op. 75,
    258, 371
" Feuerfarbe," song, op. 52, 363
Fidelio, op. 72, 29, 35, 50, 69, 120, 188,
    200, 203, 204, 207, 209, 210, 212,
    214, 215–231, 244, 252, 260, 264,
    281, 285, 347, 350, 351, 354, 368
    Overture to, in E major, op. 115, 247,
    250, 313, 319, 372
Fiesco, proposed opera, 212
" Freu dich des Lebens," canon, 379
" Freundschaft ist die Quelle," canon, 375
Fugue for organ, 360
" Fur Elise," pf. piece, 372
" Fuss about a lost penny, A," op. 129,
    rondo in G for pf., 100, 142, 376

" Gedenke mein," song, 377
" Gedenket heut an Baden," canon, 379
" Gegenliebe," song, 365
Gellert, songs after, op. 48, 369
German Dances (12) for orch., 330, 362
German Dances (6) for pf. and vn., 365
" Germania," chorus, 375
" Glaube und hoffe," canon, 377
Glorious Moment, see Cantatas
" Glorreiche Augenblick," see Cantatas
" Gluck der Freundschaft," op. 88, song
    369
" Glück zum neuen Jahr," canon, 375
" Gott ist eine feste Burg," canon, 273
    379
" Gottes Macht und Vorsehung," song, op.
    48, 258
" Great Mass," see Mass in D
" Gretels Warnung," song, op. 75, 256,371

" Herz, mein Herz," song, op. 75, 256
    257, 371
" Hol euch den Teufel," canon, 377
" Höre, die Nachtigall singt," song, 373

" Ich denke dein," song, 371
" Ich, der mit flatterndem Sinn," song, 363
" Ich war bei Chloe ganz allein," song, 377
" Ich zieh ins Feld," song, 375
" Ihr weisen Gründer," chorus, 375
" In questa tomba " (arietta), 201, 253
    371
Italian song, fragment, 379

Judith (proposed oratorio), 32
Jupiter Ammon, proposed opera, 212

" *Kennst du das Land*," song, op. 75, 256, 257, 371

King Stephen, incidental music for, 27, 206, 231, 232, 246, 349, 372

" *Klage*," song, 363

Klärchenlieder, songs, 256, 257

" *Kleine blumen, kleine blätter*," song, op. 83, 256, 257, 373

Kreutzer sonata, *see* Sonatas for pf. and vn., op. 47

Kühl nicht, lau nicht," canon, 379

" *Kurz ist der Schmerz*," 2 canons, 373, 375

" Last musical thought " in C, 378

Lebewohl sonata, *see* Sonatas for pf., op. 81*a*

Leonora, 24, 29, 66, 69, 70, 180, 188, 189, 265, 368
   Overture No. 1, op. 138, 233, 234, 235, 240, 247, 313, 316, 368
   Overture No. 2, op. 72, 233, 234, 235, 236, 237, 238–240, 243, 313, 316, 347, 368
   Overture No. 3, op. 72, 233, 234, 236, 237–241, 243, 313, 316, 370

Leonora Prohaska, incidental music for, 209, 372

"*Lied aus der Ferne*," song, 371

" *Lob auf den Dicken*," 369

" *Lösch aus mein Licht*," song, 377

Macbeth, proposed opera, 205, 211, 303

" *Man strebt, die Flamme zu verhehlen*," song, 363

March, harmonised, in C, 372

March, for a parade of the watch, 374

Marches
   2, military, 370
   3, op. 45, for two pianos, 368

Mass in C, op. 86, 24, 180, 204, 265, 266, 267, 279, 281, 306, 313, 348, 349, 371

Mass in C sharp minor (studies for), 32, 354, 379

Mass in D (*Missa solemnis*), op. 123, 32, 35, 38, 41, 45, 55, 70, 134, 137, 188, 189, 211, 247, 251, 266, 267–276, 278, 279, 281, 306, 320, 324, 325, 327, 333, 353, 354, 355, 379

" *Meeresstille und gluckliche Fahrt*," *see* Cantatas

Melusine, proposed opera, 32, 212, 213, 214, 354

Merkenstein, song, 375

Minuets, 12 for orch., 362

Missa solemnis, see *Mass in D*

" *Mit Mädeln sich vertragon* " (song), 201, 363

Mödling dances (11), 376

Monks' Song, from *William Tell*, 351, 377

Mount of Olives, The, op. 85, oratorio, 22, 201, 262, 263, 264, 265, 279, 347, 351, 369

" *Nameday overture* " in C, op. 115, 64, 191, 233, 246, 247, 250, 262, 269, 313, 319, 351, 372

" *Nord oder Süd*," song, 377

" *Nur wer die Sehnsuchtkennt*," song, 256, 257, 371

" *O Tobias Haslinger*," canon, 377

" *O welch ein Leben* " (*aria*), 201, 365

Octet for wind insts., op. 103 in E flat, 284, 285, 297, 308, 363

Opferlied, song, op. 121*b*, 262, 365, 369, 371, 377

Pastoral symphony, *see* Symphonies, No. 6

sonata, *see* Sonatas for pf. op. 28

Pathétique, sonata, *see* Sonatas for pf., op. 13.

Polonaise, op. 89, in C, 29, 141, 351, 372

Preludes (2) for pf., op. 39, 95, 360
   (1) in F mi., 360

Primo amore piacer del ciel, aria, 253

Prometheus, The Men of, ballet, op. 43, 22, 159, 163, 164, 165, 201, 231, 233, 234, 236, 237, 250, 262, 263, 346, 366

"*Prüfung des Küssens* " (aria), 201, 363

Punschlied, song, 363

Quartets for pf., vn., viola and 'cello :
   No. 1 in E flat, 21, 94, 292, 361
   No. 2 in D, 94, 292, 361
   No. 3 in C, 94, 292, 361
   arrangement of op. 14. i, 369

Quartets for 2 vns., viola, and 'cello :
   op. 18. i in F, 94, 283, 297, 306, 308, 310, 315, 357, 367
   ii in G, 94, 283, 297, 306, 308, 310, 315, 367
   iii in D, 94, 283, 297, 306, 308, 310, 315, 367
   iv in C mi., 94, 283, 312, 313, 314, 367
   v in A, 94, 283, 311, 367
   vi in B flat, 94, 283, 312, 367
   op. 59 " *Rasumovsky* :
   i in F, 24, 130, 260, 306, 315, 316–318, 348, 371
   ii in E mi., 24, 130, 260, 306, 315, 316–318, 371
   iii in C major, 24, 130, 260, 306, 313, 315, 316–318, 371
   op. 74 in E flat, 181, 269, 306, 318, 326, 371

Quartets for 2 vns., viola, and 'cello (*continued*) :—
op. 95 in F mi., 181, 269, 306, 319, 329, 373
op. 127 in E flat, 32, 280, 283, 319, 320, 325, 326, 328, 356, 379
op. 130 in B flat, 32, 73, 135, 274, 280, 327, 328, 331–333, 336, 337, 357, 379
op. 131 in C sharp mi., 32, 36, 283, 327–329, 333–335, 357, 358, 379
op. 132 in A mi., 32, 73, 190, 280, 283, 327–332, 356, 357, 379
op. 135 in F, 32, 73, 283, 328, 330, 333, 335–337, 357, 379
op. 133, fugue in B flat, 199, 283, 332–335, 379
Quartet arrangement of pft. son. op. 14 1, 315
Quintet :
for pf., oboe, clar., horn, and bassoon, op. 16 in E flat, 287, 289, 290, 365
for strings :
op. 4 in E flat, 284, 285, 297, 308, 314, 315, 365
op. 29 in C, 313–315, 367
op. 104, 314, 315, 377
op. 137, fugue in D, 314, 377
for wind insts. (fragment), 365

Rasumowsky quartets, 24, 130, 260, 306, 313, 315–318, 348
Requiem (projected), 32
Ritterballet, 16, 201, 231, 344, 362
Romances for vn. and orchestra :
op. 40 in G, 123, 368
op. 50 in F, 123, 366, 368
Romulus und Remus, projected opera, 209
Rondino for wind insts., E flat, op. 103, 284, 285, 363
Rondos :
for pf. in A, op. 51, 105, 360
for pf. and orch. in B flat, 366
for pf. and vns. in G, 369
for pf. op. 51. i, in C, 364 ; op. 51. ii, in G, 366
" *capricioso*," in G, 100, 142, 376
" *Ruf vom Berge*," song, 377
Ruins of Athens, The, 27, 141, 206, 212, 231, 232, 246, 349, 350, 372
Ruins of Babylon, proposed opera, 207, 208, 209

" *Sankt Petrus war ein Fels*," canon, 377
Saul (proposed oratorio), 32, 264, 357
Schilderung eines Mädchens, song, 361
Schöne Schusterin Die, prelude to, 201
" *Schwenke dich*," canon, 379
" Seine Kaiserliche Hoheit," canon, 377

Septet, op. 20 in E flat, 21, 282, 283, 288, 290, 346, 357, 367
Serenades :
op. 8 in D, 297, 308, 309, 315, 365
op. 25 in D, 297, 308, 365
" *Seufzer eines Ungeliebten*," song, 365
Sextet :
for wind insts., op. 71, 283, 284, 286, 287, 365
for str. quartet and two horns, op. 81*b*, 285, 289, 365
Shottisches (6) for pf., 376
in E flat, 378
12 for 2 vns. and bass, 370
polonaise, 372
" *Si non per portas*," canon, 379
Sieg des Kreuzes (plan for an oratorio), 32, 264
" *Soll ein Schuh nicht drücken*", (*aria*), 201, 365
Sonatas for pf. :
3 dedicated to Elector, 6, 11, 94, 292, 304, 344, 360
op. 2. i in F mi., 21, 95, 96, 97, 102, 109, 294, 362
ii in A, 21, 95, 96, 97, 98, 104, 109, 294, 362
iii in C, 21, 95, 96, 97, 100, 121, 294, 362
op. 7 in E flat, 21, 98, 99, 102, 104, 108, 111, 115, 294, 364
op. 10. i in C mi., 99, 100, 101, 102, 103, 109, 312, 364
ii in F, 99, 100, 102, 108, 109, 312, 364
iii in D, 64, 99, 100, 101, 102, 113, 114, 184, 312, 364
op. 13 in C mi. (*Pathétique*), 99, 101, 102, 103, 104, 139, 289, 293, 298, 312, 319, 366
op. 14. i in E, 64, 99, 103, 104, 289, 366
ii in G, 64, 99, 103, 104, 113, 127, 366
op. 22 in B flat, 94, 99, 103, 104, 105, 309, 366
op. 26 in A flat, 106, 113, 126, 161, 209, 310, 366
op. 27. i in E flat, 106, 107, 108, 109, 113, 119, 130, 310, 366
ii in C sharp mi., 106, 109, 110, 111, 113, 119, 366
op. 28 in D (*Pastoral*), 110, 112, 113, 114, 115, 366
op. 31. i in G, 109, 113, 115, 117, 119, 128, 368
ii in D mi., 64, 99, 109, 110–114, 115, 117, 119, 128, 368
iii in E flat, 110, 115, 117, 127, 128, 303, 368
op. 49. i in G, 105, 288, 290, 364
ii in G mi., 105, 364

Sonatas for pf. (*continued*) :—
op. 53 in C (*Waldstein*), 24, 109, 110, 117–121, 131, 132, 133, 173, 313, 368
op. 54 in F, 24, 107, 110, 126, 127, 129, 368
op. 57 in F mi., 24, 64, 89, 104, 109, 110, 117, 119, 120, 126, 132, 133, 139, 171, 303, 316, 368
op. 78 in F sharp, 126, 127, 129, 303, 370
op. 79 in G, 129, 137, 303, 370
op. 81*a* in E flat (*Lebewohl*), 80, 101, 126, 128, 129, 370
op. 90 in E mi., 29, 80, 103, 104, 112, 126, 128–130, 372
op. 101 in A, 130–132, 137, 302, 305, 374
op. 106 in B flat, 86, 99, 110, 133–136, 137, 138, 142, 143, 186, 190, 199, 269, 270, 274, 305, 333, 376
op. 109 in E, 80, 129, 137, 138, 376
op. 110 in A flat, 73, 108, 127, 137, 138, 139, 299, 376
op. 111 in C mi., 120, 137, 139, 140, 141, 312, 314, 376
op. 6 in D, duet, 105, 364
in C (fragment), 95, 362
duet (projected), 32
Sonata for pf. and horn, op. 17, 282, 287, 289, 297, 346, 367
for pf. and flute, 287, 363
Sonatas for pf. and vn. :
op. 12. i in D, 94, 298, 301, 367
ii in A, 94, 298, 301, 367
iii in E flat, 94, 301, 367
op. 23 in A mi., 298, 299, 300, 367
op. 24 in F, 298, 299, 367
op. 30 (*Alexander*), i in A, 298, 299, 300, 351, 369
ii in C mi., 298, 299, 300, 312, 351, 369
iii in G, 298, 299, 351, 369
op. 47 (*Kreutzer*) in A, 23, 297, 298, 299, 300, 305, 316, 369
op. 96 in G, 27, 181, 297, 298, 299, 300, 350, 373
Sonatas for pf. and 'cello :
op. 5. i in F, 94, 297, 301, 365
ii in G mi., 94, 297, 301, 365
op. 69 in A, 301, 371
op. 102. i in C, 29, 283, 298, 301, 302, 304, 305, 313, 375
ii in D, 29, 283, 298, 301, 302, 304, 305, 375
Sonatina and adagio for mandoline and cembal, 365
Sonatinas (2) for pf. in G and F, 362
Song-cycle, see " *An die ferne Geliebte* "

Symphonies :
No. 1, op. 21 in C, 26, 148–151, 152, 159, 262, 281, 309, 346, 347, 348, 366
No. 2, op. 36 in D, 151–153, 159, 166, 167, 168, 184, 263, 269, 295, 347, 348, 357, 368
No. 3, op. 55 in E flat (*Eroica*), 23, 69, 70, 89, 107, 109, 110, 118, 126, 151, 153–155, 159–166, 167, 170, 171, 173, 176, 177, 181, 185, 187, 188, 190, 192, 194, 195, 197, 222, 231, 233, 234, 243, 270, 274, 280, 315, 317, 324, 347, 348, 349, 357, 368
No. 4, op. 60 in B flat, 24, 109, 167–169, 170, 177, 181, 184, 185, 187, 190, 193, 194, 197, 280, 317, 348, 370
No. 5, op. 67 in C mi., 24, 75, 100, 108, 109, 170–174, 176, 177, 180, 181, 186, 187, 190, 194, 197, 230, 233, 265, 272, 280, 312, 314, 317, 318, 329, 348, 370
No. 6, op. 68 in F (*Pastoral*), 24, 43, 65, 66, 109, 126, 176–181, 188, 190, 193, 197, 254, 255, 260, 348, 370
No. 7, op. 92 in A, 109, 181–188, 197, 260, 301, 304, 318, 319, 350, 351, 352, 372
No. 8, op. 93 in F, 109, 126, 146, 181–188, 193, 197, 269, 281, 290, 318, 319, 324, 335, 350, 372
No. 9, op. 125 in D mi. (*Choral*), 32, 92, 114, 137, 147, 174, 188–197, 198, 199, 248, 251, 254, 260, 265, 268, 269, 270, 275, 276, 278, 280, 281, 306, 319, 320, 355, 356, 376
No. 10 (studies for), 32, 197, 199, 378
studies for, in C mi., 360
in B mi., 374

Tarpeja, march for, 209, 372
" *Tata*," canon, 373
" *Te solo adoro*," canon, 379
" *Tremate, empi, tremate*," terzet (vocal), 253, 350, 355, 373
Trios :
for 2 oboes and cor anglais, op. 87 in C, 286, 363
for pf., flute and bassoon in G, 287, 361
for pf., vn. and 'cello, op. 1. i in E flat, 21, 94, 288, 293, 294–296, 297, 304, 345, 363
op. 1. ii in G, 21, 94, 288, 294–296, 297, 304, 305, 363
op. 1. iii in C mi., 21, 94, 288, 294–296, 297, 304, 305, 312, 314, 345, 363

Trios *(continued)* :—
op. 70. i in D, 24, 99, 181, 269, 296, 297, 302, 303, 305, 356, 357, 371
ii in E flat, 24, 181, 269, 296, 297, 302, 303, 305, 318, 356, 357, 371
op. 97 in B flat, 27, 181, 262, 269, 283, 303, 304, 305, 350, 356, 357, 373
in B flat (one movement), 283, 304, 373
in F mi. (study), 304, 375
in E flat, 363
for pf., clar. and 'cello, in B flat, op. 11, 94, 287, 288, 289, 290, 297, 365
for strings, op. 3 (?) in E flat, 297, 308, 309, 363
op. 9. i in G, 297, 306, 308, 309, 312, 315, 365
ii in D, 297, 306, 308, 309, 312, 315, 365
iii in C mi., 297, 306, 308, 309, 312, 315, 365
" Trocknet nicht," song, op. 83, 255, 257, 373
Turkish march from *King Stephen*, 231

Urians reise um die Welt, song, op. 52, 363

Variations for pf. :
in C mi., on a march by Dressler, 9, 94, 344, 360
in F, op. 34, on an original theme, 116, 117, 118, 120, 366
in E flat, op. 35, on a theme from *Prometheus*, 117, 118, 163, 231, 368
in D, op. 76, on an original theme, 141, 232, 370
in C, op. 120, *Diabelli*, 32, 80, 142, 143, 188, 304, 305, 313, 376
in C mi., on an original theme, 141, 370
in F, on a Swiss song, 364
in D, on *Rule Britannia*, 368
in C, on Grétry's " *Une fièvre brûlante*," 117, 366
in D, on Righini's " *Venni amore*," 117, 362
in A, on Dittersdorf's " *Es war einmal*," 362
in D flat, on Salieri's " *La stessa, la stessissima*," 117, 366
in F, on Süssmayr's " *Tändeln und scherzen*," 117, 366

Variations for pf. *(continued)* :—
in G, on " *Nel cor più non mi sento*," 364
in A, on " *Quant' è più bello*," 364
in C, on a " *Menuett à la Vigano*," 364
in A, on a theme from " *Das Waldmädchen*," 117, 364
in F, on Winter's " *Kind willst du ruhig schlafen*," 366
in C (duet), on a theme by Waldstein, 362
in D (duet), on original theme " *Ich denke dein*," 366
for pf. and vn., on Mozart's " *Se vuol ballare*," 363
for pf., vn. and 'cello, in G, on Müller's " *Kakadu*," 32, 283, 304, 305, 377
in E flat, op. 44, on an original theme, 304, 363
for pf. and 'cello, in G, on a march from Handel's *Judas Maccabeus*, 304, 305
in F, on Mozart's " *Ein Mädchen oder Weibchen*," 304, 365, 366
in E flat, on Mozart's " *Bei Männern, welche Liebe fühlen*," 304, 367
for 2 oboes and cor anglais, on Mozart's " *La ci darem*," 286, 308, 365
6 variations for pf. and flute or vn., 260, 377
10 variations for pf. and flute or vn., 377
" *Vom Tode*," song, op. 48, 258

Waldstein sonata, *see* Sonatas for pf., op. 53
Waltzes :
in E flat, 378
in D, 378
" *Was zieht mir das Herz*," song, op. 83, 256, 257, 373
Weihe des Hauses, overture in C, op. 124, 32, 137, 212, 233, 247, 248, 249, 250, 269, 313, 319, 354, 355, 376
" *Welch ein wunderbares Leben*," song, 373
" *Wellington's Victory*," see *Battle* symphony
" *Wenn die Sonne niedersinkt*," song, 377
" *Wer ist ein freier Mann*," song, 363
" *Wir irren allesamt*," canon, 379
" *Wo blüht das Blümchen*," song, 375

Zerstörung Jerusalems, proposed oratorio, 264